The art of *The Faerie Queene*

MANCHESTER
1824

Manchester University Press

The
Manchester
Spenser

The Manchester Spenser is a monograph and text series devoted to historical and textual approaches to Edmund Spenser – to his life, times, places, works and contemporaries.

A growing body of work in Spenser and Renaissance studies, fresh with confidence and curiosity and based on solid historical research, is being written in response to a general sense that our ability to interpret texts is becoming limited without the excavation of further knowledge. So the importance of research in nearby disciplines is quickly being recognised, and interest renewed: history, archaeology, religious or theological history, book history, translation, lexicography, commentary and glossary – these require treatment for and by students of Spenser.

The Manchester Spenser, to feed, foster and build on these refreshed attitudes, aims to publish reference tools, critical, historical, biographical and archaeological monographs on or related to Spenser, from several disciplines, and to publish editions of primary sources and classroom texts of a more wide-ranging scope.

The Manchester Spenser consists of work with stamina, high standards of scholarship and research, adroit handling of evidence, rigour of argument, exposition and documentation.

The series will encourage and assist research into, and develop the readership of, one of the richest and most complex writers of the early modern period.

General Editors   Joshua Reid, Kathryn Walls and Tamsin Badcoe
Editorial Board   Sukanta Chaudhuri, Helen Cooper, Thomas Herron, J. B. Lethbridge, James Nohrnberg and Brian Vickers

Also available
Literary and visual Ralegh   Christopher M. Armitage (ed.)
A Concordance to the Rhymes of The Faerie Queene   Richard Danson Brown & J.B. Lethbridge
A Supplement of the Faery Queene: By Ralph Knevet   Christopher Burlinson & Andrew Zurcher (eds)
A Companion to Pastoral Poetry of the English Renaissance   Sukanta Chaudhuri
Pastoral poetry of the English Renaissance: An anthology   Sukanta Chaudhuri (ed.)
Spenserian allegory and Elizabethan biblical exegesis: A context for The Faerie Queene   Margaret Christian
Monsters and the poetic imagination in The Faerie Queene: 'Most ugly shapes and horrible aspects'   Maik Goth
Celebrating Mutabilitie: Essays on Edmund Spenser's Mutabilitie Cantos   Jane Grogan (ed.)
Spenserian satire: A tradition of indirection   Rachel E. Hile
Castles and Colonists: An archaeology of Elizabethan Ireland   Eric Klingelhofer
Shakespeare and Spenser: Attractive opposites   J.B. Lethbridge (ed.)
Dublin: Renaissance city of literature   Kathleen Miller and Crawford Gribben (eds)
A Fig for Fortune: By Anthony Copley   Susannah Brietz Monta
Spenser and Virgil: The pastoral poems   Syrithe Pugh
The Burley manuscript   Peter Redford (ed.)
Renaissance psychologies: Spenser and Shakespeare   Robert Lanier Reid
European erotic romance: Philhellene Protestantism, renaissance translation and English literary politics   Victor Skretkowicz
God's only daughter: Spenser's Una as the invisible Church   Kathryn Walls

The art of *The Faerie Queene*

RICHARD DANSON BROWN

Manchester University Press

The right of Richard Danson Brown to be identified as the author of this work has been asserted by him in accordance with the Copyright, Designs and Patents Act 1988.

Published by Manchester University Press
Altrincham Street, Manchester M1 7JA, UK
www.manchesteruniversitypress.co.uk

British Library Cataloguing-in-Publication Data is available

ISBN 978 0 7190 8732 5 hardback
ISBN 978 1 5261 5179 7 paperback

First published by Manchester University Press in hardback 2019

This edition published 2020

The publisher has no responsibility for the persistence or accuracy of URLs for any external or third-party internet websites referred to in this book, and does not guarantee that any content on such websites is, or will remain, accurate or appropriate.

Typeset by Toppan Best-set Premedia Limited

For J. B. Lethbridge and David Lee Miller

Contents

Illustrations

Acknowledgements

This book has been lucky in its friends. My main debts are recorded in the dedication: Julian Lethbridge has encouraged me over many years since our first meeting in Doneraile in 1999, particularly through his energetic interest not only in all things Spenserian, but in me and my work. His invitation to collaborate with him on *A Concordance of the Rhymes of The Faerie Queene* was serendipitous, and enabled me to work up closely with the poem in the service of that collaborate project. The odd format of the lists of rhymes (initially in massive PDF files; later in the elegant format of the printed book) helped both to refocus my enthusiasm for Spenser and to see the poem in different ways, thus inspiring the first seeds of this book. During the course of writing, Julian has given me access to his unpublished digital Concordance of *The Faerie Queene*, and has extracted data sets for me at short notice. One of the most striking aspects of collaborating with Julian was the way in which the data provoked different critical responses in us as readers. He will not agree with everything I say in this book, but, at the same time, will not hold our disagreements against me, even as we offer contrasting accounts of Spenser's forms. Julian's work on The Manchester Spenser series is testimony to the abiding agreement between us and the subject community that Spenser continues to matter, and that we as scholars need to find new ways to keep this (in a phrase of Louis MacNeice's) 'forgotten truism' alive.

David Lee Miller's contribution has been different in kind but related. Since working with David on *Spenser Review* in 2014, we have corresponded at length both about the journal and about our current projects. David read the complete manuscript, and it has been significantly improved by his judicious, stringent and witty comments. Our friendship has been an education in Spenser, the sometimes perplexing differences in English idioms between America and Britain, and the ongoing need for humour.

I have profited much from discussions with other scholars, many of whom have read and commented on parts of what follows. In particular, I'd like to thank Francesca Benatti (for checking my translations from Italian), Craig Berry, Claire Eager, Jonathan Gibson, Jane Grogan, Andrew Hadfield, Syrithe Pugh, and Yulia Ryzhik. The following gave help and encouragement at different times: Judith Anderson, Helen Barr, John Brannigan, Nick Havely, Beca Helfer, Joseph Loewenstein, Willy Maley, Nicola Watson, David Scott Wilson-Okamura, and Andrew Zurcher. Being a part of the International Spenser Society, especially through the work of *Spenser Review*, has been an ongoing stimulus to my work. It is a fine thing in these days of hard borders to be part of a community which isn't ashamed to proclaim its international ambitions and trajectory. Needless to say, all errors and exaggerations are my own responsibility.

Much of this book was written – or rather was a longed-for, deferred joy – while I was Dean of Arts and then of the new Faculty of Arts and Social Sciences at The Open University. I'd like to thank a number of people who helped me during this period, and tolerated my not infrequent Spenserian allusions at times when it felt like 'the world is runne quite out of square' on an hourly basis. (This is not one of my exaggerations.) My thanks to Sue Dutton, Ian Fribbance, Laura Meadows, Annika Mombauer, Elaine Moohan, Emma Rowney, Sarah Smith, Kim Woods: while it is sometimes possible to get academic work done while taking on leadership roles, the challenges are significantly ameliorated by having sympathetic colleagues. The Open University Library has been a mainstay, both through the calibre of its excellent digital resources and through the speed of its Document Delivery system. I'm grateful too to my colleagues on The Open University module *English Literature from Shakespeare to Jane Austen* (A334), who finally succumbed to my insistence that extracts from *The Faerie Queene* would be a good choice, and to the students who have responded so positively to the poem. Manchester University Press has been a conducive publisher, and I'm grateful particularly to Matthew Frost for his patience. The text was edited by Judith Oppenheimer and the index was prepared by Isobel McLean, and the book has been materially enhanced by their careful work. My friends Clive Baldwin, Olly Bond, David McDade, and Jim MacLeod have contributed in their idiosyncratic ways to my good humour.

Some portions of Chapters 2 and 3 have appeared in other forms: 'Wise Wights in Privy Places: Rhyme and Stanza Form in Spenser and Chaucer', in *Spenser and Chaucer*, ed. Tamsin Badcoe, Gareth Griffith, and Rachel Stenner (Manchester University Press, forthcoming), and '"And dearest loue": Virgilian Half-lines in Spenser's *Faerie Queene*', in *Proceedings of the Virgil Society* 29 (2017), 49–74. My thanks to the editors and publishers of these works for permission to reuse.

Finally, I want to thank my family: Pat, Chris, Heather, Neil, Amber, Jean, Jonathan, and now Oliver and Eleanor. Though *The Faerie Queene* is not the first book any of them would turn to, their support – as well as being a good thing in itself – has sharpened my reading of the poem over the years. Love is the lesson, even if the pupils are listening to different stations.

Abbreviations

Unless otherwise stated, quotations from *The Faerie Queene* are from Hamilton's revised second edition (2001, 2007). Quotations from Spenser's shorter poems are from Oram's Yale edition, and quotations from the prose are from the *Variorum*.

Quotations from early books are, unless otherwise stated, from Early English Books Online and Eighteenth Century Collections Online. Where these databases have digitised more than one copy of a work, I have identified which copy I am quoting from.

EEBO	Early English Books Online: https://eebo.chadwyck.com via the Open University Library
ELH	*English Literary History*
FQ	Spenser, Edmund (2001, 2007) *The Faerie Queene*, Revised Second Edition, ed. A. C. Hamilton with Hiroshi Yamashita and Toshiyuki Suzuki. Harlow: Pearson
ODNB Online	*Oxford Dictionary of National Biography*: https://oxforddnb.com via the Open University Library
OED Online	*Oxford English Dictionary*: https://oed.com via the Open University Library
PMLA	*Publications of the Modern Language Society of America*
PQ	*Philological Quarterly*
Prose	Spenser, Edmund (1949) *Spenser's Prose Works*, ed. Rudolf Gottfried; Vol. 10 of *The Works of Edmund*

	Spenser: A Variorum Edition. Baltimore: Johns Hopkins Press
SSt	*Spenser Studies*
SP	*Studies in Philology*
Var	Spenser, Edmund (1949) *Spenser's Prose Works*, ed. Rudolf Gottfried; Vol. 10 of *The Works of Edmund Spenser: A Variorum Edition.* Baltimore: Johns Hopkins Press
Yale	Spenser, Edmund (1989) *The Shorter Poems*, ed. William A. Oram, Einar Bjorvand, Ronald Bond, Thomas H. Cain, Alexander Dunlop and Richard Schell. New Haven and London: Yale University Press

Introduction: tightrope walking in an afflicted style

The 'afflicted stile' of *The Faerie Queene* is part of the poem's opening gambit, the Proem to Book I. In a text which imitates the spurious opening of the *Aeneid* (still seen as genuine during the Renaissance),[1] invokes an ambiguous Muse[2] and the amorous, dysfunctional family of Venus, Mars, and Cupid, Spenser finally turns to the 'Goddesse' who is his subject: Elizabeth is 'The argument of mine afflicted stile' (Pr. I.iv).[3] Inevitably, it also offers a tempting opening for a study of the forms of the epic: what are the implications of an 'afflicted stile'? What did Spenser have in mind in adopting this formulation? Lesley Brill offers cautious guidance about reading the Proems as self-conscious texts which never quite say as much as readers and critics might like them to:

> The proems announce the speaker's attitude towards the poem, but his attitude becomes as much a point of departure as a fixed point of reference … [They] offer fertile and compact areas for considering such issues as the character and status of the narrator of the epic, the multiple framings of the poem, its relation to the historical and fictional materials it incorporates, and, broadly, what we mean and what Spenser may have understood by the elusive entity that we call the text of *The Faerie Queene*.[4]

1 On the spurious opening, see David Scott Wilson-Okamura, *Virgil in the Renaissance*, 83–85.
2 Probably either Clio, Muse of History, or Calliope, Muse of Epic; see Hamilton's note in *FQ*, 30.
3 Though as Lesley Brill notes, 'the Elizabeth of the proems is more than an historical monarch'; '*The Faerie Queene*, proems', 294. See also Susanne L. Wofford, '*The Faerie Queene*, Books I–III', 106.
4 Brill, '*The Faerie Queene*, proems', 294. As Hamilton notes, 'Proem' (like 'Argument') is an editorial convention rather than a Spenserian usage (*FQ*, 29).

A point of departure is a good way of explaining a line which is at one level no more than a studied modesty topos.[5] At the beginning of his epic, Spenser disclaims literary skill in a passage which is paradoxically one of the most rhetorically ornamented in the 1590 *Faerie Queene*; 'afflicted' has the sense of 'cast down' or 'humble', implying that the poem and the poet need to be uplifted by the Goddess, who will 'raise my thoughtes too humble and too vile' (Pr. I.iv).[6] Like all modesty topoi, the line is conventional and asks to be read as a formal gesture of obeisance the poet doesn't altogether mean. As Brill implies, we should be cautious before generalising from this about Spenser's understanding of the necessarily 'elusive' *Faerie Queene*. It might be better to say Spenser's style is 'afflicted' only inasmuch as it pleases himself to label it as such at this moment; in the Mutabilitie Cantos at a similarly self-conscious moment, the narrator suggests that he will temporarily 'abate the sternenesse' of his 'stile', a description more in keeping with conventional ideas of epic (VII.vi.37).[7]

As this discussion implies, 'afflicted stile' is usually read in terms of the poet-narrator's attitude towards his poem.[8] Yet as Brill points out, the Proems are also concerned with the reader's understanding of the poem.[9] So it might be reasonable to consider 'afflicted stile' as a way of characterising how we read *The Faerie Queene* – that this is a troubled style which in some ways deliberately seeks to impede its readers,[10] or at the very least, to slow them down, to force them to work harder at the business of interpretation. Such a suggestion would add an edge to the modesty topos: though Spenser may be humble in respect of Elizabeth, he may at the same time be aggressive or indifferent to the comforts of his readers.

Spenser's use of 'afflicted' is unusual. Though widely used, particularly in pietistic contexts – afflicted ghosts and spirits are commonplace in late sixteenth-century texts – it is not typically a word associated with

---

5 On modesty topoi, see Ernst Robert Curtius, *European Literature and the Latin Middle Ages*, 83–85.

6 See Hamilton's note in *FQ*, 30, and "afflicted, adj. and n.". *OED Online*.

7 See Richard Danson Brown, "'I would abate the sternenesse of my stile'", 275–94, particularly 279–80.

8 See A. Leigh DeNeef, *Spenser and the Motives of Metaphor*, 92, 94.

9 See Brill, '*The Faerie Queene*, proems': 'the proems condition the reader's understanding of the following narratives', 294.

10 See the earlier reference to the *OED* definition of 'afflicted', a term which comprises meanings such as downtrodden, troubled, tormented, and humiliated – *OED* cites this passage in relation to the latter meaning.

poetic style.[11] Anne Dowriche's account of the 'beastlie butchers' who
kill French Protestants demonstrates the way in which the word tends to
adhere to religious content: 'Not like to men, but rather as some furies
had been sent/From hell, to stop the course of Gods afflicted word'.[12]
Dowriche's 'afflicted word[s]' are unambiguously biblical – as the full title
of her poem declares, she records the 'most famous bloodie broiles that
haue happened in France for the Gospell of Iesus Christ'.[13] In contrast,
Spenser's 'afflicted stile' is polysemous, a usage which at once comprises
notions of humility and humiliation, but whose fundamental purpose is
to provoke the reader's alert curiosity about the poem it precedes and
elliptically describes. Indeed, in arriving at this striking collocation Spenser
conceivably was remembering aspects of Petrarch's *Rime Sparse*. Though
Petrarch never uses precisely this phrase, Poem 332, the double sestina, 'Mia
beninga foruna e'l viver lieto', is in effect an evocation of stylistic affliction
in response to Laura's death; he laments his 'agro stile' and 'debile stile'
(bitter and weak style), and the poem as a whole is a concerted abjection
of an afflicted poet-speaker. In other poems, Petrarch uses the adjective
'afflitto' in ways which are again suggestive of poetic self-consciousness.[14]
As a piece of lexis, then, 'afflicted' is tonally challenging and uncertain,
evoking simultaneously notions of both religious and erotic persecution,
and positioning the speaker of this epic poem in a kind of stylistic no
man's land.

In making the suggestion that Spenser's style is deliberately troubled
and elliptical, part of me is profoundly uncomfortable: since first reading
The Faerie Queene and Paul Alpers's brilliant discussion of the way it
works syntactically, I have inclined to the view that the aesthetic singularity
of the poem lies in 'a rule that Spenser's verse almost never makes us
violate: follow the path of least resistance'.[15] As Alpers demonstrates,
Spenser's syntax, his organisation of meaning in lines of verse, is significantly

11 See for example Jean Calvin, *Sermons of John Calvin*, sig. A6v ('his tender and afflicted
spirit') and Samuel Daniel, *Delia and Rosamund*, sig. E6r ('My poore afflicted ghost').
12 A[nne] D[owriche], *The French Historie*, 33 [v], sig. I4v. On Dowriche, see Bronwen
Price, 'Women's Poetry 1550–1700', 288, and Kate Aughterson, 'Dowriche, Anne (*d.* in
or after 1613)', *ODNB Online*.
13 D[owriche], *The French Historie*, sig. A1r.
14 See Francesco Petrarca, *Petrarch's Lyric Poems*, 524–29. For 'afflitto' elsewhere in Petrarch,
see 64–65 (Poem 23, l.97: 'vertute afflitte'), 204–05 (Poem 102, l.5: 'l'imperio afflitto'),
and 234–35 (Poem 120, l.13: ''l cor vostro afflitto'). My thanks to David Lee Miller for
alerting me to these echoes.
15 Paul J. Alpers, *The Poetry of The Faerie Queene*, 84.

easier to follow than the syntactic styles of his contemporaries: by following this semantic path, you accommodate yourself to the sometimes 'extreme permissiveness' of *The Faerie Queene* as a poetic narration.[16] Yet it takes time and patience to get to the easy familiarity with Spenser's syntactic structures which Alpers's study exemplifies. The point is not so much whether the style of *The Faerie Queene* is easy or difficult as that at a key moment in the poem, Spenser chooses a word with troubling connotations, implying that the reader's progress through the poem may be similarly impeded. And at a time when Spenser's position in the English studies curriculum is 'curious' – a major canonical writer who is almost habitually seen by students as an obstacle to be avoided – an 'afflicted stile' might be seen as the worst form of self-promotion.[17]

My concern in this study is not Spenserian difficulty per se, a topic which would demand encyclopaedic coverage. Rather, I'm interested in the way in which Spenser's style might be experienced as a blockage to comprehension and enjoyment. Since Sir Philip Sidney's *Defence of Poetry* onwards, commentators have seen Spenser's archaism as his fundamental stylistic difficulty, and it is the unfamiliarity of his idiom which alienates many fledgling readers.[18] *The Faerie Queene* shows a patina of archaism throughout, such as the inflected past participle 'Ycladd' in the first stanza of Book I, but its unfamiliarity is not only a matter of *whilomes* and *sithences*. What arrests a new reader in the following stanzas is a mixture of syntactic difficulty alongside variety of allusion:

> Firebrand of hell first tynd in Phlegeton,
>> By thousand furies, and from thence out throwen
>> Into this world, to worke confusion,
>> And set it all on fire by force vnknowen,
>> Is wicked discord, whose small sparkes once blowen
>> None but a God or godlike man can slake;
>> Such as was *Orpheus*, that when strife was growen
>> Amongst those famous ympes of Greece, did take
> His siluer Harpe in hand, and shortly friends them make.

---

16 Alpers, *The Poetry of The Faerie Queene*, 83. See pp. 77–82 for comparisons of Spenser with Milton, Marlowe, and Drayton. For a contrasting position, see Carol V. Kaske, *Spenser and Biblical Poetics*, 2, who suggests that 'Spenser's style is often ornate and seldom plain, as conventional wisdom considers that of the Bible to be'.

17 John D. Staines, 'The Historicist Tradition in Spenser Studies', 733.

18 Sir Philip Sidney, *A Defence of Poetry* in *Miscellaneous Prose of Sir Philip Sidney*, 112. Archaism is widely discussed by linguists and Spenserians, with most authorities suggesting that the quantity of archaic diction has been exaggerated; see Manfred Görlach, *Introduction to Early Modern English*, 144, 202, and Chapter 1 below for further discussion.

Or such as that celestiall Psalmist was,
    That when the wicked feend his Lord tormented,
    With heauenly notes, that did all other pas,
    The outrage of his furious fit relented.
    Such Musicke is wise words with time concented,
    To moderate stiffe minds, disposd to striue:
    Such as that prudent Romane well inuented,
    What time his people into partes did riue,
Them reconcyld againe, and to their homes did driue. (IV.ii.1–2)

This is in some ways an uncharacteristic passage, which is what makes it stylistically provocative. In the first place, these stanzas are canto openers, a subset which have their own particular styles and registers, and in which the narrator typically makes space outside of the narrative to address moral questions or the reader directly.[19] But even in this specialised discursive space, these are extraordinary stanzas. In the first, syntax flows beyond line lengths in lines 2, 5, 7, 8, and even 4 (despite its ostensibly conclusive comma); the subject of the first sentence is delayed until the beginning of the fifth line, by which stage the reader is feeling some of the confusion ascribed to discord as s/he tries to work out what the 'Firebrand of hell' is and who the 'force unknowen' might be which is causing this chaos. The meaning of 'tynd' is a smaller problem, perhaps, but the verb is strongly marked metrically in the first line, and adds to the confusion of both the Firebrand and the ensuing Phlegton. 'Tynd' is easy enough to gloss, and was probably unproblematic to readers in the 1590s; it means 'kindled'.[20] As so often in the Spenserian stanza, the fifth line is the hinge between two halves of the stanza, as noted by William Empson.[21] In this case, the fifth line renews the stanza's syntactical challenges: 'Is wicked discord' retroactively explains some of the riddles of the first four lines, but 'whose small sparkes once blowen' runs into the oracular sixth line and the story of Orpheus's reconciliation of the warring Argonauts. Overall, the stanza operates in a way which is in sharp contrast with Alpers's rule that 'individual lines of verse work independently, even

19 See Jerome S. Dees, 'Narrator of *The Faerie Queene*' (1990), 498–500, on the uncertainty and '"provisional" authority' of canto openings (499). I give dates to distinguish this essay from Dees's earlier essay with an almost identical title, 'The Narrator of *The Faerie Queene*' (1971). See further discussion in Chapters 5 and 6 below.
20 See "tind, v.". *OED Online. OED*'s citations indicate that 'tynd' was still being used in the Elizabethan period, particularly in poetic contexts.
21 William Empson, *Seven Types of Ambiguity*, 33–34.

when they are based on the same narrative event'.[22] It is difficult to read lines like 'Is wicked discord, whose small sparkes once blowen' and 'Amongst those famous ympes of Greece, did take' as independent lines. Rather, the reader has to work against the structure of the line and with the syntax of the sentence to recode the second half of the stanza as 'Only a God or godlike man can slake the fires of discord, as is shown by Orpheus, who, when strife grew amongst those famous youths of Greece, took his silver harp and made them friends again'. This is not poetry, but something like this transposition is what Spenser's verse demands of its readers here.

The second stanza presents related and different challenges. Syntactically, the sovereignty of the individual line is re-established as the poet-narrator warms to his theme: as the ordering function of poetry overwhelms the principle of discord, so its 'outrage' is more properly controlled – or 'relented' – in the more linear syntax of this stanza. The fifth line, 'Such Musicke is wise words with time concented', exemplifies the theme and restores the syntax to the organising authority of the line. But even here, Spenser's syntax may strike the reader as unusual with its repeated use of the (to modern ears) outdated, supremely 'poetic', device of inversion. In the first two lines, the main verb is relentlessly transferred to the rhyming position: in place of the normative subject-verb-object syntax of 'such as *was* that celestiall Psalmist' and 'when the wicked feend *tormented* his Lord', Spenser prefers patterns which delay the verb, thus maximising his rhyming options and adding a distinctive, verbal quality to his syntax. The same trick repeats throughout the stanza, as in the final line, which would read more easily as 'reconciled them again and drove them to their homes'. As well as missing the rhyme, such reordering loses the semantic emphasis Spenser throws on the key verbs of the C-rhyme, *striue: riue: driue*, all of which stress the theme of confusion reconciled by harmonious speech or music.[23] But it is Spenser's mythological thinking which poses the major difficulty in this stanza. After the Greek exempla of the previous stanza, this stanza draws on the Hebrew Bible and on Livy for the examples of David ('that celestiall Psalmist') and Menenius Agrippa ('that prudent Romane'). In

---

22 Alpers, *The Poetry of The Faerie Queene*, 37. See also Catherine Addison, 'Rhyming Against the Grain' for the related idea that 'the reader has been educated by thousands of stanzas of nine self-contained lines each to pause even when the grammar does point onwards beyond the line ending' (346).

23 On the unusually high incidence of verbal rhymes in Spenser, see Addison, 'Rhyming Against the Grain'. On the semantic and affective qualities of rhyme, see Richard Danson Brown, '"Charmed with Inchaunted Rimes": An Introduction to *The Faerie Queene* Rhymes Concordance'.

both cases, the characters are named by epithet rather than directly, a device of omission which underlines the narrator's learning while implying the familiarity of the allusions. An educated sixteenth-century reader would need little help with either of these exempla – for Sir Philip Sidney, Menenius's fable of the belly was 'notorious, and as notorious that it was a tale'.[24] At the same time, the allusive texture of *The Faerie Queene* is dynamic, fusing tales from different traditions, and demanding similar dynamism from its readers, or at the very least readers equipped with good critical editions. The verse continues to impede the reader through specific choices of diction, such as 'tynd' in the first stanza, and the rare coinage 'concented' in the second.[25] Alpers notwithstanding – and as this study will demonstrate, I write in a tradition stemming from his work – Spenser's poetic idiom is challenging, strewn with stylistic, rhetorical, and above all interpretive impedimenta. I aim to clear some of this rubble, or at least to enable the reader to negotiate it in new ways.

So far I have used metaphors of obstruction and blockage to evoke the effect of Spenser's 'afflicted stile'. In doing so, I am drawing on Viktor Shklovksy's suggestive model of literary style in *Theory of Prose* (1929). His remarks about poetic language are congruent with most readers' first experience of *The Faerie Queene*. He sees it as a device of 'enstrangement', or defamiliarisation.[26] In Shklovsky's terms, poetic language is artificially distanced from ordinary language in order to slow the reader down to enhance the text's semantic and artistic charge. Such 'impeding language', he suggests, is 'the very hallmark of the artistic':

> an artifact has been removed from the domain of automatized perception. It is 'artificially' created by an artist in such a way that the perceiver, pausing in his reading, dwells on the text.[27]

Shklovsky interrogates why writers adopt particular forms: 'A crooked, laborious poetic speech, which makes the poet tongue-tied, or a strange

---

24 Sidney, *Miscellaneous Prose*, 93. See *FQ*, 419 for Hamilton's notes. For the centrality of the Psalms to the sixteenth-century English experience of the Bible and to Spenser in particular, see Kaske, *Spenser and Biblical Poetics*, 12–13.
25 For concented, see "† concent, v.". *OED Online*.
26 Viktor Shklovsky, *Theory of Prose*, 12–14. See Shur's remarks about the difficulty of rendering Shklovsky's term *ostaniene* – Shur rejects the more usual translation 'defamiliarization' in favour of 'enstrangement' on the grounds that the latter has cognate roots to Shklovsky's Russian neologism (xviii–xix).
27 Shklovsky, *Theory of Prose*, 13, 12. In the same passage, Shklovky notes (following Aristotle) the 'outlandish' quality of poetic language, and includes the use of archaism in a brief inventory of obstructing techniques (13).

unusual vocabulary, an unusual arrangement of words – what's behind all this?'[28] The tongue-tied poet is a good evocation of the tongue-twisting involutions performed by Spenser in the 'Fireband of hell' stanza. According to Shklovsky, the main reason for such styles is to make the reader dwell on the text, to reduce 'automatized perception' in favour of a more questing response to the artistic structures of the text in question. My approach is rooted in Shklovsky's thinking: Spenser's manipulation of poetic form constitutes a series of enstranging devices, which aim to provoke and engage the reader. These devices are the means through which Spenser positions and repositions the reader in relation to the poem. Modulations of rhyme, metre, stanza, episode, and interpretative framework are dynamic aspects of the poem in progress which cumulatively resist evaluative stasis. Put another way – and to adapt a related remark of Shklovsky's – my aim is to show why and how Spenser walks the poetic tightrope in an afflicted style.[29]

'Enstrangement' has a bearing on two further aspects of my work. Firstly, I am interested in *The Faerie Queene*'s relationship to its medieval precursors. The question of how early modern writing negotiates the influence of the medieval is a developing topic, covered by several important collections,[30] and the formal consequences of Spenser's reading of 'the Renaissance Chaucer' need reconsideration, especially in the light of the growing consciousness of both the continuity and the oddness of Middle English idioms in the later sixteenth century.[31] Though Sidney's adverse comments on *The Shepheardes Calender*'s archaism are the most well known contemporaneous response, Everard Guilpin provides a glimpse of the enstranging qualities of Spenser's diction at the end of the 1590s:

> Some blame deep *Spencer* for his grandam words,
> Others protest that, in them he records
> His maister-peece of cunning giuing praise,
> And grauity to his profound-prickt layes.

Spenser's 'grandam words' follow Guilpin's amused report of related carping at 'reuerend *Chawcer*' and a Gower past his literary sell-by date: poetic diction was a subject of debate and tastes were changing whilst Spenser

28 Shklovsky, *Theory of Prose*, 15.
29 Shklovsky, *Theory of Prose*, 15.
30 Theresa M. Krier (ed.), *Refiguring Chaucer in the Renaissance*; Gordon McMullan and David Matthews (eds), *Reading the Medieval in Early Modern England*.
31 Alice S. Miskimin, *The Renaissance Chaucer*; Andrew King, *The Faerie Queene and Middle English Romance*.

was publishing *The Faerie Queene*.[32] As Guilpin suggests, opinions had not coalesced about Spenser's language, nor indeed about the medieval past. This vignette shows a culture attempting to value a literature which was becoming enstranged from its own readers; as Edmund Waller would ask much later, 'who can hope his lines should long/Last in a daily changing Tongue?'[33] 'Enstrangement' also provides a way of re-reading the 'bad' or phatic parts of *The Faerie Queene*. The sense that *The Faerie Queene* is an uneven poem has been articulated by generations of readers and has been used as evidence of Spenser's compositional processes; Josephine Waters Bennett used the varying stylistic qualities of different parts of the poem to suggest the sequence in which it might have been written.[34] Interventions since the turn of the millennium respond to similar perceptions: the work of J. B. Lethbridge and others pays renewed attention to the formulaic aspects of *The Faerie Queene* to suggest that its poetic texture is more conventional and ready made than previous scholars have recognised.[35] As Bennett's work inadvertently suggests, badness is often in the eye of the beholder;[36] conversely, I am interested in whether the weak parts of *The Faerie Queene* are bad by design or writerly inattention.[37] Lethbridge's work suggests that Spenser's epic was written under different aesthetic criteria from the largely unhistoricised notions of stylistic consistency invoked by Bennett. These are debates to which I will return.

Formalism vs historicism?

That my thinking about the forms of *The Faerie Queene* draws on the work of Shklovsky and Alpers poses a broader question: what is the place of formalist approaches when historicism has become the dominant critical paradigm in Renaissance literature and Spenser studies? There are two

32 Everard Guilpin, Satire VI, ll.73–76, 67–72, in *Skialetheia*, 90.
33 Edmond Waller, *Poems*, 234. Waller goes on to lament that '*Chaucer* his Sense can only boast,/The glory of his numbers lost', underlining the widespread difficulty early modern readers had with Chaucer's metres (235).
34 Josephine Waters Bennett, *The Evolution of The Faerie Queene*. The longevity of Bennett's modelling of the composition is shown by Andrew Hadfield's reliance on her work in his account of the writing of the poem in *Edmund Spenser: A Life*, 254–55, 444 fn. 221.
35 See J. B. Lethbridge's study, 'The Bondage of Rhyme in *The Faerie Queene*: Moderate "this Ornament of Rhyme"', in Brown and Lethbridge, *A Concordance*, 76–180.
36 See Bennett, *The Evolution of The Faerie Queene*, 21, on Spenser's 'struggle for rhymes', and my discussion in '"Charmed with Inchaunted Rimes"' in *A Concordance*, 12, 22.
37 See David Lee Miller, 'Laughing at Spenser's *Daphnaida*', 241–50, for a recent example of an argument based on the 'bad by design' model.

main ways of answering this question. The first is to argue that the dominance of historicist approaches has been counterproductive in terms of the understanding of the literary qualities of Spenser's work. As Mark David Rasmussen suggests (in an essay which incidentally makes searching criticism of my earlier study of the *Complaints* volume), though formalist approaches are 'less influential' than historicist ones, both approaches suffer from overlapping weaknesses: where formalism can overlook context, historicism can fail 'to fully engage the poems'.[38] Inevitably, I want to suggest that despite the enormous value and range of historicist approaches to *The Faerie Queene*, something of the aesthetic richness of the poem – and particularly the demands which it lays on its readers – has been mislaid or, rather, side-stepped since the 1980s.[39] Richard A. McCabe's remarks about his decision to place a group of essays on 'Poetic Craft' at the heart of his *Oxford Handbook of Edmund Spenser* strike an interesting balance between historicism and formalism:

> Without his literary skills, Spenser would be indistinguishable from the scores of secretaries, civil servants, and colonists who sought personal advancement on the fringes of empire ... Without his literary skills, he could never have produced the works ... upon which his reputation rests.[40]

McCabe's careful, anaphoristic sentences insist on both the claims of the historical and those of the literary. In this regard, the New Critical position which privileges literary texts as self-sustaining entities, or icons which exist outside of time and space, has little purchase. McCabe's Spenser is emphatically both literary and historical; similarly, it is my contention that there is no intrinsic incompatibility between these approaches.[41] Yet, in the course of this study I will have little to say about Spenser's engagement with Ireland or the complex web of patronage relationships in which he was involved throughout his career.[42] In a related fashion, there are formal

---

38 Mark David Rasmussen, '*Complaints* and *Daphnaïda*', 222. Though Rasmussen's comments relate primarily to *Complaints*, they have broader application, and mirror some of the trends mapped by David Scott Wilson-Okamura ('The Formalist Tradition') and Staines ('The Historicist Tradition in Spenser Studies') in the same volume.

39 Staines, 'The Historicist Tradition in Spenser Studies', 733, is again germane in observing that Spenser is rightly seen as both 'the poet's poet' and 'a historian's poet', 'a fruitful paradox that opens up the richness of his literary achievement'.

40 Richard A. McCabe, 'Introduction', *The Oxford Handbook of Edmund Spenser*, 4.

41 See Brown, '"Charmed with inchaunted rimes"', in Brown and Lethbridge, *A Concordance*, 27–31.

42 See for example Judith Owens, *Enabling Engagements*, Thomas Herron, *Spenser's Irish Work*, and more recently, Richard McCabe, *Ungainefull Arte*, and Rachel E. Hile, *Spenserian Satire*.

approaches which are not developed here: I do not engage in detail with numerological or topomorphical approaches, because my primary concern is with the text as the reader experiences it moment by moment as well as with the still controversial bases of such interpretations.[43] Such omissions do not betoken a lack of interest or engagement, but are, rather, a concomitant of attempting to re-read the poem formally, and for what its formal engagements and experiments tell us about interpretation and allegory.

The second approach to the question of the place of formalism is the corrective advanced by David Scott Wilson-Okamura. Taking the longer view of Spenserian reception, formalism is the dominant tradition:

> Critics have been writing about Spenser for more than four centuries, and for the first three of those centuries, most critics wrote about subjects which today would be classified as formalist ... the recurring issues in Spenser criticism – the ones that critics have come back to, not just decade after decade, but century after century – have historically been questions about form.[44]

This is not simply a fact about the reception of Spenser: it is also a truth about the literary culture which shaped Spenser. Early modern education was rooted in the acquisition of rhetorical fluency and the laborious analysis of sentences in Latin and other ancient languages. As has widely been recognised, such a rigorous, painstaking (in all senses of the word) grounding in the mechanics of syntax, translation from and back into Latin, and the mastery of rhetorical tropes equipped educated Elizabethans with a formidable battery of linguistic and cultural resources.[45] Unsurprisingly then, Renaissance criticism remains perplexed by and fixated on questions

43 See Maren-Sofie Røstvig, 'Canto Structure in Tasso and Spenser', 179, for the use of 'topomorphical'; for an overview, see Alexander Dunlop, 'Modern Studies in Number Symbolism'. Though numerological approaches are widely referenced (Hadfield makes repeated use of them in *Edmund Spenser: A Life*), a comprehensive review of numerology in the light of historical and textual evidence remains a pressing need in the critical literature. At any event, numerology demands readers willing to juxtapose the textual reading of the poem with various forms of counting and tallying of fictive incident to symbolic number.
44 Wilson-Okamura, 'The Formalist Tradition', 718.
45 See Hadfield, *Edmund Spenser: A Life*, 29–30, for the curriculum at Merchant Taylors, and 57–59, for Cambridge. Herbert D. Rix, *Rhetoric in Spenser's Poetry*, 11–18, is still useful on the question of curriculum. See also Brian Vickers, *In Defence of Rhetoric*, 264; Peter Mack, 'Spenser and Rhetoric', 425–28; Jonathan Bate, *Shakespeare and Ovid*, 19–23, for an empathetic evocation of the 'limited but intense' education grammar school boys received (19), and Jeff Dolven, *Scenes of Instruction in Renaissance Romance*, 15–64. For the physical pains of early modern education, see Gordon Campbell and Thomas N. Corns, *John Milton*, 152–54.

of genre and form, in particular the legitimacy of those formal choices. Formal legitimacy underlines both Sidney's assessment of *The Shepheardes Calender* and Spenser's own defensive remarks about *The Faerie Queene* in the 'Letter to Raleigh': Sidney 'dare[d] not allow' the archaic diction of the *Calender*, [46] while Spenser's letter attempts to forestall '*gealous opinions and misconstructions*' by clarifying his '*general intention and meaning*' (*FQ*, 714). As Wilson-Okamura argues, the thinking which underlies these and many similar interventions is implicitly formalist: what is the proper diction for a pastoral collection in English? What is the basis of Spenser's epic – what does an intelligent reader need to know in order to make sense of that poem in terms of genre ('*being a continued Allegory, or darke conceit*' [*FQ*, 714])? These are naturally not the only questions we might ask about Spenser's poetry now, nor are they superior to the questions which have been asked of the poems by historicist critics. As others have suggested, historicist approaches do not preclude close reading, while the renewed attention to the textuality of context arguably sharpens the practice of close reading while certainly making its practitioners more ideologically self-conscious. In seeking to re-read the formal bases of *The Faerie Queene*, I am not attempting to rescue Spenser from his contexts, nor to suggest that aesthetic questions can or should be insulated from the cultures which produced them. Indeed, the consequence of many of my readings is to underline the unfixed, unsettled quality of *The Faerie Queene*'s narrations and descriptions; Spenser, I think, was wholly serious in his recognition that '*the most part of men delight to read*' what he calls '*historical fiction … rather for variety of matter, then for profite of the ensample*' (*FQ*, 715). [47] In other words, variety of matter, with all the mediation and complexity such variation necessarily entails, frequently occludes the profit of the example; the darkness of the dark conceit may be constitutive of a reader's experience. Wilson-Okamura makes the broader claim that formal questions have historical and methodological priority: 'To insist on the importance of style, in a period obsessed with style, is not mere formalism; it is also good historicism.'[48] While this remains debatable – for a materialist,

46 Sidney, *Miscellaneous Prose*, 112.
47 Jane Grogan, *Exemplary Spenser*, 27–34, argues that both the 'Letter to Raleigh' and the poem as a whole are serious about their claims to ethical teaching. Though my emphasis is different, Grogan's sense of the playfulness of the Letter is helpful: 'The Letter's aim, it seems, is not to furnish an accurate *précis* of Spenser's poetics but to entice, poke and point readers towards a deeper understanding of the poetics of the poem by making them work through the challenges of a genial but tricksy familiar letter, one that simultaneously *embodies* the principles it states' (33).
48 Wilson-Okamura, *Spenser's International Style*, 3.

politics will always take precedence over competing discourses[49] – it points to the fact that historicists can underestimate the changeable history of literary forms and their impact on what and how we read.

Formal reading is a challenging and potentially delusive discipline: the things which I see in the text may not be there; I will overlook many of the things which are there. This is particularly the case with a text which deploys conventions which are unfamiliar or have been rusting for centuries. T. S. Eliot's bemused contempt for the pleasures of Spenser – 'who except for scholars, and except the eccentric few who are born with a sympathy for such work ... can now read through the whole of *The Faerie Queene* with delight?' – captures this dilemma.[50] Since *The Faerie Queene* is an antiquarian enthusiasm, it takes antiquarian sympathies (or eccentricities) to enjoy it. A more nuanced way of putting this would be that Spenser demands historical sympathy, broadly conceived, from his readers – that is, an interest in the history of the language and style as well as an interest in English and European history. Formal reading of *The Faerie Queene* entails the deployment of a range of reading styles in the service of a broader attentiveness to a text which is always dynamic, always on the point of further qualifications or amendments. To misapply a Neil Young song: rust never sleeps; the processes of historical change and decay on the language and forms of the poem mean that the reading of it is never steadied or fixed. The formal reader needs to have an informed understanding of a wide range of discourses and practices such as: sixteenth-century rhetoric; Spenser's knowledge of other poetries and literatures, including the Bible; versification and contemporaneous debates about metre; the impact of book history on the understanding of the physical forms in which Spenser's poems circulated; the relationship between Spenser's language and Early Modern English, itself a distinct linguistic phenomenon.[51] In its perhaps relaxed complexity, Spenser's approach to poetic meaning is analogous to the unaligned modus vivendi Louis MacNeice outlined in his 'Ode' in the mid 1930s:

> I cannot draw up any code
> There are too many qualifications
> Too many asterisk asides
> Too many crosses in the margin[52]

49 See for example Jameson's claim that 'the political perspective' is 'the absolute horizon of all reading and all interpretation'. In Michael Hardt and Kathi Weeks (eds), *The Jameson Reader*, 33.
50 T. S. Eliot, *Selected Essays*, 451.
51 See individual chapters for full references on these topics.
52 Louis MacNeice, 'Ode' in *Collected Poems*, 37. On MacNeice and Spenser, see my 'MacNeice in Fairy Land', 352–69.

'Ode' is a poem of paternal advice to MacNeice's new-born son; as such, it is both pseudo-oracular and skittish in the service of a serious scepticism. How do you give advice which doesn't want to be seen as advice? Those 'qualifications' and 'asterisk asides' are a useful way of approaching *The Faerie Queene*, and the work of its critics, whether formalists or historicists. How do you *'fashion a gentleman or noble person in vertuous and gentle discipline'* with an 'afflicted stile' (*FQ*, 714)? To develop this idea further, I add some 'crosses in the margin' about the risks and ambiguity of formal reading. These are not only those diagnosed by Rasmussen of neglecting context for form. Gordon Teskey has suggested that close reading techniques of microscopic analysis may be counterproductive to understanding Spenserian allegory:

> There is no poet for whom the techniques of close reading are more unsuitable if relied on exclusively, or more likely to mislead if mechanically applied. When we read *The Faerie Queene* we need a long memory and a distanced, somewhat relaxed view of its entanglements even more than we need the capacity for paying minute attention. Matters are complicated and deepened in Spenser's verse by continually widening contexts ... Meaning in *The Faerie Queene* is like meaning in life: it is always entangled with the real.[53]

The notion of the relaxed entanglements of *The Faerie Queene* serves as a warning against mechanistic close reading: again, Spenser's epic is not a verbal icon, and does not always respond well to the kinds of microscopic close reading practised by writers like Empson.[54] Teskey's maxim that *The Faerie Queene*'s meaning 'is like life' strikes a MacNeicean note, or certainly the MacNeice of 'Ode', who goes on to claim that he would as 'mystic and maudlin/Dream of both real and ideal/Breakers of ocean.'[55] Any formal reading of *The Faerie Queene* has to strike a balance between 'minute attention' and a more 'relaxed' overview, which must recognise that no individual case is conclusive. The disrupted syntax of IV.ii.1 does not disprove Alpers's model of a linear syntax, rather the reverse; again, this is a point of departure, rather than a fixed point of reference. The breakers of ocean are both real and ideal, both specific forms and dynamic phenomena.

53 Gordon Teskey, 'Thinking Moments in *The Faerie Queene*', 103–24 (111).
54 As Empson himself recognised: see *Seven Types of Ambiguity*, 33. See also Theresa Krier, 'Time Lords', 1–19, for the notion that *The Faerie Queene* actively encourages readers to experience semantic drift in the white spaces between individual stanzas.
55 Louis MacNeice, *Collected Poems*, 37.

In a book published in the same year as Teskey's article, Andrew Zurcher offers a lengthy footnote which attempts to specify the kind of reading demanded by *The Faerie Queene*. Working from a close reading of I.ii.4–6, Zurcher notes that an annotated edition like Hamilton's Longman necessarily cannot reproduce the attention he has just paid to the semantics of individual words like 'suddenly' and 'yblent', and which 'we can suppose Spenser would have expected from his first readers'.[56] The footnote richly elaborates on this expectation:

> It might at first seem obvious that the interpretation of a rhetorically or conceptually complicated work should require studious application over time; and yet at the same time the apprehension of beauty or meaning in a text seems to occur in a vanishing moment, in the course of any single reading experience. The experience of coming-to-know a text like *The Faerie Queene* … must thus be one of successive layering of momentous apprehensions. This successive layering can take place if the reader invests time and effort, between readings, in the analysis of the constituent elements of the text; these sundry inquiries will themselves provoke proleptically the pleasures of a further reading, as the synthesizing intuition, stored with new information, interacts with the memory, but the real effect of synthesis will occur most pleasurably at the next reading.

The work of the reader envisaged here is certainly not relaxed: Zurcher's focus is on a 'studious' reading and re-reading with the aim of producing aesthetic pleasure; as he goes on to note, this method of reading for 'temporal synthesis (where the experience of times past and that of the present are gripped as in a handful) is physically delighting'.[57] Zurcher's reader follows Sir Walter Ralegh, who by following Spenser's advice '*may as in a handful gripe al the discourse*' of *The Faerie Queene*, but where Spenser offers an aide-memoire to his diffuse text, Zurcher repurposes this resonant phrase to evoke the delight of re-reading (*FQ*, 718). Whether Ralegh was a delighted re-reader of *The Faerie Queene* is a different order of speculation.[58] The hesitancies in Zurcher's formulation are exemplary of the difficulties still facing formalists: should we talk of 'beauty or meaning'? (The second term reads as a neutral-seeming afterthought to qualify what might

56 Andrew Zurcher, *Spenser's Legal Language*, 5.
57 Zurcher, *Spenser's Legal Language*, 5 n.2. See also Zurcher's discussion of the 'Letter to Raleigh' in the context of the *sensus germanus* of Renaissance lawyers, 17–49, in particular his remarks about the 'desperation' the reader may feel in attempting to analyse the poem (49).
58 Hadfield suggests that Spenser's attitude towards Ralegh was to become progressively more hostile and critical; in *Edmund Spenser: A Life*, 172–73, 307, 340.

otherwise seem an unguarded admission). Does finding aspects of *The Faerie Queene* beautiful problematise our objectivity as critics? I would put the question the other way around: how can we study, much less teach, *The Faerie Queene* without some measure of recognition that it can be beautiful?[59] As before, beauty is not a get-out clause from the realities which flow from '*the wel-head*' of history (*FQ*, 718); that *The Faerie Queene* is a great poem does not make the Smerwick massacre any less repellent, nor obviate the treatment of the native Irish by Spenser and fellow settlers. Indeed, as Zurcher has suggested elsewhere, the poetry of *The Faerie Queene* draws vividly for both serious and comic effects on the bloodthirsty transactions in which Spenser was complicit as both witness and participant.[60]

What makes this footnote so valuable is its painstaking articulation of the cognitive processes which go into the re-reading of *The Faerie Queene*. Such a model is in tension with Teskey's scepticism about close reading – Zurcher's reader remains preoccupied with 'the analysis of the constituent elements of the text'.[61] Nevertheless, these models do not cancel one another out. If Teskey's relaxed entanglements point to the way the poem enacts the processes of thinking through its extraordinary variety of episode and thus to its overall construction, Zurcher's successive layerings speak to the reader's apprehension of the same poem line by line and page by page in the processes of reading and re-reading. The challenge for formal reading is to reconcile these different yet related imperatives. *The Faerie Queene* is at once a record of complex historical processes, a text (to adopt a quasi-New Historical rhetoric) in which the tensions within certain ideologies are played out and negotiated, and a complex, layered work of art

---

59 See Wilson-Okamura, *Spenser's International Style*, for the related argument that students legitimately expect from their teachers some grounding in the basics of literary composition. This is related to the other subversive classroom question: 'Yes, but is it any *good*?'. Like Wilson-Okamura, my view is that we fail to respond to our students' enthusiasm for literature when we brush this off as a jejune or inappropriate question.

60 Edmund Spenser, *Selected Letters Other Papers*, ed. Christopher Burlinson and Andrew Zurcher, Introduction, lix–lxiv, citing Gordon Teskey, *Allegory and Violence*. See Hadfield, *Edmund Spenser: A Life*, 100–01, for the argument that Spenser witnessed the execution of Murrough O'Brien at Limerick in 1577, later described in *A View of The Present State of Ireland*.

61 Although perhaps not wholly: Teskey goes on to clarify the 'Thinking Moments' of *The Faerie Queene* through analogies to the way in which philosophers arrest and slow down discursive flow, connecting Hegel and Plato with the 'continual oscillation between narrative movement and symbolic tableau' in *The Faerie Queene* (114–15), a model which mirrors Zurcher's emphasis on 'momentous apprehensions'.

which demands plural readings and approaches. My ambition is to contribute to this debate by exploring how the poem works from the level of the individual word upwards to the poem as a totality, always conscious of what Teskey refers to as 'its sheer bigness' and 'the noetic entanglement' of its episodes.[62] There have been several important moves to revitalise formal reading, which have reminded readers of Spenser's unique literary skills. My debts to these scholars will be evident throughout, but in particular I want to demarcate my approach in this book from David Scott Wilson-Okamura's *Spenser's International Style* and my earlier collaboration with J. B. Lethbridge on the *Concordance to the Rhymes of The Faerie Queene*. Wilson-Okamura's brilliant study focuses on the literary contexts for Spenser's style, particularly the commentarial tradition on Virgil and others which helped to constitute the humanist and Renaissance poetics in which Spenser and others were educated; as he concedes at the outset, 'In what follows there is almost no close reading.'[63] Like Teskey, he suggests that such approaches may not be the best suited to the reading of *The Faerie Queene*: 'for a long poem, there are better ways to prove something about its style: by adducing statistics; or, when those are unavailable, by appealing to the *consensus sapientum*, the convergence of scholarly or critical opinion over a long period.'[64] Lethbridge and I have made a contribution to the tools available for the formal analysis of the poem through the *Concordance to the Rhymes of The Faerie Queene*, and further work remains to be done in this field. However, this is mostly an analytical study rather than a statistical one – my emphasis here is on reading for meaning.

Such perspectives notwithstanding, in this study I concentrate on readings of *The Faerie Queene*, albeit readings which are consciously provisional, and which are informed by relevant contexts (historical, literary, political, and, in places, contexts by analogy). Wilson-Okamura partly adopts the term 'historical formalism';[65] a related formulation would be provisional rather than definitive close readings – readings which aim for the dynamism which is characteristic of the poem. Spenser's comments in the metaphysical laboratory of the Gardins of Adonis are germane to

---

62 Teskey, 'Thinking Moments', 111.
63 Wilson-Okamura, *Spenser's International Style*, 4. See also Wilson-Okamura, *Virgil in the Renaissance* for his earlier work on the commentarial tradition.
64 Wilson-Okamura, *Spenser's International Style*, 5.
65 Wilson-Okamura, *Spenser's International Style*, 5–6.

such an enterprise: 'formes are variable and decay,/By course of kinde, and by occasion' (III.vi.38). Though the main referent is the distinction between the 'substaunce' which is 'eterne' and the transitory 'outward fashion' of appearances (III.vi.37–38), Spenser's biologies mimic and reflect upon his literary choices. Indeed, the textual changes to this canto – in particular the introduction of a half line to stanza 45 in the 1609 folio, which appears as an incomplete eight-line stanza in both the 1590 and 1596 editions – suggests a witty consciousness of the vagaries through which 'sweet Poets verse' might give 'endless date' to its subjects (III. vi.45).[66] Traditional close reading is inappropriate to such a text because it so continuously evokes within itself notions of the mutability and plasticity of all forms. Yet the business of making sense remains paramount, and my readings try to do limited justice to the challenges the poem poses to its readers. My hope is that this study and Wilson-Okamura's will be complementary, providing readers with different approaches to related problems. This does not mean that we are wholly in agreement at all points. I remain sceptical about Wilson-Okamura's contention that Renaissance thinking valued ornament and ornamentalism for its own sake, and that such ornaments are separable from questions of poetic meaning, as will become clear.[67] In contrast, I tend to read Spenser's style semantically. That is, I am ready to look for meaning as and when the forms of *The Faerie Queene* diverge and mutate under pressure of the events he narrates or the objects he describes; my reading of the 'Firebrand of hell' stanza above is exemplary of this tendency.[68] The more important commonality between this study and Wilson-Okamura's is in the broad contours of our interests and in our conviction that style matters centrally to Spenser and the interpretation of *The Faerie Queene*.

   This study is structured in two complementary parts. The first half concentrates on detailed accounts of the key compositional units of *The Faerie Queene*: words and lexis (Chapter 1), line and metre (Chapter 2), rhyme (Chapter 3), and stanza (Chapter 4); this part is aimed at giving an overview of the microscopic aspects of Spenser's art. In contrast, the second half offers panoptic views of *The Faerie Queene*'s macrocosmic

66 See *FQ*, 745 for textual commentary. I discuss this stanza in greater detail in '"And dearest loue": Virgilian half-lines in Spenser's *Faerie Queene*'.
67 See Wilson-Okamura, *Spenser's International Style*, Chapter 5, 'Ornamentalism'.
68 The counter position – that Spenser is aesthetic rather than a mimetic metrist, whose formal effects aim for pleasingness of sound but which do not affect 'the lexical meaning of the poem's statement' – is advanced by Susanne Woods, *Natural Emphasis*, 15, 137–61, and more recently by Jeff Dolven, 'Spenser's Metrics', 390.

structures, focusing on canto (Chapter 5) and, finally, narrative structure (Chapter 6). These demarcations are necessarily not absolute: rhyme as a device is discussed in and across several chapters; choices of lexis are particularly relevant to Chapter 1, but are discussed throughout. As will become clear, I have been conscious throughout of the risks of what I later call 'synecdochical formalism'; that is, the selection of one or two examples which serve as illustrations of larger tendencies. The selection of examples is perforce one of the hazards of close reading: even as I warn against it, I embrace it.

1

Doubtful words: the vocabulary of *The Faerie Queene*

> Although indeed the senate of poets hath chosen verse as their fittest raiment, meaning, as in matter they passed all in all, so in manner to go beyond them: not speaking (tabletalk fashion, or like men in a dream) words as they chanceably fall from the mouth, but peising each syllable of each word by just proportion according to the dignity of the subject. (Sir Philip Sidney)

> For the poet's first business is *mentioning* things. Whatever musical or other harmonies he may incidentally evoke, the fact will remain that such and such things – and not others – have been mentioned in his poem. (Louis MacNeice)

> Spenser definitely does not belong to the class of writers who call a spade a spade. (Herbert Rix)[1]

The focus of this chapter is outwardly a simple one: the vocabulary of *The Faerie Queene*. But there is nothing simple about such a topic, which is at once vast and all-pervasive. Any discussion of Spenser's epic is sooner or later concerned with the words of the poem, no matter what the methodological approach adopted by its writer. My focus is more narrowly on the lexis of *The Faerie Queene*: the diction and choices of word in the poem, and how those choices affect the reader's understanding. I am concerned with questions which relate to the rhetorical character of Elizabethan thinking and the styles Spenser deploys and the choices he makes in the construction of his poem at a local level. To quote MacNeice

---

1 The quotations are: Sidney, *Miscellaneous Prose*, 82; Louis MacNeice, *Modern Poetry*, 5; Rix, *Rhetoric in Spenser's Poetry*, 71.

again: it is a 'forgotten truism that words are what poems are made of'; my aim is to remind readers of the peculiarities of Spenser's words as we process them in the act of reading.[2] Such a truism brings out the profound differences between Renaissance and modern assumptions about the words in poems.[3] Both Sidney and MacNeice are concerned with diction in the passages cited above. Sidney's conception of words being suited to subject matter articulates a long-standing tradition[4] that language clothes ideas – that diction is a form of rhetorical dressing-up, a 'fittest raiment', which re-presents familiar ideas in new forms for the edification and delight of its readers.[5] As Shakespeare puts it in his version of the dressing-up conceit, in keeping 'invention in a noted weed' to praise his beloved, he is 'dressing old words new'.[6] In contrast, MacNeice implies a closer relationship between things and words; as he writes elsewhere in the same book 'New subject-matter ... needs a new diction.'[7] While this is a self-conscious exaggeration, MacNeice's assumptions are closer to contemporary views suspicious of rarefied poetic diction and the claims of formal rhetoric.[8] The poet who mentions things may be said to take a constitutive as opposed to an allegorical approach to the words of poetry, although Spenser is more adept at the business of mentioning concrete things than he is usually given credit for. The cultural distance which separates Sidney and MacNeice draws attention to the different expectations early modern and contemporary readers have of poetic diction. My discussion will endeavour to shed light on these ongoing questions.

The work of Judith H. Anderson and Andrew Zurcher has been influential in returning critical attention to the language Spenser uses, particularly in terms of the materiality of Renaissance words, and Spenser's adaptation

2 Louis MacNeice, *Selected Literary Criticism*, 205.
3 For the preference of 'Renaissance' over 'Early Modern' in such contexts, see Judith H. Anderson, *Words That Matter*, 5–6, and Wilson-Okamura, *Virgil in the Renaissance*, 8.
4 As David Bellos notes, even Saussure's radical *Course in General Linguistics* 'firmly maintained the long tradition of treating language as the dress of thought', in *Is That a Fish in Your Ear?*, 325.
5 See John Webster, 'Rhetoric', for the brilliant observation that in the *Defence of Poetry* 'In a projection worthy of the best of alchemists, Sidney transmutes the central values which Cicero defined as those of oratory into those of poetry' (599).
6 Shakespeare, Sonnet 76 in *Complete Sonnets*, 533.
7 MacNeice, *Modern Poetry*, 139.
8 See Vickers, *In Defence of Rhetoric*, for an assertion of both of the enduring values of rhetoric and a history of attacks against it from Plato onwards. Modern linguists, such as Ronald Carter, *Language and Creativity*, emphasise the artifice inherent in 'common talk', thus chiming with MacNeice's broader claims that 'The poet is a specialist in something which everyone practises', *Modern Poetry*, 31. See Richard Danson Brown, '"Can't We Ever, My Love, Speak in the Same Language"' for commentary.

of legal idioms.[9] Both their studies extend historical understanding of
The Faerie Queene whilst refocusing attention on issues of form and word
choice and the values associated with such usages. My approach is both
more traditional and (I hope) differently radical in its focus on lexis. This
discussion entails consideration of traditional topics, such as archaism and
rhetoric, alongside newer concerns such as the poem's formulaic qualities,
and reflection on Spenser's use of the English language at a point when
it was undergoing considerable change and flux.[10] At the same time, as
Eleanor Cook stresses, 'The primary rule for thinking about lexis is that
words in a poem always exist in relation, never in isolation'; individual
words in *The Faerie Queene* always impinge on the interpretation of its
larger structures.[11] This imperative relates to my concern with how we
closely read the poem: is this possible, or does its diction actively resist
the kind of analysis prized by New Criticism? A related question is more
troubling: what is the purpose of the lexis of *The Faerie Queene*? Is the
poem, as Hazlitt suggested, a form of literary narcotic in which the sound
of verse lulls 'the senses into a deep oblivion of the jarring noises of
the world'?[12] Though Hazlitt has been something of a whipping boy to
modern Spenserians (chiefly because of his notorious advice to nervous
readers that 'If they do not meddle with the allegory, the allegory will not
meddle with them'),[13] the questions he raises in his brilliant evocation of
the sensuous experience of reading the poem remain provocative.[14] In
this context, Rix's common-sense insistence on the rarefied qualities of
Spenser's diction is relevant. On a literal level, Spenser was perfectly capable
of calling a spade a spade: the Brigants 'neuer vsde to liue by plough nor
spade'; in the pageant of the months, 'sturdy *March*' carries both a spade
and a seed bag (VI.x.39; VII.vii.32). Things are constantly mentioned in
The Faerie Queene: the first stanza itemises a knight, his arms and shield
(including their condition), his horse and its apparel, and the plain on
which they ride (I.i.1); it is a stanza which strikingly bears out the justice
of MacNeice's characterisation of what poetry does. Spenser's poetry is
at once deictic and ornamental; this is a tension which will be played

9 Anderson, *Words that Matter*; Zurcher, *Spenser's Legal Language*.
10 See Görlach, *Introduction to Early Modern English*.
11 Eleanor Cook, 'Lexis', 688.
12 Hazlitt in Paul J. Alpers (ed.), *Edmund Spenser: A Critical Anthology*, 138.
13 Hazlitt in Alpers (ed.), *Edmund Spenser: A Critical Anthology*, 133–34. As Gordon
     Teskey has pointed out, scholars have often misread this as a denial of allegory; in
     'Thinking Moments', 104–05.
14 See Alpers, *The Poetry of The Faerie Queene*, pp. 70–76; David Bromwich, 'Hazlitt,
     William', 349–50; and David Scott Wilson-Okamura, 'The Formalist Tradition', 724–25.

out throughout this book. Rix's remark articulates a widespread sense that Spenser is a poet of circumlocution, of involution, and of rhetorical elaboration.[15] Redcrosse is clothed in '*mightie* armes and *siluer* shielde';[16] his horse is not just 'angry' but gets a complete line evoking its impatience, 'As much disdayning to the curbe to yield'. Certainly, this is a poetry which doesn't yield to the curb of compression or to the more dubious truism that poetry is an art of the fewest possible words.[17] Spenser's choice of lexis – the words he uses and the restrictions he places on the vocabulary of *The Faerie Queene* – are telling evidence of the ways he expected to be read.

Compression or reduplication?

How did Spenser use words poetically? Again, this sounds like a deceptively simple or naïve question, but even in formal criticism, there are sharp divisions between those who argue that Spenser's vocabulary is ornamental and those who view it as semantic. Consider William Empson's account of why Spenser did not fully fit his approach in *Seven Types of Ambiguity*:

> Ambiguity is a phenomenon of compression. Thus it is seldom that one finds relevant ambiguities in Spenser or Marlowe, because their method is by a variety of means to sustain a poetic effect for so long that the poetic knot can be spread out at length, and one does not see that the separate uses of a word would be a pun if they were drawn together.[18]

It is relatively easy to find examples which contradict Empson's ruling: the lavatorial pun about the working of the Port Esquiline in the House of Alma, 'It was auoided quite, and throwne out priuily', shows Spenser's readiness to deploy concise ambiguity (II.ix.32). Empson's approach is illustrative of conventional assumptions about Spenser's lexis, reflecting the value which he and other Modernists found in the pre-eminently ambiguous Donne. For Empson, because Spenser's control of rhythm

---

15 See for example Kaske, *Spenser and Biblical Poetics*, for the view that Spenser's style is 'ornate', or at least more ornate than the Bible; 2, 52.
16 My emphases.
17 See Don Paterson, *Reading Shakespeare's Sonnets*, 490, for a typical statement of this belief: 'since poetry is largely the art of saying things once and only once, a pithy summary *within* the poem is thoroughly redundant – because poetry *is* the art of pithy summary'. Paterson is objecting to Shakespeare's often 'otiose' couplets in the Sonnets, but without reflecting on the historical differences in taste and education between Shakespeare's period and our own.
18 Empson, *Seven Types of Ambiguity*, 31.

works over long passages, 'it was not necessary for him to concentrate on the lightning flashes of ambiguity'.[19] Though the critical terminology is different, Empson's approach is congruent with Rix's description of Spenser as a specialist in modes of periphrasis and related schemes rather than those of direct statement.[20]

Similarly, J. B. Lethbridge has re-emphasised the formulaic character of *The Faerie Queene*: as much as two-thirds of the poem may take the form of almost prefabricated poetic expressions; such phrases become generative Spenserian clichés.[21] Indeed, there are large portions of the poem which work to dampen linguistic particularity through the relentless deployment of formulae: steeds are great, ladies are fair, knights are redoubted, and so on. Although Lethbridge's lists are statistically impressive, his study necessarily avoids detailed analysis of the instances he assembles: his point is that it is a matter of semantic indifference what 'goodly' does in lines as dispersed as 'Which to a goodly Citty led his vew' and 'Both goodly Castle, and both goodly Towne' (I.x.55; V.x.26). 'Goodly' is metrical filler which efficiently contributes to pentameters when such a colourless adjective is needed. Lethbridge problematises the conventional assumption that Spenser's words should be closely read for inference. Yet the question for criticism is not so much whether *The Faerie Queene* uses formulae but whether they are invariably to be read as little more than phatic poetic clichés. Is every 'redoubted knight' dreaded only in formulaic terms because this is a convenient qualifier with appropriate metrical and attributive contours, or are these ostensibly blunt terms sharpened by use and poetic context? The first usage of this formula hints at the complexities of this question: 'Her doubtfull words made that redoubted knight/Suspect her truth', a formulation which blends the trustworthiness of language within the poem with a neat metamorphic doubling of the key term 'doubt' (I.i.53).[22] Lethbridge's work points in similar directions to Empson and Rix: Spenser's poetic language is one of reduplication and variety rather than of pointed utterance. These observations are worth testing and my argument responds to the challenge Lethbridge poses to readers of *The Faerie Queene*: what are the implications of a formulaic lexis to the

19 Empson, *Seven Types of Ambiguity*, 34
20 Rix, *Rhetoric in Spenser's Poetry*, 21, 46.
21 Lethbridge 'The Bondage of Rhyme' in Brown and Lethbridge, *A Concordance*, 134–57, 480–533.
22 See *FQ*, 43, for Hamilton's notes on the complex ways in which the Redcrosse Knight is 'redoubted'. This is admittedly an unfair example. However, the extent to which Spenser modifies the reading of familiar terms remains as remarkable as his dependence on formulae. In this light, 'goodly' can be simultaneously phatic *and* evaluative.

interpretation of the poem? This chapter deploys two test cases to explore Spenser's vocabulary: first, I consider the debate around archaism as both a conceptual and a practical problem for editors and readers. Second, I re-read the infamous episode of the Giant with the Scales from Book V in terms of its concern with the relationships between allegory, violence, and choices of word.

'Olde and obsolete wordes'

The idea that formulae might be sharpened by use recalls Spenser's innovative suggestion in 1580 that English poets might legitimately wrench pronunciation from convention to suit the requirements of a classically based quantitative metre. 'Rough words must be subdued with Vse,' he wrote to Harvey, imagining the vowel patterns of *Carpenter* being reshaped to elongate the central syllable and so conform to rules of Classical prosody.[23] However one reads Spenser's involvement in the quantitative experiments, the Letters show an ambitious writer willing to recognise that the practice of poetry may conflict with the dynamics of the spoken language and to act on the implications of this shortfall.[24] What matters for Spenser is not English tradition so much as English potential; how poetry should be written trumps how language is actually used.

Though the quantitative experiment was ultimately a dead end, Spenser's readiness to adapt his practice in the light of theory is evident throughout his career. His commitment to archaism is the most notorious example of this privileging of theory.[25] The use of archaism is a complex gesture which, as scholars have noted, points in several directions at once. Paula Blank emphasises Spenser's participation in a broader culture of archaic usage: throughout the sixteenth century, the use of Chaucerian vocabulary

---

23 *Prose*, 16. See Derek Attridge, *Well-Weighed Syllables*, 146–49, for Harvey's horrified reaction.
24 Hadfield, *Edmund Spenser: A Life*, 106–09, reviews the evidence of the Areopagus sceptically, viewing the Letters as evidence of a 'casual symposium' rather than a serious group committed to metrical reform (108).
25 There is an extensive secondary literature on archaism. In addition to the foundational work of W. R. Renwick, Emma Field Pope, and Bruce McElderry (see Bibliography), the following are particularly useful: Nathan A. Gans, 'Archaism and Neologism in Spenser's Diction'; Barbara Strang, 'Language'; T. V. F. Brogan, 'Archaism'; Richard Danson Brown, *The New Poet: Novelty and Tradition in Spenser's Complaints*, 65–71; Paula Blank, 'The Babel of Renaissance English', 283–86; Zurcher, *Spenser's Legal Language*, 7–8, 28–41; and 'Spenser's Studied Archaism'; Dorothy Stephens, 'Spenser's Language(s)'; and Wilson-Okamura, *Spenser's International Style*, 57–66.

could mark nationalist resistance to the importation of foreign loan words, or 'inkhorn' terms, into English.[26] But equally, archaic speech could be seen as an olde-worlde affectation; according to the rhetorician Thomas Wilson, 'the fine Courtier wil talke nothyng but Chaucer.'[27] Nevertheless, to write like Chaucer two centuries after his death is a significantly larger project than to try to talk like Chaucer. Wilson-Okamura summarises the conflicting positions encoded in Spenser's use of archaism:

> The paradox of Spenser's archaisms is that they are local and global, medieval and humanist, all at the same time. Insofar as they are drawn from medieval authors – Chaucer, Gower, Langland, and Lydgate – they are native, English, 'Gothic,' residual, atavistic; but insofar as they are pure and originary, the products of historical research, they are also modern, progressive specimens of the new, international style in classical scholarship and literary authorship.[28]

The point is well made: by adopting a medievalising diction, Spenser is at once looking back to Chaucer, Gower, and metrical romance whilst at the same forging a new kind of written style unlike that of his predecessors. Similarly, Zurcher's discussion of E. K.'s Epistle to Harvey – the document which most fully articulates Spenser's theory of archaism – stresses the 'nose-thumbing at authority' which underpins that theory alongside the international scholarship which informs it.[29] The self-assertive flash of E. K.'s prose marks it as an audacious act of entrée to ongoing debates about both language and literature. Where Wilson had accused speakers of 'outlandishe Englishe' of becoming incomprehensible to their own mothers,[30] E. K. brusquely bats the accusation of maternal neglect back: Spenser's diction restores 'as to theyr rightfull heritage such good and naturall English words' to 'our Mother tonge' (*Yale*, 16).[31] Archaism is a deliberate tactic

---

26 Blank, 'The Babel of Renaissance English', 283–86. See Willy Maley, 'Spenser's Irish Language', for the argument that Spenser's distinctive vocabulary is properly understood as an imitation of linguistic usage in Ireland.

27 Thomas Wilson, *The Art of Rhetorique* (1553), quoted in Görlach, *Introduction to Early Modern English*, 220. This remark comes in a passage which robustly attacks the use of 'straunge ynkehorne termes' in place of plain English; unlike E. K., Wilson was not persuaded that Chaucerianisms had any value – his ideal was to 'speake as is commonly receiued' (219).

28 Wilson-Okamura, *Spenser's International Style*, 59.

29 Zurcher, *Spenser's Legal Language*, 31. As Zurcher suggests, the Epistle is the 'closest' we may come to Spenser's 'explicit views on language and interpretation' (30); like Zurcher, I think it is a matter of indifference whether 'E. K.' denotes a real person, or was a convenient front for Spenser himself (30 n.30).

30 In Görlach, *Introduction to Early Modern English*, 220.

31 See Zurcher, *Spenser's Legal Language*, 31, for commentary on E. K.'s subsequent analogy between 'natural speach' and breast milk.

in a project which encompasses both the renewal of the English language and the creation of a new sort of poetry. In a key passage, E. K. stresses firstly the literary decorum which Spenser's vocabulary brings to the *Calender* and secondly the 'grace' and 'auctoritie' which archaisms give to the verse. Again, this is the language of someone with a point to prove, wordily yet wittily underlining his rectitude – 'sure I think, and think I think not amisse' – while deflating the positions of his opponents and stressing the deliberation (and incipient cultural capital) which underlies Spenser's diction:

> albe amongst many other faultes it specially be objected of Valla against Livie, and of other against Saluste, that with over much studie they affect antiquitie, as coveting thereby credence and honor of elder yeeres, yet I am of opinion, and eke the best learned are of the lyke, that those auncient solemne wordes are a great ornament both in the one and in the other; the one labouring to set forth in hys worke an eternall image of antiquitie, and the other carefully discoursing matters of gravitie and importaunce. (*Yale*, 14–15)

E. K. urges that if it was legitimate for Livy and Sallust to 'affect antiquitie', so it must be for the New Poet, despite the objections of humanists as distinguished as Valla. As Zurcher observes, 'This harnessing of classically sanctioned arguments in defence of distinctively unorthodox ideas is precisely what makes E. K.'s *Epistle* so clever'.[32] Cleverness, innovation, and self-confidence are all evident in this writing – indeed, it is a text which both flaunts its learned opinionatedness ('the best learned are of the lyke', and who are *you* to think differently?) and solicits precisely the kinds of objection which it received.

Spenser's contemporaries thus could not fail to notice the aggressive novelty of his diction. As the testimony of writers like Sidney, Guilpin, and Jonson (representing literary opinion over a more than fifty-year period)[33] demonstrates, Spenser's archaisms were seen as a distinctive choice which materially affected the reception of his poetry; in Jonson's

---

32 Zurcher, *Spenser's Legal Language*, 32.
33 Sidney's *Defence* was probably written around 1579–80 before its publication in 1595; see *Miscellaneous Prose*, 62, 65–66. Guilpin's *Skialetheia* was published in 1598 and probably written 'within a year or perhaps eighteen months of its entry' on the Stationers' Register; see *Skialetheia*, 3–5. Jonson's *Timber*, his commonplace book, was published posthumously in 1640 but had been written over many years beforehand; see Ian Donaldson, *Ben Jonson*, 13. Jonson's views had a constitutive influence on later Neo-Classical criticism, conveniently assembled by R. M. Cummings (ed.), *Spenser: The Critical Heritage*, particularly 299–314.

infamously backhanded formulation, '*Spencer*, in affecting the Ancients, writ no Language: Yet I would have him read for his matter; but as *Virgil* read *Ennius*.'[34] Like Sidney before him, Jonson responds to E. K.'s self-confidence in kind, and sharply distinguishes between dress and what lies beneath; *that* is what justifies Spenser's work, not the flim-flam of his diction.[35] Another way of understanding these criticisms is that Spenser's diction did its work by provoking comment, separating the New Poet decisively from contemporary styles.

Indeed, it could be argued that the strategy worked too well. Though the Epistle is clear that Spenser's archaisms should be read in terms of ideas of pastoral decorum – this is a language 'fittest for such rusticall rudenesse of shepheards' – readers have assumed that all of his work participates in the same manoeuvre, when the truth is that archaism is significantly less prominent in his other works (*Yale*, 14).[36] *The Faerie Queene* uses archaism, but it is not the only nor even the most prominent facet of its diction. Nevertheless, the poem looks and feels archaic to modern readers through vocabulary like 'Lo', 'whilome', and 'areeds', not to mention the Latinate typography which prints moderns *us* and *vs* and vice versa, as well as *js* as *is* ('vnfitter'; 'hauing'; '*Ioue*').[37] Zurcher's remarks about the way in which generations of Spenserians have curated the lexical forms of Spenser's texts are pertinent:

> Spenser's fussy archaism … has subsequently … been adduced to the defence of old-spelling editions of his work, in a conservative campaign so successful that, alone among the works of any one his contemporaries, his poetry and prose survive in modern editions entirely in the original spelling. Subtle academic readers congratulate themselves not only on their initiated capacity for understanding this spelling and this language, but on their determination to secure and protect it … The marginalization of Spenser's writings in the

34 In Cummings (ed.), *Spenser: The Critical Heritage*, 294. Jonson's attitude to Spenser is significantly more complex than this often cited soundbite allows for; see James A. Riddell and Stanley Stewart, *Jonson's Spenser*, 35–36, for contextual commentary on this passage from *Timber*. See S. P. Zitner, 'Spenser's Diction and Classical Precedent', 364, for discussion of the 'inadequacy' of Jonson's view in terms of the classical authorities he cites.
35 See Hadfield, *Edmund Spenser: A Life*, 76, 128, for the suggestion that Spenser courted a certain brusque rudeness, particularly in his relations with social superiors.
36 See Zurcher, *Spenser's Legal Language*, 8. Drawing on McElderry's work, he notes that there are around 300 archaisms in Spenser and that most of these are concentrated in the *Calender*. Görlach, *Introduction to Early Modern English*, 140, shows that 'Spenser had no intention of using old words exclusively'.
37 All examples taken from I Proem, stanzas 1 and 3.

university curriculum, with their almost total disappearance from mainstream literary culture … has been considered a plausible or at least a necessary price to pay for the preservation of Spenser's original, however difficult, diction and spelling.[38]

As I was told – or rather reassured – as a graduate student by the editor of a modern-spelling series of drama texts, Spenser's orthography is a 'special case' which no one would dream of modernising. Yet as Zurcher suggests, the costs of this conservative exclusivity are considerable. Spenser's text has been rarefied from prevailing editorial norms to maintain its status as an elite classic; it has become a masterpiece of archaic subtlety, conserved in its singularity by the self-sustaining patina of its distinctive usages.[39] The specialness of Spenser's orthography was partly reinforced by broader movements in criticism, such as the New Bibliography in the earlier twentieth century, and later New Historicism, both of which in different ways and for different reasons supported the reprinting of other contemporary texts in old-spelling editions.[40] In this respect at least, Spenser has looked less eccentric to modern scholars. Yet as Zurcher suggests, the unmodernised text has significant consequences in terms of who reads Spenser now and for what purposes. Our old-spelling editions encourage the misconception that Spenser's archaisms are a form of literary fogeydom – that to use archaisms is equivalent to the affectation of Wilson's courtiers – rather than a commitment to radical and international literary values. Barbara Strang suggested that 'The reader of Spenser should approach the text as being in Spenser's language, which is a very different matter from reading him as if he were writing modern English with intermittent lapses into strange expressions which require glossing.'[41] This is surely a sentiment with which most Spenserians concur, but the problem is that the distinction Strang advances is more meaningful to academic readers than to students faced with *The Faerie Queene* for the first time. And yet, implicit in Zurcher's discussion is the recognition that modernising *The Faerie Queene* would be difficult because it would do violence to the intricate structures of meaning encoded in its lexis. Here is Book II Canto

---

38 Zurcher, *Spenser's Legal Language*, 7.

39 *Yale* provides an example of partial modernisation, by adopting modern conventions in i/j and u/v; see *Yale*, 781.

40 See John Jowett, 'Editing Shakespeare's Plays in the Twentieth Century', for an overview.

41 Strang, 'Language', 426; also cited by Cook, 'Lexis', with the relevant warning that 'readers and critics must be vigilant not to read modern assumptions about lexis back into older poetry' (689).

III stanza 26 as it appears in Hamilton's 2001 edition of the poem, a text closely based on the 1590 *Faerie Queene*:

> So faire, and thousand times more faire
> She seemd, when she presented was to sight,
> And was yclad, for heat of scorching aire,
> All in a silken Camus lylly whight,
> Purfled vpon with many a folded plight,
> Which all aboue besprinckled was throughout,
> With golden aygulets, that glistred bright
> Like twinckling stares, and all the skirt about
> Was hemd with golden fringe

How might this be modernised? Some changes would be relatively trivial: updating *faire* to *fair* and *seemd* to *seemed* would make little difference to the meaning of the verse, and there are examples of the modern forms elsewhere in the poem.[42] Similarly, little would be lost be modernising *lylly* to *lily* and even *aygulets* to *aglets*, though in this case the gains would be small since this remains a recondite term for a metallic stud.[43] But what about words that are now clearly archaic, like *yclad*, the past tense of *clothe*, showing Spenser's characteristic use of archaic verb-tense inflections,[44] or *Purfled*, an obsolete word meaning adorned with embroidery? *Plight* is an eye-rhyme for *pleat*, so should a modernised version regularise the spelling of the word to aid the reader's comprehension? *Whight* for *white* shows the same deliberate distortion: as the *Concordance to the Rhymes of The Faerie Queene* shows, the usual rhyme is *white*, outscoring *whight* seven to one, a neat statistical illustration of Spenser's general preference for modern forms over archaic.[45] If you make these changes, inevitably you lose something of the aesthetic shaping of the original spelling, since *pleat* is at best a half-rhyme with *sight*, *whight*, and *bright*. Moreover, *plight* is a different unit of lexis from *pleat*, with a separate listing in *OED*;[46] such a modernising would be an over-zealous intervention, materially altering the look and feel of Spenser's verse. It may stretch interpretive credulity to suggest a buried pun on 'plight' in the sense of

---

42 Other semantically insignificant changes could be made to *aire, glistred, twinckling, starres*, and *hemd*. Throughout the following discussion, Hamilton's notes in *FQ*, 184, are germane.

43 See "aglet, n.2.a". *OED Online.*

44 See Herbert W. Sugden, *The Grammar of Spenser's Faerie Queene*, 104.

45 Though there are several rhymes on 'white', this is only rhyme on 'whight'; indeed, it is the only usage of this form in the poem. See Brown and Lethbridge, *A Concordance*, 342, 384. For Spenser's preference for visual rhymes, see Toshiyuki Suzuki, 'Irregular Visual Rhymes in *The Faerie Queene*, Part I (Books I–III)'.

46 See "† plight, n.3". *OED Online.*

a pledge or undertaking,[47] yet Belphoebe is certainly pledged to keep her 'stedfast chastity' (III.v.55), so this single term may also allude to the binding language analysed by John Kerrigan in Shakespeare.[48] Similarly, to update *besprinckled* and *silken* to their contracted modern forms would alter the scansion of these artfully regular pentameters. If you roughen the accents by modernising (try speaking 'All in a silk chemise lily white') you mislead readers both about Spenser's diction and his intentions in this blazon.

The problems with this putative modernisation coalesce on 'Camus'. To modern readers, this looks wildly eccentric – an eccentricity possibly cued by its initial capitalisation,[49] but as *OED* explains, this is a Spenserian neologism based on the Romance word for a shirt, such as *chemise* in French or *camiza* in Spanish.[50] As Nathan A. Gans has remarked, 'neologism could itself be a form of archaism. One way of imitating the old poets – Chaucer, Lydgate, Occleve, and Hawes – was to neologize, since the sixteenth-century reputation of these writers depended, in part, on their enriching the language with new words.'[51] Although it's clear what Spenser means in context, the word is an example of the phenomenon observed by David Bellos about translators' use of 'foreign-sounding' loan words: 'Either it will be disregarded as a clumsy, awkward or incomplete act of translation, or it will be absorbed, reused, integrated, and become not foreign at all.'[52] *Camus* has not been absorbed into Standard English, where the etymologically related *chemise* has been.[53] Could the term be changed to *chemise*, an easier word, albeit with the stress on the second rather than the first syllable?[54] The problem is precisely that 'Camus' is

47 See "plight, n.1". *OED Online*.
48 John Kerrigan, *Shakespeare's Binding Language*, see 78–79, and 224, on the complex etymologies in *pledge*, *plight*, and *play*. More broadly, Kerrigan's work is exemplary of the complex cultural values encoded in the language of binding oaths.
49 See Görlach, *Introduction to Early Modern English*, 49, for the inconsistency of capitalisation practices during the period.
50 For 'Camus', see "† 'camis | camus, n.". *OED Online*. March 2013. See also V.v.2, 'All in a Camis light of purple silke', describing Radigund.
51 Gans, 'Archaism and Neologism in Spenser's Diction', 379. Gans's broader argument warns against McElderry's over-reliance on *OED's* datings to determine whether Spenser's usages were felt as archaisms by contemporaries.
52 Bellos, *Is That a Fish in Your Ear?*, 55. See also Frederick M. Padelford, 'Aspects of Spenser's Vocabulary', 280–82.
53 See "chemise, n.". *OED Online*.
54 See Chapter 2 below. Spenser was not above manipulating stress against convention; see 'In gilden buskins of costly Cordwayne' in the following stanza. This is a metrically irregular line. In a foot-based scansion, it could be seen as two iambs followed by a pyrrhic and two trochees, with the need to shift the accent to the final syllable of 'Cordwayne' to secure the full rhyme on *trayne*.

an instance of Spenser's enstranging diction whereas 'chemise' would not be. In the process of blazoning Belphoebe, Spenser deploys a consciously inflated vocabulary where words are chosen partly for their unfamiliarity and partly for their ornamental glitter. Words like 'Purfled', 'plight', 'besprinckled' and 'aygulet' contribute to a richly ornate poetic vocabulary which underlines Belphoebe's exceptional exceptionalness: 'So faire, and thousand times more faire/She seemd'. Spenser, we might say, polishes the surface of his verse to convey verbally a sense of Belphoebe's bewildering shimmer 'That quite bereau'd the rash beholders sight' (II.iii.23). As T. V. F. Brogan remarks, 'one should proceed with caution in appraising archaism, for its strategies are various and not easily disentangled from innovation'.[55] A contemporary illustration of the justice of this remark comes from Philip Pullman's *His Dark Materials* trilogy, which uses a series of neologistic archaisms like *anbaric* (meaning electric) and *cthonic* (meaning earthy) to convey the weird like-not-likeness of Lyra's world to our own.[56]

Throughout this episode, Spenser's choice of lexis shows a similar inventiveness: 'belgardes' and 'retrate' are coinages from Italian (II.iii.25),[57] while 'Cordwayne' is Spanish (II.iii.27).[58] The bravura archaism of 'full faire aumayld' from the same stanza, which *OED* aptly describes as an 'archaistic refashioning' of the already recherché noun 'amel' for 'enamel' into an adjectival form, underlines the way in which the appearance of Spenser's vocabulary is an intrinsic part of its meanings.[59] Modernise it, and you almost invariably find yourself rejigging its metre, impoverishing its semantic content, or disguising the enstranging effects Spenser put into his text. 'With curious antiques,[60] and full fair enamelled' maybe easier than 'With curious antickes, full faire aumayld', but it speaks to a different sensibility than the sometimes deliberately bizarre formulations of the early editions. In this case, Spenser is concerned to refashion the appearance of his vocabulary to mirror 'the antique Image of thy great auncestry', he promises Elizabeth in the Proem to Book II. It is antick for a reason.

55 Brogan, 'Archaism', 94.
56 See http://en.wikipedia.org/wiki/Glossary_of_His_Dark_Materials_terminology [accessed 2 December 2013] for a useful glossary of these terms, with some derivations.
57 See "† bel'gard, n.", and "† retrait, n.". *OED Online*.
58 See "cordwain, n.". *OED Online*.
59 See "aumail, n.", and "† 'ameled | 'amelled, adj.". *OED Online*.
60 'Antickes' is of course a false friend to the naïve moderniser, since Spenser's word means elaborate, grotesque figures, mirroring contemporary Italian decoration; see "antic, adj. and n.". *OED Online*. Again, this underlies the moderniser's dilemma: 'antics' would possibly be a better – but differently misleading – attempt at re-rendering Spenser's word.

Mot juste: the Gyant and his words

Book V is remarkable for its anxieties about language.[61] The fate of the Guizor, Pollente's skinhead toll-gatherer, begins with a radical conflation of word with exemplary violence, which the narrative seems to endorse:

> Who as they to the passage gan to draw,
> A villaine to them came with scull all raw,
> That passage money did of them require,
> According to the custome of their law.
> To whom he aunswerd wroth, Loe there thy hire;
> And with that word him strooke, that streight he did expire. (V.ii.11)

Artegall, it seems, doesn't need to draw breath: one invidious demand by a member of the lower orders[62] meets an instantaneous response, fusing a rather weak play on 'hire' with the literally unanswerable action of the mortal stroke.[63] Guizor is illustrative of the summary justice which is characteristic of Artegall's actions in the early cantos of Book V.[64] Language, lexis, and poetry do not just represent the violent actions of the poem – they are allegorically involved in those actions to an extent which remains disturbing; as Paul Alpers puts it in relation to the Giant with the scales, which forms the second half of this canto, 'The problem with this episode is not the basic political assumptions, but their poetic manifestations.'[65] Though critics since the 1908s have been significantly more troubled by those political assumptions,[66] Alpers's sense of a disturbance in the poetry remains valuable. He continues: 'The limitations of the poetry here, the loss of complexity and poise of understanding found in Artegall's speech,

---

61 See Anderson, *Words That Matter*, 187–88; Kirsten Tranter, '"The sea it selfe doest thou not plainely see?"', 84.

62 There is some confusion about Guizor's rank: while this stanza identifies him as a 'villaine' (and V.ii.6 as 'a groome of euill guize' with a haircut which denotes his function as someone who 'pols and pils the poore'), V.vi.32–33 suggests that he is the son of the former knight, Dolon. See *FQ*, 517, 551, for Hamilton's notes.

63 'Hire' plausibly recalls the Proem's lament of the golden age 'When Iustice was not for most meed outhyred', since Munera is a Lady Meed figure (V.Proem.3), although the echo serves again to emphasise the incongruity between the lament for an idealised past and Artegall's pre-emptive actions. Echoes of the Proem feature prominently in this Canto, as I discuss below.

64 See Richard Chamberlain, *Radical Spenser*, 98; Zurcher, *Spenser's Legal Language*, 65–67, emphasises 'the peculiarly native English character of the allegory in Book V' (65).

65 Alpers, *The Poetry of The Faerie Queene*, 300.

66 See Stephen Greenblatt, 'Murdering Peasants', in *Learning to Curse*, 160–66; Annabel Patterson, 'The Egalitarian Giant'; and Andrew Hadfield, 'Was Spenser a Republican?', 178–79, for readings of the episode's complex politics.

come from the fact that political attitudes are now being expressed as action.'[67] This is a precise diagnosis of what happens to Guizor: by blending Artegall's 'word' with his 'strooke', Spenser curtails discourse, implying that the only appropriate response on the part of the reader is one of awed approval of such acts of exemplary violence. Moments such as this dramatise the tensions within the didactic project of *The Faerie Queene*'s teaching of '*vertuous and gentle discipline*'. Since violence supplements discourse to the extent of supplanting it, why bother with '*continued Allegory*' at all?

Critics have come up with various strategies for coping with these tensions, from C. S. Lewis's suggestion that implementing Elizabethan policy in Ireland corrupted Spenser's imagination to the more robust work of those informed by New Historicism and postcolonial perspectives which explores the collision between realpolitik and humanist idealism in Book V.[68] Allegory continues for these critics, but the humanist confidence that reading poetry is reformatory is jolted by the repeated acts of violence administered in the service of Justice. The confrontation between the Giant and Artegall, which follows directly from the killings of Guizor, Pollente, and Munera, is exemplary of these tendencies, in which Book V's allegory is founded on images of judicial violence, and a debate weighted to the side of traditional authority against the forces of 'innouation' (V.ii.52). As Judith Anderson observes, it is 'a profoundly disturbing locus of meaning' because of the fissures it exposes in Spenserian symbolism.[69] It is also an urgently appropriate context in which to discuss Spenser's lexis because of its thematic concern with language, allied with its manipulation of epithet, rhetoric, and the precise semantic weight which adheres to the choice of individual words. The debate turns on whether words can be literally weighed in the Giant's balances (V.ii.43–44). Spenser's narrative almost inevitably backs Artegall's nuance over the Giant's literalism,[70] yet

67 Alpers, *The Poetry of* The Faerie Queene, 300. Compare Greenblatt, 'Murdering Peasants', 166, who insists 'upon the allegorical separation of rhetoric and violence' in this episode.
68 C. S. Lewis, *The Allegory of Love*, 348–49; Elizabeth Jane Bellamy, '*The Faerie Queene* (1596)', 279–84, for a summary of recent work on Book V; Elizabeth Fowler, 'The Failure of Moral Philosophy', 59–66, is the classic recent statement that the episode enacts 'an epistemological crisis about justice' (59) in the light of colonial and legal contexts.
69 Anderson, *Words That Matter*, 169.
70 See for example Kathleen Williams, *Spenser's Faerie Queene: The World of Glass*, 181; Judith H. Anderson, *The Growth of a Personal Voice*, 186; Michael O'Connell, 'Giant with the Scales', 331–32; and *FQ*, 520, for Hamilton's notes on the weighting of the argument in Artegall's favour numerically.

there is a sense in which the words of poetry are uneasily marshalled to support this view. As this chapter's first epigraph implies, the 'peising' of words is a key part of the poet's job: rather than speaking 'words as they chanceably fall from the mouth', Sidney's poet weighs 'each syllable of each word by just proportion according to the dignity of the subject'. Although this formulation partly reflects humanist admiration of the 'just proportion' of Classical metres,[71] the idea that the poet is a specialist in the measuring of words is clear. Spenser's Giant falls partly because of his failure to recognise that 'winged words' will not be contained on a set of scales (V.ii.44). Nevertheless, Spenser must have realised that he and Artegall perform a species of poetic legerdemain similar to that of Malengin in conflating words with the more abstract concepts of wind, light, and thought.[72] Poets do measure words, even if not on actual scales.[73] Though the Giant goes about his measuring project too crudely and too earnestly – and with too little a sense of the complexity of his medium – the work he attempts is crudely analogous to the poetic weighing of words. From this perspective, traditional criticism has perhaps taken the 'weighting' of the episode too much on trust, in one case quoting almost exclusively from Artegall's biblically informed and rhetorically authoritative speeches to the virtual exclusion of the Giant.[74] Rather than adjudicating between the disputants, my reading tries to magnify this sense of unease by focusing on how the episode is told and refractory choices of word, as poetic *mot juste* collides with Artegall's militant language of justice.

Elsewhere I have used the notion to 'strategic blandness' to evoke the evasive and self-protecting quality of Spenser's writing about his style.[75] The concept is also useful when considering *The Faerie Queene*'s lexis since it gives a framework for reading the seemingly colourless descriptions in which Spenser specialises. Compared with the adjectival fireworks of

71 See Attridge, *Well-Weighed Syllables*, 1, 175.

72 For Malengin as a specialist in 'legierdemayne', see V.ix.13. See also *Mother Hubberds Tale*, l.701, 'But he so light was at legier demaine', describing the Ape, another amorphous, poetic villain, and Richard Danson Brown, *The New Poet*, 193–200.

73 Compare Fowler, 'The Failure of Moral Philosophy', 63: 'Measuring… is not wrong in itself'. Fowler pursues this observation in the light of contemporary equity theory rather than poetic practice; I am endebted to her sense that Artegall 'narrow[s]… the discourse of justice' (63), thus setting an epistemological trap into which the Giant inevitably falls.

74 Williams, *Spenser's Faerie Queene*, 181–85. Williams's reading remains valuable for its tallying of the biblical and Lucretian echoes which underpin Artegall's speech. But my point is that she sees no conflict – for her the Giant is exclusively an emblem of 'gigantic simplemindedness' and argumentative 'nonsense' (181).

75 Richard Danson Brown, '"I would abate the sternenesse of my stile"', 277–80.

Donne or Shakespeare, Spenser is often content with standard formulations – 'This wicked woman had a wicked sonne'; 'he was full stout and
tall' (III.vii.12; VI.i.2) – rather than the more recherché ambiguities like
'th'hydroptic earth' or 'sluttish time'.[76] To an extent, these differences
are functions of genre: lyric poetry can sustain an intense focus on the
individual epithet because of its comparative brevity where epic cannot.
Yet this remains a fragile generalisation. *Amoretti* has many examples
of the same sort of knowing blandness: 'Fayre ye be sure, but cruell and
unkind'; 'Most happy letters fram'd by skilful trade' (LVI; LXXIIII); not all
Renaissance epics follow Spenser's stylistic example.[77] Equally, Spenser's
lexis is neither consistently nor universally bland. The line of epithets
which initially describe Talus – 'Immoueable, resistlesse, without end'
(V.i.12) – compactly demonstrates his ability to use precise, semantically
rich adjectives; I will return to this description to understand Talus's role
in the Giant's killing.[78] John Webster suggests that Spenser's unemphatic
epithets should not obscure the fact that the poem's language 'can reveal
surprisingly intricate insights on the poem's allegory' since 'the context
of language and narrative around an epithet can make its normally vague
and formulaic use become specially meaningful'.[79] As Webster suggests,
Spenser's style is 'divided': in his argument, between oral and literary models
of composition, or in mine, between the neutrality of strategic blandness
and a more evaluative approach to character and situation in the processes
of narration.[80] The implication is that although Spenser does not typically
focus on Empson's 'lightning flashes of ambiguity', the reader is nevertheless
implicated in a way of writing which is evaluatively dynamic, not static.
Like the poet, we must keep peising the different words which structure
his narrative. In this episode, these lexical effects are achieved through the
recycling of phrases and images, often with very different implications,
and – related to this – a seesaw between neutral and evaluative epithets. My
approach is based both on close reading and an unpublished concordance
prepared by J. B. Lethbridge, the Yamashita Concordance to the 1590 *Faerie*

76 John Donne, 'A Nocturnal Upon Saint Lucy's Day', in *The Complete Poems*, 227;
    Shakespeare, Sonnet 55, in *The Complete Sonnets and Poems*, 490–91.
77 *Fayre, cruell,* and *happy* are amongst the commonest adjectives in *Amoretti*, with several
    poems (like the ones cited) which are constructed from variations on such standard
    epithets. The implication is that Spenser expected his bland adjectives to do work as
    malleable semantic counters in different genres.
78 'Immoueable' and 'resistlesse' are rare and only used in Books V and VI; for 'immoueable',
    see V.ii.35.6 (quoted below) and V.iii.26.9; for 'resistlesse', see V.viii.32.4 and VI.xi.43.2.
79 John Webster, 'Oral Form and Written Craft', 86.
80 Webster, 'Oral Form and Written Craft', 76 fn. 5.

Queene, and digital resources such as the *Early Modern Print* text-mining site, used in conjunction with the invaluable *Early English Books Online* website.[81] Concordances are invaluable for seeing frequency and variety of usage, but such data is only meaningful inasmuch as it tallies with Eleanor Cook's dictum that choice of lexis is understood 'in relation, never in isolation'.[82] Or: concordances perforce isolate – it is the job of the reader to relate.

My interest is in what might be called the choreography of description in the episode. This oscillation between contrasting points of view is shown by the use of the formulaic phrase *much admire* in consecutive stanzas, V.ii.29–30. At first it describes Artegall and Talus's reaction to the crowd gathered around the Giant:

> They saw before them, far as they could vew,
> Full many people gathered in a crew;
> Whose great assembly they did *much admire*.
> For neuer there the like resort they knew.[83]

There are eleven other uses of the *much admire* formula, all from the second instalment of *The Faerie Queene*; usually it denotes approval (of a woman's beauty or a knight's bravery), or at worst critical wonderment.[84] In most of these examples (and the lines just quoted) it typifies Spenser at his blandest. Yet in context the phrase conveys a sense of process in Artegall and Talus's evaluation of what they see. In the next stanza, the same formula is used to evaluate the Giant's project:

> … all the world he would weigh equallie,
> If ought he had the same to counterpoys.
> For want whereof he weighed vanity,
> And fild his ballaunce full of idle toys:
> Yet was *admired much* of fooles, women, and boys.[85]

81 Lethbridge, *Concordance to The Faerie Queene*; Hiroshi Yamashita, *A Comprehensive Concordance to the Faerie Queene, 1590*; for *Early Modern Print*, see https://earlyprint.wustl.edu [accessed 30 July 2017]. See Brown and Lethbridge, *A Concordance*, xv, for the limitations of the old Osgood Concordance.
82 Cook, 'Lexis', 688.
83 My emphases.
84 The other usages are: IV.v.38.1; IV.ix.11.2; IV.ix.16.9; IV.x.31.1; IV.xii.33.4; V.viii.12.8; VI.ii.13.1; VI.ii.24.5; VI.ii.34.2; VI.vii.28.6; VI.xii.37.9. The latter encapsulates the distinction between two different kinds of admiration, first applied to the captured Blatant Beast, and second to Calidore: 'And much admyr'd the Beast, but more admyr'd the Knight'.
85 My emphases.

As in the killing of Guizor, Spenser's narration leaves little room for ambiguity: instead of being a marvel, the Giant is recoded as something admired only by an unreliable audience. Elizabeth Fowler counters that rather than being 'synonyms for scorn', these lines list 'those who are not full citizens': the narration enacts Artegall's aristocratic failure to recognise the legitimate aspirations of the socially excluded to their full legal rights.[86] Perhaps so, but the problem remains that the narrative is primarily concerned to direct the reader's estimation of what happens in ways that chime with Artegall and Talus's responses. Even the disruption to the iambic regularity of the alexandrine – in which the spondaic crash of '**fooles, wo**men' upsets the more natural rhythm of '**wo**men, **fooles**' – coercively implies that women are fools, or that fools take precedence over women, and that neither have any status in terms of judgement.[87] And yet Fowler's reading honours the tensions in the way Spenser shapes his story. The hesitancy between the consecutive uses of the *much admire* formula suggests an ambiguity not usually remarked on: although by the end of the episode, the narrative has resolved the 'great assembly' into a 'rascall crew' (itself a correction of the earlier 'Full many people gathered in a crew' from stanza 29), Artegall and Talus's first reaction to the gathering is one of alert curiosity.[88] The self-correcting variation of *much admire* across these two stanzas is indicative of the ways in which Spenser can use formulae to make precise semantic discriminations – in this case, a term of neutral admiration is rapidly shaded into critical evaluation. At the same time, it indicates the interpretive pressures on lexis as the episode oscillates between alternate ways of seeing the same events.

This evaluative flux is illustrated by the presentation of the Giant and Artegall. Spenser's epithets for the Giant contrast intriguingly with those deployed by critics, who have tried a range of inventive terms for him: the egalitarian giant, the democratic giant, the Equality Giant, a communist, a leveller, an Anabaptist, or the more descriptive 'Giant with the scales'.[89]

86 Fowler, 'The Failure of Moral Philosophy', 60.
87 My emphases. See Hamilton's note on Warton's proposed emendation of this line in Spenser, *The Faerie Queene* (1977), 539.
88 'Crew' is widely used in *The Faerie Queene*, typically as a neutral way of describing a large gathering; compare I.iv.23.9 (the Seven Deadly Sins) with I.xii.5.4 (attendants on Una's parents). See '"crew, n.1.", particularly 3 a. *OED Online*.
89 This is by no means an exhaustive list: Graham Hough, *A Preface to The Faerie Queene*, 194 ('communist giant'); Patterson, 'The Egalitarian Giant'; Anderson, *Words That Matter*, 168 ('leveling Giant'); Rebeca Helfer, *Spenser's Ruins*, 265 ('Equality Giant'); see O'Connell, 'Giant with the Scales', for an overview. Tranter, '"The sea it selfe doest thou not plainely see?"', 83, opts for the 'Mighty Gyant' (from V.ii.30), and prefers the Spenserian spelling 'Gyant' throughout.

The index of one study comes up with the 'Giant of False Justice', an elegant formulation which mirrors 'righteous *Artegall*' (his signature epithet in Book V),[90] yet one which has no warrant in the text of *The Faerie Queene*.[91] To be sure, describing the otherwise unnamed Giant can be helpful, and these epithets summarise the issues which modern scholarship has found in the episode.[92] In practice, Spenser's terms oscillate between empathy and hostility. The Giant is initially 'mighty' (V.ii.30), a common adjective which elsewhere describes figures as diverse as Jove (VII.vii.45), the Giants Argante and Ollyphant (III.vii.37, 48) and Gloriana herself (V.i.4; V.xii.3).[93] 'Mighty' conveys a sense of the Giant's scale and his potential to unsettle established order, but it remains in context a neutral modifier: it is only in the fourth line of stanza 30 that the narrative unambiguously evaluates the Giant's measuring activities as 'surquedrie', an apparent archaism for arrogance or pride.[94] As the debate develops, Spenser's modifiers focus on the Giant's emotional reactions. In stanza 37, he is 'wroth' when responding to Artegall's assertion of the correct ordering of the world (stanzas 34–36); by stanza 44 he is 'much abashed' by Artegall's comprehensive assault on the bases of his thinking. The narrative develops incrementally on this sense of the Giant's growing confusion: in stanza 47, he 'greatly grew in rage' to the point of almost breaking his scales in pique, an action Talus will perfect a few stanzas later.

It is here worth exploring the proximity between the way the narrative presents the Giant and Artegall. The hierarchy between the disputants is at one level clear; where the Giant is boastful, Artegall is 'righteous':

> Of things vnseene how canst thou deeme aright,
> Then answered the righteous *Artegall*,
> Sith thou misdeem'st so much of things in sight? (V.ii.39)

---

90 The usages in Book V are: Proem 11 ('righteous doome'); V.i.4 ('righteous lore'); V.i.11 ('righteous balance'); V.ii.39 ('righteous *Artegall*'); V.iv.1 ('righteous doome'); V.iv.16 ('righteous man'); V.vii.1 ('righteous lore'); V.vii.22 ('righteous Knight'); V.ix.2 ('righteous *Artegall*'); V.ix.23 ('righteous doome'); V.ix.31 ('righteous *Themis*'); and V.x.4 ('righteous *Artegall*'). See also Zurcher, *Spenser's Legal Language*, 266, for a gloss on *right*.
91 Williams, *Spenser's Faerie Queene*, 238.
92 See *FQ*, 520, for Hamilton's note about the Giant's namelessness.
93 There 154 instances, either of *mightie* or *mighty* in *The Faerie Queene*; see Brown and Lethbridge, *A Concordance*, 450.
94 E. K. glosses it as 'pryde' when it occurs in 'Februarie', l.49 (*Yale*, 41, 49); see also Bruce McElderry, 'Archaism and Innovation', 153, for the fact that the term was used by contemporary poets; see also *OED*, "† 'surquidry | 'surquedry, n.". *OED Online*.

This is an unambiguous nudge to the reader, tilting the argumentative balance in the knight's favour and underlining the limitations of the Giant's project: as his 'deeming' is fundamentally suspect, so the narrative insists that his opponent is cleverer, better, righter. And as Michael O'Connell observes, 'Spenser gives Artegall some of the most rhetorically impressive poetry in Book V to defend the established social order'.[95] At the same time, there are significant tensions between Artegall's assertion of the monumental stability of creation – 'The earth was in the middle centre pight,/In which it doth immoueable abide' – and the Proem's more anxious sense that 'Me seemes the world is runne quite out of square' (V.ii.35; V.Proem.1). Artegall, it seems, does not share the narrator's anxieties, which suggests that Spenser himself is unsure of his cosmology, or that Artegall's confident rhetoric is not endorsed by the poem as a whole. As some commentators have argued, the tension between these two positions impinges on the coherence of Book V's political philosophy.[96] Even within this episode, Artegall's behaviour is not quite so authoritative as the strength of his rhetoric might imply. In keeping with the doubleness of the *much admire* formula, Spenser describes an Artegall who can't quite make up his mind how to deal with his opponent. Initially he matches the Giant's 'surquedrie' with disdain: 'All which when *Artegall* did see … In sdeignfull wize he drew vnto him neare' (V.ii.33). The archaistic 'sdeignfull' suggests both Artegall's contempt for the Giant's arguments and the consciousness of his own rank which will become inhibiting by the end of the canto.[97] Yet by stanza 47, Artegall attempts to comfort the enraged Giant ('*Artegall* him fairely gan asswage'), a gesture Fowler describes as 'condescendingly conciliatory',[98]

---

95 O'Connell, 'Giant with the Scales', 332.
96 Greenblatt, 'Murdering Peasants', 162; Anderson, *Words That Matter*, 173; Tranter, '"The sea it selfe doest thou not plainely see?"', 87; these positions are congruent with those taken by Fowler, 'The Failure of Moral Philosophy', and Patterson, 'The Egalitarian Giant'.
97 Elsewhere variations on *sdeign* are used for Radigund's anger in her fight Artegall ('sdeignfull pride'; V.iv.43.3); a simile about fighting tigers comparing knights in battle ('either sdeignes with other to partake', IV.iii.16.8). *OED* implies that *sdeignfull* was seen as a Spenserian coinage, with quotations from Fairfax's Tasso and Shenstone's *Schoolmistress*; see '† 'sdeignful, adj.'. *OED Online*. This is confirmed by a usage in R[obert] T[ofte]'s 1598 translation of *Orlando Inamorato*, 'They lay on load, with blowes themselues to smother,/Frowning with sdainfull lookes, and collor great'; see *Orlando inamorato*, sig. D4r.
98 Fowler, 'The Failure of Moral Philosophy', 63, arguing that Artegall's ostensible advocacy of equity serves his own interests rather than those of society more broadly conceived. See also Anderson, *Words That Matter*, 182, for a gloss on the use of 'betoken' in this stanza to suggest that Artegall does not explain away the Giant's insistence on the existence of inequality.

while in stanza 52, after the Giant's death, Artegall replicates the confusion earlier felt by the Giant:

> Which lawlesse multitude him comming too
> In warlike wise, when Artegall did vew,
> He much was troubled, ne wist what to doo.
> For loth he was his noble hands t'embrew
> In the base blood of such a rascall crew;
> And otherwise, if that he should retire,
> He fear'd least they with shame would him pursew.

What is most striking here is the language of social hostility between Artegall's chivalric and aristocratic ethos and 'the base blood of such a rascall crew'.[99] Spenser emphatically underlines both Artegall's squeamishness and his fear of the 'shame' which will overtake him at the end of the Book (V.xii.42). Yet his confusion is also noteworthy, and inevitably recalls the Giant's of only a few stanzas earlier:

> yet did he labour long,
> And swat, and chauf'd, and proued euery way:
> Yet all the wrongs could not a litle right downe lay. (V.ii.46)

Spenser writes confusion convincingly with a deft, mostly monosyllabic simplicity. As so often in *The Faerie Queene*, empathy with character depends on choices of diction which enable the reader to have emotionally compelling insights into unsettled states of mind. In both cases, Spenser weighs simple words effectively. The Giant's intensive activity is presented through a sequence of unavailing verbs which ironically stress the physical action he inappropriately takes to make sense of an intellectual conundrum ('labour', 'swat', 'chauf'd', 'proud'). Conversely, Artegall's reluctance to take action is shown through a sequence of adjectival verbs and conditionals ('was troubled', 'loth he was', 'if that he should … He fear'd') which betoken his paralysis. Again, this is not to argue that the Giant is 'right': my point is rather that Artegall's mirroring of the Giant's confusion exposes a careful mismatch between the outcome of the debate and the outcome of the episode. Artegall wins the former because, *pace* O'Connell, he has the best lines and strongest-seeming argument. In the latter, however, winning and losing are significantly more problematic, and Spenser's lexis continues to fluctuate between the two antagonists. To understand this further, we need to look at the Giant's downfall.

The Giant's failure to weigh the abstract qualities and words enables the narrative to offer a more stringently negative assessment of his behaviour:

> But he the right from thence did thrust away,
>   For it was not the right, which he did seeke;
>   But rather stroue extremities to way,
>   Th'one to diminish, th'other for to eeke.
>   For of the meane he greatly did misleeke.
>   Whom when so lewdly minded *Talus* found,
>   Approching nigh vnto him cheeke by cheeke,
>   He shouldered him from off the higher ground,
> And down the rock him throwing, in the sea him dround. (V.ii.49)

The first half of this stanza casts the Giant as a 'lewdly minded' extremist, who perversely rejects 'the meane' revealed to him by Artegall, in which the extravagant eye rhyme 'misleeke' might be taken as a witty demonstration of the distorting effects of the Giant's extremism.[100] But the second half is more troubling in the poetic shift from evaluating the Giant's intellectual failures to the punishment Talus inflicts. Elizabeth Fowler assumes that this passage shows Talus losing his temper with the Giant, but again Spenser's text is less determined than this implies.[101] Though Book V later comically miscasts Talus as the bringer of bad tidings to Britomart,[102] here he shows no emotional reaction. 'Immoueable, resistlesse, without end': like later robots, Talus lacks the circuits for anger. As in the first half of the canto, his role is to enact a rigid interpretation of Justice, underlining his allegorical function as an embodiment of 'the common law's inflexibility' and the principle of retributive justice (V.i.12).[103] This is part of the poetic and lexical point of this canto: where the Giant and Artegall are 'troubled' by their encounter, Talus the robot is incapable of such qualms (V.ii.52). Rather, the stanza stresses both the automatic quality

---

100 Rhymes on *-eek* with words usually spelled *-ike* are not unusual among Spenser's contemporaries; see Samuel Daniel, *The ciuile wars*, 1.32 (*mislike: seeke: weake*), 9 (sig. C 1 r) and 5.12 (*alike: mislike: seeke*), 116 (sig. K2v).
101 Fowler, 'The Failure of Moral Philosophy', 60, 65. The episode shows the Giant and to a lesser extent Artegall losing their tempers.
102 V.vi.9: 'The yron man, albe he wanted sence/And sorrowes feeling, yet with conscience/ Of his ill newes, did inly chill and quake,/And stood still mute'. Book V is not often praised for its humour, but the spectacle of Britomart telling Talus to 'be bold' shows him ludicrously out of his emotional depth.
103 Zurcher, *Spenser's Legal Language*, 138, the best recent gloss on the relationship between Artegall and Talus. See *FQ*, 512, for the connection between Talus and 'talion' or redistributive justice.

of this punishment – Talus evaluates and punishes the Giant in the space of three lines – and the intimacy of an execution which takes place 'cheeke by cheeke'.[104]

The precision of Spenser's lexis is shown by the verb *shouldered*. Though used sparingly, this is something of a favourite in *The Faerie Queene*, with connotations of violent natural change, insurrection, or jockeying for position. In Book I, it is used in an epic simile for the wounded dragon, which compares his cries with the noise of 'rolling billowes' which 'beat the ragged shore,/As they the earth would shoulder from her seat' (I.xi.21). Later it encapsulates Mutabilitie's ambitions in a usage congruent with Talus's action: 'T'attempt th'empire of the heauens hight,/And *Ioue* himselfe to shoulder from his right' (VII.vi.7).[105] But the most remarkable proleptic use of the verb occurs in the Proem to Book V, where it describes the shifting of the constellation Aries from its ancient location eastwards: 'that same fleecy Ram … Hath now forgot, where he was plast of yore/And shouldered hath the Bull, which fayre *Europa* bore' (V.Proem.5). Aries's westward migration is another instance of the general process of cosmic change deplored in the Proem — unlike Artegall, the narrator sees no stability in 'the heauens'. Given that Jove was the father of Taurus, these lines anticipate Mutabilitie's insurrection: sharp shoulders are essential if you want to change government. Such lexical contexts do not on their own suggest that Talus's action is to be read negatively. But they do underline the fact that Spenserian shouldering is poised between acts of rebellion and violent incursions against natural order; in this light, Talus's punishment feels something like an act of God, a not inappropriate idea given his origins as Astraea's 'groome' (V.i.12).

The tension between an 'Immoueable' conception of justice and a more complex emotional reality is underlined in the simile which describes the Giant's death:

> Like as a ship, whom cruell tempest driues
> Vpon a rocke with horrible dismay,
> Her shattered ribs in thousand peeces riues,
> And spoyling all her geares and goodly ray,
> Does make her selfe misfortunes piteous pray.

104 See Hadfield, *Edmund Spenser: A Life*, 100–01, for Spenser as an eyewitness of executions in Ireland. One of the realist strengths of Book V is that its acts of violence are always intimate and unsettling; compare Talus's disembowelling of Malengin at V.ix.19.

105 'Shoulder' as a noun is more widespread, as in VII.vi.18, where Mercury places his caduceus on Mutabilitie's shoulder in a direct rebuke to her earlier ambition. See also II.vii.47.3 for 'close shouldring' courtiers, and II.xii.23.6 for 'sea-shouldring Whales'.

> So downe the cliffe the wretched Gyant tumbled;
> His battred ballances in peeces lay,
> His timbered bones all broken rudely rumbled,
> So was the high aspyring with huge ruine humbled. (V.ii.50)

The epithets perform a dance between different forms of evaluation which cumulatively does little to offer a single line: as the image of shipwreck is 'cruell' and 'horrible', so the damage done to the Giant is metaphorically 'piteous' as *his* 'geares and goodly ray' – the 'battred ballances' and the form of his formerly 'mighty' body – lie 'all broken rudely rumbled'.[106] Annabel Patterson comments that 'the simile patently *mourns* the Giant before the official, editorial comment [of the alexandrine] can condemn him'.[107] Certainly, the empathetic itemisation of the damage done to the Giant's body suggests that his death should be read in a range of poetic contexts. Patterson notes the closeness of the shipwreck image to Spenser's self-conscious images of *The Faerie Queene* as a vessel,[108] but perhaps more remarkable is the recuperation of this simile later in Book V in the fight between Arthur and Geryoneo's monster, where the simile is applied to the shaking Arthur after he is bashed by the monster's tail:

> As when the Mast of some well timbred hulke
> Is with the blast of some outragious storme
> Blowne downe, it shakes the bottome of the bulke,
> And makes her ribs to cracke, as they were torne,
> Whilest still she stands as stonisht and forlorne:
> So was he stound with stroke of her huge taile. (V.xi.29)

The proximities are striking: 'cruell tempest' becomes 'outragious storme'; the metaphor of the Giant's 'timbered bones' becomes the realistic description of the ship's 'timbred hulke'; conversely, the Giant's 'shattered ribs' become the cracked metaphorical ribs of the vessel's interior.[109] This homogenisation of the Giant with Arthur as the subjects of these similes supports Patterson's sense that Spenser's presentation of the Giant's arguments is profoundly ambivalent.[110] Is the reader really supposed to equate

---

106 The Giant's fate counterpoints Munera's (V.ii.25–27), but without the clear sense of appropriate punishment – see in particular Talus's chopping off of her hands 'Which sought vnrighteousnesse, and iustice sold' (26), and the image of the stream washing away 'her guilty blood' (27).
107 Patterson, 'The Egalitarian Giant', 113.
108 Patterson, 'The Egalitarian Giant', 113–14, citing I.xii.42 and VI.xii.1.
109 See "rib, n.1. II. 6. a". *OED Online*. March 2013. Oxford University Press. 29 April 2013.
110 See Helfer, *Spenser's Ruins*, 18–19, for ambivalence as 'a keyword in Spenser studies to describe a Spenser divided against himself'.

Arthur with the Giant as s/he reads the later canto (or even to remember the earlier episode?), or is this another illustration of Teskey's rule that too much close reading can impair a reader's understanding of the allegory? If this is so, then the shipwreck simile would itself be a formulaic property which may be applied indifferently through the course of the poem.[111] What matters in this view isn't so much the genetic similarity between the similes as the moral realities at the heart of the Book. Yet it's hard to resist the sense that in both cases the simile mobilises the reader in sympathy with its unlike subjects, and that therefore those moral realities are held in greater suspension than traditional allegoresis has recognised.

In the same way, it is difficult to sustain the view that Spenser was a poet who was lexically careless, or uninterested in the evaluative and connotative properties of individual words. As this discussion has shown, considerable interpretive pressure is placed on relatively unusual words like *shouldered* and *immoueable*, which seem to have been reserved for early parts of Book V. At the same time, Spenser's handling of the simplest items of lexis – epithets, verbs, formulaic phrases like *much admire* – repeatedly rewards the reader's attention and shows the complex styles he used throughout *The Faerie Queene*. At one level, the episode of the mighty Giant is a singular one precisely because it shows Spenser's growing sense of what Fowler calls 'the failure of moral philosophy' whilst Artegall and the Giant engage in what turns out to be deadly game about the definitions of words and the feasibility of 'peising' the abstract with the literal. Yet at another level, precisely because this is an episode so concerned with judgement and the behaviour of 'winged words', it is an ideal introduction to Spenser's lexis. As I have suggested, Spenser's typical choice of phrase, idiom, and individual word is repeatedly and almost aporetically subject to revision, recasting, and reassessment. The words the Giant tries to weigh fly away from containment, proving the strength of Artegall's challenging contention that 'The eare must be the ballance, to decree/And iudge' (V.ii.47).[112] And yet these fleeting words show the

111 For nautical imagery, particularly the traditional metaphor of poems as ships, see Curtius, *European Literature and the Latin Middle Ages*, 128–30; Jerome S. Dees, 'Ship Imagery', 655–56; and Philip Edwards, *Sea-Mark*, 19–49. The shipwreck simile is a subset of this broad tradition. Dees's remark that Spenser's development of it 'create[s] a rich symbolic texture dominated by a sense of mutability' suggests some of the problems in seeing any of this imagery as formulaic (656).
112 On the primacy of hearing and listening in *The Faerie Queene*, see Teskey, 'Thinking Moments', 120–21, who stresses the difficulty of this image: 'The ear as a balance … is a wonderful image because it cannot be visualized as such. It requires thinking about the balance as a symbol of creation by God … and of judgement by men' (120).

elusiveness which characterises Spenser's use of words throughout *The Faerie Queene*.

Finally, I want to return to Hazlitt's evocation of reading Spenser:

> Spenser was the poet of our waking dreams; and he has invented not only a language, but a music of his own for them. The undulations are infinite, like those of the waves of the sea: but the effect is still the same, lulling the senses into a deep oblivion of the jarring noises of the world.[113]

In this chapter, my argument has resisted the kind of aesthetic intoxication of reading which Hazlitt so powerfully evokes; my emphasis has been on the utility of Spenser's lexis and the work to which he puts different kinds of vocabulary, including both the rarefied, archaistic idiom of 'a silken Camus lylly whight' and the ordinary, almost conversational register of 'yet did he labour long,/And swat'. To this extent, I have argued for reading Spenser's lexis functionally: it is a language which does what it needs to do in a range of contexts. 'Doing what it needs to' covers subtle aesthetic manoeuvres, such as the blazon of Belphoebe, in which the vocabulary works to enstrange its subject as a singular mythological being, and the episode of the Giant, in which Spenser's divided, fluctuating choices of epithet enact the complex issues at stake between the antagonists. Yet the peculiarity and particularity of Spenser's idiom has rarely been better put than by Hazlitt. This is partly due to the lyrical panache of *his* style, alongside his concern to explain the sensuous experience of reading, as in the earlier remark that Spenser's language 'is a labyrinth of sweet sounds … that would cloy by their very sweetness, but that the ear is constantly relieved and enchanted by their continued variety of modulation', a perception which curiously anticipates Barbara Strang's more analytical essay on language in *The Spenser Encyclopedia*.[114] Aesthetic intoxication is, I would contend, a measurable part of *The Faerie Queene* but, unlike Hazlitt, my suggestion is that this is not done so much to cast the reader into 'a deep oblivion' as to warn of significant shifts of register and tone.[115] Artegall's speeches to the Giant are examples of this sort of writing, where the alert

---

113 In Alpers (ed.), *Edmund Spenser: A Critical Anthology*, 138.
114 In Alpers (ed.), *Edmund Spenser: A Critical Anthology*, 138; Strang, 'Language', 428: '[Spenser's] capacity for variation is demonstrated by the fact that up to the end of Book VI one is still recording new patterns'.
115 In this context, see Krier, 'Time Lords', an important essay which explores the ways in which *The Faerie Queene* exploits the physical spaces in between stanzas and imagines readers who are subject to fluctuating attention and moments of drift.

reader is intended to weigh an apparently 'immoueable', unanswerable rhetoric in the light of the rest of the poem and individual choices of lexis. In this context, the sentencious as well as sensuous maxim 'Ill can he rule the great, that cannot reach the small' is not a rebuke to the Giant alone (V.ii.43.9).

2

Uncommon lines: lineation and metre

To what extent was Spenser stylistically conservative? This is one of the central questions which this book seeks to address; as the previous chapter suggested, questions of stylistic radicalism frequently overlap with the more widely debated question of Spenser's politics. In relation to lexis, I argued that Spenser's procedures were both functional and unpredictable, making it difficult to resolve particular usages one way or another. The episode of the mighty Giant is provocative partly because its vocabulary seesaws between incompatible positions, as in the final simile which compares his dead body with a shipwreck whilst simultaneously evaluating him as an example of failed ambition. Spenser's lexical choices aim to implicate the reader in the business of interpretation whilst at the same time enstranging the objects of Faery land (things, places, characters) through a catholic amalgam of archaism, neologism, linguistic borrowing, and ostensibly colourless formulae. To quote again from Hazlitt, this produces 'a poetical language rich and varied and magnificent beyond all former, and almost all later example', with the rider that such poetic exceptionalness is often achieved through strategies of blandness and repetition.[1] Though contemporary criticism fights shy of richness and magnificence, these are not intrinsically extravagant claims.

This chapter is concerned with line and metre. My suggestion is that literary historians have underestimated the extent of Spenser's radicalism.

---

1 In Alpers (ed.), *Edmund Spenser: A Critical Anthology*, 138. Hazlitt's remarks relate to the Spenserian stanza, the complexity of which he argues is responsible for Spenser's language.

Or rather, although he refines and modifies an existing tradition, Spenser the technical innovator – someone whose works stretch and revise the accepted paradigms of the English poetic line – has been displaced by the familiar caricature of Spenser the stylistic conservative. This argument entails discussion of reception history and some revision to accepted literary history, before turning to the question of the semantic role of the Spenserian line in *The Faerie Queene*. My scope is ambitious: this chapter considers questions of lineation, metre, and syntax, though I return to Spenser's syntax in later chapters. Though most studies separate line from metre, my work reflects the fact that for the reader this is often a tricky or an artificial procedure; when reading *The Faerie Queene*, the apprehension of the shape of a line and its metre is usually simultaneous, if not necessarily something that the ideal reader considers in precise detail. Hence this chapter attempts to discuss two closely related phenomena in the same textual space.

Line and metre

'Line' is an appropriately flexible term which can be stretched to accommodate a wide range of meanings.[2] Though *The Faerie Queene* only uses a fraction of the many listed by *OED*, the term evokes ideas of lineage (II.x.50.3), the lead for Una's lamb (I.i.4.9), as well as lines of writing ('on his shield *Sans loy* in bloody lines was dyde'; I.iii.33.9) and the verse of the poem itself ('my frayle eies these lines with teares do steepe'; I.iii.2.3).[3] The most provocative instance of 'line', however, is one where the predominant meaning is the now archaic sense of rule, precept, or standard practice:[4]

> Let none then blame me, if in discipline
> Of vertue and of ciuill vses lore,
> I doe not forme them to the common line
> Of present dayes, which are corrupted sore (V Pr. 3.1–4)

Not to follow the 'common line/Of present dayes' is a characteristically primitivist gesture, as Spenser aligns his thinking with 'the antique vse

---

2 See "line, n.2". *OED Online*. The Lethbridge Concordance records fifteen instances of *line* or *lines*, one of which relates to *OED*'s "line, n.1" (V.vii.6.4), meaning linen. The other usages are all variants of "line, n.2".

3 See also I.xii.26.2 (the 'sad lines' of Duessa's letter); III.xii.36.7 (Busirane's 'bloudy lynes'). IV.ii.48.4 uses the idiom 'lines of life'; see "line, n.2", I.1 †g, *OED Online*.

4 See "line, n.2", †5, *OED Online*, citing this passage. See also the related V.i.7.4 ('the line of conscience').

… When good was onely for it selfe desyred' (V Pr. 3.5–6).[5] This phrase
also gestures towards the work which the lines of *The Faerie Queene* are
doing, and Spenser's sense of his distinction from contemporary poetic
practice. While the Proem ventriloquises a weary social conservatism
(partly at odds with the Book which follows),[6] the resistance 'to the common
line' is an assertion of aesthetic singularity. In the face of a 'corrupted'
present, Spenser backs his own judgement about 'ciuill vses lore' and,
implicitly, about the writing of poetry. It is this divergence from common
practice which this chapter seeks to illuminate.

The importance of the line was demonstrated most thoroughly by Paul
Alpers's *The Poetry of The Faerie Queene*. He argues that the Spenserian
line is a paradoxically complex instrument, relentlessly tending to semantic
and syntactic independence. This tendency leads to a characteristic simplicity and 'lucidity of diction'.[7] Alpers's work builds on C. S. Lewis's observation
that much of *The Faerie Queene* is '"a poetry of statement". The typical
Spenserian line tells you what somebody did or wore or where he went,'[8]
as in these two lines from the beginning of the poem: 'Vpon a great
aduenture he was bond'; 'A louely Ladie rode him faire beside' (I.i.3.1,
4.1). Lewis's 'poetry of statement' mirrors MacNeice's poet who mentions
things, cited in the previous chapter: through the medium of the poetic
line, Spenser's poetry is demonstrative, repeatedly pointing who did what
to whom and in what contexts. For Alpers, even the apparently strong
enjambments and marked caesurae of lines like 'Of needments at his
backe. Thus as they past' or 'Amid the thickest woods. The Champion
stout' (I.i.6.4,11.7) are less strongly felt than they would be in Spenser's
contemporaries. Indeed, the elastic recoil to endstopped forms in the
succeeding lines ('The day with cloudes was suddeine ouercast,'; 'Eftsoones
dismounted from his courser braue,') demonstrates the sovereignty of the
line, as though Spenser's syntax were spring-loaded to return to the ordered
familiarity of the independent line. The reader of *The Faerie Queene* is
– in Catherine Addison's elegant restatement of Alpers's model – 'educated
by thousands of stanzas of nine self-contained lines each to pause even
when the grammar does point onwards beyond the line ending'.[9] The

---

5   See William Keach, 'Primitivism' in *The Spenser Encyclopedia*, 557, for the problematics
    of Spenserian primitivism.
6   See Chapter 1 above.
7   Alpers, *The Poetry of The Faerie Queene,* 71; more generally, see 36–106.
8   C. S. Lewis, *English Literature in Sixteenth Century Excluding Drama*, 391.
9   Addison, 'Rhyming Against the Grain', 346.

brilliance of Alpers's work lies in its sensitivity to the work done by Spenserian manipulation: by conceptualising the individual line as the poem's basic measure of sense, Alpers furnishes the reader with an expansive sense of the rhetorical variations inherent in *The Faerie Queene*. His comparisons with Ariosto, Marlowe, and Drayton help to explain the ways in which Spenser's lineation is atypical of sixteenth-century poetry: rather than imitating a Latinate, periodic syntax, Spenser harnesses his line as a syntactic unit in its own right with its own particular cadences, modalities, and values.[10] For Alpers, the independence of the line controls, and to an extent minimises, the syntactic possibilities generated by the stanza form. Though Alpers remains central to any understanding of the Spenserian line, I will register some caveats to his model later in the chapter.

Lineation is clearly related to metrics, yet in practice, discussions have tended to run on lines which are parallel and contradictory. Alpers cites John Thompson's *The Founding of English Metre*, but chiefly to register the New Critical preference for Donne and Sidney as poets of the mimetic speaking voice rather than to marry his approach with Thompson's comparative work on the development of metre.[11] Similarly, although Susanne Woods in *Natural Emphasis* dissents from Alpers, arguing that Spenser's core verse unit was the hemistich, this disagreement is surfaced in a footnote rather than in detailed discussion.[12] Jeff Dolven follows Woods in seeing Spenser as metrically conservative: 'Spenser the metrist is at his most experimental near the beginning of his career', particularly in *The Shepheardes Calender*; in consequence, his career moves from youthful errantry to the 'massive commitment to iambic movement' of *The Faerie Queene*.[13] But although this discussion takes place in a section called 'The Line of *The Faerie Queene*', it includes no consideration of lineation per se, nor reference to Alpers. Because for Dolven, Spenser's metre is conservative, so the working of his line can be subsumed within a description of its metrical operations.

More than most branches of literary history, formal history tends to read in ways which are both teleological and evolutionary: *The Faerie Queene* is a step on a road which leads from *The Canterbury Tales* to

---

10 Alpers, *The Poetry of The Faerie Queene*, 77–95.
11 Alpers, *The Poetry of The Faerie Queene*, 72–73, citing John Thompson, *The Founding of English Metre*, 140.
12 Woods, Natural Emphasis, 141, 177 n.10.
13 Dolven, 'Spenser's Metrics', 387, 389.

Paradise Lost and even to *The Waste Land*.[14] Literary history becomes a positivist discipline, with an implied commitment to the idea that forms develop to 'classic' formulations. Thompson's study is structured by the quasi-nation-building metaphor of 'founding'; it culminates with Sidney because 'in his poetry the metrical principles that dominated English verse for three centuries were fully and systematically developed'.[15] Both 'developed' and 'dominated' suggest that literary tradition is shaped by individual talents whose work provides suasive and indeed coercive templates which become constitutive for later writers.[16] Similarly, Wright discusses 'The demise of iambic pentameter as the chief meter of English poetry', which 'probably owes much to its coming to be understood even by poets themselves as an available prosodic form, a metre to write poems "in", a Roman road, rather than as a kind of heroic adventure or even a haunted house'.[17] Later poets (and perhaps literary historians) are tormented by their own belatedness: what was once dangerous and radical turns through the passage of time into something straight and predictable. Such narratives of rises and falls – of developments and hauntings – are post facto reconstructions with more than a hint of artificiality.[18] There is some comfort in a straight road which leads to classics like *Astrophil and Stella* or *Hamlet* – at least we know that there was growth and development, even if these are forerunners of an inevitable demise. Yet there are two significant problems with this image. Firstly, as I have implied, formal history is not necessarily best understood as an evolutionary narrative. Though the long view of literary history suggests that (for example) free verse develops out of blank verse, such views disguise the literary experience of writers and readers at specific moments in time. As we shall see in later chapters, early reaction to the Spenserian stanza shows the confusion which this

14 See Thompson, *The Founding of English Metre*, Woods, *Natural Emphasis*, George T. Wright, *Shakespeare's Metrical Art*, and O. B. Hardison, *Prosody and Purpose*. These are each in different ways major contributions to the understanding of sixteenth-century metre, and my work is particularly indebted to Wright's lucid and practical book. At the same time, each study tends towards this kind of evolutionary teleology, as Chaucer gives way to Wyatt, Wyatt to Gascoigne, and so on forwards in time.

15 Thompson, *The Founding of English Metre*, 3. See Richard Helgerson, *Forms of Nationhood*, 1–18, for the relevance of Spenser's discussion of metrics in the Letters to the project of English self-representation.

16 See T. S. Eliot's influential 'Tradition and the Individual Talent' (1919); *Selected Essays*, 13–34.

17 Wright, *Shakespeare's Metrical Art*, 18.

18 Harold Bloom, *The Anxiety of Influence*, is the classic statement of this evolutionary and pathological model of poetic development in relation to the individual poet, in which novelty is generated by competitive uncertainty.

kind of innovative model could generate among contemporary readers. The grand narrative displaces the individual achievement and sees it as symptomatic of broader tendencies which may not have been evident at the time. Whilst abandoning evolutionary metaphors may be impossible, I want to suggest that temporarily shelving the received narrative of progressive change can be helpful in understanding the forms of *The Faerie Queene*. The second, related, problem is that for sixteenth-century readers, what confronted them was not a Roman road so much as a range – perhaps even a chaos – of competing styles and different kinds of line.

Nevertheless, the work of Thompson, Wright, Woods, and Hardison provides useful maps of this chaos which show the way in which discussion of *The Faerie Queene*'s metre has been framed. There is significant agreement about the poets and texts that mattered in the development of English verse during the sixteenth century. All of these scholars discuss Chaucer and the problem of how Elizabethan readers scanned his metre.[19] All handle the work of Wyatt and Surrey and its problematic presentation in print in the 1550s.[20] And all agree that Gascoigne's *Certayne Notes of Instruction* (1575) is a valuable codification of contemporaneous practice, written by a pivotal figure between different sixteenth-century poetic generations.[21] Such mappings suggest a relatively lucid story of chaos resolving into order; of a more or less poorly understood ten-syllable iambic line in the early part of the century becoming the accepted norm in texts like *The Faerie Queene* and *Tamburlaine* by the 1580s and 1590s. Within this agreed narrative, there are differences of emphasis, terminology, and methodology which underline the difficulties inherent in formal history. Prosodic vocabulary is a case in point. Thompson retains the traditional classicising terminology of iambic pentameter because of its dominance in later writing and because 'it provides the best symbolic model of our language'.[22] For Hardison and Woods, such terms do not

---

19 Thompson, *The Founding of English Metre*, 2, 16, 93; Woods, *Natural Emphasis*, 21–68; Wright, *Shakespeare's Metrical Art*, 20–37; Hardison, *Prosody and Purpose*, 4–19.

20 See in particular Hardison, *Prosody and Purpose*, 127–47, who argues that John Day's 1554 edition of Surrey's *Fourth Boke of Virgill* preserves a text closer to Surrey's intentions than the more familiar Tottell edition of 1557.

21 See Gillian Austen, *George Gascoigne*, 101–03, for the text's ironic humour and its importance for William Webbe's *Discourse of English Poetrie* (1586). Indeed, Webbe freely plagiarises Gascoigne's ideas; see Brown, '"Charmed with inchaunted rimes"', in Brown and Lethbridge, *A Concordance*, 70.

22 Thompson, *The Founding of English Metre*, 12.

adequately describe the development of English verse. Following the work of comparative metrists like Jespersen, they argue that English scansion is part of the Romance tradition, which depends on syllable counting, not accentual feet.[23] Wright, in contrast, is sceptical of such manoeuvres, suggesting that flexibility is inherent within iambic pentameter because it accommodates both metrical and phrasal orders simultaneously.[24] While precise metrical systems are not crucial to my present argument, in this debate, I side with Wright and also Dolven in retaining the vocabulary of the iambic pentameter: it is more widely used then and now (Gascoigne laments that 'we vse none other order but a foote of two sillables') and is consequently so embedded in critical discourse that to uproot it would pose as many problems as it solves.[25] At the same time, my suspicion remains that Spenser's method of composition was a combination of stress and syllable counting, to produce lines which are usually decasyllabic, and which may be described according to a consciously flexible definition of 'iambic pentameter'. It is not saying much to suggest that Spenser had a superlative ear, nor that he had a knack of making most lines settle on ten syllables, but these sorts of observation do capture the range of his achievement.

This overview of how scholars have conceptualised Spenser's place in the history of sixteenth-century verse suggests some of the difficulty in demarcating line from metre, and in bringing these two related categories of formal analysis to bear on the phenomena of metrical verse lines. T. V. F. Brogan's essays in *The New Princeton Encyclopedia of Poetry and Poetics* clarify the interrelations and interdependencies between the concepts. Since the invention of writing and printing, poetry has had dual visual and auditory realities, which means that the 'concept of the line is fundamental to the concept of poetry itself, for the line is the differentia

---

23 Woods, *Natural Emphasis*, 11, 37–47, 69–72; Hardison, *Prosody and Purpose*, 8–10 and passim.

24 Wright, *Shakespeare's Metrical Art*, 10–12, 17. See also the crucial caveats made by T. V. F. Brogan, 'Meter', 773, on the inadequacy of classical foot theory as a description of the working of English verse: '"trochaic substitutions" are not and never were felt to be violations of the iambic meter', so that an accentual iambic pentameter must be understood as inherently flexible and indeed permissive form. For a linguistic approach to related issues (including large-scale data sets), see Marina Tarlinskaja, *Shakespeare and the Versification of English Drama, 1561–1642*, and note Paul J. Hecht's perceptive review, 'Marina Tarlinskaja, Shakespeare and the Versification of English Drama, 1561–1642'.

25 George, *Certayne Notes of Instruction* (1575) in G. Gregory Smith (ed.), *Elizabethan Critical Essays*, I, 50.

of verse and prose'. Equally, the idea of metre as regular patterns of contrasting syllabic stress, pitch, or duration necessarily depends on line.[26]

Lines of verse are the fundamental units of printed poetry. They are simultaneously agents of convention, in which line length signals familiar metrical patterns, and of innovation, in which typographical distortion can be the harbinger of broader forms of disruption. 'My lines and life are free; free as the rode,/Loose as the winde, as large as store', George Herbert writes in a poem which exploits the appearance of freedom to enforce the reality of psychological dependence: by bending the expected line shape, you can – as in much contemporary poetry – induce swerves in readerly perception.[27] Thus 'The Collar' assays an anarchic lineal freedom in the bulk of the text before recoiling to the apparently settled order of its closing quatrain. In the case of a Renaissance epic like *The Faerie Queene*, lineation plays a special role in the manipulation of metrical effect. My approach entails re-reading and querying previous approaches: Woods and Dolven offer a powerful consensus that Spenser's lines and metres are 'aesthetic' rather than 'mimetic': Spenserian syntax tends to a harmonious uniformity (in which syntax and line length elegantly cohere) rather than the jagged edges of Sidney and Donne's attempts to accommodate credible speaking voices to the artifice of the iambic pentameter.[28] There is much value in this approach, and I will not suggest a Herbertian, much less a Williamsesque, Spenser.[29] Yet as Dolven recognises, the distinction between aesthetic and mimetic is 'somewhat rough and ready', as is the notion that spatial disruption necessarily betokens a poetry whose goal is to mimic the speaking voice. My suggestion is that Spenser has appeared conventional, especially when read through the filters of Shakespeare, Donne, Jonson, and Milton: as a medial figure between different literary generations, he has been almost automatically overshadowed by

26 T. V. F. Brogan, 'Line', 696, 694, 'Meter', 773. The complexity of the issues developed during the twentieth century by the emergence of free verse: 'In metrical verse … line-forms were mainly determined by history and convention … free verse … foregrounded visual space and posited the line within a two-dimensional matrix where blanks, white spaces, drops, gaps, vectors, and dislocations became possible' ('Line', 696). As we shall see, Spenser's 'imperfect' stanzas exploit analogous techniques.

27 'The Collar', ll.5–6, in George Herbert, *The English Poems*, 524–29; see Wilcox's note on the self-consciousness of these lines (527) and her summary of critical opinion about the mood of the closing quatrain (525). Again, Brogan, 'Line', 696, is germane for the observation that poetry's 'seen/heard … duality' is intensified by the emergence of free verse. For discussion of line in modern poetry, see James Longenbach, *The Art of the Poetic Line*.

28 Dolven, 'Spenser's Metrics', 390; Woods, *Natural Emphasis*, 15, 161.

29 Although I do explore analogies between Williams' lineal poetics and Spenser's below.

what followed.[30] In place of these acknowledged technical innovators (not to mention writers of the first rank who learned much of their technique from reading Spenser), *The Faerie Queene* also needs to be read in the lineal contexts of less celebrated (and often less competent) writers like Tusser and Phaer, and writers like Skelton whose significance to the history of metre is often minimised or overlooked.

One final rider is that I focus on English sources in this chapter, not to minimise the huge influence of continental European and Neo-Latin poetry on Spenser, but rather because these sources have been so fruitfully explored by David Scott Wilson-Okamura.[31] Indeed, his focus on Spenser's properly international affiliations may serve to blunt awareness of Spenser's responses to sixteenth-century English verse. In terms of the specifics of metre and lineation, reaction to English poetry was certainly a pivotal aspect of Spenser's dynamic practice. In this context, I stress that a focus on English sources should not be allegorised to any narrow nationalism: Spenser was not a Brexit laureate; his reading was catholic, even if his religion was not.[32]

Common lines (1): Tusser and Skelton

What follows is not an exhaustive history of sixteenth-century metre but, rather, focuses on two extreme outliers to highlight the range of English verse with which Spenser would have been familiar. My aim is not to prove the direct influence of these texts on *The Faerie Queene*. The generic and formal differences between them are considerable; Spenser is not in any straightforward way 'like' Tusser or Skelton, nor is he unproblematically indebted to them in formal terms. Rather, I want to dramatise the culture of formal assumptions and possibilities in which Spenser participated. This culture was shaped partly by unorthodox works as well as by the

---

30 See Wright, *Shakespeare's Metrical Art*, 61–65. This approach is also common to Thompson, Woods and Hardison: Spenser is read chiefly in terms of wider narratives of the development in prosody during the sixteenth and seventeenth centuries. So Spenser is (perhaps) a stop on the Roman road which leads to the real path finders – for Thompson, this means Sidney; for Woods, Milton and Dryden; for Wright, the later Shakespeare; and for Hardison, Milton. My approach suffers from the converse vulnerability: of too much focus on Spenser to the exclusion of broader developments.

31 Wilson-Okamura, *Spenser's International Style*, in particular 167–79. While I am sceptical about his ornamental reading of feminine rhyme, his emphasis on its antecedents in French and Neo-Latin verse is exemplary.

32 For the complexity of Spenser's religious position, see Hadfield, *Edmund Spenser: A Life*, 47 and passim, and Claire McEachern, 'Spenser and Religion'. For Spenser and Brexit, see Willy Maley, 'Spenser and Europe: Britomart after Brexit'.

experimental courtly verse of *Tottel's Miscellany* and Gascoigne, which have long been key markers in the narrative of the development of English verse. My snapshots of Tusser and Skelton aim to extend the range of texts relevant to the study of *The Faerie Queene*'s metre while continuing to bring the discussion of metre consciously into line with that of lineation.

Literary history habitually excludes Thomas Tusser from the mainstream of English poetry.[33] Yet *A Hundreth Good Pointes of Husbandrie*, later expanded to *Five Hundreth Points of Good Husbandry*, went through 'eighteen editions between 1557 and 1599', which makes it 'probably the biggest-selling book of poetry in the reign of Elizabeth I.'[34] Size doesn't matter in itself, yet, as the thrift-conscious Tusser would have argued, neither is it wholly irrelevant. Literary historians ignore Tusser chiefly because his verse is relentlessly practical and has no pretensions to literariness of any kind, eschewing ornament and ambiguity alike. Lewis's judgement articulates a complex doubleness: 'In a sense … Tusser is of no importance: the course of English poetry would be the same if he had never written.' This encapsulates the tendency towards progressive narratives, while at the same time partially resisting its exclusionary direction. Does it matter that Tusser stands outside the progressive 'course of English poetry'? Though for Lewis, Tusser's 'homely verses' are 'scarcely art', 'You cannot read long without feeling earth between your fingers': the palpable life the text evokes and engages with somehow salvages it in spite of orthodox literary taste.[35] Tusser's verse is often described as doggerel,[36] yet *Five Hundreth Points of Good Husbandry* contains a range of forms, including acrostics, sonnets, and sixains. The results are remote from Skeltonics in terms of their elaborate strategies of metrical control, if not in their effects; 'doggerel' highlights the mnemonic function of the text as practical and moral advice to be remembered through the working cycle of the year. As Wendy Wall has argued, Tusser's concern for his book as an artefact complicates any notion that his work is without artifice. 'The Preface' displays a writer very much aware both of the forms he was

---

33 See for example Thompson, *The Founding of English Metre*, 1–2.

34 Andrew McRae, 'Tusser, Thomas (c.1524–1580)', *ODNB Online*.

35 Lewis, *English Literature in Sixteenth Century*, 263. As Lewis implies, literary taste isn't everything; Wendy Wall has characterised Tusser's text as a 'how to' manual of understanding the protocols of the printed book; see 'Literacy and the Domestic Arts', 387–90.

36 See for example Steven Doloff, 'Polonius's Precepts and Thomas Tusser's *Five Hundreth Points of Good Husbandry*', 227–28, where the text is described as 'Written almost entirely in doggerel verse' (227).

using and the discursive differences between his work and that of his
more elevated contemporaries:

> What lookest thou here for to haue?
>   Trim verses, thy fansie to please?
> Of Surry (so famous) that craue,
> Look nothing but rudenesse in these.[37]

This poem exemplifies the mobile construction and emergent self-
consciousness of Tusser's text. It was added after the first edition of 1557;
I quote here from the 1570 edition. Later editions changed the third line
to 'Of manye my betters that craue', presumably as memories of Surrey's
work faded.[38] Tusser and Surrey shared a publisher in Richard Tottel,[39]
so the allusion is pointed: in place of the 'Trim verses' of *Songs and Sonets*
or the *Aeneid* translation, this is a work self-consciously structured by
'rudenesse', as Tusser emphasises the huge social gap between himself and
Surrey. This primitivist aesthetic is a knowing rejection of courtly norms
and milieu; 'The Preface' thus rejects 'Termes painted with Rhetorike'
because 'Good husbandrie seeketh not that'.[40] Tusser's poem makes good
on his promise:

> Now leekes are in season, for pottage full good,
>   and spareth the milchcow, and purgeth the blood.
> These hauing, with peason for pottage in Lent:
>   thou sparest both otemell and bread to be spent.

This stanza comes towards the end of 'Marches husbandrie'; the ensuing
'Aprils abstract' shows Tusser at his most sing-song as he summarises the
contents of the next month's advice:

> Get swineherd for hog,
> but kill not with dog.
> Wher swinheard doth lack
> corne goeth to wrack.[41]

37 Thomas Tusser, *A hundreth good pointes of husbandry* (1570), sig. A2r. The fuller text
    is Tusser, *Fiue hundred pointes of good husbandrie* (1580), which is the basis for Geoffrey
    Grigson's 1984 edition; see Tusser, *Five Hundred Points of Good Husbandry*, xxi.
38 The first edition to exclude Surrey was printed in 1573; see Tusser, *Fiue hundreth points
    of good husbandry* (1573), sig. B3r. On Tusser's social position, see McRae, 'Tusser,
    Thomas (c.1524–1580)'.
39 See Wall, 'Literacy and the Domestic Arts', 387–88.
40 Tusser, *Fiue hundred pointes of good husbandrie* (1580), sig. B4v.
41 Thomas Tusser, *Fiue hundred pointes of good husbandry* (1580), sigs. L4v–M1r.

Tusser has no interest in ambiguity, or complication of perspective; his writing presents the activities it describes as directly as possible. Hence the first stanza above tells the reader nothing more complicated than that eating leeks in season is economically and physiologically beneficial. The metrical forms he employs are unusual. Lewis uncertainly described them as '"anapaests"'; Emrys Jones, more confidently, opts for 'amphibrachs whose vigorous galloping or jouncing is unflaggingly maintained throughout the entire volume'.[42] Certainly, there is something amphbrachic about Tusser, but a more accurate description would be syllabic: his long lines have eleven syllables (or twelve, if the rhymes are feminine) and four stresses; medium lines have eight or nine syllables with three stresses; short lines have five or six syllables and two stresses.[43] The pattern is, as Jones indicates, easy to follow, and the fall of phrases into rhythmic shapes of the lines is certainly memorable, as in the following advice to young men not to be led astray by talkative women:

> x / x x / x x / x x /
> With hir that will clicket, make daunger to cope,
> x / x x / x x / x x /
> least quickly hir wicket, seeme easie to ope.[44]

A foot-based scansion of these lines would characterise this as three amphibrachs followed by an iamb in the final position (or perhaps a curtailed amphibrach, lacking its final syllable); Tusser reliably produces lines of eleven syllables with this strongly marked metrical pattern. The internal rhyme *clicket: wicket* enhances the verses' mnemonic function and draws attention to the almost unvarying position of the caesura after the sixth syllable, another device aimed at facilitating memorisation.[45] Aside from the deliberately utilitarian finish in which didactic intention and formal design coincide to an almost unparalleled extent, the importance of Tusser is that he demonstrates that metrical verse can be written on the basis of syllable counting and almost completely predictable stresses. Again, this is not a poetry of any technical sophistication, but it offers

---

42 Lewis, *English Literature in Sixteenth Century*, 262; Emrys Jones (ed.), *The New Oxford Book of Sixteenth Century Verse*, xxxiv. See also 186–92 for representative excerpts; Jones is alone amongst recent anthologists in including Tusser.

43 See T. V. F. Brogan, 'Amphibrach', 66, for the suggestion that accentually amphibrachic metre 'may not exist except as an experiment'.

44 Tusser, *Fiue hundred pointes of good husbandrie*, sig. S3v.

45 Grigson's edition removes many of these caesural commas, unwisely from the perspective of metrical history; see Tusser, *Five Hundred Points of Good Husbandry*, 165.

technical certainty based on syllabics where the courtly writers of the previous generation (in particular Sir Thomas Wyatt) could seem chaotic in the extreme.[46] Spenser may also have learned something about sequencing a poem on the calendar year from Tusser's precedent, and the ghost of his 'amphibrachs' may be detectable in 'Februarie', 'Maye', and 'September', with the caveat that these texts were certainly not written on the basis of syllable counting. *The Faerie Queene* seldom sounds like *Five Hundreth Points of Good Husbandry*, nevertheless it offers an artisanal template of metrical writing which Spenser probably read with interest.[47]

In contrast with Tusser, Skelton's literary reputation is secure. Nevertheless, despite his acknowledged influence on Spenser,[48] there is little discussion of him in work on the sixteenth-century metre or lineation, again because of his (perceived) eccentricity.[49] The sense that Skelton is a marginal figure goes back to the sixteenth century, and humanist outrage at his failure to reach the expected standards of a courtly poet. Puttenham could scarcely mention him without disdain: 'Skelton; usurping the name of a poet laureate, being in deed but a rude, railing rhymer, and all his doings ridiculous: he used both short distances and short measures, pleasing only the popular ear. In our courtly maker we banish them utterly.'[50] While this gibe may partly be actuated by Skelton's 'doings' in Elizabethan jest books,[51] contempt for his poetic technique is palpable. 'Short distances and short measures' are equated with catering to popular taste; as a specialist in such forms, Skelton reveals himself as an imposter. Indeed, the printing of Skelton's works mirrors this story of Elizabethan critical disdain: after

46 On Wyatt, see Woods, *Natural Emphasis*, 70–86, and Alan Swallow, 'The Pentameter Lines in Skelton and Wyatt'.
47 Hadfield, *Edmund Spenser: A Life*, 228–29, makes the same point from the opposite direction, stressing Spenser's likely interest in works about husbandry as a landowner. He also notes that Harvey owned a copy of Tusser, while Jonson intriguingly owned a volume which bound together *The Shepheardes Calender* with *Five Hundred Points of Good Husbandry*.
48 See Kinsman, 'Skelton, John', 660–61, and Heale, 'Spenser and Sixteenth-century Poetics', 590–91, 94, for Spenser's adoption of Colin Clout from Skelton's satirical poem.
49 Thompson discusses 'Edward IV', included in *The Mirror for Magistrates* and attributed to Skelton but possibly written earlier, *The Founding of English Metre*, 37–38; Woods argues that the Skeltonic 'was not an important influence on the direction of English verse'; *Natural Emphasis*, 70, 96 n.4; Wright and Hardison discuss other aspects of Skelton's work than Skeltonics: Wright, *Shakespeare's Metrical Art*, 29–30; Hardison, *Prosody and Purpose*, 155, 156, 172.
50 George Puttenham, *The Art of English Poesy: A Critical Edition*, 173; see also 148, 150.
51 See Andrew Hadfield, 'Spenser and Jokes', 5, for jest books based on Skelton's apocryphal 'doings'.

its heyday in the 1550s and 1560s, none of Skelton's major poems was printed in the 1570s, 1580s or 1590s.[52]

Spenser surely felt differently. As Elizabeth Heale suggests, Spenser was 'a close reader' of Skelton's *Collyn Clout*; she detects resonances of this text in the 'September' eclogue as Diggon Davie 'adopts the same self-protective technique of reporting and denying other men's criticisms.'[53] Though 'September' is not written in the same verse form, its discursive self-consciousness in the passage Heale cites suggests that Spenser was mimicking the 'flatt' style of the earlier Colin Clout:

Then playnely to speake of shepheards most what,
Badde is the best (this english is flatt.)
Their ill haviour garres men missay,
Both of their doctrine, and of their faye.
They sayne the world is much war then it wont,
All for her shepheards bene beastly and blont. ('September', ll.104–09)

And yf ye stande in doute
Who brought this ryme aboute,
My name is Collyn Cloute.
I purpose to shake oute
All my connyng bagge,
Lyke a clerkely hagge.
For though my ryme be ragged,
Tattered and jagged,
Rudely rayne-beaten
Rusty and mothte-eaten
Yf ye take well therwith
It hath in it some pyth.[54]

There have been more far-fetched analogies for Spenser's loose, four-beat couplets than Skelton's 'Rudely rayne-beaten' short measures. Diggon's self-conscious aside '(this English is flat)' suggests a continuity of rhetorical awareness between Skelton and Spenser of the uses to which literary

52 The *English Short Title Catalogue* shows numerous reprints of the major Skeltonic poems in the 1540s, 1550s and 1560s. After John Stow's collected edition of 1568 (*Pithy pleasaunt and profitable workes of maister Skelton, Poete Laureate*, printed by Thomas Marshe), there is no reprint of Skeltonic verse until 1609. See the *English Short Title Catalogue* at http://estc.bl.uk/ [accessed 5 September 2013]; Hadfield, *Edmund Spenser: A Life*, 466 n.3, suggests that Spenser would have used the Stow edition. Naturally, much of Skelton's work is topical satire of the 1520s (*Collyn Clout*; *Why Come Ye Nat to Courte?*), but the collapse in editions of Skelton's work also underlines a shift in literary taste.
53 Heale, 'Spenser and Sixteenth-century Poetics', 590.
54 Skelton, *The Complete English Poems*, 248.

'rudeness' might be put as the flouting of conventional decorum enables the satiric utterance of otherwise unsayable truths. Unlike Tusser's careful syllable counting, what unites 'September' and the Skeltonic is a scansion constructed from stress counting:

x   /   x x   /   x   /   x   x   /
Then playnely to speake of shepheards most what,

/   x x   /   x   / x x   /
Badde is the best (this english is flatt.)

x   /   x   /   x   /   x
For though my ryme be ragged,

/ x x x   /   x
Tattered and jagged

As with all such scansions, this is a loose approximation for texts which advertise their stylistic licence. Is Skelton's 'Tattered' tri- or disyllabic? Does it matter whether we hear 'Badde is' as trochaic or iambic? How should one approach scanning a line like 'Marrie that great *Pan* bought with deare borrow' ('September', l.96)?[55] What these extracts emphasise is the proximity between Skelton and Spenser in terms of a readiness to challenge conventional courtly idioms in explicitly satirical texts. Nevertheless, it is significant that 'September' does not follow Skelton in more radical ruptures of lineation. Where Skelton courts what Puttenham would see as chaos by hovering between three and two stresses per line, Spenser maintains a firmer metrical contract, in which despite varying syllable counts, generally four strong beats are discernible. And yet, though Skelton is indifferent about the precise number of stresses in a given short line, it should also be noted that the Skeltonic is typically anchored by the authority of the individual line. Syntax necessarily carries on over

---

55 This line can be approached as a five beat, rough iambic:

/ x   x   /   x   /   x   /   / x
Marrie that great *Pan* bought with deare borrow,

though it would be equally plausible to stress almost any of the monosyllables in the heart of the line. A four beat scansion might produce:

/ x   x   /   x   /   x   x   / x
Marrie that great *Pan* bought with deare borrow,

But the permutations remain considerable; as throughout 'September', 'Febraurie' and 'Maye', Spenser depends if not on a speaking voice then on phrase rhythm. At the same time, the integrity of the line anchors the reader in the sense that this is metrical writing.

several of these short measures, but almost invariably Skelton wants the reader to pause on his rhymes, thus signalling the force of the line as a unit. Consider a passage from *Why Come Ye Nat to Courte?*:

> Suche a prelate, I trowe,
> Were worthy to rowe
> Thorow the streytes of Marock
> To the gibbet of Baldock.
> He wolde dry up the stremys
> Of ix kingis realmys,
> All ryvers and wellys
> All waters that swellys;
> For with us he so mellys
> That within Englande dwellys.
> I wolde he were somewhere ellys[56]

Within this extract, line length varies from around five syllables to eight per line, but each line both builds the punch of Skelton's joke while maintaining its own syntactic domain through rhyme. The comic force of the short measure is that it insists that the reader recognises each rhyme and the comic potential within each accumulating cluster; as Elaine Spina suggested, this is probably connected with the fact that such poems were written for oral performance rather than print.[57] In this case, the bathetic final line works partly because the diminished scale of 'somewhere ellys' contrasts with the huge extent of Wolsey's influence (related of course to his huge greed and size)[58] in the previous lines. As in 'September', the value of the individual line is clear; what orientates the reader in both texts is the sense that each line is a coherent unit of sense, even if the metre is less fixed. At one level, the Skeltonic poems remain remote from *The Faerie Queene*. They are nevertheless a neglected part of Spenser's literary culture, underlining what Robert Starr Kinsman has aptly characterised as a literary relationship which is 'ambivalent, complicated, important, yet incomplete'.[59]

56 Skelton, *The Complete English Poems*, ll.953–63; 303.
57 Elaine Spina, 'Skeltonic Meter in *Elynour Rummyng*', 665.
58 See ll.213–26 for Wolsey's greed, in *The Complete English Poems*, 284.
59 Robert Starr Kinsman, 'Skelton, John', 660. Kinsman's article is valuable for articulating many of these difficulties, particularly in relation to the Colin Clout persona. He also touches on the linguistic debt, seeing elements of Skelton in 'Maye' but less so in 'Julye'. Another writer who felt differently was Michael Drayton, who cites Skelton with qualified admiration in his *Odes*; see *Poems [1619]* for 'To Himselfe, and the Harpe' (''Tis possible to clyme,/To kindle, or to slake,/Although in SKELTON'S ryme', 283), and 'A Skeltoniad', which somewhat backhandedly imitates the Skeltonic, 301–02; the *Odes* has been published in a different form in 1606.

Common lines (2): longer and shorter lines

Earlier I evoked the almost chaotic variety of English lines and scansion in the sixteenth century. Part of what continues to make the poetry of this period stylistically exciting is that dominant styles have not yet become fully paradigmatic norms in which available forms are prescribed by an authoritative tradition. The concern for correctness which would become characteristic of neo-classical criticism makes only limited inroads onto a literary culture which remains in important respects confused and contradictory. Roger Ascham's *The Scholemaster* (1570), in part an earnest assertion of classical rectitude by one of England's leading humanists, did not herald a revolution in prosody.[60] The vices (or more neutrally, trends) deplored by Ascham – that 'rash ignorant heads ... can easely recken vp fourten sillabes, and easelie stumble on euery Ryme' – continue unabated in the 1570s and beyond.[61] In this section, I look at two of the dominant line forms of this period: the long line forms of the fourteener and poulter's measure and a particularly influential format of the shorter iambic pentameter. If Tusser and Skelton are formal outliers, these examples constitute the mainstream of English metrical writing.

The fourteener and poulter's measure are closely related forms: the former is a couplet in which each line has seven stresses and fourteen syllables; the latter substitutes a twelve-syllable hexameter for the first line. In each case, the iambic beat is strongly marked as in the first line of Robert Southwell's 'A childe my Choyce', 'Let folly praise that fancie loves, I praise and love that child'.[62] Both forms are sometimes described as 'common metre' because of their similarities to ballad stanza, though this term is usually used in referring to texts where the long line forms are typographically resolved into their smaller constituent units of alternating lines of eight and six syllables.[63] Fourteeners and poulter's are used in a wide range of texts and genres. A selective list would include the translations of classical epics by Thomas Phaer, Arthur Golding, and George Chapman; lyrics in *Tottel's Miscellany* by Surrey and others; pastorals, epistles, and satires by the major writers of the 1560s and 1570s, Barnabe

---

60 See Attridge, *Well-Weighed Syllables*, the most complete account of the quantitative revival. The reasons for its failure are complex, but the lack of wide agreement on how to scan English on a quantitative basis alongside the popularity and flexibility of rhyming verse remain significant factors. See also Gavin Alexander's illuminating Introduction to William Scott, *The Model of Poesy*, xliv–li.

61 Ascham in Smith (ed.), *Elizabethan Critical Essays*, I, 31.

62 Southwell, *The Poems*, 13.

63 See T. V. F. Brogan, 'Ballad', 117. Beth Quitslund, *The Reformation in Rhyme*, 22–23, suggests that Sternhold's verses 'are essentially a transitional form between fourteener couplets and iambic quatrains' (23).

Googe, George Turberville, and George Gascoigne; and the hugely popular
metrical psalters of Thomas Sternhold and John Hopkins. As I have already
implied, writing about these forms as 'long lines' needs careful qualification
since these same lines might be written or printed either in the long form
of Golding's *Metamorphoses*, or as the short quatrains of the Sternhold-
Hopkins Psalms. Michael Drayton's first publication, *The harmonie of the
church* (1591) exemplifies this typographical flexibility where a number
of texts set the first couplet as a quatrain before reverting to longer line
layout for the remainder of the poem:

> Oh Lord, the God of *Simeon*,
>   my soueraigne Father deare:
> To whom thou gauest strength and might,
>   the sword in hand to beare.
> To take reuenge on those which first, the maidens wombe did tame,
> And spoiled her virginitie, with great reproach and shame.[64]

Whether through artistic design, or the concern of the compositors to
use space as economically as possible, Drayton's text graphically captures
the doubleness of the form.[65] It underlines the fact that many long-line
fourteeners can be relineated as quatrains with the regular caesuras after
the eighth syllable (or sixth in the case of poulter's) transmuted to line ends.
One of the most celebrated lyrics of the period, Southwell's 'The burning
Babe', appears as long lines on its first print publication and in quatrains
in some contemporary manuscripts.[66] What is the difference between

> With this he vanisht out of sight, and swiftly shrank away,
> And straight I called unto minde, that it was Christmasse day

64 M[ichael] D[rayton], 'The Praier of Iudith', in *The harmonie of the church*, sig. E2r. See
   also 'The Song of Deborah and Baracke', sig. D1r; 'The Eight Chapter' of his paraphrase
   of 'The Song of Solomon', sig. C3r, is reproduced in Kenneth Borris and Meredith
   Donaldson Clark, 'Hymnic Epic and *The Faerie Queene*'s Original Printed Format:
   Canto-Canticles and Psalmic Arguments', 1166, which shows the way in which the
   large initial capital of each text creates a need for relineation.
65 The layout of other poems in the volume suggests that changes were made to fit the
   available space. In several poems only the second line is relineated – see 'The fift
   Chapter', sig. C1r; 'The sixt Chapter', sig. C2r; 'The seventh Chapter', sig. C2v; 'The
   Song of Annah', sig. C3v, and 'The Song of Iudith', sig. E2v. The same patterns are largely
   retained in the 1610 reprint, *A heauenly harmonie of spirituall songes*.
66 See Southwell, *The Poems*, 124, for McDonald and Brown's commentary; this process
   also affected 'A childe my Choyce' (123). See David Norbrook and H. R. Woudhuysen,
   The Penguin Book of Renaissance verse 1509–1659, 535, for 'The burning Babe' set in
   long lines. See also Joseph Loewenstein, 'Tudor Verse Form: Rudeness, Artifice, and
   Display' (forthcoming) who notes a parallel process in the *mise en page* of Turberville's
   1567 Mantuan translation, in which the octavo format of the book necessitates the
   presentation of poulter's measure and fourteeners as short lines. I am indebted to
   Professor Loewenstein for advance sight of this illuminating essay.

and

> With this he vanisht out of sight,
> And swiftly shrank away,
> And straight I called unto minde,
> That it was Christmasse day?[67]

The lines certainly look different, and layout may have a perceptual influence on the sense the reader makes of the text. Different lineations may also encode different generic signals. In the epic translations of Phaer, Golding, and Chapman, the long-line forms evoke the dactyllic hexameter by typographic resemblance if not any exact metrical similarity. Conversely, the line breaks (cued by initial letter capitalisation) McDonald and Brown give to 'The burning Babe' encourage the reader to approach it as a lyric quatrain. Long-line forms are also useful space and paper savers, a particular concern for longer texts like epics, but possibly germane to the presentation of 'The burning Babe' in print in 1602.[68] Yet there is a case for saying that there is very little difference between the two presentations of 'The burning Babe': orthography and punctuation are identical, it is only lineation which changes. And in effect, the short-line form emphasises the force of the caesuras in the long-line form; the flexible appearance of these forms is at once a key to their success and an index to their limitations.

John Thompson long ago pointed out the tendency of caesura in poulter's and the fourteener to predictability. Such caesuras (respectively after the eighth syllable in the fourteener and the sixth syllable in the hexameter line of poulter's) become constitutive metrical patterns from which it is difficult to break. For Thompson, this helps to account for the ultimate triumph of the shorter iambic pentameter line, which is freer and less predictable in its placement of caesura. Though, as we shall see, there are exceptions to this rule, the point remains that in the fourteener, metrical pattern tends to 'overwhelm' speech rhythm and the rhythm of phrase.[69] In Robert Lowell's evocative summary, Golding's fourteener 'seems like some arbitrary and wayward hurdle, rather than the very backbone of

---

67 Southwell, *Saint Peters complaint* (1602), sig. L4v; Southwell, *The Poems*, 16.
68 McDonald and Brown argue for quatrains, on the basis that the 1602 edition of *Saint Peters complaint* was pressed for space, an argument enhanced by the fact that the preceding poem, 'New Prince, new pompe', also in fourteeners, is there printed as quatrains; see Southwell, *The Poems*, 124, and Southwell, *Saint Peters complaint*, sigs L4r-v.
69 Thompson, *The Founding of English Metre*, 36.

what is being said'.[70] Another way of putting this is that the fourteener sets an unusually high premium on the subordination of language to metrical pattern. The close of 'The burning Babe' exemplifies that process, showing how a skilled poet may work in harmony with the form's demands. What makes the poem so lyrically effective is its precise coincidence of syntax and metre: the recording of the date in the final line(s) seems to fall without constraint into the familiar metrical pattern, but it is of course with this sense of achieved inevitability that Southwell transforms the commonplace into poetry.

Nevertheless, to subordinate is necessarily to constrain; as Drayton was to put it in a related context, 'all Stanza's are in my opinion but Tyrants and Torturers, when they make inuention obey their number, which sometime would otherwise scantle it selfe'.[71] Any reader of fourteeners will come across examples of such tortuous obedience to formal pattern. Sternhold's Psalter is a text which puts a strong emphasis on obedience; these are poems which 'exhorteth vs/to leue in godly feare', and which are equally ready to subordinate language to the beat of the metrical pattern to make the biblical texts as memorable as possible to readers and auditors in particular.[72] His contraction of rhyme words exemplifies this process:

> Ponder my words O lord aboue
> my studye lorde consider,
> And heare my voice my king my God
> to the I make my prayer.[73]

Though Sternhold allows himself a trochaic opening with 'Ponder', the rhyme of 'consider' with 'prayer' shows the extreme subordination of polysyllabic words to metrical pattern as the reader is forced to swallow 'consi-' and wrest the emphasis to the final syllable. My point is not that this is bad writing, but that much of Sternhold's success as a populariser lies in his readiness to sacrifice word accent to metrical pattern, thus creating texts which might easily be sung. As Beth Quitslund demonstrates, Sternhold's reputation as a type of an incompetent poet derives largely

70 Cited by Thompson, *The Founding of English Metre*, 36 FN 2. For the full essay, see Lowell, *Collected Prose*, 152–60, in particular 154–56.
71 Drayton, 'To the Reader of The Barons Warres' in *Poems [1619]*, sig. A3v. See "† 'scantle, v.". *OED Online*. As *OED* demonstrates, this term was a favourite of Drayton's; here it conveys the sense of make scant or restrict.
72 Thomas Sternhold, *Certayne psalmes*, sig. B6v. This quotation is from Sternhold's argument to Psalm 34.
73 Sternhold, *Certayne psalmes*, sig. A7v.

from seventeenth-century anti-puritanical controversies in which the
long-dead courtier was a convenient fall-guy. His writing is better understood as 'economical' and transitional.[74] Later in the same psalm, he writes
'And thou wylt hate the bloude thirstye/And the deceitefull man', which
demands that a reader stress the final syllable of 'thirstye' and stress 'the'
in the second line.[75] In Drayton's terms, invention obeys number, but the
broader point is that Sternhold makes the psalms into credible popular
poetry rather than a text for private reading.[76]

    In a radically different literary context, similar effects can be seen in
Phaer's *Aeneid* translation, in which Virgil's epic syntax is made to conform
to the twenty-eight syllable units of the fourteener. Though not as widely
cited as Golding's Ovid, Phaer's translation remains an historically significant
work which has much to say about early Elizabethan metrics and taste.[77]
William Webbe patriotically saw in Phaer's version a demonstration of
the heroic potential of English, even going so far as to suggest that 'the
coppy it selfe [i.e. Virgil's poem] goeth no whit beyond it [i.e. Phaer's]'.[78]
Phaer's version of Dido's speech at the beginning of Book IV exemplifies
the virtues and the vices of the fourteener as a medium for epic:

> Dere sister Anne, what dreames be these yt th[us] my slepes affrights
> What wondrous gest is this that thus among us newly lightes?
> How like a lord? how valiaunt strong of hart & armes he semes?
> I see right wel no fables ben that men of God esteemes.
> Of kind of gods he is doubtles, by drede ar dastardes knowen.
> Alas what warrs hath he gon through, what destnyes him hath thrown …
> Synce of my husband first the death and fatall end I knew,
> And that my brother with his blood his alters did embrew:
> This only man hath bent my hart, & sore my mind doth moue,
> I know the steppes of old, I feele the flames of former loue.[79]

74 Quitslund, *The Reformation in Rhyme*, 1–4, 22–23. See also 70–71 for the convincing
     argument that rather than being an adaptation of popular forms, Sternhold's psalter
     actually provided a template for those forms.
75 Sternhold, *Certayne psalms*, sig. A8r.
76 See Christopher Hill, *The English Bible and the Seventeenth-Century Revolution*, 355–56,
     who contextualizes Sternhold's versions in communal singing in the sixteenth and
     seventeenth centuries.
77 See Brown "'Charmed with Inchaunted Rimes'" in Brown and Lethbridge, *A Concordance*,
     49–50, for the differing fortunes of Golding and Phaer's translations.
78 Webbe in Smith (ed.), *Elizabethan Critical Essays*, I, 259. For Webbe's 'conference' of
     Phaer with Virgil, see 256–62. For Webbe's use of the word to mean original, see *OED
     Online*, "copy" IV. 8 a, citing this passage.
79 Virgil, *The nyne fyrst bookes of the Eneidos of Virgil*, sig. H4r.

This passage shows the uneasy dance Phaer has to perform between faithfully rendering the Latin and the exigencies of the fourteener. Though he works to vary caesura position to mirror the skittish syntax of Dido's Latin, it is something of an uphill struggle to combat the normative structures of the verse form.[80] The third line here, 'How like a lord? how valiaunt strong of hart & armes he semes?' bears some resemblance to Virgil's 'Quem sese orc ferens? quàm forti pectore, et armis?'[81] Similarly, Phaer's rendering of the celebrated phrase 'agnosco verteris vestigia flammae' as 'I know the steppes of old, I feele the flames of former loue' is a limited success. Adapting an image from Surrey's translation, Phaer contrives an early caesura after the sixth syllable and renders the Virgilian phrase with forceful alliteration.[82] Nevertheless, the line exemplifies Phaer's tendency to say too much, or to yoke phrases into lines which Virgil keeps separate. Phaer in fact latches onto Surrey's image of Dido's steps as a means of filling out his line; as so often, English translators stretch Virgil to suit the different demands of English syntax and metre. Similarly, 'Of kind of gods he is doubtles, by drede ar dastardes knowen' makes one semantically incoherent line from Virgil's more adroit disposition of Dido's half-connected ideas into separate lines and sentences: 'Credo equidem (nec vana fides) genus esse deorum./Degeneres animos timor arguit.'[83] Metrical subordination is shown by the strong accent Phaer puts on the second syllable of 'doubtles'. Spenser shows evidence of a similar readiness to wrest pronunciation to metrical conformity,[84] but in poetic context, Phaer's surrender to the metre is unfortunate because it distracts attention from the meaning of the passage. Surrey's version, though substituting two lines for one original, is more poised in throwing emphasis onto the semantically significant terms which continuously point to the ways in which Dido sees Aeneas: 'Truly I think (ne vain is my belefe)/Of Goddish race some

---

80 Like Golding, Phaer elsewhere employs rhyming triplets, which allow for a more extended syntax. He also mimics Virgil's unfinished hemistichs: just after this passage Virgil's 'Germaníque minas?' becomes 'And of your brothers threatnings?'; see Virgil, *Pub. Virgilii Maronis opera*, 204, and Virgil, *The nyne fyrst bookes of the Eneidos*, sig. H4v.
81 Virgil, *Pub. Virgilii Maronis opera*, 203. As Wilson-Okamura, *Virgil in the Renaissance*, 4, cautions it is important to quote from Renaissance Virgils rather than only the Loeb Virgil. In this passage, Bynneman's text is close to that of modern editions.
82 Virgil, *Pub. Virgilii Maronis opera*, 203. Surrey's version, published the year before Phaer's first edition, is 'Now feelingly I tast the steppes of mine old flame', a powerful hexameter amidst his pentameters; see Virgil, *Certain bokes of Virgiles Aeneis*, sig. D3v.
83 Virgil, *Pub. Virgilii Maronis opera*, 203.
84 Though *The Faerie Queene*'s one usage of 'doubtlesse' scans it conventionally: 'For doubtlesse death ensewed, if any him descryde' (I.v.52.9).

off spring shold he be'.[85] Where the dactylic hexameter excels in showing Dido's abrupt changes of focus and emotion, the fourteener offers only a ponderous regularity. Phaer tries to resist it, yet the fourteener's enclosing patterns of emphasis and syntax predominate in his *Eneidos*. The radical potential of the fourteener as a heroic medium would have to wait for Chapman's brilliant and still experimental translation of the *Iliad*.[86]

Of course, as well as being an essential part of Spenser's literary culture, the fourteener contributes to *The Faerie Queene*, albeit without much acknowledgement. The arguments to each canto are seventy-four couplets of fourteeners, usually presented in four-line quatrains rhyming *Abxb*, though this particular example falls pleasingly into *Abab*:

> *Calidore hostes with Meliboe*
> *and loues fayre Pastorell,*
> *Coridon enuies him, yet he*
> *for ill rewards him well.* (VI.ix.arg)

Such verses are as metrically predictable and conservative as both Sternhold and Phaer; this example shows metrical subordination as Spenser opts for the trisyllabic 'Pastorell' over the full form of 'Pastorella'.[87] The arguments were likely designed to work as rough and ready counterpoints to the more polished verse of the poem proper, picked out in italic to distinguish them from the roman of the main text, and which knowingly allude to older forms of English verse.[88] In an illuminating essay of 2011, Kenneth Borris and Meredith Donaldson Clark demonstrate that these texts recall the arguments used by Sternhold and Hopkins in their psalms.[89] Like their counterparts in *The Faerie Queene*, Sternhold's arguments use a different

---

85 Virgil, *Certain bokes of Virgiles Aeneis*, sig. D3r.

86 See Chapman, *Homer's Iliad*, 1–18, for Robert S. Miola's judicious summary of Chapman's achievement.

87 The Lethbridge Concordance shows 'Pastorell' outscoring 'Pastorella' 26 to 15, though the character is typically referred to in the longer form; see for example Richard T. Neuse, 'Pastorella', 532–34. As this example implies, 'Pastorell' is a much more convenient rhyming term: see Brown and Lethbridge, *A Concordance*, 288 and passim; there are 13 rhymes on 'Pastorell' and none on 'Pastorella'. Such forms of subordination are essential in the writing of a long narrative poem in rhyme.

88 See Brown, '"Charmed with Inchaunted Rimes"' in Brown and Lethbridge, *A Concordance*, 49, 64.

89 Borris and Clark, 'Hymnic Epic', 1148–93. An important strand of Borris and Clark's argument is that the subhead 'Cant.' in early editions of *The Faerie Queene* is an abbreviation of 'canticle' rather than, as commonly assumed in critical editions, 'canto'. They connect this with their contextualisation of the arguments in terms of the Sternhold psalter to amplify their sense that *The Faerie Queene* makes significant paratextual allusion to the form of sacred song. See the discussion in Chapter 5 below.

font (roman where the psalms are in black letter), and offer what are often allegorical summaries of the psalms they gloss. Sternhold's argument for Psalm 3 asserts 'The passion here is fygured,/and how Christ rose agayne', a technique which is particularly analogous to the arguments of Book I: '*The guilefull great Enchaunter parts/The Redcrosse Knight from Truth*' (I.ii. arg).[90] For Borris and Clark, the Sternhold psalter offers the fullest analogue for *The Faerie Queene*'s arguments. While many contemporary poems have arguments, typically they are not in the precise form of common metre quatrains.[91] Elizabethan versions of Italian epics have ottava rima arguments, 'the same form that they used for the narrative'.[92] This suggests that the 'formal significance' of the arguments depends on the reader's registering their hymnic forerunners: 'The arguments provide means to assimilate epic endeavor to Protestant poetics and to reconcile vaulting literary ambition with religious beliefs that privilege humility'.[93]

Although this essay is the most substantial recent contribution to the understanding of the arguments' paratextual function, in my view Spenser was not alluding exclusively to Sternhold's work. As Borris and Clark recognise, the hymnic analogy works best in relation to Book I: 'Correlations of tone, rhetoric, and substance are strongest in the arguments of book 1, the Legend of Holiness, which provides the epic's fundamental English Protestant curriculum'.[94] It is harder to read the argument from Book VI quoted above – which is a relatively straightforward summary of Calidore's pastoral séjour – in these contexts. Indeed, the arguments in the later books tend to be compact résumés of narrative rather than the more leading symbolic glosses of Book I: '*The Witch creates a snowy Lady/like to Florimell*'; '*The battell twixt three brethren with/Cambell for Canacee*', and so on (III.viii.arg; IV.iii.arg). What is being recalled here is traditional poetry broadly conceived; as I have suggested elsewhere, they are fossils of older forms of writing which Spenser has set in the topsoil of his poem and which serve to counterpoint its bolder styles.[95]

---

90 Sternhold, *Certayne psalms*, sig. A6r.
91 For examples, see Chapman's Homer, which translates the long and short verse arguments from Jean de Sponde, in Homer, *The Iliad*, 3, 413; Drayton's *Barons Warres* (the same ottava rima stanzas as the main narrative), and *Englands Heroicall Epistles* (no more than 14 lines of pentameter couplets, the same form as the poems), in Drayton, *Poems [1619]*, 1, 105 and passim.
92 Borris and Clark, 'Hymnic Epic', 1170.
93 Borris and Clark, 'Hymnic Epic', 1170, 1176.
94 Borris and Clark, 'Hymnic Epic', 1175.
95 In Brown '"Charmed with Inchaunted Rimes"' in Brown and Lethbridge, *A Concordance*, 49.

The layout in the early editions lends support to this view. These editions are inconsistent in their allocation of initial capitals to lines 2 and 4 of the arguments. In the 1609 folio (the fullest edition because of its inclusion of the Mutabilitie Cantos), there are forty-seven arguments where lines 2 and 4 do not have initial capitalisation and twenty-seven which do.[96] The argument of II.ii illustrates the uncapitalised model; all early editions follow the same pattern:

> *Babes bloody handes may not be clensd,*
> *   the face of golden Meane.*
> *Her sisters two Extremities:*
> *   striue her to banish cleane.*[97]

This is the same layout used in Sternhold's *Certayne psalms*: the common metre quatrain is made up of two connected units of longer and shorter lines where the long line only takes an initial capital. Conversely, the argument of II.i differs from edition to edition. In 1590, it reads:

> *Guyon by Archimage abusd,*
> *   the Redcrosse kniggt awaytes,*
> *Fyndes Mordant and Amauia slaine*
> *   With pleasures poisoned baytes.*[98]

The compositor of 1590 seems unclear whether to capitalise the beginnings of lines 2 and 4 and in this case opts for an amalgam which was corrected in 1596,[99] although this edition is as inconsistent as 1590 in its overall policy about initial capitals in the arguments. Such evidence perhaps doesn't tell us much beyond the fact that early editions had a complex manuscript to print which may itself have been inconsistent in practice. More significant

---

96 Based on a copy of the 1609 folio in my possession. Proper names complicate this calculation. I have counted III.x as uncapitalized because the fourth line is '*to turne she doth refuse*' even though the second line is '*Malbecco her pursewes*'. But I count IV.ix as capitalized, where the relevant lines are '*Poeana takes to wife*' and '*Prince Arthur stints their strife*'. See Spenser, *The Faerie Queene* (1609), 171, 228.

97 Spenser, *The Faerie Queene* (1590), 205. Huntington Library copy. David Lee Miller points out to me that this is one of the few arguments to include characteristic quirks of wordplay: 'hands' anticipates 'face' and 'Extremities'; 'clensd' morphs to 'cleane' (email correspondence, August 2017).

98 Spenser, *The Faerie Queene* (1590), 187. Huntington Library copy. Other copies correct '*kniggt*'; see the Folger Shakespeare Library copy, also reproduced on EEBO.

99 1596 reads: '*Guyon by Archimage abusd,/The Redcrosse knight awaytes,/Findes Mordant and Amauia slaine/With pleasures poisoned baytes.*'; *The Faerie Queene* (1596), 187. Huntington Library copy. 1609 makes minor changes to spelling ('*abus'd*'; '*awaites*'; '*baites*') but keeps the same initial capitals; *The Faerie Queene* (1609), 60.

are arguments where the metre points to the likelihood that the lines were composed as couplets of fourteeners rather than as quatrains. This occurs when the longer lines stretch to nine or more syllables, as in the argument to II.iii:[100]

> *Vaine Braggadochio, getting Guyons*
> *horse is made the scorne*

The compositor of 1609 clearly felt something was awry here and introduced a comma, '*horse,*' which enhances the sense that this is a long line which has been roughly cut into two units. Indeed, in a couple of cases in the 1590 *Faerie Queene*, such metrical irregularity is partially corrected by hyphenating the long terms which would otherwise transgress the eight-syllable boundary:

> *Prince Arthure meets with Vna great-*
> *ly with those newes distrest* (I.vii)

> *Fights with Cymochles, whiles his bro-*
> *ther burnes in furious fyre* (II.vi)[101]

For I.vii, the compositor of 1609 was so disturbed by the appearance of his text that he changed it to '*Prince Arthur meets with Vna/greatly with those newes distrest*,'[102] a correction which rather gives the game away: I would suggest that Spenser wrote these lines as complete fourteeners which were subsequently disposed into rather awkward quatrains. Certainly it makes better metrical sense to read lines like

> *Besieged of many foes whom straunger knightes to flight compell*

or

> *The maske of Cupid, and th'enchanted chamber are displayd*[103]

as Spenserian versions of the heroic fourteener rather than as fully coherent common metre stanzas. This is not to say that Spenser was making specific allusion to Phaer or Golding, but that the form of these arguments underlines what I called earlier a culture of formal assumptions. In this

---

100 Other examples occur at I.iv, II.ix, III.viii (quoted above), and III.xii. Spenser generally avoided such lines in arguments for Books IV–VI, which tend to be metrically smoother than those in Books I–III. See *The Faerie Queene* (1609), 69, for the argument to II.iii.
101 Spenser, *The Faerie Queene* (1590), 89, 256. Huntington Library copy.
102 Spenser, *The Faerie Queene* (1609), 29.
103 II.ix.arg and III.xii.arg, relineated and with the initial capital on '*Chamber*' silently amended.

view, the fourteener is an intrinsic part of Elizabethan notions of both sacred and epic poetry, and which participate in Spenser's poem through these paratexts.

The larger point which arises from these materials is that *The Faerie Queene* resembles John Thompson's brilliant description of *The Mirror for Magistrates* as 'an extraordinary museum of metre', with the difference that what was a consequence of the multiple contributors to *The Mirror* is a deliberate part of *The Faerie Queene*'s design.[104] Or rather, Spenser's poem is a special collection of key Elizabethan lines and styles (iambic pentameter, fourteener and common metre, hexameter) which showcases the changing history of those styles. The arguments show a writer fully versed in the tonalities of common metre, and perhaps comedically aware of its limitations as a medium for epic. They are knowingly rough summaries which most readers pass over and forget in the process of reading what I earlier called 'the poem proper'. This is not to say that the arguments are 'improper', it is rather to register the radical asymmetry between these texts and the narrative they summarise. Borris and Clark's analogies with translations of Italian epic are telling here: where Harington and Fairfax construct arguments which are formally similar to their poems, Spenser deploys an argument form which in no real way resembles that of his poem. By incorporating such traditional metrical shapes within his poem, Spenser emphasises the difference and the novelty of the main body of that text. At the same time, the roughened forms of Spenser's arguments underline the mechanics of subordination, as name and word forms mutate under the pressure of common metre.

Common lines (3): the '4/6' line

It would be a mistake, however, to view iambic pentameter as an intrinsically freer verse form than the fourteener. The development of the iambic pentameter line in the sixteenth century suggests the reverse, as the uncertain measures of key writers like Wyatt and Chaucer were regularised into stricter forms, in which syllable count and number of stresses were more stringently enforced. In this final illustration, I examine an extreme permutation of the iambic pentameter line. There is no agreed name for this line, so the easiest way to describe it initially is by citing a number of examples:

104 Thompson, *The Founding of English Metre*, 37.

The Nightingale, (whose happy noble hart),
No dole can daunt, not fearefull force affright,[105]

Swete were the sawce, would please ech kind of tast,
The life likewise, were pure that never swerved,[106]

My threed is cutt, and yet it was not spunn –
And nowe I liue, and nowe my life is donn.[107]

Let *Gryll* be *Gryll*, and haue his hoggish mindc; (II.xii.87.8)

These texts encompass a surprisingly wide number of stanza and verse forms, from Gascoigne's blank verse satire, the rhyming sixains of Ralegh and Tichborne, to *The Faerie Queene* itself. Carlo Bajetta evokes the line's distinctive *mise en page* and 'rather odd punctuation' which produces 'an iambic pentameter verse marked by a very heavy pause after the fourth syllable'.[108] The appearance of the lines coercively signals how they should be read. For convenience, I call it the 4/6 line because of its strict syllabic pattern with an unvarying mid-line pause and rigid endstopping. In the examples discussed by Bajetta, this almost asphyxiating form, in which syntax and word form are subordinated to syllabic pattern, is used throughout the poems he discusses, whether this is a short lyric or a discursive poem running to several hundred lines.[109] Bajetta sees the 4/6 line as a characteristic of poets associated with the Inns of Court in the 1570s. Using evidence from presentation manuscript copies to confirm his reading of printed works, he suggests that Gacoigne, Ralegh, Googe, and Churchyard – all writers with Inns of Court connections – consciously developed the line as a stylistic calling card. That this form was something of a constitutive norm of what a line of iambic pentameter in English should look like is borne out by Gascoigne's *Certayne Notes of Instruction*: despite recognising that caesura placement is an issue for the 'discretion of the wryter', he counsels that 'in a verse of tenne [the caesura] will best be placed at the end of the first foure sillables'.[110]

105 George Gascoigne, *The steele glas*, sig. B1r.
106 Sir Walter Ralegh, 'Walter Rawely of the middle *Temple, in commendation of the Steele Glasse*', in *The Poems*, 1.
107 Chidiock Tichborne, 'Tichborne's Lament', in Richard S. M. Hirsch (ed.) 'The Works of Chidiock Tichborne', 310.
108 Carlo M. Bajetta, 'Ralegh's Early Poetry and its Metrical Context', 392.
109 See Bajetta, 'Ralegh's Early Poetry', 392 n. 7 for the very few lines in *The Steele Glas* which do not have this punctuation.
110 In Smith (ed.), *Elizabethan Critical Essays*, I, 54; see also Bajetta, 'Ralegh's Early Poetry', 392.

Bajetta's work is valuable both in drawing attention to this phenomenon and in underlining the importance of *mise en page* to metrical effect. However, that the 4/6 line was not exclusively an Inns of Court phenomenon is shown by my second two examples. The Babington conspirator Chidiock Tichborne's self-lament was written in the days leading up to his execution in 1586. It was one of the most popular lyric poems of the period, surviving in twenty-eight manuscripts, and was also set to music.[111] Though not every line is punctuated in manuscript or in print in precisely the 4/6 pattern, Tichborne's poem follows the precedent of Gascoigne and Ralegh by relentlessly splitting 'every line identically into two segments'.[112] While at one level this is an 'obsessive design', Tichborne displays with some elegance how such a pattern might be harnessed to poetic effect as antithetical pairings bleakly and with appropriate relentlessness underline the speaker's position. As Wright acknowledges, 'the two-step move to the pause, and then the three-step sweep to the line's end … evidently gave distinct pleasure to Elizabethan listeners'.[113] More pressingly, the device gives a flavour of metrical formality common to all of these examples. This is also clear in the Palmer's judgement on Gryll, and can be seen in another text which helped to make the iambic pentameter line an established norm in the 1580s. The death of Tamburlaine encourages Marlowe to employ a flurry of such lines:

> Farewel my boies, my dearest frends, farewel,
> My body feeles, my soule dooth weepe to see
> Your sweet desires depriu'd my company,

111 See Hirsch, 'The Works of Chidiock Tichborne', 305–06, 314–18, for the contexts and transmission of the poem from manuscript to print. Tichborne (?1558–1586) came from a recusant aristocratic family in Hampshire. Neither Hirsch nor *ODNB* records any contact with the Inns of Court, though Babington had some connection with Lincoln's Inn; see Penry Williams, 'Babington, Anthony (1561–1586)', *ODNB online*. Tichborne's poem reflects the prestigious styles of the day: his two other surviving poems are written in fourteeners and common metre quatrains; in Hirsch, 307–08.
112 Wright, *Shakespeare's Metrical Art*, 45. For a facsimile of the Tanner MS and variants between different manuscripts and the printed edition, see Hirsch, 'The Works of Chidiock Tichborne', 314–18. Wright's point is well made: even lines which do not have a medial comma in either manuscript or print, like line 4, 'And all my good is but vaine hope of gaine', suggest a pause after the fourth syllable. The smug answer poem in the printed edition by T. K. (probably Thomas Kyd) shows itself incapable of following the 4/6 pattern throughout; T. K.'s final taunt is the feeble 'And this, O *Tychborne*, hath thy treason done', a line which serves to point up the sombre majesty of 'And now I liue, and now my life is done'; Tichborne, *Verses of Prayse and Ioye*, sigs. A2v-A3r.
113 Wright, *Shakespeare's Metrical Art*, 45.

For *Tamburlaine*, the Scourge of God must die.
Amy[ras] Meet heauen & earth, & here let al things end[114]

Like Tichborne, Marlowe seems to associate the 4/6 line with a certain kind of metrical formality and solemnity: the predictable pattern of pauses could be said to enforce a plangent catch in the voice as Tamburlaine realises his mortality. For Marlowe and Spenser, the line is a traditional property which can be manipulated at will, but which need not dominate their texts to the exclusion of all others.

The 4/6 line presents an extreme pattern of subordination which emphasises the restrictive ways in which Elizabethans conceptualised verse form. A striking example of this is Churchyard's 'Thomas Wolsey', which first appeared in the 1587 edition of *The Mirror for Magistrates*.[115] This uses the 4/6 line throughout its 490 lines of rhyme royal. It is at once an impressive and monotonous achievement, which betrays both the morphological effects of subordination, and some of Churchyard's skill in overcoming this self-imposed schema.[116] The following lines show Churchyard's readiness to manipulate word form and orthography to fit the line's metrical demands:

> The King at length, sent mee beyonde the seas,
> Embastour then, with message good and greate:
>
> His Amner to, hee made mee all in haste,
> And threefolde gyftes, hee threwe vpon mee still:
> His counslor straight, listewise was *Wolsey* plaste,
>
> A sumptuous house, a stately worke in deede.
>
> The worlde will thinke, thy sprits are growne so weake,[117]

There is a sense in which 'Thomas Wolsey' is simply an extreme example of the technique of syllabic syncopation: to get the metre, you expect your

114 Christopher Marlowe, *Tamburlaine the Great*, sig. L2v. As so often in Elizabethan, 'heauen' is monosyllabic; compare 'To see th'vnkindly Impes of heauen accurst' (I.i.26.2).
115 The poem's full title is 'How THOMAS WOLSEY did arise vnto great authority and gouernment, his maner of life, pompe, and dignity, and how hee fell downe into great disgrace, and was arested of high treason'; Lily B. Campbell (ed.), *The Mirror for Magistrates*, 495.
116 Bajetta, 'Ralegh's Early Poetry', 401–03, suggests that adherence to the form was an 'authorial habit' (403). See also Wilson-Okamura, *Spenser's International Style*, 31, who suggests that Churchyard's rigid adherence to the 4/6 line produces 'a kind of metrical arthritis'.
117 Churchyard, 'Thomas Wolsey', ll.92–3, 99–101, 272; in Campbell (ed.), *The Mirror for Magistrates*, 498, 499, 504.

readers and performers to be able to swallow syllables as occasion requires. Barabas in *The Jew of Malta* has been 'Hard harted to the poore, a couetous wretch': the actor syncopates 'couetous' into a disyllabic word without difficulty.[118] *The Faerie Queene* relies on these conventions: 'As lurking from the view of couetous guest' performs the same syncopation (II. xii.55.4).[119] Yet what is remarkable about Churchyard's text is the extent to which orthography is reformed to indicate accent. 'Ambassador' becomes 'Embastour', 'almoner' becomes 'Amnor', 'counsellor' becomes 'counslor', and 'spirits' 'sprits'. As these examples demonstrate, Churchyard's readiness to subordinate is closely linked to his adoption of the 4/6 line: in line 93, he needs a trisyllabic word with a medial stress to satisfy the demands of the first hemistich; in line 272, the disyllabic 'spirits' would over balance the second hemistich. Formal compliance dictates lexical form. It is illuminating to turn from Churchyard to Spenser, since the extreme template of 'Thomas Wolsey' shows how flexible and strategic Spenser was in his approach to metrical compliance. On the one hand, he often prefers compressed forms: though he does not use 'sprits', he tends to prefer the monosyllabic 'sprite' and 'sprights' for similar reasons to Churchyard.[120] In his only use of 'almoner', Spenser follows Churchyard: 'The second was as Almner of the place' (I.x.38.2), where the disyllabic form is preferred for metrical reasons. On the other hand, his single use of 'counsellors' is emphatically trisyllabic: 'On which her six sage Counsellours did ryde' (I.iv.18.2). Metre is again the primary reason for the choice, but in both these examples, Spenser's approach to verse and word form is hardly as mechanistic as his letter to Harvey had implied: rough words are *not* subdued by use; rather word shape and the flexibility of Early Modern English are exploited as poetic resources which enable him to continue his long poem without monotony.[121] In the case of 'Counsellours', Spenser's

---

118   Christopher Marlowe, *The famous tragedy of the rich Iew of Malta*, sig. G2v. See also Marlowe, *The Jew of Malta*, 148 (IV.i.53). The play is usually dated 1589 or 90; see Bawcutt in *The Jew of Malta*, 1.

119   But Spenser is not consistent: in two of the six occurrences of the word, it is fully sounded with the final syllable taking a stress: 'And couetous desire with his huge threasury'; 'And couetous aspects, all cruel enimyes' (II.vii.4.9; II.xi.8.9). Both these examples are alexandrines, which illustrates the way in which Spenser adapted convention to suit metrical context within his poem.

120   See Brown and Lethbridge (eds), *A Concordance*, 418, for tallies of the different usages of the cognate terms 'spirit[e]', 'spright[e]' and 'sprit[e]'. Including plurals, the totals are respectively 37, 95 and 12, which shows Spenser's preference for monosyllabic forms. The broader conclusion must be that Spenser changes morphology for a variety of reasons including metrical and poetic context.

121   *Prose*, 16; see Chapter 1 above for further discussion. See also S. P. Zitner's still useful notes on Spenserian metaplasm in Spenser, *The Mutabilitie Cantos*, 67–71.

choice of the unsyncopated form is revealing: the initial capitalisation and full syllabic value emphasise the word's importance as Lucifera's six deadly followers are satirically compared with government officials. Churchyard's compressed usage has little of this covert political charge.

Spenser took a similarly flexible approach to the 4/6 line. Like Marlowe, he recognised it as an effective rhythmic resource. There are many such lines in *The Faerie Queene*: from the first page to the last, lines like 'For soueraine hope, which in his helpe he had:' or 'Whose flowring pride, so fading and so fickle,' are common, yet are almost always set in more varied verse contexts than is the case with Churchyard or Gascoigne (I.i.2.6; VII. viii.1.8). When the reader is sensitised to this device, it becomes clear that this arrangement is something of a ground bass motif on which Spenser could perform inventive variations. Consider a stanza from shortly before Gryll's appearance:

> His warlike Armes, the ydle instruments
> Of sleeping praise, were hong vpon a tree,
> And his braue shield, full of old moniments,
> Was fowly ra'st, that none the signes might see;
> Ne for them, ne for honour cared hee,
> Ne ought, that did to his aduauncement tend,
> But in lewd loues, and wastfull luxuree,
> His dayes, his goods, his bodie he did spend:
> O horrible enchantment, that him so did blend. (II.xii.80)

The 4/6 line predominates here, with as many as five or six lines following the pattern. Yet, unlike 'Thomas Wolsey', there is no sense of passive or automatic conformity. Instead Spenser uses the line as a means of framing how the reader interprets Verdant, with variations to the pattern signifying changes in the way the poem expects to be read. Thus the strong enjambment between lines 1 and 2 subtly alters the convention. This is more than a case of a missing comma: 'the ydle instruments' is semantically double jointed, both qualifying 'His warlike armes' and anticipating 'Of sleeping praise'. The medial phrase is synonymic forwards and backwards: 'Armes' become 'instruments' and 'ydle' morphs to 'sleeping' as the stanza initiates the process of evaluating the blissed-out Verdant through his accoutrements. As so often in Spenser, apparent repetition turns into a languorous enactment of the processes described: as Verdant surrenders masculine agency to the debilitating effects of sexual indulgence, so the syntax slackens to evoke the loosening of temperate control. The 4/6 line is the basis of how Spenser presents Verdant to the reader, but in almost every case, his use of the line form is self-aware and purposive. A modern reader might assume that 'ra'st' is an example of metrical subordination, since the word conveys the rubbing out of 'old moniments' from Verdant's shield, but Spenser's word is the earlier form he uses later to describe Malfont's disgrace: '*bon* that once had written bin,/Was now raced out' (V.ix.26.4–5).[122] In this context, the 4/6 line becomes a tool for pointed evaluation, by connecting the erasure of knightly accomplishments from his shield with what can be seen of his behaviour. It shows Spenser's lively awareness of the textuality of his poem as it plays on the doubleness of what can be seen as against what may be read: within the Bower of Bliss no one can see the signs of Verdant's valour, but anyone may read the signs of his 'sleeping praise' on the pages of *The Faerie Queene*.

The second half of the stanza shows a more varied approach to caesura position. Lines 5 and 6 adjust the caesura leftwards in support of the narrator's rhetorical lament over Verdant. Though I would argue that the stanza modifies Alpers's model of the independent line, it richly conforms to his characterisation of the poem as a continuous rhetorical address: 'Even where there is a sense of fictional action, it is in the service of direct address to the reader.'[123] The heavy pauses after the third and second syllables respectively enable Spenser to emphasise the abstract qualities of 'honour' and 'aduancement' which Verdant is neglecting. Another way of putting this is that the rhetorical schema of polysyndeton (consecutive clauses connected by 'ne') displaces the metrical schema of the 4/6 line.[124] That pattern seems to be reasserted in lines 7 and 8, but as with lines 1 and 2, these lines are not formed on the conventional model. In line 7, the patterning of sound modifies the iambic beat: Spenser allows stress to adhere to the dominant 'l' sound, producing what is in effect a pyrrhic iamb followed by a spondaic iamb:[125]

$$\text{x x} \quad / \quad / \quad \text{x} \quad / \quad \text{x} \ / \ \text{x} \ /$$
But in lewd loues, and wastfull luxuree,

---

122 See Hamilton's note, *FQ*, 285. *OED* dates the first usage of 'erase' to 1605, though this is from an unrevised portion of the dictionary; see "erase, v.". *OED Online*.

123 Alpers, *The Poetry of The Faerie Queene*, 7.

124 See Rix, *Rhetoric in Spenser's Poetry*, 31, citing definitions from Joannes Susenbrotus's *Epitome Trophorum ac Schematum* (1563) and Henry Peacham's *The Garden of Eloquence* (1577).

125 See Wright, *Shakespeare's Metrical Art* for these terms and the concept of Shakespeare's 'syllabic ambiguity', 149. Wright suggests that Spenser was 'more restrained in his treatment of syllabic value' than Shakespeare (158); as will become clear, the bulk of Spenser's variations of the iambic pattern still take place within the context of 10 (or in some cases 11) syllable lines. Nevertheless, Spenser's experimentalism was a vital paradigm for Shakespeare.

Spenser frequently uses this line form in *The Faerie Queene*: it is a device which at once emphasises the poem's dependence on monosyllables, enables a vital variation in rhythm, and – as in this case – allows certain terms to be emphasised.[126] Thus the spondaic foot 'lewd loues' anticipates the intoxicated sensuality of 'wastefull luxuree'; again, sound pattern underlines the force of the poem's address to the reader. The last two lines of the stanza present further complications. 'His goods, his days, his bodie he did spend' transforms the 4/6 line into a 2/2/6 variation. This comprehensive assessment of Verdant's predicament uses the rhetorical device of zeugma (in this case hypozeugma) to compartmentalise how Verdant's sexual expenditure diminishes his goods, days, and body.[127] As lines 5 and 6 prefer polysyndeton to the 4/6 pattern, so this line rewires the metrical formula to the stringent yet witty syntactic demands of zeugma. That this stanza partly depends on the reader's awareness of shifting caesura position is underlined by the alexandrine, which veers away from its habitual pattern of two hemistichs of six syllables each into the more unusual 7/5 pattern.[128] The line itself – 'O horrible enchantment, that him so did blend' – embodies the horror the narrator feels at Verdant's condition as the first hemistich topples into the syllabic space of the second, while the rhyme on 'blend' is a reminder of the flexibility of Early Modern English. Rather than being a distortion of 'blind', this is a now obsolete term with the same meaning employed by Spenser and others, often as a rhyming prop.[129]

Such writing is deeply indebted to the work of Gascoigne, Ralegh, and Churchyard in that it depends on the technical resource of the 4/6 line. Spenser takes what had been a relatively clumsy means to achieving regular ten-syllable lines and redirects that pattern into more fluid forms and structures: a static convention becomes the backbone of a new poetry which is closely in touch with the metrical past yet far surpasses that past

---

126 This line shape is common, particularly in lines which include adjectival noun phrases like 'lewd loues'; compare I.i.31.3 ('Of a staunge man I can you tidings tell'); II.viii.37.8 ('From the third brunt of this my fatall brond'); III.vi.48.5 ('For that wilde Bore, the which him hath annoyd'); IV.xi.8.7 ('But the proud Nymph would for no worldly meed'); V.i.30.2 ('For his great iustice, held in high regard'); VI.iv.23.4 ('From his soft eyes the teares he wypt away').

127 Rix, *Rhetoric in Spenser's Poetry*, 33–34. Hypozeugma is (according to Peacham) 'where the common worde is put in the last clause' (34).

128 The 6/6 pattern is the commonest hexameter line used in *The Faerie Queene*, but is not used monotonously. In stanzas 77–87 of this canto, for example, there are six alexandrines which follow this pattern (whether the caesura is signalled be a comma or not), with several variations such as 4/8 (stanza 77), 8/4 (78), 4/4/4 (81 and 84), and 7/5 (80). See further below on the Spenserian alexandrine.

129 See "† blend, v.1". *OED Online*.

in achievement. The evidence of 'A Vision upon this conceipt of the Faery Queene' suggests that even if he had not read the whole of the first install-ment, Ralegh was a keen student of the metre and *mise en page* of Spenser's poem. In place of the unvarying form of his *Steele Glas* poem, Ralegh produces a text with only two unequivocal 4/6 lines and a more Spenserian sensitivity to the disposition of pauses within verse lines.[130]

Negotiating the metrical contract[131]

My closing sections attempt to amplify a sense of the variations of metre and line form within *The Faerie Queene*. This cannot be comprehensive, and all such work necessarily runs the risk of magnifying particular cases at the expense of the poem as a whole.[132] These caveats notwithstanding, to respond to the opening question about the extent to which *The Faerie Queene*'s style is conservative demands detailed engagement with the words of the poem. What the reader needs to bear in mind is that no single reading is conclusive, while it is one of the pitfalls of close reading to ascribe intelligent design and formal self-consciousness to passages which may be textually faulty, hurriedly written, or just plain bad.[133] The other side of this equation, of course, is that many readers remain unclear about what *is* good about *The Faerie Queene*, and close reading remains one of the key means of demonstrating that a text has sophisticated claims on its readers' attention. In what follows, I examine how Spenser negotiates the terms of his iambic contract, and then how he exploits variations of differing kinds (to metre, to lineation, and to types of line) to maintain his poem's formal interest and his readers' engagement.

I have previously cited Jeff Dolven's view that *The Faerie Queene* shows 'a massive commitment to iambic movement'. He suggests that Spenser was more conservative than Sidney, who privileges the 'spoken vitality' of English over metrical pattern, whereas in Spenser the 'conformal pressure' of that pattern tends to minimise rhythmic variation.[134] This decorative

---

130 Ralegh, *The Poems*, 2. The 4/6 lines are ll.3 and 5, although its residual rhythm is audible in lines like 'And from thenceforth those graces were not seene'. For the problematics of the Ralegh-Spenser friendship, see Hadfield, *Edmund Spenser: A Life*, 173; and James P. Bednarz, 'The Collaborator as Thief'.

131 The idea of a 'metrical contract' comes from John Hollander, 'Romantic Verse and the metrical Contract', cited by Dolven, 'Spenser's Metrics', 387.

132 See again Gordon Teskey, 'Thinking Moments', 111 and Introduction above.

133 See Paterson, *Reading Shakespeare's Sonnets*, 301–02 and passim, for the risks of analytical overload.

134 Dolven, 'Spenser's Metrics', 389.

Spenser always opts for a line which scans conventionally over disruption
or rhythmic dissonance. It is certainly the case that there are numerous
stanzas in *The Faerie Queene* which could be used as textbook illustrations
of how to write iambic pentameter. This example describes Phaedria's
attempts to divert Guyon on her island:

> And she more sweete, then any bird on bough,
>   Would oftentimes emongst them beare a part,
>   And striue to passe (as she could well enough)
>   Their natiue musicke by her skilfull art:
>   So did she all, that might his constant hart
>   Withdraw from thought of warlike enterprize,
>   And drowne in dissolute delights apart,
>   Where noyse of armes, or vew of martiall guize
> Might not reuiue desire of knightly exercize. (II.vi.25)

Spenser's object in this stanza is not to mimic the speaking voice. Indeed,
its mimicry is rather different, as Phaedria skilfully 'striues to passe' the
'quire of birds' that 'did sweetly sing' on the island (II.vi.24.8). The euphony
of the stanza partly depends on its seemingly effortless achievement of
iambic uniformity, as in 'And drowne in dissolute delights apart', where
the intricate pattern of polysyllabic words never destabilises the strongly
felt iambic pattern, carried through the majority of the line by marked
alliteration. There is some limited subordination: 'martiall' is disyllabic,
where elsewhere the trisyllabic form is used as a rhyme word.[135] The
overall metrical effect, however, is of the graceful satisfaction of the iambic
standard. How, then, does Spenser avoid monotony? One answer is, as
in the preceding section, through the variation of caesura position. Lines
1, 3, 5, and 8 follow the 4/6 pattern; note again its tendency towards
formal description, as in line 1, or rhetorical distinction, as in line 8.[136]
Elsewhere caesuras are either ignored (lines 2, 4, 7, and 9), or hinted but
not resolved (line 6 suggests but does not demand the 4/6 pattern). Similarly,
the relative absence of subordination helps to 'naturalise' the sound of
the verse; it has a kind of hypnotic inevitability (implicit in the accentual
iambic) which helps to underline Phaedria's harmonious assault on Guyon's

135 See Brown and Lethbridge, *A Concordance*, 276, for the seven rhymes of 'martiall';
    II.iii.37c is typical: 'Through deeds of armes and prowesse martiall;/All vertue merits
    praise, but such the most of all'. When not used as a rhyme, 'martiall' tends to be
    disyllabic: 'The mightie martiall hands doe most commend' (II.vi.35.5).
136 1609 prints line 1 as 'And shee, more sweet then any bird on bough', which may be a
    better annotation of the line than the more familiar version of 1590 and 1596; see *The
    Faerie Queene* (1609), 84.

determination. The stanza is, like the majority of those which surround it, massively yet not monotonously iambic, and this is partly achieved through varied caesura position.

Another answer is to say that it is monotonous, and deliberately so. In context, Phaedria is doing all she can to divert Guyon, and this stanza levelly participates in a mimetic game of drowning – or perhaps muffling – his moral sense 'in dissolute delights'. The mimetic effect is shown both in the first half of this stanza, in which Phaedria imitates the bird song, and by the preceding stanza's insinuation that the island is a product of her artifice: 'Such as he saw, she gan him lay before,/And all though pleasant, yet she made much more' (II.vi.24.4–5). In this light, the lines attempt to pull off the same trick Phaedria had done earlier with Cymochles of lulling him 'fast a sleepe', in this case by hypnotic rhythms (II.vi.18.1). The problem with this reading is precisely the size of the poem and the number of stanzas where similar regularity might be observed.[137] This observation perhaps lends itself to larger discriminations between Spenser and his contemporaries: *The Faerie Queene* line is not mimetic in the same way that Sidney and Donne are; Spenser's poem is not speech, nor does it pretend to be. Nevertheless, this is writing which is highly alert to the interplay between fictional context and metrical pattern. Thus when a few stanzas later Cymochles wakes 'out of his ydle dreme' (II.vi.27.2), it is not surprising that Spenser varies accent to register his character's anger:

> Eftsoones he gan to rage, and inly frett,
> Crying, Let be that Ladie debonaire ...
> Loe, loe already, how the fowles in aire
> Doe flocke, awaiting shortly to obtaine
> Thy carcasse for their pray (II.vi.28.3–9)

The variations here are limited: a trochaic opening to the second line quoted, and the spondaic bluster of 'Loe, loe already'. Allied to this, caesura position is more unsettled than in the stanza discussed above. The point bears repeating that although Cymochles speaks, Spenser does not aim to replicate the effects of real speech. Rather, it's as though Spenser is hurrying his writing up, and that slight acceleration is audible metrically and visible through the *mise en page* of unusual caesurae and metrical

---

137 It should also be noted that that Phaedria's song to Cymochles is not as rhythmically uniform as this stanza, with several lines having trochaic openings: 'Wilfully make thy selfe a wretched thrall, ... Seeking for daunger and aduentures vaine' (II.vi.17.3–5).

emphases. This is the essence of how I would modify Dolven's position: *The Faerie Queene* is the supreme Elizabethan demonstration of the poetic capacity of the iambic, ten-syllable line. That capacity is most strongly felt in the sometimes minute alterations Spenser makes to the pattern in which he invests so much. This means that we need to be prepared to read him for variation and to attune ourselves to the slight changes of semantic emphasis which may be implied by tweaks to the metrical pattern.

This point bears exploration through a different passage with a contrasting narrative function. Where Phaedria's seduction of Guyon is in the broadest sense a quasi-dramatic action, the entrance to the Cave of Despair is a static description:

> Ere long they come, where that same wicked wight
>   His dwelling has, low in an hollow caue,
>   Far vnderneath a craggie clift ypight,
>   Darke, dolefull, drearie, like a greedie graue,
>   That still for carrion carcases doth craue:
>   On top whereof ay dwelt the ghastly Owle,
>   Shrieking his balefull note, which euer draue
>   Far from that haunt all other chearefull fowle;
> And all about it wandring ghostes did wayle and howle. (I.ix.33)

The conventional view would be that only the trochaic inversion 'Shrieking' in line 7 shows any marked deviation from iambic norms, and this is an acceptable variance of practice which Spenser repeats on numerous occasions.[138] Every other line can be scanned as regular iambic pentameter, or hexameter in the case of the alexandrine. The sixth line shows the lengths to which Spenser went to secure an iambic pattern through its use of the semantically minimal 'ay' which fills out the iambic measure:

$$x \;/\quad x\;\; /\; x \quad/\quad x\quad/\quad x\quad/$$
On top whereof ay dwelt the ghastly Owle[139]

---

138   In the same canto, see I.ix.4.6 ('*Vnder* the foot of *Rauran* mossy hore'); I.ix.5.1 ('*Thether* the great magicien *Merlin* came'), I.ix.11.5 ('*Nothing* is sure, that growes on earthly grownd'), my emphases; altogether I count eight examples of this technique in this canto, where a line begins with a two-syllable word with a natural stress on the first syllable.

139   For simplicity, my scansions of Spenser indicate only unstressed syllables and primary stress. It is easy to deduce feet from such markings, but this does not mean that Spenser necessarily composed according to such rules. He was clearly aware of 'foot' as a technical term, hence the puns in 'I follow here the *footing* of thy *feete*' (IV.ii.34.8; my emphases), referring to Chaucer.

But although it's possible to read the stanza in this way – as a to-the-letter fulfilment of the iambic contract – I suggest that what we experience in reading is significantly more varied, and that this variation is crucial to the poem's metrical success. Line 2 might be read as

x   / x / / x x / x /

His dwelling has, low in an hollow caue,

in which the inversion of the third foot would emphasise the 'ow' sound which later reverberates in 'hollow'. Certainly, 'low' is more semantically significant and sonally dominant than 'in', but in effect this is the same kind of metrical 'substitution' as 'Shrieking': instead of the expected iamb, Spenser can occasionally introduce a trochee, or a spondee, or a pyrrhic; like Wright, I prefer to label these substitutions as 'iambic' trochees, spondees, or pyrrhics, since Spenser's use of them seldom destabilises the reader's overall perception of rhythm. More radically, line 4 demands that the reader is ready to register the strong metrical markedness, cued by heavy alliteration, of its opening:

/   / x / x x x / x /

Darke, dolefull, drearie, like a greedie graue

Spenser is particularly fond of this effect of clustering mono- and disyllabic words at the start of the line, here to produce a spondaic effect of consecutive stressed syllables. This canto repeats the effect on several occasions: 'Thee, **fool**ish man'; '**Sleepe aft**er toile'; '**Ease aft**er warre'; '**Feare, sick**nesse, age'; '**Come, come** away'. In these later examples, the spondaic effect is related to the persuasive speeches of first Despair, then Una: by clustering emphases at the start of the lines, they impress on Redcrosse and the reader the urgency of their cases.[140] Again, these lines can be scanned in an orthodox manner, but punctuation and grammar suggest a blurring of the iambic towards the spondaic. Many metrists and linguists have been unwilling to acknowledge the possibility of the accentual spondee.[141] Since commentary has agreed for hundreds of years about the mellifluous quality of his 'sugred penn', the notion of a spondaic Spenser seems to ally his

140 See stanzas 38.2; 40.8–9; 44.6; 53.1. In each case I have emphasised the spondaic opening.
141 Compare Robert Pinsky, *The Sounds of Poetry: A Brief Guide*, 65, with Catherine Addison, 'Stress Felt, Stroke Dealt: The Spondee, the Text, and the Reader', 153–74. For an overview of the debate, see T. V. F. Brogan, 'Spondee', 1206–07; my approach is congruent with that of Wright, *Shakespeare's Metrical Art*, who argues for spondaic and pyrrhic iambs (9 and passim).

work with that of writers like Marston and Donne who specialised in an aesthetic of angry syllabic collision, particularly in their satires.[142] Yet spondees are not exclusively markers of anger. In the Cave of Despair, the spondaic effect tends to the emphatic, as the narrator tries to highlight the spiritual danger represented by Despair through the rhythmic marking of the adjectival cluster which begins the line. T. V. F. Brogan's remarks about perception of pattern in metre are pertinent:

> The paradigm of iambic pentameter … is not statistically preponderant – it appears only about 25% of the time. But the principles of perceptual psychology and information theory show that once a pattern is recognized, even if unconsciously, it need be reproduced only often enough to reconfirm it, and even then not always wholly.[143]

What I am suggesting is that *The Faerie Queene* repeatedly reconfirms the iambic pattern in readers' minds even though in practice it may eschew the paradigmatic iambic pentameter line. Spenser still conforms to the broad outlines of the decasyllabic line described by Susanne Woods,[144] yet the precise metrical patterning is less predictable and more potentially meaningful than an unambiguous iambic realisation of the line would have been. Where Spenser differs from Marston and Donne is in his stricter observance of syllable count. The effect the latter exploit of extending the length of a pentameter beyond ten or eleven syllables, so as to suggest the rupture of conventional poetic syntax, is something which Spenser generally avoids. In this case, 'Darke' and 'dolefull' require a consecutive emphasis which the middle of the line does not, partly because of the psychological horror of the environment Redcrosse is entering.[145] This is not to say that the Spenserian line is invariably mimetic, but rather to underline that it is a flexible unit which is capable of making small changes of emphasis semantically significant. Thus the iambically unstressed *Far*s which introduce lines 3 and 8 may take a stronger, spondaic, or trochaic edge as the reader recognises the discrimination implied by this repeated separation of Despair from all forms of sociability and natural

142 Francis Thynne, 'Spencers fayrie Queene' (1600) in Cummings (ed.), *Spenser: The Critical Heritage*, 107. See Richard Danson Brown, '"Such ungodly terms": style, taste, verse satire and epigram in *The Dutch Courtesan*', paragraphs 3–4, for commentary on Marston's *The Scourge of Villanie* (1598).

143 Brogan, 'Meter', 771.

144 Woods, *Natural Emphasis*, 137–82.

145 The metrical shape of this line inverts that of line 2, which is dominated by the spondaic cluster of '**has, low**' in the centre of the line.

process.[146] If metre is a contract between the writer and the reader, Spenser in practice repeatedly renegotiates its terms without ever fully jeopardising the reader's confidence that he will keep delivering on his side of the bargain.

Spenserian experiment

As Edward Lucie-Smith long ago observed: 'Spenser, though it takes some effort to think of him as an experimentalist and a revolutionary, was both of these things, and on a truly formidable scale.'[147] Most scholars follow Dolven in seeing such experimentation as products of Spenser's youth rather than his maturity: the blank verse sonnets of *A Theatre for Worldlings*, the variety of formal experiments contained in *The Shepheardes Calender*, and the stringent advocacy of metrical reform counselled in the Letters to Harvey.[148] Lucie-Smith was thinking of texts of this kind: his *Penguin Book of Elizabethan Verse* includes 'Iambicum Trimetrum', a poem of which most scholars remain dismissive.[149] The poem's interest is primarily formal, as it accommodates conventional Petrarchan sentiment to the quantitative metrical pattern of its title. In the process, particularly at the beginning of the poem, Spenser creates what looks like a radical *mise en page*:

> Vnhappie Verse, the witnesse of my vnhappie state,
>   Make thy selfe fluttring wings of thy fast flying
>   Thought, and fly forth vnto my Loue, whersoeuer she be:
> Whether lying reastlesse in heauy bedde, or else
>   Sitting so cheerelesse at the cheerfull boorde, or else
>   Playing alone carelesse on hir heauenlie Virginals.
> If in Bed, tell hir, that my eyes can take no reste:
>   If at Boorde, tell hir, that my mouth can eate no meate:
>   If at hir Virginals, tell hir, I can heare no mirth. (*Prose*, 7)

---

146 The 1596 *Faerie Queene* has 'Farre' in both cases, a spelling which emphasises the possible sonal strength of the word more than 1590's 'Far'; see *The Faerie Queene* (1596), 128. 'Farre' is retained in both lines by 1609; see *The Faerie Queene* (1609), 41.
147 Lucie-Smith, *The Penguin Book of Elizabethan Verse*, 19, referring chiefly to the quantitative movement.
148 Dolven, 'Spenser's Metrics', 387, comparing the *Calender* with *The Faerie Queene*.
149 Lucie-Smith, *The Penguin Book of Elizabethan Verse*, 262. Lucie-Smith shows a marked interest in quantative experiments, including such poems by Stanyhurst (263–65), Campion (62–63), Sidney (240–41), and the perennially enigmatic A. W. (34–35). For an overview of 'Iambicum Trimetrum', see Joseph Campana, '*Letters* (1580)', 188.

It's worth registering the graphic oddness of this text: in these lines, syntax overflows line ends, producing what for Spenser are strangely modern-looking line ends and caesurae. Though again he wasn't aiming for a conversational aesthetic, on a first reading, it is possible to mistake phrases like 'thy fast flying/Thought' and 'or else/Sitting so cheerlesse' as attempts to loosen the normative practice of Elizabethan verse through the kind of freewheeling enjambment which would become the norm in later dramatic blank verse.[150] That the layout of the poem was felt to be eccentric in the period is shown by the fact that when it was reprinted in 1602 in Davison's *Poetical Rhapsody*, the lineation of lines 2–3 was normalised to 'Make thy selfe fluttring wings of thy fast flying thought/ And fly forth vnto my Loue, whersoeuer she be', a 'correction' which awkwardly amends Spenser's quantitative design to the pattern of rough accentual hexameters.[151]

'Iambicum Trimetrum' is an inconsistent experiment. At one level, these enjambments can be explained in terms of the task Spenser had set himself. In the second line, 'flying' is scanned with a long final syllable to produce a quantitative iamb, following the prosodic rule that short vowels followed by double consonants are long by position. In turn, this means that another long syllable, 'Thought', is thrust from its phrase unit to the start of the third line; similar metrical considerations account for the enjambment in lines 4 and 5.[152] Nevertheless, Spenser manages to avoid such enjambments in the rest of the poem, which suggests that the lineation is more than just a function of the metre. By the end of the poem, the coincidence of phrase unit with line length has reverted to the heavily marked antithetical pattern of lines 7 to 9; Spenser reinstates something like the lineal patterns, if not the metrical basis, of *The Shepheardes Calender*:

> And if I waste, who will bewaile my heauy chaunce?
> And if I starue, who will record my cursed end?
> And if I dye, who will saye: *this was, Immerito?* (*Prose*, 8)

The antithetical and anaphoristic patterns here give the lines the illusion of sounding like English alexandrines of the kind which would complete

150 See Wright, *Shakespeare's Metrical Art*, 91–107, for the variations Shakespeare introduced to blank verse practice.
151 Francis Davison, *A poetical rapsody* (1602), sig. L6r.
152 See Attridge, *Well-Weighed Syllables*, 9–10 and 64 for the rule of position, and 190, for a scansion of the first four lines of 'Iambicum Trimetrum'.

each *Faerie Queene* stanza, an impression which is enhanced by the repeated use of Gascoigne's preferred caesura after the fourth syllable. It's as though Spenser's accentual ear is fighting with his intellectual commitment to quantity:

> x / x /   x   / x /   x   / x   /
> And if I waste, who will bewaile my heauy chaunce?

Needless to say, it would be impossible to repeat this illusion with the poem's opening lines. What emerges from this discussion is that the poem is a twofold experiment: in addition to the attempt to domesticate quantitative metrics, it shows Spenser in the act of trying out new forms of lineation, in which phrase unit and line length do not necessarily coincide. For 'Iambicum Trimetrum', the value of these experiments is nugatory, because there's no compelling poetic reason why 'Thought' should be sundered from 'fast flying'. Though it might be read as a mimetic gesture, inasmuch as the speaker's thoughts are speeding so quickly at the start of the poem that he lacks the means to integrate the word with the line, the coincidence of line and phrase by the end does not signal that any integration takes place in the course of the 'Vnhappie Verse': Immerito is as dejected at the end as he was at the beginning. A different way of putting this is that in place of Spenser's usual adherence to a parsing syntax – in which line length and phrase unit coincide – 'Iambicum Trimetrum' partly showcases an annotating syntax, in which phrasal emphasis cuts against line units.[153]

As an experiment in form, 'Iambicum Trimetrum' can attune the reader to those rare moments in *The Faerie Queene* where the formal pattern of line and stanza is broken, whether accidentally or by design. Scholars have pointed to the half lines of the *Aeneid* as a classical licence for the few half lines in Spenser's epic.[154] The contrast with 'Iambicum Trimetrum' could not be stronger; nevertheless, the mimetic charge of the ruptured alexandrine which hands II.viii.55 to 56 exemplifies the kind of revolutionary technical experiment we may find in *The Faerie Queene*:

> As to the Patrone of his life, thus sayd;
> My Lord, my liege, by whose most gratious ayd

---

153 See Longenbach, *The Art of the Poetic Line*, 53–56, for discussion of annotating and parsing syntaxes. Longenbach credits J. V. Cunningham with the idea of a parsing syntax, and John Hollander with annotating syntax, in his work on Milton.

154 See J. C. Smith's introduction to his edition of *The Faerie Queene* (1909), vii. Ironically, the *Aeneid*'s half lines are indicative of the incomplete state in which Virgil left it; see Wilson-Okamura, 'Belphoebe and Gloriana', 49, and *Virgil in the Renaissance*, 101–03, and my '"And dearest loue": Virgilian half-lines in Spenser's *Faerie Queene*'.

I liue this day, and see my foes subdewd,
What may suffise, to be for meede repayd
Of so great graces, as ye haue me shewd,
But to be euer bound

To whom the Infant thus, Faire Sir, what need
Good turnes be counted, as a seruile bond,
To bind their dooers, to receiue their meede?
Are not all knights by oath bound, to withstond
Oppressours powre by armes and puissant hond?
Suffise, that I haue done my dew in place. (II.viii.55–56)

The suggestion that Arthur interrupts Guyon, and so truncates the expected alexandrine, goes back to Ralph Church, who noted that because neither the 1596 nor 1609 editions complete the hemistich, he was 'inclined to think *Spenser* never intended to fill it up. The speech of Sir *Guyon* is plainly unfinished: The Prince breaks in upon him: -*Faire Sir*, &c'.[155] Church's reading is lent further support by the way in which the B- rhyme of stanza 56 modulates from Guyon's interrupted word, *bound*. In interrupting Guyon, Arthur suggests that he needn't be 'bound … as a seruile bond'; appropriately, the narrative moves forward with the line 'So goodly purpose they together fond', in which the past participle of *find* punningly comprises the fondness which is developing between the two knights 'Of kindnesse and of courteous aggrace'. Again, these are relatively small gestures, yet it should be remembered that they take place against the backdrop of Pyrochles's repudiation of Arthur's 'princely bounty' and his subsequent decapitation (II.viii.51–52). In the wake of John Kerrigan's *Shakespeare's Binding Language*, which pays meticulous attention to the language of bond and obligation in Shakespeare, this passage shows the way in which Spenser was similarly attuned to the register of social contract and (here) amicable or chivalric obligation. As Kerrigan notes: 'During Shakespeare's lifetime the cluster of words around *bind*, *bound*, and *bond* was used of so many kinds of connection – bonds of kin, allegiance to a monarch, material threads and cords, being bound by good will or service … that usage was coloured with implications that allow binding as act and description to draw fields of meaning together'.[156] Guyon's truncated alexandrine, with its restitution in the following stanza, shows a Spenser prepared to manipulate lineation on the basis of hints he found in the *Aeneid* for symbolic effect. In Kerrigan's terms, Arthur repudiates the notion of the 'seruile bond' outlined

---

155 See *FQ*, 234, and *The Faerie Queene* (1758) II, 164–65.
156 Kerrigan, *Shakespeare's Binding Language*, 10–11.

by Guyon, to reassert the old-fashioned – yet still operative within the idealist structures of *The Faerie Queene* – chivalric oath which binds knights 'to withstond/Oppressours powre'. Meanwhile, these literal, metaphorical, and textual works of severing and restoration anticipate the allegory of the human body in the House of Alma in the next canto.

At this point, it is worth considering Spenser's lineation in the light of modern discussions of the function of poetic line. Contemporary attention to issues of lineation is partly the product of the importance of free verse or 'open forms' to modern poetry.[157] Much of this thinking, especially in America, posits an 'evolutionary' model in which traditional metres and lineal shapes are superseded by the new: in 1959 William Carlos Williams suggested 'Present day practitioners of the art are dissatisfied with the cultured patter of the iambic pentameter, even at the hands of Shakespeare, and look toward wider horizons.'[158] 'Cultured patter' is a neat way of surfacing the politics of such stylistic distinctions: in Williams's view, iambic pentameter is an Old World form not properly at home in America; the land of 'wider horizons' demands prosodic innovation. The distinction between parsing and annotating syntaxes referred to above derives from this sort of thinking. James Longenbach compares the radical 'annotating' style and the more traditional 'parsing' style of lineation. Like Denise Levertov's 1979 essay 'On the Function of the Line', Longenbach's work is careful to qualify 'evolutionary' thinking:

> Neither a parsing nor an annotating line is inevitably preferable; there is nothing wrong or right about any particular way of ending the line. But by placing line so utterly in service of syntax, reducing the tension between syntax and line, a poem dominated by the parsing line can make its own lineation seem increasingly unnecessary.[159]

Though Longenbach is considering primarily modern poems (this extract comes from a comparison of the contrasting styles of the earlier and the later Williams), it would be reasonable to say that the line of *The Faerie Queene* is, in the main, 'utterly at the service of syntax'. This is in effect

---

157 Denise Levertov, 'On the Function of the Line', 30, uses the term 'open forms' in preference to free verse.

158 William Carlos Williams, *The Collected Poems: Volume II 1939–1962*, 511. The text is from a note Williams added to his sequence 'Some Simple Measures in The American Idiom and The Variable Foot' when it was first printed in *Poetry*; see 418–23 for the sequence. See Levertov, 'On the Function of the Line', 30, for a qualification to the 'evolutionary' model: 'I do not mean to imply that I consider modern, non-metrical poetry "better" or "superior" to the great poetry of the past, which I love and honor.'

159 Longenbach, *The Art of the Poetic Line*, 56.

a restatement of Alpers's model. Yet by 'reducing the tension between syntax and line', Spenser doesn't make his lineation seem unnecessary so much as clarify syntax and lineation by making the two more than usually cognate. As in many of the examples I have already used, the point is that Spenser derives much of his variation from the tension between largely prescribed syllabic norms alongside greater freedoms with stress marking (hence pyrrhic and spondaic iambs), caesura position, and occasionally line shape. And as 'Iambicum Trimetrum' and II.viii.55–56 demonstrate, Spenser was capable of breaking lineal convention and annotating his syntax when he chose to – it's just that for the most part, he chose not to.

What's interesting about this work is that while it presupposes an almost Manichean split between tradition and modernity, at its best it also describes the effects writers like Spenser and Herbert were aiming for in their printed texts. Levertov's description of the effects of line breaks is closely linked to her sense that the 'open forms' of modern poetry mimic the hesitating processes of thinking, and mimetically catch the melodious pitch of the speaking voice:

> The line-break is a form of punctuation *additional* to the punctuation that forms part of the logic of completed thoughts. Line-breaks – together with intelligent use of indentation and other devices of scoring – represent a peculiarly *poetic*, a-logical, parallel (not competitive) punctuation.[160]

For Levertov, effective lineation mimics the 'a-logical' randomness of thought patterning. Williams's 'Perpetuum Mobile' wittily connects the movements of 'all the girls/of all ages/who walk up and down on//the streets of this town' with the backwards and forwards momentum of his own mischievous line breaks:

> one two they
> pause sometimes before
> a store window and
>
> reform the line
> from here
> to China everywhere
>
> back and
> forth and back and forth
> and back and forth[161]

160 Levertov, 'On the Function of the Line', 31. See 32–36 for her ideas about the connection between line-breaks, pitch and melody.
161 Williams, *The Collected Poems: Volume II*, 419.

As the girls 'reform the line' of their walking, so Williams makes his lines form and reform 'back and/forth' in a series of mimetic movements. By functioning as additional punctuation, Williams's line breaks pirouette around ostensibly identical words to imitate the cumulatively like-and-unlike rhythms of different forms of walking; as Longenbach observes of another Williams poem, 'The line looks the same, but we hear the line differently.'[162] There is a virtuous circle between the movements described and the verse shapes through which those movements are represented. Though these devices are the hallmarks of poetic modernity, such use of line breaks, 'together with intelligent use of indentation and other devices of scoring', are nevertheless visible in *The Faerie Queene*. Of course, Spenser's verse is not as 'open': it is shaped by predetermined line lengths. Nor is it a metaphorical speech act to be 'scored' in the way envisioned by Levertov; as I have stressed already, Spenser does not imitate speech, and in this he remains significantly unusual amongst both traditional and modern writers. Yet the disposition of phrases into lines – the way in which the placement of phrases within the interlocking structures of line and stanza can enhance the action described – is evident throughout *The Faerie Queene*:

> Which when the valiant Elfe perceiu'd, he lept   →
>   As Lyon fierce vpon the flying pray,
>   And with his trenchand blade her boldly kept   →
>   From turning backe, and forced her to stay:
>   Therewith enrag'd, she loudly gan to bray,
>   And turning fierce, her speckled taile aduaunst,
>   Threatning her angry sting, him to dismay:
>   Who nought aghast, his mightie hand enhaunst:
> The stroke down from her head vnto her shoulder glaunst. (I.i.17)

In many ways, this stanza is a typical example of Spenserian redundancy, as poetic space seems to exceed narrated incident: what happens is that the Redcrosse Knight blocks Error's retreat, at which she threatens him with her sting, which prompts him to strike her a blow which glances from her head to her shoulders. But, as Alpers argues, such a stanza is always more than the sum of its narrative raw materials.[163] The movements

---

162 *The Art of the Poetic Line*, 17. See Levertov, 'On the Function of the Line', 33–34, for discussion of Williams's earlier poem, 'To a Poor Old Woman', whose variations on the phrase 'They taste good to her', provide a key example of the aesthetics of the line break.

163 See Alpers, *The Poetry of* The Faerie Queene, 36–69, in particular 54–69 for the argument, based on a comparison of the Phedon narrative in Book II with its source in *Orlando*

from Redcrosse to Error and back are a complex, quasi-balletic series of gestures scripted in lines the shapes and patterns of which self-consciously comment on the incidents narrated. Lineation is an intimate part of the processes of description, and ultimately of Spenser's poetic evocation of and metaphorical commentary on Redcrosse's quest as the Knight of Holinesse. In lines 1–4, the relatively strong enjambments in lines 1 and 3 (marked above) enact Redcrosse's 'fierce' valiance as he forces 'her to stay': the quatrain pens Error in and prevents her 'From turning backe' through the movement from the mobile syntax and caesurae of lines 1–3 to the containment described and mimicked in line 4. The next lines evoke Error's attempts to break from this trap through variations on the same familiar formula of the 4/6 line:

> Therewith enrag'd, || she loudly gan to bray,
> And turning fierce, || her speckled taile aduaunst,
> Threatning her angry sting, || him to dismay:
> Who nought aghast, || his mightie hand enhaunst:

Spenser's critical use of the 4/6 pattern conveys something of the formality and predictability of Error's manoeuvres: it might be argued that the noise of her 'braying' is partly rendered by the recurrence of this metrically familiar pattern. But the subtler point is that this stanza is concerned with Redcrosse's initial, ultimately overconfident attempt to master his enemy 'As Lyon fierce vpon the flying pray', a line in which the absence of caesura may in turn hint at an absence of reflection.[164] In this view, what animates the stanza is the tension between forms of restraint and forms of resistance which prove to be closely related. Lines 4, 6 and 8 follow similar metrical and grammatical structures while narrating different actions in the conflict. 'And turning fierce, her speckled taile aduaunst' resists the restraint of 'From turning backe, and forced her to stay', while 'Who nought aghast, his mightie hand enhaunst' seeks to reimpose that restraint.[165] In between, line 7 introduces variation: firstly through its trochaic first foot, and secondly by postponing the caesura until after the sixth syllable to isolate 'him to

---

Furioso, that 'The climax of the episode is not an action at all, but a rhetorical scheme, a formal arrangement of words – precisely a stanza of poetry, and nothing else' (69).

164 See Hamilton's note in *FQ*, 35. At the same time, the line can be read as having an unmarked pause after the fourth syllable since the 4/6 line was so ubiquitous; see Bajetta, 'Ralegh's Early Poetry', 391–95, and above.

165 Note the way that assonantal and alliterative vocabulary, as well rhyme, also helps to script the conflict: 'aghast' anticipates 'enhaunst' and responds to 'aduaunst'; the unrealized threat of 'her angrie sting' anticipates the unsuccessful 'stroke' of line 9.

dismay', anticipating some of the challenges Redcrosse will undergo in subsequent cantos.[166] The largely monosyllabic alexandrine further modifies the confident heroism Redcrosse exhibited at the beginning of the stanza by showing the failure of 'his mightie hand' to wreak real damage. 'The stroke down from her head vnto her shoulder glaunst' exemplifies what might be called Spenser's comedic control of lineation as it moves from heroic gesture to the reality of a stroke which misses its target. As in the middle of the stanza where Spenser plots the action through two different kinds of turning, so 'glaunst' itself glances back to 'perceiu'd' in line 1, and corrects the assumptions of both Redcrosse and the reader about the nature of this encounter.

Levertov's point that line breaks and devices such as indentation are a form of poetic punctuation is handsomely borne out by this stanza.[167] The difference between Spenser and Williams is in terms of their use of predetermined versus 'open' line shapes: neither form is intrinsically superior, unless you adopt the cultural politics which underpins Williams's concept of the variable foot. This is not to suggest that formal discussion can or should be decontaminated of politics: as the work of critics like Helgerson demonstrates, the language of form and the language of politics overlap; it's not accidental that 'line' can describe both a line of verse and a line of succession.[168] Nevertheless, comparing the lineal poetics of Williams and Spenser suggests that both depend on the reader's ability to register the effects of similarity with difference. Williams expects his readers to appreciate the mimetic weight of his divisions, so that Chloe in another poem from the 'Some Simple Measures' sequence becomes a sexy version of Williams himself 'idly/tilting her weight/from one foot//to the other'.[169]

166　It's possible to hear in 'him to dismay' the first sounding of the riff which will become so crucial to Redcrosse's story in later cantos: 'Disarmd, disgraste, and inwardly dismayde' (I.vii.11.6); see *FQ*, 94, for Hamilton's note, and also I.vii.47.8 ('The groning ghosts of many one dismaide'), and I.vii.51.3 ('Who him disarmed, dissolute, dismaid'). Such an approach is linked to Kaske's 'concordantial' method, where the reader is enjoined to compile 'a mental concordance' of related 'hook-words'; *Spenser and Biblical Poetics*, 19, 21.

167　Spenserian indentation is an interesting subject in its own right: early editions of *The Faerie Queene* justify lines 1 and 9 of each stanza to the left, with the body of the stanza indented to the right, the form followed in all authoritative modern editions. Though for the most part, this is a convention, it is not a necessarily a neutral part of the physical composition of the text; Spenser's exploitation of the white spaces on the printed texts as metaphors for allegorical suspension is discussed by Krier, 'Time Lords', 1–19.

168　Helgerson, *Forms of Nationhood*, 1–18 and passim. For a broad cultural poetics of line, see Tim Ingold, *Lines: A Brief History*.

169　Williams, *The Collected Poems: Volume II*, 421–22.

Similarly, Spenser's lines partly depend on the reader's readiness to register small changes of emphasis, such as the counterpoint of form and meaning in lines 4, 6, and 8 of I.i.17, all of which are variants of the 4/6 line, and of the mock heroic downturn of the alexandrine.

To draw them longer out: Spenser's alexandrines

For the final illustration of *The Faerie Queene*'s complex formal amalgam of traditional and innovative line forms, I turn to one which occurs on every page of the poem, yet which remains relatively little discussed: the twelve-syllable alexandrines or hexameters which conclude almost every stanza.[170] Unlike his Janus-faced stanza, there is no mystery about where Spenser got this form from: he had ample precedents in the work of the French poets of the Pléiade, for whom the alexandrine was an innovative alternative to the decasyllabic line across a range of genres. Ronsard and Du Bellay used the alexandrine throughout poems rather than as a component within stanzaic verse.[171] It was also prevalent in native forms like poulter's measure, where, as we have seen, the first line of each couplet is a hexameter, usually with a rigid mid-line caesura as in the opening of one Surrey's poems from *Tottel's Miscellany*, 'Wrapt in my carelesse cloke, as I walkt to and fro'.[172] To those critical of Spenser, the alexandrine has always been something of a technical blemish: James Fenton singles out *The Faerie Queene* as symptomatic of the English alexandrine's tendency 'to contain one otiose word'.[173] What is at issue here is not the quality of the alexandrine per se, nor the symbolic meaning of Spenser's adoption of this form.[174] What I'm interested in is the ways in which Spenser's

---

170 The title of this section comes from IV.ii.50.2: not in this case an alexandrine, but Spenser's account of Agape's concern to extend the lives of her children.

171 For literary contexts, see David Scott Wilson-Okamura, *Spenser's International Style*, 42, 46, 68. John Hollander, 'Alexandrine', 15–16, provides a rich summary. See also Hollander, *Melodious Guile*, 124–25, 167–70, for comment on specific lines.

172 *Tottel's Miscellany*, 35–36, where it is given the editorial title 'A carelesse man, scorning and describing, the suttle usage of women towarde their lovers'. See also 'Of the wretchedness of this world', 156, a poem of sixteen lines in which every hexameter follows the 6/6 pattern.

173 Fenton, *An Introduction to English Poetry*, 39. See also 71, which ironically imagines Spenser devising his stanza form, which Fenton characterises as 'a tall order', particularly the alexandrine. For criticisms by Spenserians, see Wilson-Okamura, *Spenser's International Style*, 68–69, on the views of John Hughes (1715) and O. B. Hardison (1989), that the alexandrine is inappropriate to epic, citing Hardison, *Prosody and Purpose*, 217.

174 See Wilson-Okamura, *Spenser's International Style*, 46, for the cautious suggestion that the Spenserian alexandrine works as a 'functional equivalent or analogy' to Virgil's

alexandrines orientate his poem stylistically – in other words, are they indicative of conservatism or experiment? At one level, Fenton's criticism is well made: many Spenserian alexandrines can feel at least a word or a foot too long. On many occasions, the alexandrine could be used to illustrate Spenser writing to the form: because he has twelve syllables to fill, he will often produce qualifiers which are strictly redundant:

> The Lyon whelpes she saw how he did beare,
> And lull in rugged armes, withouten childish feare. (I.vi.27.8–9)

> His name was *Guzior*, whose vntimely fate
> For to auenge, full many treasons vile
> His father *Dolon* had deuiz'd of late
> With these his wicked sons, and shewd his cankred hate. (V.vi.33.6–9)

> No gate, but like one, being goodly dight
> With bowes and branches, and did broad dilate
> Their clasping armes, in wanton wreathings intricate. (II.xii.53.7–9)

I have given more than just the alexandrines to locate them in semantic context; as will become clear, alexandrines always work in relation to their parent stanzas and are seldom syntactically isolated. Working on the basis of a poetics of concision, an editor might circle 'rugged', 'childish', 'wicked', and 'cankred', not to mention the metaplasmic 'withouten' which enables Spenser to satisfy his metre.[175] In the third example, it would be hard to know where to start: arms are sui generis 'clasping'; 'wanton wreathings intricate' seems to amplify what's said in the first half of the line without any real semantic gain. An unsympathetic paraphrase might read: 'the arms of the boughs and branches (which were clasping) were intertwined in such a way that was both complex and morally dubious'.[176] Why not simply say 'did broad dilate/Their wanton armes'? Spenser of course did not write to such a style guide, and this exercise emphasises the real presence of redundancy in *The Faerie Queene*, alongside the difficulty of

---

final spondee in the hexameter line, an idea further discussed by Paul J. Hecht, 'Prosody', 208–09.

175 See S. P. Zitner's discussion of metaplasm in Spenser, *The Mutabilitie Cantos*, 67–69. This is an example of paragoge, the extension of the end of a word for rhetorical or metrical effect.

176 See "wreathing, n. 3", *OED Online*, citing this passage. Paraphrase is a notoriously untrustworthy critical tool; see Paterson, *Reading Shakespeare's Sonnets*, which heavily relies on critical paraphrase to amplify Paterson's sense that many of the sonnets are poetically feeble. The criticism may be well founded, but to paraphrase is always in some way to distort.

deciding when and where such redundancy is sharpened into semantic activity.[177] Hamilton's note on the final example is germane: 'The line conveys the labyrinthine twisting it describes.'[178] The line is mimetic of the processes it describes, and its feel of gathering repetition is deeply appropriate to the visual and moral involutions it describes, as well as the potential hold of these delusive beauties on Guyon and the Palmer. Again, the mimetic qualities of Spenser's lines are connected with the fictive contexts of his poem, as syntax is shaped to imitate the thing described.

It would be hard to make similar defences of the other two alexandrines: the highlighted terms have little semantic charge, although they contribute to the satisfaction of the pattern. My zealous copy editor might save a few words, but would in so doing undermine the poem's broader formal device. We may not need to know that Satyrane's arms are 'rugged' (though the adjective amplifies the joke that he is fiercer than the wild animals he plays with) or that he is (still) a child during this episode; as readers we expect the satisfaction of the formal pattern ahead of the need for sharply pointed epithets. The drawn-outness of the alexandrine remains a key part of the line's function in *The Faerie Queene*. As we have seen, such extension is a traditional part of English poetry in the sixteenth century, particularly in the long line forms of the fourteener and poulter's measure. This might lead to the conclusion that the alexandrine is a traditional property which advertises Spenser's stylistic conservatism. And as noted above, many iterations of the alexandrine in *The Faerie Queene* take the traditional form of two equally divided hemistichs of six syllables each; the first two examples are in just this form. To gauge the difference between Spenser's practice and that of his literary forebears, consider the final stanza of 'Upon sir James Wilfordes death' from *Tottel's Miscellany*. This lament for a dead soldier, written in alexandrines and the *Ababcc* sixain,[179] shows something of the sombre feeling post-Henrician poets could wrest from the alexandrine:

> The fates have rid him hence, who shal not after go,
> Though earthed be his corps, yet florish shall his fame,
> A gladsome thing it is that ere he stepte us fro,
> Such mirrours he us left our life thereby to frame,
> Wherfore his praise shall last aye freshe in Brittons sight
> Till sunne shall cease to shine, and lende the earth his light.[180]

177 See Chapter 1 above, particularly my discussion of Lethbridge's model of formulae.
178 FQ, 279.
179 See *Tottel's Miscellany*, 477, for notes on the poem's literary and historical context.
180 *Tottel's Miscellany*, 156–57.

Though caesurae are marked in only three of these lines, they are felt in every one. The pause between 'A gladsome thing it is' and 'that ere he stepte us fro' is as necessary to the rhythm as that between 'Though earthed be his corps' and 'yet florish shall his fame'. The poet clearly structured his poem in six-syllable hemistichs with a rise and fall motion not inappropriate to the poem's elegiac function. As with poulter's measure and the fourteener, these verse forms tend towards spatial and metrical strictness: the twelve-syllable iambic pattern dictates syntax and breathings in ways which must have been aesthetically pleasing, or which were felt to be decorous.[181] Though *The Faerie Queene* is strikingly different from such texts, it none the less uses similar devices such as the equal hemistich and a preference for mono- and disyllabic words,[182] which are simpler to fit into iambic patterns of six syllables. As Gascoigne had counselled, monosyllables both sound more English (so avoid the taint of the 'smell of the Inkhorne') and are easier to fit into a verse 'as occasion requireth' metrically.[183] The key difference, however, is the flexibility of use in poetic context. Spenser can evoke the formal decorum of the *Tottel's Miscellany* poet, as in famous lines like 'Yet nothing did he dread, but euer was ydrad' (I.i.2.9), or 'O helpe thou my weake wit, and sharpen my dull tong' (I.Proem.2.9), yet his lineal palate is not restricted to this kind of writing. As these lines suggest, a favourite device is to use the alexandrine for the purposes of antithesis. Stanzas often close with a word play ('dread' to 'ydrad') which momentarily slows the reader down and enforces the pause between stanzas.[184]

A demonstration of the relational quality of Spenser's alexandrine naturally means we have to read it in the metrical context of its parent stanza:

> Within the Barbican a Porter sate,
>   Day and night duely keeping watch and ward,
>   Nor wight, nor word mote passe out of the gate,
>   But in good order, and with dew regard;
>   Vtterers of secrets he from thence debard,

181 See again Wright, *Shakespeare's Metrical Art*, 45 and passim.
182 This poem includes only one trisyllabic word which is sounded as such: 'When rash upon misdede they all *accorded* bee' (my emphasis); though 'triedly' looks trisyllabic, in context it is clearly disyllabic: 'So triedly did he treade ay prest at vertues beck'. *Tottel's Miscellany*, 156.
183 Gascoigne, *Certayne Notes of Instruction*, in Smith (ed.), *Elizabethan Critical Essays*, I, 51.
184 See Empson, *Seven Types of Ambiguity*, 33–34; for the intervals between stanzas, see Krier, 'Time Lords', 1–19.

> Bablers of folly, and blazers of crime.
> His larumbell might lowd and wide be hard,
> When cause requyrd, but neuer out of time;
> Early and late it rong, at euening and at prime. (II.ix.25)

What is good metrical order, 'with dew regard', in the House of Alma? Spenser's allegory of the oral cavity and the tongue suggests that metrical order may imitate the qualities the verse describes. Once again, the technical adjustments Spenser makes are small yet pervasive: he uses trochaic substitution in lines 5, 6, and 9 to highlight the groups excluded ('Vtterers … Bablers … blazers') and then to mimic the tongue's interventions 'Early and late'.[185] Spenser's joke is that the 'larumbell' sounds 'Early' in the line as he returns to the trochaic pattern for the alexandrine with its early onset of stress. The line may also seem another example of redundancy, since 'at euening and at prime' is implicit in the first hemistich. Yet the wit of the stanza lies in its overall concern with 'good order': 'at euening and at prime' looks back to the second line, which emphasises the tongue's stewardship of spoken language. The 'larumbell' is repeated 'but neuer out of time' because the tongue must be vigilant both in the choice of words and in the avoidance of the politically unacceptable activities detailed in lines 5–6. This is densely mimetic writing, which exerts tight prosodic control not in the service of imitating speech. Rather, Spenser onomatopoeically evokes the sounds of conversation ('Barbican … Bablers … blazers') and the interruption of the tongue as a 'lowd … larumbell', while remaining rooted in what Alpers calls the 'rhetorical mode' of its address to the reader.[186] At the same time, the linguistic politics of the stanza are kept firmly under pressure, as rhythmic variation ultimately reinforces the need to police how and what we speak. Never a babbler nor a blazer be, even in the context of verse forms which may seem to maximise the opportunities for wandering garrulously.[187]

In this chapter, I have related the poem's metrical forms to its lineal patterns to suggest that its major technical innovation is to use the iambic line, whether this is the decasyllabic or the alexandrine, in such a way

---

185 The trochaic pattern is anticipated by line 2, which may be scanned as a regular iamb but at the expense of the natural emphasis on 'Day' rather than 'and'. The spondaic tension between 'night' and 'duely' underlines the surveillance the Porter has to perform in this stanza. Everything is on guard here; the custody of spoken language is absolute and neither Spenser not his porter show any inclinations towards notions of freedom of speech.
186 *The Poetry of The Faerie Queene*, 3–35.
187 Adapted from Empson, *Seven Types of Ambiguity*, 33.

that anticipates what Wright calls Shakespeare's 'syllabic freedom'.[188] To
be sure, Spenser's forms are usually more tethered to iambic norms than
Shakespeare's were to become in the seventeenth century. But for the alert
reader of *The Faerie Queene* in the 1590s, this poem must have seemed
an intoxicating amalgam of the traditional and the previously unheard
in English. On the opening pages, such a reader would have encountered
familiar forms like the 4/6 and 6/6 lines alongside lines where the accent
would have seemed new and rhythmically fresh. The alexandrine I quoted
earlier from the first proem – 'O helpe thou my weake wit, and sharpen
my dull tong' – may legitimately be scanned as an orthodox iambic
hexameter. Yet when you read the line aloud, something strange happens
as the marked parallelism between 'weake wit' and 'dull tong' suggests
you need to read these as spondaic iambs. It's a new kind of line – regular
yet ambiguous, free yet restricted, vocative and rhetorical – with which
early readers would soon become familiar.

188 *Shakespeare's Metrical Art*, 155.

3

Proportionable returns: rhyme, meaning and experience

In a treatise drafted in 1599, but not published until 2013, William Scott identifies rhyme as a particular grace of English poetry, congruent with rhythm and metre, yet distinctive in effect:

> Now our verse to make the delight more perfect hath to this proportion of number added another ear-pleasing grace unknown to the Greeks and Latins: the like sounding of last words or ends of our verses which we call *rhyme*.

After a discussion of the differences between rhyming in European languages, heavily informed by Sidney's *Defence of Poetry*,[1] Scott goes on to stress the complex patternings afforded by stanzaic verse: 'by the varying and transposing the rhymes to some convenient distance, we grow to have another proportion of number called a *stanza* or *staff* that is of divers verses in a proportionable return of the rhyme and number crossed and intermingled, that gives a great delight to the ear'.[2] Scott makes a good point of entry to this chapter because he writes in full awareness of the work of Sidney and Spenser.[3] Unlike the treatises on poetry published in the 1570s and 1580s, Scott's attitude towards rhyme is overwhelmingly positive: this is a technique which brings sonal delight to its auditors

---

1 See Alexander's notes in William Scott, *The Model of Poesy*, 207–08.
2 Scott, *The Model of Poesy*, 62–63.
3 Scott cites Sidney throughout; for Spenser, see *The Model of Poesy*, 19, where his discussion of epic includes 'Master Spenser's moral invention, shadowed so naturally and properly under the persons in his *Faerie Queene*.'

through its 'proportionable return[s]'.[4] The most influential statement of
the negative view of rhyme is in Roger Ascham's *Scholemaster*, posthumously
published in 1570, where the device encapsulates the shortfall of English
verse in comparison with Greek and Latin poetry. For Ascham, the English
taste for rhyme shows an unaccountable preference for Northern barbarism
over the learning of the Classical South: 'surelie to follow rather the *Gothes*
in Ryming than the *Greekes* in trew versifiyng were euen to eate ackornes
with swyne when we may freely eate wheate bread emonges men'.[5] It is
the work of texts like *The Faerie Queene* which helps to account for this
change in cultural politics: Spenser and Sidney rhyme in such a way as
to produce musical delight rather than disgust.

The debate about rhyme is, then, one which stretches back to the
sixteenth century, and which bears on the ways in which humanist thought
was received and hybridised in English verse.[6] What we see is a shift from
a painful sense of cultural inadequacy to a renewed confidence in the
distinctiveness of English as a literary language, in which the absence of
Classical precedents for rhyme turns from an impediment to an advantage.
As Samuel Daniel puts it in *A Defence of Rhyme* (1603), 'all our vnderstand-
ings are not to be built by the square of *Greece* and *Italie*'.[7] In this chapter,
I am not directly concerned with the story of the attempted revival of
quantitative metrics, nor indeed with the ultimate dominance of rhyme,
much though these engagements between poetic form and intellectual
history can teach about Elizabethan culture in the dialectical seesaw between
opposing positions in the 1570s and 1580s and the synthesis of the 1590s
and beyond. Rather, my focus is on what Scott calls the ear-pleasing
graces of *The Faerie Queene*, to try to illuminate how Spenser used rhyme
in relation to his poetic forebears, notably Chaucer, and to clarify the

4 Scott repeatedly stresses the aural quality of poetry; in his opening comparison of
  poetry with painting (referring to Sidney and drawing on a tradition going back to
  Plutarch), he contrasts the painter working 'by the eye only in colours' and the poet
  'by the ear in words'; *The Model of Poesy*, 6. For discussion of early modern theories
  of hearing, see Mark Robson, *The Sense of Early Modern Writing: Rhetoric, Poetics,
  Aesthetics*, 146–68. For the 'visual turn' to literary thinking in the 1590s and in Scott's
  poetics, see Alexander's Introduction, li.
5 Ascham in Smith (ed.), *Elizabethan Critical Essays*, I, 30.
6 See the discussions in Attridge, *Well-Weighed Syllables*, 89–162; Wilson-Okamura,
  Spenser's International Style, 50–103, and my study in Brown and Lethbridge, *A Concordance*, 10, 52, 71–75.
7 In Smith (ed.), *Elizabethan Critical Essays*, II, 366. Though Daniel represents something
  of a special case because of his extreme formal patriotism, his position here could
  legitimately be described as Spenserian; see Lawrence Manley, *Convention 1500–1750*,
  199–202.

relationship between sound, meaning, and experience in the practice of his rhymes. If at one level these Renaissance debates about rhyme are incomprehensible to twenty-first-century readers – used to experimentation in verse form and rhyme across a range of media – at another, both the conceptual and empirical problems of rhyme remain almost ignored. T. V. F. Brogan observed that 'reliable *facts* about rhyme are very few and far between': he cites an absence of statistics, suggesting that the prevalence of theory in the later twentieth century tended to neglect the 'collection of useful data' about rhyme.[8] In terms of Spenser studies, the *Concordance of Rhymes to The Faerie Queene* (2013) which I edited with J. B. Lethbridge was a step towards the empirical data Brogan was looking for. This chapter aims to be more than a restatement of my study in that volume, where I considered in depth the reception of Spenser's rhymes in relation to conflicting theories of rhyme, though inevitably it extends arguments and observations made there. Rather, it considers Spenser's rhymes in relation to Chaucer's, while pursuing the proposition that Spenser's rhymes make poetic capital from semantic recurrence: in my view, the sonal 'reuolt' of rhyme – that is, its recurrence to similar sounds and echoic patterns – is frequently also a turning back from formal decoration into symbolic content (III.xi.25.9).[9]

Merlin's prophecy

I begin with a discussion of a passage of *The Faerie Queene* from the perspective of rhyme to describe the sorts of techniques Spenser uses and the compromises and distortions these productively entail. The passage is Merlin's prophecy in III.iii.25–55. This canto, deriving from yet extending familiar precedents in the *Aeneid* and *Orlando Furioso*, has received illuminating commentary, particularly in relation to the complex politics of the multiple mirrors it provides for Elizabeth.[10] Like Book II Canto X, because of its background in chronicle history, it is rich in proper names

---

8 Brogan, 'Rhyme', 1060–61.
9 See 'revolt, v.' *OED Online*. Particularly germane to my discussion is the word's etymology and its relationship to the French *révolter*, meaning to turn, and the Italian, *rivoltare*, which means to turn back or around as well as to rebel. See particularly entries 4 and 5, citing Golding's *Metamorphoses* and this passage, which is discussed below.
10 See Bart van Es, *Spenser's Forms of History*, 164–71, citing previous scholarship and analogues while attentive to the verbal patternings within the episode; for useful overviews, see Harry Berger, Jr, 'The Structure of Merlin's Chronicle in *The Faerie Queene* III.iii', in *Revisionary Play*, 118–30, Colin Burrow, *Edmund Spenser*, 37–38, and William Blackburn, 'Merlin', 471–72.

which must be accommodated into the structure of verse lines and rhymes; in other words, studying a passage like this shows how Spenser manipulates (and is in turn manipulated by) his sources.[11] My focus is on the way in which rhyme works in this prophecy, or rather, the way in which Spenser's chosen form inflects the words and word forms he chooses.

The constraints which rhyme imposes on Spenser are readily evident in this passage. Word forms and syntax are repeatedly distorted to secure the desired rhyme, particularly when new names are introduced:

> But sooth he is the sonne of *Gorlois*,
> And brother vnto *Cador* Cornish king,
> And for his warlike feates renowmed is (III.iii.27.1–3)

This is one Spenser's favourite devices, whereby the main verb is delayed to secure the rhyme, whilst also suggesting how the reader might vocalise '*Gorlois*'. Unlike modern poets, Spenser makes no attempt to sound conversational. Indeed, the illusionism of this verse lies partly in the way that such techniques deliberately enstrange Merlin's idiom from ordinary language acts. 'And for his warlike feates renowmed is' is a characteristic flourish of Spenserian syntax, as the auxiliary verb is postponed to the end of the verse line. Fitting the formal pattern almost always trumps normative syntax; inversion is positively encouraged throughout *The Faerie Queene*. 'And brother vnto *Cador* Cornish king' is a perfectly comprehensible as a line of epic genealogy, but makes no concessions to prose idiom. The verbal quality of Spenser's rhymes has received detailed analysis from Catherine Addison, and was implicit in Hazlitt's bravura description of the way the stanza works.[12] Merlin's prophecy shows several examples of the kind of techniques observed by Addison, such as Spenser's fondness for auxiliary forms which allow him to rhyme on infinitives rather than past tenses; stanza 26 has another example of this, where the final line of the B-rhyme, 'Whiles yet in infant cradle he *did crall*'[13] enables rhymes on the more complex polysyllables '*Artegall*' and 'terrestriall'. Stanza 43 climaxes with a couplet of auxiliary + infinitive rhymes: 'But shall their

---

11 See Brown, '"Charmed with Inchaunted Rimes"' in Brown and Lethbridge, *A Concordance*, 57–60, for a discussion of polysyllabic rhyme. In this passage, there are around nine rhymes on proper names. Spenser's usual method is thus to put names in mid line, as in the Welsh kings in stanza 45 ('And *Howell Dha* shall goodly well indew… Then *Griffyth Conan* also shall vp reare'), but there are also striking examples of using names as rhyme words, discussed below.

12 Addison, 'Rhyming Against the Grain', 337–51; Hazlitt in Alpers (ed.), *Edmund Spenser: A Critical Anthology*, 137–38; see also Brown and Lethbridge, *A Concordance*, 19–21, 67–69.

13 My emphases.

name for euer *be defaste*,/And quite from off the earth their memory *be raste?*[14] In this case, Spenser expects the reader to register the close proximity between his rhyming terms over a number of syllables, where the linked sounds convey the urgency of Britomart's anxiety.

Such devices nevertheless remain forms of distortion and compromise, as Spenser manipulates syntax and morphology in ways which few subsequent poets have been able to emulate because of the growth of linguistic standardisation in the seventeenth and eighteenth centuries.[15] Stanza 33 provides a typical example:

> Great *Gormond*, hauing with huge mightinesse
> Ireland subdewd, and therein fixt his throne,
> Like a swift Otter, fell through emptinesse,
> Shall ouerswim the sea with many one
> Of his Norueyses, to assist the Britons fone. (III.iii.33.5–9)

There are thirteen rhymes on 'fone' in *The Faerie Queene*; in each case, the word takes the place of the more usual plural 'foes'.[16] 'Fone' is a characteristic rhyming archaism: Spenser uses it in 'The Visions of Bellay' as a rhyme word, as does Edward Fairfax in his Spenserian translation of Tasso, *Godfrey of Bulloigne*.[17] If this is a rhyming prop which shows Spenser's readiness to warp language to suit his rhyme scheme, the use of 'Norueyses' is more individualistic. Most Elizabethans preferred the modern form of

---

14 My emphases.
15 Any such generalisation is precarious: it excludes dialect poets like William Barnes and writers who developed their own idiosyncratic approaches, such as Thomas Chatterton and John Clare. The central point is that the progressive standardisation of English in subsequent centuries exerts a centripetal influence on poetic diction, and that Spenser enjoyed freedoms largely unknown to later writers. See James Milroy and Lesley Milroy, *Authority in Language*, 22–36. The work of more recent linguists suggests that the power of standardisation has been overstressed; see for example Ingrid Tieken-Boon Van Ostade, 'English at the Onset of the Normative Tradition', 298–339, which notes that a range of writers were still coining neologisms in the later eighteenth century.
16 Brown and Lethbridge, *A Concordance*, 244. Note that there are five rhymes on 'foes'.
17 'The Visions of Bellay', l.66 ('When lo a barbarous troupe of clownish fone', rhyming with 'grone'). Fairfax's Tasso uses *fone* on six occasions, always as a rhyme word: VIII.78, XVIII.97, XIX.54, XX.14, XX.90, XX.117, in Tasso, *Godfrey of Bulloigne*, 291, 516, 532, 556, 575, 582. Emma Field Pope long ago suggested that such archaic plurals 'are not to be classed as unusual' ('Renaissance Criticism and the Diction of *The Faerie Queene*', 610); an EEBO-TCP key words in context query on the *Early Modern Print* website produces 38 hits, with results in *The Mirror for Magistrates*, Turberville and Brooke among others. The examples from Spenser and Fairfax are the only verse instances from the 1590s which is perhaps indicative of changes of taste against archaic plurals. Such data is necessarily limited by the number of full texts on EEBO at the time of writing (October 2014); on this, see Martin Mueller, 'The EEBO-TCP Phase I Public Release'.

the word, as in Holinshed's description of the Battle of Stamford Bridge: 'In this conflicte Harolde Harfager King of the Norwegians was slain.'[18] Metrically, 'Norueyses' and 'Norwegians' are identical, so Spenser's preference of his own version of the word is a characteristic touch of rarefied diction. The line at once demonstrates *The Faerie Queene*'s subservience to rhyme and its resistant idiosyncrasies of diction and vocabulary.[19]

In a sense, what is striking about Spenser's rhymes is the way they can flaunt their transgression of ordinary usage. This runs counter to Lethbridge's suggestion that 'rhyme often disappears into the page, and the verse appears to aspire to the condition of blank verse': the evidence of this passage is that Spenser anticipated readers willing to register rhyme as an important part of *The Faerie Queene*'s construction and soundscape.[20] Consider the following two A-rhymes. Stanza 48 begins with another extravagant morphological distortion:

> Tho when the terme is full accomplishid,
> There shall a sparke of fire, which hath long-while
> Bene in his ashes raked vp, and hid,

This is the only rhyme on 'accomplishid' in the poem, and there is no attempt to disguise the fact that this is a transactional distortion which primarily enables Spenser to fulfil the terms of his rhyme scheme.[21] In this case, the distortion is emphasised by the relative weakness of the final syllable of 'accomplishid': by rhyming it with 'hid', Spenser flaunts the opportunistic formation of his past participle. Indeed, the distortion is almost humourously advertised by the choice of 'hid' as the rhyming term. While rhyme may indeed vanish into the page, Spenser does not hide the phonetic happenstance on which his stanzas depend.

18 Holinshed, *The firste [laste] volume of the chronicles of England, Scotlande, and Irelande*, 285. Again, the *Early Modern Print* website suggests that 'Norwegian' was the dominant form at the time; 'Norueyses' is unique to *The Faerie Queene*.
19 Note too the close phonetic proximity between the C-rhyme of stanza 33 and the A-rhyme of stanza 34, *ouerronne: fordonne*. *The Faerie Queene* overflows with linkages of this kind, which I have characterized elsewhere as interstanzaic knitting; see Brown, '"Charmed with Inchaunted Rimes"' in Brown and Lethbridge, *A Concordance*, 60–63, and below.
20 Lethbridge, 'The Bondage of Rhyme', in Brown and Lethbridge, *A Concordance*, 109. See also Wilson-Okamura's related argument that Renaissance style is primarily ornamental and does not necessarily have a relationship with meaning; in *Spenser's International Style*, 140–79, and my review: 'The Scope of Spenser's Strangeness'.
21 Brown and Lethbridge, *A Concordance*, 184. The only other appearance of the word in *The Faerie Queene* follows the usual inflected ending of the preterite: 'Accomplished, that many deare complaind:' (III.ix.42.7), where the –ed must be sounded to secure the iambic pattern.

Conversely, the A-rhyme of stanza 42, while no less ostentatious, turns on the reader's receptivity to extreme repetition, as well as a culture in which biblical turns of phrase were ubiquitous:

> Then *woe*, and *woe*, and euerlasting *woe*,
>> Be to the Briton babe, that shalbe borne,
>> To liue in thraldome of his fathers *foe*[22]

As Hamilton points out, the first line recalls Revelation 8.13, 'Wo, wo, wo, to the inhabitants of the earth', endowing the Saxon conquest of Briton with an apocalyptic resonance.[23] Rhyme here does not disappear so much as break out into a chorus of 'future woes', in which identical rhyme underlines the gravity of the events Merlin forecasts (III.iii.43.3). At the same time, this passage doubles the A-rhyme into an unlikely quadruple, a characteristic flourish of bravura repetition.[24]

As this evidence suggests, it is difficult to sustain an argument which equates morphological distortion with poetic inattentiveness, period of composition, or the quality of the writing.[25] The point is rather that, because of the intricacy of the stanza form, Spenser repeatedly made use of the relative malleability of Early Modern English to make and remake his poetic language to fit his formal patterns; in a very real sense, the rhymes of *The Faerie Queene* show a writer at work who implemented his cocky plan to subdue 'rough words ... with Vse' (*Prose*, 16). Unlike the scheme to impose quantitative metrics onto English, however, Spenser's acts of linguistic violence are typically done in the context of rhyming. Distorted forms cannot in any simple way be equated with bad or ineffective writing. On the contrary, Merlin's prophecy shows a high degree of formal inventiveness and rhyming for meaning. Consider a further example. When Glauce asks 'How shall she know, how shall she finde the man?' (itself a resonant example of the 4/6 line discussed in the previous chapter) Merlin uses a cluster of C-rhymes which reverberate at important moments in what follows:

> Then *Merlin* thus, Indeed the fates are firme,
>> And may not shrinck, though all the world do shake:
>> Yet ought mens good endeuours them confirme,
> And guyde the heauenly causes to their constant terme. (III.iii.25)

22 My emphases.
23 Hamilton, *FQ*, 318; *The Geneva Bible*, Ggg1r.
24 For related examples, see Brown, '"Charmed with Inchaunted Rimes"' in Brown and Lethbridge, *A Concordance*, 68–70, where I discuss linked stanzas and stanzas which include two rhymes only.
25 See Bennett, *The Evolution of The Faerie Queene*, 21, who uses evidence of Spenser struggling for rhyme as ways of dating the composition of the poem.

Though this is not much of an answer to Glauce's practical query, it insists on the prophetic character of this episode, and its necessary concern with 'heauenly causes' and 'constant terme[s]'.[26] Though *terme* is relatively common in *The Faerie Queene*, this is the only occasion on which it is used as a rhyme.[27] This may simply indicate that Spenser found these terminations difficult to rhyme, perhaps because of a felt paucity of workable rhymes.[28] Nevertheless, these unusual rhymes echo through the rest of the prophecy. Stanza 27 describes Britomart's eventual marriage with Artegall in a direct echo of the C-rhyme of 25: 'From thence, him *firmely* bound with faithfull band,/To this his natiue soyle thou backe shalt bring'; the firm fates produce the firm bonds of a faithful marriage on the right terrain.[29] Similarly, at the further edges of Merlin's prophecy, Spenser returns to *terme*, albeit not in the rhyming position. As we have seen, stanza 48 reassures Britomart of the eventual return of the Britons through Henry VII, 'Tho when the *terme* is full accomplishid'; earlier Merlin makes the point in a related context that 'the *terme* (he sayd) is limited,/That in this thraldome *Britons* shall abide' (III.ii.44.1–2).[30] Merlin's prophecy as a whole is concerned with the sometimes tenuous control of historical anxieties;[31] the rhymes on 'constant terme[s]' are, in this sense, would-be comforting sonal markers of the prophet's attempts to control his audience,

26 See van Es, *Spenser's Forms of History*, 165, for the connections between prophecy, Tudor ideology and providential history.
27 There are 14 instances of *terme*, 28 of *termes*, and 1 each of *termd* and *termed*; see Brown and Lethbridge, *A Concordance*, 418, 327. This cluster is striking in including three one-off rhymes; see also *A Concordance*, 213 and 242 for *confirme* and *firme*.
28 There is some evidence to suggest that Spenser was not alone in avoiding rhymes on –*erm*/-*irm* terminations. An EEBO keyword full text search of verse published between 1590 and 1600 reveals relatively few examples of *term* and cognates as a rhyme word, although the word itself is extremely common in mid-line positions because of its multiple connotations, as in *Mother Hubberds Tale*, ll.41, 309 ('Ile write in termes, as she the same did say'; 'Expired had the terme, that these two iauels'). John Marston's *Scourge of Villanie* (1598) has an interesting example which suggests the difficulty of finding these sorts of rhyme. 'Proemium in librum secundum' adopts the unusual form of sixain, rhyming *Axaabb*, where the second line is the unrhymed: 'Or brand my Satyres with som Spanish terme'. While this may alliterate with the second line of the second stanza ('Seeking conceits to sute these Artlesse times'), more likely Marston was intending a characteristic effect of satiric roughness – the unrhymed lines inevitably underline the point being made; *The scourge of villanie*, sig. D9r.
29 My emphasis.
30 My emphases.
31 See again van Es's discussion. As he comments, Merlin's address 'puts a heavy burden on its recipient', while at the same failing to reconcile the 'disquieting' possibilities signalled by the rupture of Merlin's prophecy in stanza 50 as it reaches the contemporary world of Elizabeth's own reign; *Spenser's Forms of History*, 168.

to 'confirme' Britomart at least for the moment in a confident sense of providential design 'though all the world do shake'. Yet III.iii.25.c also verbalises the tension between these ambiguous 'termes', underlining the difficulty of guaranteeing the firmness of such a historical design authoritatively. The climax of the prophecy in stanzas 49–50 is similarly anxious, as it hurries from the Virgilian anticipation of the 'sacred Peace' of Elizabeth's reign to the abrupt close of Merlin's speech, 'But yet the end is not'.[32] Merlin's prophecy is only a partial discovery of the future, where it is the uncertainties of outcome which ultimately reverberate in the reader's and Britomart's minds, as in the uncomfortable distortion in the B-rhyme of stanza 50:

> There *Merlin* stayd,
> As ouercomen of the spirites powre,
> Or other ghastly spectacle dismayd,
> That secretly he saw, yet note discoure:
> Which suddein fit, and halfe extatick stoure
> When the two fearefull women saw, they grew
> Greatly confused in behaueoure

In his 'halfe extatick *stoure*', Merlin is reluctant to '*discoure*' – rather than the more usual 'discouer' – what 'secretly he saw', which unsurprisingly makes Glauce and Britomart 'Greatly confused in *behaueoure*'.[33] Once again, Spenser's rhymes exhibit a high tolerance of morphological distortion, and those distortions can be related to the events described. 'Note discoure', with its characteristic Spenserian modal form, almost constitutes a grammatical riddle, a 'halfe extatick' puzzle in diction, which self-consciously enacts the semantic refusal it describes.[34] Rhymes such as these and those of III.iii.25.c are important facets of the complex articulation of Merlin's prophecy as a political document. Spenser's text maintains an equipoise between doubt and reassurance which cumulatively underlines the necessarily imperfect character both of prophetic writing, and of Britomart's quest itself.[35]

32 For the violent caesura in this line, see Debra Fried, 'Spenser's Caesura'.
33 My emphases. See Brown and Lethbridge, *A Concordance*, 199, 225, for rhymes on *behaueoure* and *discoure* and variants. These are relatively unusual terms, and the combination of morphological distortion and prominent polysyllables makes them hard to ignore. Nevertheless, *discouer* and related terms comfortably outscore *discoure* as rhymes, by 7 to 2. Rhymes on *powre* and *stoure* are significantly more widespread.
34 On Spenser's modal verbs, see Sugden, *The Grammar of Spenser's Faerie Queene*, 119, and more recently, Zurcher, 'Spenser's Studied Archaism: The Case of "Mote"'.
35 See van Es, *Spenser's Forms of History*, 192–96, for the contested, subversive character of prophecy in the 1580s and 90s.

At the same time, this canto is rich in the kinds of formulaic rhymes analysed by Lethbridge. Consider again stanza 26:

> The man whom heauens haue ordaynd to bee
> The spouse of *Britomart*, is *Arthegall*:
> He wonneth in the land of *Fayeree*,
> Yet is no *Fary* borne, ne sib at all
> To Elfes, but sprong of seed terrestriall,
> And whilome by false *Faries* stolne away,
> Whyles yet in infant cradle he did crall;
> Ne other to himselfe is knowne this day,
> But that he by an Elfe was gotten of a Fay.

Alongside its more recherché rhymes on 'terrestriall' and (perhaps surprisingly) '*Fayeree*' (respectively three and one instances in the poem),[36] this stanza includes some of the basic rhyming props of *The Faerie Queene*: 'bee' (164 rhymes), 'all' (110), 'away' (147), 'day' (140); even '*Arthegall*' is used as a rhyme on 32 occasions.[37] It would of course be difficult to write a long rhyming poem without using words like 'be' and 'day'; phrases like 'ordaynd to bee' and 'knowne this day' are related to the syntactical formulae inventoried by Lethbridge. Such lines thus partly bear out the justice of his observation that many of Spenser's rhymes are place holders, devices for the fulfilment of the formal problem set by the rhyme scheme.[38] The reader does not need to dwell long on the rhymes in lines like 'The man

---

36 The other two rhymes, 'crall' and 'Fay', are used on respectively 3 and 4 occasions; see Brown and Lethbridge, *A Concordance*, 356, 361. For an illuminating discussion of the origins and poetic orientation of 'Fay' particularly in II.x, see Matthew Woodcock, *Fairy in The Faerie Queene: Renaissance Elf-Fashioning and Elizabethan Myth-Making*, 131–32.

37 Brown and Lethbridge, *A Concordance*, 'Alphabetical List of Rhymes with Frequency and Distribution' for the raw data, 352, 350, 351, 356. My tally of '*Artegall*' (the usual spelling) includes the variants '*Artegale*' (1 instance with distortion to rhyme with 'scale' at V.ii.46.a) and (as here) '*Arthegall*' (4 instances); see *A Concordance*, 192 for the full listing. '*Artegall*' comfortably outscores other titular knights as a rhyme word, which suggests the pragmatism of Spenser's practice, since this name is significantly easier to rhyme than 'Guyon'. The other knights score as follows: Britomart (25) Calidore (17), Triamond (5), Redcrosse (4), while Cambel is not rhymed at all, and 'Guyons' occurs once at the end of an unrhymed line of an argument (II.iii.arg); see *A Concordance*, 374, 354, 382, 365, 253.

38 See Lethbridge, 'The Bondage of Rhyme' in Brown and Lethbridge, *A Concordance*, 134–53, for examples with argument. Lethbridge's approach is summarised as follows: 'The sheer number of repeated and generalised rhymes indicates that in the main they are not there to be attended to – they are in the main meant to pass unnoticed as having merely formal relevance' (138). For syntactical formulae, see 141–42; see also the list of 'Rhymes in "to be" and various forms', 529–30.

who, heauens haue ordayned to bee' or 'Yet is no *Fary* borne, ne sib at all/To Elfes' to understand that little semantic pressure is being brought to bear on these individual rhymes. The difficulty of course is knowing where rhymes are formulaic, and where they may snap into semantic activity. In this stanza, the characteristic interspersing of what I would prefer to call colourless rhymes with one-off, unusual rhymes inevitably complicates the reader's work. If you pay no attention at all to 'at all', should you also gloss over 'terrestriall'? The slide of the one-off A-rhyme on '*Fayeree*' to the C-rhyme on '*Fay*' also suggests the careful process of selection, echo, and development in the construction of a stanza which is in essence a genealogical rebus of a knight who is not fully known 'to himselfe' – or the reader – as Merlin speaks. As Britomart sees Artegall in a magic mirror, so Artegall is shown in a false reflection of both colourless and purposive rhymes at the moment of his naming.[39] This is a key facet of the way Spenser rhymes – the colourless and the colourful are endlessly aligned and recombined in poetic structures which it is well not to take for granted.

Merlin's prophecy does not showcase all of Spenser's rhyming devices[40] but it does suggest some preliminary conclusions which are of relevance to an understanding of *The Faerie Queene* as a rhyming poem. Spenser is unusual in his predilection for verbal rhymes, which in turn tend to remove the diction of the poem ever further from conversational English; 'Till thy wombes burden thee from them do call' (III.iii.28.6) is an appropriately extravagant, or heroic, way of saying something relatively simple: pregnancy will make you give up fighting. Allied with this, Spenser freely distorts word forms to secure rhymes. Conversely, morphological distortion does not betoken bad writing. It shows the reader that s/he is engaged in reading a poem where rhyme may 'discoure' issues of the first importance. *The Faerie Queene* inevitably abounds with rhyming formulae. Though the existence of these formulae is important, phatic language alone is not a reliable guide to poetic function. Rhyme is a trope of repetition, and to repeat even the most tired of poetic formulae can have the effect of re-energising, of recolouring, the familiar. I return to these arguments in the next section.

39 For stanzas of naming, see Brown, '"Charmed with Inchaunted Rimes"' in Brown and Lethbridge, *A Concordance*, 37–38.
40 See Brown, '"Charmed with Inchaunted Rimes"' in Brown and Lethbridge, *A Concordance*, 38–71, for a comprehensive overview of these devices, including the introduction of feminine rhyme to the 1596 edition.

Rhyme in theory and practice: the debt to Chaucer

As this discussion of Merlin's prophecy implies, and as I have argued at greater length elsewhere, observing the variety of Spenser's rhyming practices draws attention to the tensions between reading rhyme semantically and the anti-rational potential of rhyme. The sonal linkage of words is always potentially at variance with the idea that content and meaning should dictate choice of word; that sound should be subservient to sense.[41] Guy Cook's statement of this tension is provocative, particularly in the context of *The Faerie Queene*. Where criticism tends almost as a reflex to look for the 'deep' structures of a given text – their dark conceits, their allegorical 'cores' – rhyme is a potentially subversive device of the surface, a shallow randomiser, which by 'its very focus on form rather than meaning may create new meanings, by bringing together units which schematic thinking would often keep apart'.[42] In III.iii.vi, the final line of the B-rhyme exemplifies this potential. Where the previous six lines describe Britomart's strange viewing of Artegall in the mirror (with rhymes on 'Damosell', 'tell', and 'dwell'), the seventh and eight lines take an unexpected detour: 'For though beyond the *Africk Ismael*,/Or th'Indian *Peru* he were'. Arguably, Spenser hadn't thought of Northern Africa, or indeed Peru, before he was put to the task of finding the fourth rhyme.[43] This is not to say that this continental excursion is inappropriate – it readily gives a sense of the geographical scale to Britomart's 'infinite endeuour' to seek Artegall – the point is rather that it is the randomising trick of rhyme which facilitates the concrete example of '*Africk Ismaell*', and in turn underlines the hyperbolical quality of Britomart's quest.

As so often, Sidney's *Defence of Poetry* provides the orthodox humanist scepticism about rhyme in relation to the impact it has on sense. Discussing contemporary poetry, he laments that often 'one verse did but beget another, without ordering at the first what should be at the last; which becomes a

---

41 See Brown, '"Charmed with Inchaunted Rimes"' in Brown and Lethbridge, *A Concordance*, 13–16, citing influential work by W. K. Wimsatt and others on the idea that rhymes across different parts of speech are intrinsically more demanding than rhymes on nouns alone.

42 Guy Cook, 'Genes, Memes, Rhymes', 389. See also Brown, '"Charmed with Inchaunted Rimes"' in Brown and Lethbridge, *A Concordance*, 16 n.96. Cook's work problematises literary criticism's habitual privileging of deep layered meaning, or allegory, over the phonetic surface of a literary text.

43 Spenser's rhymes on place names are frequently one-offs, as in Proem II.2 ('Who euer heard of th'Indian *Peru*?'). This is a useful counter example to the one cited above, since this is the first line of the C-rhyme. See Brown and Lethbridge, *A Concordance*, 475–78, for a list of 'Names in Rhyme Position'.

confused mass of words, with a tingling sound of rhyme, barely accompanied with reason.'[44] Though this stanza is remote from the 'tingling' chaos envisaged by Sidney, nevertheless it demonstrates the way in which sense may be guided by sound, rather than the other way around. The intellectual underpinning of poetry – the poet's 'fore-conceit' – is in practice often at the mercy of what will rhyme with what, or indeed what can be manipulated by poetic sleight of hand to rhyme with what.[45] Indeed, formal features such as rhyme can be seen as providing necessary counterweight to the Sidneyan foreconceit precisely by their antirational tendencies. The rhyme scheme, in other words, is part of their aesthetic design which endlessly works to keep this didactic poem interesting and surprising.

This suggests that Spenser's rhyming practice was both permissive and pragmatic, adaptable to the moment-by-moment contingencies of a given passage, ready to incorporate divergent and unusual terms into the body of the poem.[46] The question then arises of what were the literary antecedents for that practice. There have been two major contributions to this debate, which take antithetical approaches. David Scott Wilson-Okamura has argued that Spenser's style is best understood in terms of the continental Renaissance, and specifically, that the introduction of feminine rhymes to the second installment of *The Faerie Queene* may be traced to his reading of predominantly French and medieval Latin during the 1580s while he was living and working in Ireland, away from the London book trade.[47] Conversely, Ants Oras's empirical 1955 study argued that Spenser's rhyming practice derives more from the English tradition than the Italian.[48] Like Wilson-Okamura, Oras also saw a change between the two installments, but he characterised this as a move from a traditional, Chaucerian model, heavily reliant on *rime riche*, to a practice which is more like the rest of 1590s poetry. Though Wilson-Okamura is clearly right to remind readers

44 Sidney, *Miscellaneous Prose*, 112.
45 Sidney, *Miscellaneous Prose*, 79. For related morphological sleights of hand, see Brown, '"Charmed with Inchaunted Rimes"' in Brown and Lethbridge, *A Concordance*, 26–27.
46 See Brown and Lethbridge, *A Concordance*, 467–71, for the *hapax legomena* in rhyme position; see also 424–26 for the same information presented in a different form. This long list of both familiar ('cart') and recondite terms ('bikerment') goes some way to demonstrate the variety and pragmatism of Spenser's rhyming practice.
47 Wilson-Okamura, *Spenser's International Style*, 161–77. Earlier, Wilson-Okamura includes some discussion of English influences: see 43–44, on the origins of the Spenserian stanza. Though this is a useful discussion, he does not consider *Troilus and Criseyde* as an important precedent for *The Faerie Queene* in stanzaic verse, despite his ostensible concern with the reasons for adopting stanzas for an epic.
48 Ants Oras, 'Intensified Rhymes Links in *The Faerie Queene*', 57. For commentary on this seminal article, see Brown, '"Charmed with Inchaunted Rimes"' in Brown and Lethbridge, *A Concordance*, 23–25.

of Spenser's significant debts to continental models, my argument follows Oras in reasserting the Chaucerian qualities of Spenser's rhyming. This is not, I should stress, to advance a 'Little Englander' Spenser. It is rather to argue that while Spenser's reading was undoubtedly international (and conceivably international in directions not fully considered by existing scholarship), his rhyming forms remain rooted in absorption of, and reaction to, domestic models, amongst whom Chaucer remains, in Puttenham's phrase, 'the most renowned of them all'.[49]

Although the connection between Chaucer and Spenser is as old as *The Shepheardes Calender* – where Colin Clout and E. K. repeatedly underline the New Poet's fealty to Tityrus/Chaucer[50] – the scholarly exploration this literary relationship began in the 1970s and has continued to develop since then. Scholars have started to problematise and lift the disciplinary barriers between Medieval and Renaissance studies. It is only since the 1970s that the question of 'the Renaissance Chaucer' and the medieval imprint on Elizabethan writing has been systematically debated.[51] The work of Judith Anderson has done much to clarify the intertextual allusions which lie beneath *The Faerie Queene*. In a succession of essays, Anderson trains her readers to uncover the extent to which Spenser writes with his Chaucer – particularly *The Canterbury Tales* – close at hand, and close in mind, in the writing of *The Faerie Queene*.[52] Yet the relationship between Chaucer and Spenser in terms of rhyming remains relatively

---

49 Puttenham, *The Art of English Poesy*, 149. Puttenham's praise comes in the context of a chapter which surveys 'our English poesy' (147). On Spenser's possible library, see Hadfield, *Edmund Spenser: A Life*, 227–30.

50 See famously 'June', 81–82 ('The God of shepheards *Tityrus* is dead,/Who taught me homely, as I can, to make'), and E. K.'s gloss: 'by Tityrus is meant Chaucer'; in *Yale*, 112, 116. See also Cummings (ed.), *Spenser: The Critical Heritage*, 49, 50, 55, 98–99, 107, 109–11 for the similar tropes by other contemporary witnesses, notably Thomas Speght in his Chaucer folio (1598, 1602). For the suggestion that 'Tityrus' is more polyvalent, see Syrithe Pugh, *Spenser and Virgil: The Pastoral Poems*, 105–06.

51 See Miskimin, *The Renaissance Chaucer* (1975), Krier (ed.), *Refiguring Chaucer in the Renaissance* (1998, including key essays by Berry and Anderson), and McMullan and Matthews (eds), *Reading the Medieval in Early Modern England* (2007). Notwithstanding much excellent work, the academic self-definition as medievalist or early modernist remains enormously constitutive of how we think and talk; at the excellent 'Dan Geffrey with the New Poete' conference held in Bristol in 2014, many speakers (including the present writer) were at pains to establish the limits of their professional knowledge. Such differences were sometimes comically audible in our different readings aloud of Middle English.

52 See the essays collected in Judith H. Anderson, *Reading the Allegorical Intertext: Chaucer, Spenser, Shakespeare, Milton*.

unexplored. As Anderson's work has centred on the influence of *The Canterbury Tales* on Spenser, so the question of Spenser's reading of *Troilus and Criseyde* has to some extent been side-lined.[53] Yet arguably it is the *Troilus* rather than the *Tales* which is the key text for the Renaissance Chaucer. In what follows, I focus on the *Troilus* (with some comment on 'The Squire's Tale') because of its centrality to the sixteenth-century understanding of Chaucer, and because it is written in what Puttenham called the 'meter heroical' of rhyme royal stanzas.[54] It is the stanzaic form of the *Troilus* which makes it a key precedent for *The Faerie Queene* as a sustained heroic poem which repeatedly gestures to the forms and tropes of Classical literature.[55] A related facet of the Renaissance Chaucer which is not often remarked on is that sixteenth-century editions have the effect of making him seem a more stanzaic poet than modern collected editions do. Kathleen Forni notes that the majority of William Thynne's non-Chaucerian selections in the 1532 folio are 'composed in rhyme royal'.[56] Seen in the material contexts of the great folios, it is Chaucer's rhyming couplet poems which are eccentric. In these lights, the decision to use rhyming stanzas for an epic is perhaps less surprising than Wilson-Okamura suggests.[57]

Rime riche and changes of custom

Rime riche was something of a calling card for Chaucer and, as Oras shows, there are numerous examples in *The Faerie Queene*. By the seventeenth century, neo-classical literary opinion deemed it to be a device better avoided both because of its aura of desuetude and because of its

53 Anderson's keynote lecture at the 'Dan Geffrey' conference, 'Chaucer's *Troilus and Criseyde* in Spenser's *Amoretti* and *Faerie Queene*: Reading Historically and Intertextually', extended her work into the question of the relationship between the *Troilus* and Spenser.
54 Puttenham, *The Art of English Poesy*, 149–50; see Craig A. Berry, '"Sundrie Doubts"', 108, for Puttenham's ambivalence about Chaucer. For the broader point of the dominance of allusion to the *Troilus* in the sixteenth century, see Sidney, *Miscellaneous Prose*, 112, and Brewer, *Chaucer: The Critical Heritage* Vol 1, 17, for the popularity of the *Troilus*, and 108, 123, 126–27, for Elizabethan allusions.
55 See the invocations of the Fury Thesiphone, and the Muse of Epic, Calliope, at the beginning of *Troilus* Books I and III (I.6–7; III.45–49), and Stephen A. Barney's notes on these passages in *The Riverside Chaucer*, 1025, 1038.
56 Kathleen Forni, *The Chaucerian Apocrypha*, 90. For the full canon of apocrypha, see xv–xviii, 44–87.
57 Wilson-Okamura, *Spenser's International Style*, 18–49. See also Chapter 4 below.

international associations. Abraham Cowley, glossing one of his Pindaric odes in 1656, asserted:

> These kind of Rhymes the *French* delight in, and call *Rich Rhymes;* but I do not allow of them in *English* … They are very frequent in *Chaucer*, and our old *Poets*, but that is not good authority for us now. There can be no *Musick* with onely *one Note*.[58]

Cowley was an enthusiastic reader of *The Faerie Queene*, so he is partly writing against his own predilections. Nevertheless, his formal chauvinism underlines the extent to which Chaucer and Spenser were seen as using analogous dated forms. The idea that 'There can be no *Musick* with onely *one Note*', though dubious in itself,[59] connects with the revival of interest in the formulaic qualities of *The Faerie Queene* in that Cowley registers an objection to the monotony of the device, with the implication that such rhymes are often shortcuts to compliance with a demanding stanza form. How, then, do Chaucer and Spenser use a typical *rime riche* cluster? Consider a rhyme on different meanings of *wise* from Book I of *Troilus*; this is the kind of rhyme Oras calls 'linkings of cognate words of identical sound but different semantic functions':[60]

> The wyse eke sayth/ wo him that is alone
> For and he fall/ he hath none helpe to ryse
> And sythe thou haste a felowe/ tell thy mone
> For this nys naught certayne the next wyse
> To wynnen loue/ as techen us the wyse
> To walowe and wepe/ as Niobe the quene
> Whose teeres yet in marble ben ysene[61]

The first line quoted here incidentally dramatises the metrical uncertainty which surrounded Chaucer in the sixteenth century. All earlier printed editions (and the *Riverside*), read 'The wyse saythe/ wo hym that is alone'; Thynne's addition of 'eke' shows his failure to hear the final e- alongside his desire to produce a text of decasyllabic regularity.[62] Spenser repeats

58 Abraham Cowley, *Poems*, sig. Fff3r, original emphases.
59 Cowley, one suspects, would not have enjoyed Terry Riley's *In C*, or the work of Steve Reich.
60 Oras, 'Intensified Rhyme Links in *The Faerie Queene*', 42.
61 Chaucer, *The Works*, sig. Hh6r; see also *The Riverside Chaucer*, 483 (I.694–700).
62 The quotation is from Pynson's 1526 edition: Chaucer, *The boke of Troylus and Creseyde*, A5v. See also the editions by Caxton (B3r) and de Worde (C1r).

the same rhyme cluster in his continuation of 'The Squire's Tale' in Book IV:

> Which whenas *Cambell*, that was stout and wise,
> Perceiu'd would breede great mischiefe, he bethought
> How to preuent the perill that mote rise,
> And turne both him and her to honour in this wise. (IV.ii.37)

In the deep Chaucerian context of the Cambell–Canacee narrative, such formal proximity is unsurprising.[63] The *rime riche* pairings are formulaic: both 'stout and wise' and 'in this wise' satisfy the metrical contract while advancing the narrative. Spenser's adoption of Chaucerian technique is less semantically purposive than Pandarus's playing on notions of wisdom and expedience in love in *Troilus*, where the coupling of 'the wyse' with 'the next wyse/To wynnen loue' hints at the rooted pragmatism of his advice.[64] Yet the fact that this instance of *rime riche* is formulaic does not mean that Spenser's usage invariably follows this pattern. Earlier in the same canto, the same pairing is used to describe the false Florimell and Blandamour:

> Sometimes estranging him in sterner wise,
> That hauing cast him in a foolish trance,
> He seemed brought to bed in Paradise,
> And prou'd himselfe most foole, in what he seem'd most wise. (IV.ii.9)

Such rhymes show Spenser directly following the footing of Chaucer's 'feete': as the stanza enacts the dance of the false Florimell's flirtation, so this rhyme points to the folly of the 'wise' in which Blandamour is behaving. Illusory wisdom and delusive behaviour – the fool's 'Paradise' of Blandamour's erotic pursuit of an insubstantial illusion – are juxtaposed through identical rhyme. While Spenser works in a Chaucerian rhyming tradition here, his application of that tradition is pleasingly idiosyncratic, as the

---

63 The other *wise: wise* clusters in *The Faerie Queene* are I.i.50b and IV.ii.37c; see Brown and Lethbridge, *A Concordance*, 344. Chaucer rhymes on *wyse* three times in 'The Squire's Tale', but not as a *rime riche*; see ll.375–76 (*ryse: wyse*), 627–28 (*wyse: servyse*), and 705–06 (*wyse: suffyse*). See also 'The Knight's Tale' ll.1739–40 (*juwise: wise*), printed 'iewyse' and 'wyse' by Thynne; sig. C6r.

64 The equivocation on contrasting meanings of *wyse* is important to the characterisation of Pandarus; see also I.959–63 ('if thow werke in this wyse … as writen clerkes wyse … in sondry wyse') and I.991–92 ('for ye ben bothe wyse,/And konne it conseil kepe in swych a wyse'). Of the 27 usages of *wyse* recorded by the *eChaucer* concordance, 10 are in Book I.

symmetrical alexandrine becomes a vehicle for a pointed antithesis. As Oras suggested, the value of this device is the 'gradation' it implies between cognate yet subtly different terms.[65] The richness of this kind of rhyming lies in the complex blending of sonally identical yet semantically distinct terms to create what W. H. Auden called 'sound-metaphors'.[66]

There are, however, many ways in which Spenser's practice appears more Chaucerian than in fact it is. This is due to changes in English pronunciation between the fourteenth and sixteenth centuries.[67] Consider rhymes on *creature*. Spenser uses this as a rhyme on two occasions, both in Book IV.[68] For him, *creature* is always a feminine rhyme. Though such rhymes are virtually excluded from the 1590 *Faerie Queene*, he then 'flood[s] the second installment' with them.[69] In total, there are around 169 such rhymes. There is an ongoing debate about why Spenser made this change. Wilson-Okamura argues that he intended to produce a 'big, fat sound' in imitation of the poets of the Pléiade and Medieval Latin, whereas I have suggested that the 1596 installment aligns *The Faerie Queene* with contemporaneous long English poems. In this view, the rhyming practices of the 1590 edition are more eccentric than those of 1596.[70] Spenser was too good a technician to ignore the poetic excess and overflow which is an inbuilt fact of feminine rhyme: that it adds to a text's semantic and affective scope. Chaucer's practice is very different. He rhymes on *creature* relatively frequently: there are twenty separate instances in *Troilus*. But he scanned the word as a tri- or quadri-syllable, depending on the uncertain

65 Spenser may have remembered some of Chaucer's uses of 'paradys'; see *Troilus* 4.864: 'Her face lyke of paradys the ymage/Was al ychaunged in another kynde'; and 'The Merchant's Tale', ll.1265–66: 'That in this world it is a paradise/Thus saith this olde knyght that is so wise'. In Chaucer, *The Works*, sigs. Nn4v, H3v.
66 Auden, *Prose* I, 20.
67 See April McMahon, 'Restructuring Renaissance English', 189–218, for the historical complexity of describing these changes.
68 The rhymes on *creature* are IV.ii.44b and IV.vi.17b: note in the latter, that the A-rhyme, *endure: impure*, with the emphasis on the second syllable, half-rhymes with the *creature: nature: feature: defeature* cluster; as Hamilton notes, this 'rare duplication' of A- and B-rhymes 'seems designed to highlight' a crucial moment in the relationship between Britomart and Artegall; *FQ*, 453. There is a single rhyme on *creatures* in the Mutabilitie Cantos: *creatures: features* (VII.vii.4a), which is directly linked to the next A-rhyme of *Nature: stature* at VII.vii.5a.
69 Wilson-Okamura, *Spenser's International Style*, 162; see Brown, '"Charmed with Inchaunted Rimes"' in Brown and Lethbridge, *A Concordance*, 22. The precise figure is ambiguous because of the uncertain syllabic status of words like *powre*, which could be realised either as mono- or di-syllables.
70 Wilson-Okamura, *Spenser's International Style*, 177 (and 161–77); Brown, '"Charmed with Inchaunted Rimes"' in Brown and Lethbridge, *A Concordance*, 47–57.

value of the final –e . This pattern is followed in each of the twenty rhymes I have looked at,[71] as in Book I's description of Criseyde:

> She nas nat with the moste of hire stature
> But alle hire lymmes so wel answeryng
> Weren to wommanhode/ that creature
> Was neuer lasse mannysshe in semyng[72]

where the phonetic link between 'stature' and 'creature' is audibly on the last syllable, or syllable and a half, if the final –e is sounded. The *stature: creature* cluster has a parallel in *The Faerie Queene* in the description of the fay, Agape:

> all the powres of nature,
> Which she by art could vse vnto her will,
> And to her seruice bind each liuing creature,
> Through secret vnderstanding of their feature.
> Thereto she was right faire, when so her face
> She list discouer, and of goodly stature (IV.ii.44)

This is an example of the 'foot surgery' which Craig Berry diagnoses in Spenser's continuation of 'The Squire's Tale': 'a poet such as Spenser – with an unusually fine ear but a sixteenth-century understanding of Middle English pronunciation – could not help but feel a roughness in Chaucer's versification', and, I would add, in his some of his rhyming.[73] Spenser's 'creatures' are those of Early Modern English: in a Chaucerian narrative context, Chaucerian rhyming techniques are updated, as metrical emphasis and rhyming join is shifted towards the newly dominating first syllable in both words. Once again, Spenser's language proves to be less archaic in practice than its reputation would suggest.[74] The verse mimics Agape's practice by using poetic art to 'bind each living' syllable into cogent rhyming clusters with appropriate metrical values. Once again, Spenser's demand in the correspondence with Harvey for 'the kingdome of our owne Language' is pertinent, particularly in relation to what is usually seen as Harvey's more nuanced reply.[75] Harvey stresses the durability of linguistic custom

71 The full list is: I.104; I.116; I.283; I.570; II.417; II.717; III.13; IV.252; IV.386; IV.756; IV.767; IV.1679; V.154; V.210; V.241; V.384; V.714; V.808; V.832; V.1701. See https://machias.edu/faculty/necastro/chaucer/concordance/tr/tr.txt.WebConcordance/framconc.htm [accessed 2 May 2014].
72 Chaucer, *The Works*, sig. Hh3v; *The Riverside Chaucer*, 477 (I. 281–87).
73 Berry, '"Sundrie Doubts"', 116.
74 See Chapter 1 for the debate about archaism.
75 See *Prose*, 16. See Attridge, *Well-Weighed Syllables*, 146–49, for Harvey's reaction.

and the tyranny of Spenser's proposals to 'vsurpe … vppon a quiet companye of wordes',[76] yet Spenser's updating of Chaucerian rhymes suggests a deeper sensitivity to the mobility of linguistic usage than that shown by his donnish mentor. Words are not such 'quiet' creatures: they are mobile, and the way they work in verse shifts with time and changing linguistic custom.

Interstanzaic rhymes

Spenser's predilection for rhyming across stanzas (which I have called interstanzaic knitting) may also be fruitfully traced to his reading of Chaucer. This device uses the same or related rhyme words within episodes to make connections between different parts of the same narrative action.[77] It is a facet of the extreme technical restrictions of the Spenserian stanza. The Spenserian is a restrictive technical grid,[78] which repeatedly requires the poet to come up with new rhymes. Rather than following this prompt towards lexical novelty, as later poets did, Spenser restricts himself further (as Catherine Addison demonstrates) by his fondness for verbal rhymes, and his liking for interstanzaic repetitions.[79] Chaucer again provides a precedent: Spenser would have found many examples of rhymes across stanzas in the *Troilus*. The rhymes on *creature* in Books IV and V are cases in point. In Book IV, the repetition of the rhyme across twelve lines underscores Criseyde's sense of her desolation in having to leave Troy: 'She helde her selfe a forlost creature … Howe shulde a plante or lyues creature?/Lyue withouten his kynde nouriture?'[80] In Book V, over a span of some thirty lines, the rhyme describes first Criseyde – 'There myght ben no fayrer creature' – and then Troilus – 'One of the beste entetched creature/That is or shal/ whyle that the worlde may dure'.[81] Phrases like

---

76 See *Prose*, 473–74, for Harvey's reservations about Spenser's proposal to elongate the central syllable of *carpenter*.
77 See Brown, '"Charmed with Inchaunted Rimes"' in Brown and Lethbridge, *A Concordance*, 60–63, for commentary on the Book I Proem, and Brown, '"I would abate the sternenesse of my stile"', 282–83, for interstanzaic knitting in The Mutabilitie Cantos.
78 I borrow the term 'grid' from Anne Carson's *Red Doc>*, 77.
79 Addison, 'Rhyming Against the Grain'.
80 Chaucer, *The Works*, sig. Nn4r; *The Riverside Chaucer*, 548 (IV.755–768).
81 Chaucer, *The Works*, sig. Pp2v; *The Riverside Chaucer*, 571 (V.809–833). See also the earlier description of Criseyde as 'this woful creature', in *The Works*, sig. Pp2r; *The Riverside Chaucer*, 569 (V.714). Thynne prints 'entetched' where modern editions have 'entecced', meaning 'endowed'. Speght's list of 'The hard words of Chaucer, explaned' has relevant entries under 'enteched' ('defiled'), 'entetched' and 'enteched' (both glossed as 'qualified, or spotted'); (Chaucer, *The Works*, sig. Ttt 4v); see also *OED Online*, 'entach, entech'.

'lyues creature' and 'fayrer creature' are useful metrical props, Chaucer's repetitions articulate some of the creaturely fragility which underpins the turn towards tragedy, while the contrast between 'fayrer' and the more recherché 'entetched' emphasises economically the different ways the narrator presents the protagonists in these summary portraits.[82] Spenser would thus have learned much about the linking of stanzas through rhyme from Chaucer and the Chaucerian tradition.[83] Nevertheless, his use of the device is (to use my earlier word) more extreme, partly because the grid of the Spenserian stanza is more restrictive than that of the rhyme royal stanza. These are issues which will be discussed further in the next chapter. Because the Spenserian is intrinsically more repetitious, repetitions between stanzas are felt more vividly, more intrusively, than they are in a poem like *Troilus*.

There is a related factor in play here. Wilson-Okamura contrasts the 'hermetic box ... syntax' of *The Faerie Queene* with the 'leaking' stanza form preferred by Tasso and others, in which syntax may flow from one stanza to the next. Suggesting that Spenser mirrors an English distaste 'for stanzas that will not stay shut', he finds only four such stanzas in *The Faerie Queene*. Though he recognises that Chaucer and 'his disciples in the Renaissance' are something of an exception, he claims that sixteenth-century English practice is uptight, with the suggestion of an almost anally retentive resistance to 'leak and spill'.[84] Though the observation usefully signals the restrictions on *The Faerie Queene*'s syntax, the generalisations are precarious. Read in Thynne's edition, with its minimal punctuation (carried forward in later sixteenth-century editions), almost any stanza of the *Troilus* could be seen to 'leak' into the next.[85] Chaucer's syntax is

82 For a useful summary of critical debates about narratorial sympathy in *Troilus* and its continuations, see Forni, *The Chaucerian Apocrypha*, 121–23.

83 'The Floure and the Leafe', for example, has six rhyming clusters which include *wight* in its 595 lines; see ll.13–14 (*wight: light*); 16–19 (*night: might: wight*); 36–38 (*sight: wight*); 69–70 (*wight: might*); 310–13 (*bright: might: wight*), and 433–34 (*wight: sight*). Though most of these are formulaic variations on patterns such as 'any wight' and 'earthly wight', they demonstrate that such repetitions were a part of the Chaucerian tradition. See *The Floure and the Leafe, The Assembly of Ladies, The Isle of Ladies*, 4–19. The poem appears only in the 1598 and 1602 Speght folios, and was read there by Gabriel Harvey; see Forni, *The Chaucerian Apocrypha*, 128.

84 Wilson-Okamura, *Spenser's International Style*, 29–31. See Lethbridge, 'The Bondage of Rhyme' in Brown and Lethbridge, *A Concordance*, 106–07, for Lethbridge's argument that early editions are an unreliable guide to Spenser's precise intentions in relation to punctuation.

85 Even in a modern texts with fuller punctuation, there are a comparatively high number of stanzas which are not closed or marked off as the end of the sentence; in *Troilus* Book II (in Barney's Norton edition) I count some 24 'leaking' stanzas (that is, stanzas

usually constrained within stanzas, but it is by no means an invariable rule. In apocryphal poems like 'The Floure and the Leaf' and 'The Court of Love', leakage is extremely common to the extent that the relationship between stanza form and syntax can become uncertain as sentences – to vary the liquid imagery – meander from stanza to stanza.[86] Though *The Faerie Queene* is more syntactically disciplined, Wilson-Okamura's characterisation of a bound-in, archetypically English Spenser minimises the full extent of his technical illusionism. Spenser is not disciplined and repetitive because of his nationality but because of his interest in the poetic effects these devices might yield.

The fight between Cambell and the Brothers 'Mond in Book IV Canto III exemplifies these tendencies in a Chaucerian context. It features a striking coincidence between verbal patterning and the events narrated: as the fight seems unfinishable, so the verbal tricks Spenser uses imply stasis and a disquieting inability for the narrative to make progress. He goes out of his way to use samey devices: there are numerous anaphoras,[87] epic similes, which cumulatively become tropes of repetition by virtue of their frequency.[88] I begin with a description of three instances of inter-stanzaic linkage before considering their implications.[89]

1 Simple linkage of disparate stanzas. Stanzas 6 and 11 share related B-rhymes: of these relatively unusual terms, *abet* and *affret* are used only once or twice elsewhere.[90] The rhetorical variety of Spenser's practice is shown through the semantic variation: 'All arm'd to point his chalenge to *abet*' uses the rhyme word verbally; 'The meede of thy mischalenge and abet' is the unrelated noun meaning fraud. Nevertheless, the clear

---

concluded with a comma, semi-colon, colon or hyphen) in a book of 1757 lines; see Chaucer, *Troilus and Criseyde* (2006), 68–149. This phenomenon is partly a function of the large quantity of reported speech in the early books of the *Troilus*, but also stresses the differences between the workings of rhyme royal and the Spenserian stanza.

86 See 'The Floure and the Leafe', ll.1–42, which consists of two sentences (or possibly only one) unfolding over the space of six stanzas. In *The Floure and the Leafe, The Assembly of Ladies, The Isle of Ladies*, 4.

87 See stanzas 11 ('thy meede … The meede'); 12–13 ('let forth his wearie ghost … His wearie ghost assoyld'); 18 ('Where it was ment (so deadly it was ment)'); 21–22 ('the lifelesse corse it left.//It left …'). Puttenham's description of anaphora as 'the Figure of Report' which 'lead[s] the dance to many verses in suit' captures something of the slomo, balletic quality to these insistent repetitions; see *The Art of English Poesy*, 282.

88 For the similes, see IV.iii.15, 16, 19, 23, 27, 15, 29, 39, 41.

89 Almost every stanza in this episode has rhymes which are in some ways related to others, so the following discussion is illustrative of broader tendencies.

90 For *abet*, see VI.v.22b; for *affret*, see the related IV.ii.15c and III.ix.16a. See "† abet, n." *OED Online*.

similarity of wording means that stanza 11 recoils back to the formulation of stanza 6; this is the kind of effect which close interstanzaic linkage generates.

2 Direct linkage of neighbouring stanzas. Stanzas 10 and 11 show one of Spenser's favourite devices, where a C-rhyme produces next the A-rhyme, creating a five-rhyme form: *brake: shake: bespake* segues into *take: sake.* The effect is to create a sequence of five rhymes binding two stanzas together sonally and semantically.

3 More complex linkage of disparate stanzas. Stanza 23 uses an unusual two rhyme form, where the A- and C-rhymes are identical.[91] The B-rhyme of this stanza anticipates the C-rhyme of stanza 31. In turn, the B-rhyme of 31 anticipates the C-rhyme of 33. In the space of ten stanzas, there is a remarkable coincidence of similar rhymes and identical forms, some of which are used only in this Canto.

What are we to make of this evidence? First, the proximity of these rhymes underlines the endlessness of the fight between Cambell and his unkillable opponents. The *–ake* rhymes which link stanzas 10 and 11 underline the recurring gestures which constitute the fight; the alexandrine of stanza 11 captures the tension between renewal and repetition which lies at the heart of this episode as Priamond redoubles his efforts: 'And charging him a fresh thus felly him *bespake*'. Five stanzas later, another *–ake* cluster verbalises a sense of poetic stalemate: 'cruell battell twixt themselues doe *make* … So cruelly these Knights stroue for that Ladies *sake*' (IV.iii.16).[92] Cruel knights indulge in a cruel battle, but the logic underlying the struggle is curiously absent; what matters, rather, is the sense of impasse, which is underlined by the epic simile which compares the combatants with 'two Tygers prickt with hungers rage'.[93] As Anderson and Berry have

---

91 There are other examples of stanzas in this form in *The Faerie Queene*; see V.v.19–20 (two consecutive stanzas with two rhymes only) and my commentary in Brown, '"Charmed with Inchaunted Rimes"' in Brown and Lethbridge, *A Concordance*, 69–70; see also VII.vii.44, the binary stanza on Day and Night, which aptly adopts this binary rhyme scheme.

92 Similar observations could be made about the shared A- and B- rhymes in stanzas 17 and 18, where rhymes on *–ent* relentlessly highlight the circularity of the conflict: 'Full many strokes that mortally were ment' threaten to resolve into a stroke from Diamond that would stint 'all strife incontinent', but Cambell's last-minute swerve means that their 'fell intent' continues.

93 The tigers simile is literalised in stanza 39, which describes the lions that draw Cambina's chariot. Where the warring tigers make 'cruell battel betwixt themselues' over 'some beasts fresh spoyle', the 'grim lyons' are tamed by Cambina's influence: 'Now made forget their former cruell mood,/T'obey their riders hest, as seemed good'.

observed, Spenser's version of 'The Squire's Tale' threatens to reproduce the parent tale's endlessness; this interminability, I suggest, is audibly registered in these overlapping rhymes.[94]

Second, through similar rhymes, Spenser constructs tropes of wonderment for these at once baffling, at once repetitious deeds of arms. Virtuosity in rhyme is purposive inasmuch as it gives the reader ways of registering the amazement the narrator keeps trying to instil. Stanzas 23 and 31 give the best illustrations of this process of horrific wonder. Though rhymes on *–ight* terminals are common, that should not dilute the reader's sense of the technical accomplishment on display.[95] Stanza 23 invites the beholder's astonishment at Cambell's fortitude, and that wonder is made intelligible through the rhymes: the 'wounded ... *Knight*' becomes in the process of these rhymes 'freshly ... *dight*' like the snake; the internal rhyme focuses on the readerly astonishment of this spectacle: 'Some newborne *wight* ye would him surely weene'. Thus the recycling of the B-rhyme of 23 in the C-rhyme of 31 gives the reader a jarring sense of circularity. In this fight, nobody properly dies, and every weary warrior starts up perkily from apparent defeat:

> All vnawares he started vp anon,
> As one that had out of a dreame bene reard,
> And fresh assayld his foe, who halfe affeard
> Of th'vncouth sight, as he some ghost had seene,
> Stood still amaz'd, holding his idle sweard;
> Till hauing often by him stricken beene,
> He forced was to strike, and saue him selfe from teene. (IV.iii.31)

Both readers and combatants are caught in a poetic feedback loop of astonishing events. Christopher Burlinson and Andrew Zurcher have commented on 'the conspicuously funny element of much of Spenser's violence' in *The Faerie Queene* in relation to what he experienced at first hand in Ireland.[96] And indeed there is a cartoon quality to both the dead-but-not Triamond starting back to life and Cambell being so amazed by

94 Anderson, 'Cambell, Canacee, Cambina', 130. See Berry's related worries in "Sundrie Doubts" about the way in which both Chaucer and Spenser fail to address the question of Cambell's potentially incestuous love for Canacee: 'Jousting for the love of a lady is a common enough romance occurrence, but in what sense can Cambalo fight and "wynne" his sister Canacee? Spenser chooses not to deal with incest directly here, but he does create a situation in which the love between brother and sister is in tension with Canacee's status as a romantic object' (118).
95 Brown and Lethbridge, *A Concordance*, 431, for the top ten rhymes.
96 In Spenser, *Selected Letters and Other Papers*, lx.

this that it takes him some time to realise that he is under assault again. In this context, obtrusive interstanzaic rhyming serves to emphasise disquiet and unfamiliarity as preludes to the amity which these characters ultimately symbolise. Such readerly suspension is connected with Viktor Shklovsky's concept of *enstrangement*; in Shklovsky's terms, this is 'an artifact which has been intentionally removed from the domain of automatized perception'.[97] A less sympathetic reading might be that Spenser desperately tries to inject some excitement into yet another battle scene which doesn't fully engage his imagination,[98] yet the evident care with which he continues and develops this Chaucerian narrative tells against such a reading. The 'lookers on', including the reader, who believed Triamond to be dead are treated to a Zombie revival which – rather than crudely stretching – artfully extends our credulity.

Wonderment is, of course, a striking component of 'The Squire's Tale', where both characters and narrator are repeatedly astonished by extraordinary events and objects. Consider the mechanical horse: 'euermore her moste wonder was/Howe that it couthe gon/ and was of bras'.[99] Indeed, the narrator's repeated topoi of rhetorical incapacity are part of what makes the fragment so enigmatic: to what extent is the narrator to be believed, and to what extent is Chaucer playing an elaborate game with the limits of what is credible?[100] Certainly, Spenser's continuation is radically unlike the parent tale in terms of mode of narration, despite the connections in terms of plot and some details of imagery.[101] Spenser is, I suggest, less interested than Chaucer in destabilising his narrator, and the artful linkages of overlapping rhymes rather suggest that he took the tropes of wonderment in Chaucer and developed them without the patina of irony which is so characteristic of *The Canterbury Tales*; again, Spenser rewrites Chaucer in such a way as to correct aspects of his style and idiom which may have been seen as unachieved or poetically incomplete.[102] In this context, it's

---

97 Shklovsky, *Theory of Prose*, 12.
98 Compare Wilson-Okamura's exploration of *The Faerie Queene*'s failure to deliver on its promises of epic warfare; in *Spenser's International Style*, 184–93.
99 Chaucer, *The Works*, sig. G6r; *The Riverside Chaucer*, 171 (ll.199–200).
100 See ll.31–41, 67–75, 105–09, 245–46 and 341–42 in *The Riverside Chaucer*, 169–73. On the ambiguity of the narrator, see Berry, '"Sundrie Doubts"', 110–23, and *The Riverside Chaucer*, 890–91, for an overview.
101 The big cat imagery of stanzas 16 and 39 has clear precedents in 'The Squire's Tale', ll.419–22 ('ther nys tygre, ne noon crueel beest') and 543–44, in *The Riverside Chaucer*, 174–75.
102 For the sense of poetic shortfall in 'The Squire's Tale', see Thynne's editorial comment at the end of the tale: 'There can be founde no more of this fore said tale/ which hath ben sought i[n] dyvers places', in Chaucer, *The Works*, sig. H2v.

noteworthy that one of the narrator's more brusque gestures of narratorial ignorance – 'The horse vanysshed/ I not in what manere/Out of her syght/ ye get no more of me' – is an unrhymed couplet, where syntax plays against and minimises the normative structure of the couplet form, diminishing the effect of the enveloping rhymes.[103]

Stanzas 31 and 33 demonstrate that Chaucer's diction is never far from the surface. Spenser's tropes of renewal point back to his miraculous recovery of Chaucer's lost tale 'through infusion sweete/Of thine owne spirit' (IV.ii.34), and the Chaucerian idiom is prominent in these interlaced rhymes. Cambell's *sweard* in stanzas 31 and 33 is a strikingly Chaucerian property, reminiscent of the knight's 'naked swerde' in 'The Squire's Tale'.[104] These are the only rhymes on *sweard*, indeed, these are the only instances of the word in the poem. Spenser's usual term is the modern English *sword*.[105] Chaucer always uses *swerd*, so here the signifier is an archaistic hallmark, similar to the parody of the opening line of 'The Knight's Tale' at the start of the episode, 'Whylome as antique stories tellen vs' (IV. ii.32.1).[106] 'Reaching forth his sweard' like Cambell, Spenser marks his verse with an indelibly Chaucerian patina which wittily reinforces the gestures of recovery with which the episode began (IV.iii.33).

It should be clear that Spenser's rhyming strategies are profoundly Chaucerian. Despite the decorous obeisance of the 'June' eclogue, Spenser's relationship to 'The God of Shepheards' is characterised by the critical adoption of devices like *rime riche*, the bringing in line of Chaucer's scansion with later linguistic custom, and the stringent, potentially obsessive, development interstanzaic devices. Re-reading the fight between Cambell and the Brothers 'Mond, what we encounter is, rather than stanzaic leak and spill, flow and process within an episode through rhyming repetition between discrete stanzas. As I have implied, such rhymes are almost always more than verbal ornaments – for both Chaucer and Spenser, the formal

---

103 Chaucer, *The Works*, sig. G6v; *The Riverside Chaucer*, 173 (ll.342–43). Punctuation is significantly more minimal in Thynne's edition than in the *Riverside*, which decisively punctuates the passage so as to emphasise syntax over couplet form: '... kept among his jueles leeve and deere./The hors vanysshed, I noot in what manere,/Out of hir sighte; ye get namoore of me./But thus I lete in joye and jolitee ...'.

104 Chaucer, *The Works*, G5v; *The Riverside Chaucer*, 170 (l.84).

105 Brown and Lethbridge, *A Concordance*, 417, 427, 450. *Sword* is used as a rhyme 11 times.

106 For Chaucer's *swerd*, see the Machias Concordance and Norman Davis, Douglas Gray, Patricia Ingham and Anne Wallace-Hadrill (eds), *A Chaucer Glossary*, 148. See Berry, '"Sundrie Doubts"', 116, for the suggestion that Spenser's replacement of 'antique' for Chaucer's 'olde' filters the Chaucerian text to a sixteenth-century readership.

pattern has values of its own which are above and beyond compliance with the schema.

Revoke the forward foot: rhyme and turning back

One of the more obvious, yet least discussed, facets of rhyme is that it is a form which invites turning back; it is what Ricks calls 'a form of talking back and forth', and it may seem to be, in the psychological terms proffered by T. V. F. Brogan, 'the object of displaced fixation in consciousness which frees the subconscious mind for more creative wordcraft'.[107] Rhymed verse is less teleologically driven – less committed to the textual finishing line – than prose or unrhymed verse, where the onward progress to the paragraph break, the chapter end, the last full stop, maybe harder to resist.[108] As the reader notices the chime of the rhyme being satisfied, so her progress through the text is temporarily and pleasurably suspended, as the eye momentarily tracks back to check the structure and to enjoy the satisfaction of the formal relationship. Consider a contemporary example of this principle. Paul Muldoon's 'Dirty Data', from the *One Thousand Things Worth Knowing* collection (2015), is a long poem split up into nineteen unnumbered 'sonnets'.[109] While individual 'sonnets' follow a standard Petrarchan rhyme scheme (*Ababcdcdefgefg*), the first rhyme of each line of each sestet – the e-rhyme – provides the second rhyme of each succeeding 'sonnet' – the b-rhyme. In this schema, the orphan b- and e-rhymes of the final 'sonnet' (*line: swine; turpentine: dine*) revert to the b- and e-rhymes of the first one (*design: spine; pine: intertwine*), again underlining the tendency of rhymed texts to circularity as much as conclusion.[110] To borrow

107 Christopher Ricks, *Dylan's Visions of Sin*, 42, discussing Dylan's 'You're Gonna Make Me Lonesome When You Go', which this formulation paraphrases; T. V. F. Brogan, 'Rhyme', 1060.
108 This is not to suggest that the reader of prose or unrhymed verse does not track back, or reads in one direction only. The point is rather that it is an intrinsic condition of rhymed verse to make the reader return to the initiating rhyme.
109 Paul Muldoon, *One Thousand Things Worth Knowing*, 99–117. I use the term 'sonnets' since 'Dirty Data' both is and isn't a sonnet sequence: on the one hand, it may be described as a poem made up of 19 unnumbered sonnets; on the other hand, it may be equally well described as a poem of 266 lines which is printed with 14 lines per page. My own experience is that once you notice the sonnet structure, you read the poem as a sequence of sonnets, which makes the interlacing rhymes – with their insistence on the connections between the otherwise discrete sections – all the more challenging and rewarding. Like Spenser, Muldoon is a poet who demands readers as formally aware as he is.
110 Muldoon, *One Thousand Things Worth Knowing*, 117, 99.

Muldoon's terms, the intertwining rhymes constitute a formal spine, a
rhyming design which is at once intricate, delightful, and weirdly appropriate
to the poem's recursive meditation on (amongst others) civil rights in
Northern Ireland, Lew Wallace, his novel *Ben-Hur*, the 1959 movie of the
book, and the death of Churchill. The following extract, from the third
and fourth 'sonnets', shows the principle of rhyming intertwining in action,
as Muldoon's helter-skelter syntax, varying line lengths, and quick-shifting
thought-associations are held in check by the firming order of the overlapping rhymes. It is because of the free-ranging quality of Muldoon's syntax
that a long passage is needed to illustrate the way the rhymes hold the
text in check:

> Dense, too, the fog when each Halloween Ben ducks in an enamel basin
>
> for an enamel *apple*
> and comes up with a botched job.
> Such is the integrity of their kraal the horses will find no slot
>
> in the funeral cortege of Winston Churchill from the Royal *Chapel*
> to Woodstock. As his carriage passes the dolphins bob
> for a commoner's mere 19- rather than a no-stops-pulled 21-gun salute.
>
> [*page break*]
>
> Along the Thames, meanwhile, even the cranes will bow
> and scrape as the coffin passes the Isle of Dogs and the citizenry will
>   *grapple*
> with their sense of loss. The *Havengore*'s prow
> will no more shake off a water *dapple*
>
> than we'll concede we've been excluded from a race.[111]

The readerly effects of such recursion are readily shown by Muldoon's
fondness for putting feminine rhymes in the e/b position. In this passage,
the *apple: Chapel; grapple: dapple* sequence is so ostentatious that it forces
the reader to 'grapple' with the poem's formal structure as she tries to
make sense of what is happening.[112] At the same time, the structure is
partly concealed by the page break which comes between '21-gun salute'
and 'Along the Thames'; note, too, that page 102 is a verso sheet, so the
reader must flip back and forwards across the page boundary to appreciate

---

111 Muldoon, *One Thousand Things Worth Knowing*, 101–02, my emphases highlight the
      e- and b-rhymes. I have added an in-text note of where the page break occurs.
112 See note 109 above: if you read without heeding the form, rhymes like *grapple: dapple*
      throw you back to the page you have just turned over, as they forcefully echo *apple:
      Chapel*.

the structure at work. Later, over three apparently separate 'sonnets', Muldoon rhymes on *swivel: drivel; Divil's: privi-; snivel: frivols;* and at last *shrivel: civil*, as well as (at the start of a line) 'The *pivotal* point of Bloody Sunday …'.[113] This is almost the pivotal point of 'Dirty Data', as the eleventh 'sonnet', and the rhymes prod the reader into pivoting backwards and forwards from the 'Barret semiautomatic' which is 'seen to swivel' on page 108 to the 'attempt to cut down all that civil//rights stuff' on page 110. Muldoon's work is playfully rhyme-driven – even or especially as the subject matter he deals with is historically and politically dense and problematic – and, like Spenser, he expects readers who are willing to read backwards as well as forwards.

The extent to which *The Faerie Queene* is teleologically determined is a well-established topic. In 1976 James Nohrnberg made a useful distinction between commentaries which follow 'the path of the physical traveler, who assumes that because he is always facing forward he must also always be traveling in the same direction', and the transit of the 'the mental traveler, who at some point parts company with his fellow to see the poem coming back against itself'.[114] This retrogressive motion is at its clearest in relation to recurring and related echoic pattern of rhyme. The Spenserian poetic unit is calibrated to emphasise the tension between moving forwards both in the local context of the individual stanza and in the larger context of the episode, and the epic, as a whole. I turn now to rhymes which express movement backwards to enable further reflection on rhyme as a trope of 'displaced fixation'.[115] These examples are intended to afford an opportunity to debate the relationship between sound and sense. Are these rhymes decorative forms which might be substituted with pliant synonyms which still fulfil the rhyme scheme, or do they communicate something of the wider importance to the poetic matter in hand? What is the value of, and the aesthetic claim of, the poetic surface as we read *The Faerie Queene*? As discussions by Heather James, Leah Whittington and others indicate, Spenser's decorative surfaces remain in crucial ways enigmatic and debatable. Whittington searches for 'ways not to rush past the encounter with a text, but to allow it to open into a period of sustained attention, to wallow and get lost in a rigorous way such that conscious absorption becomes a mental discipline full of texture and

---

113 Muldoon, *One Thousand Things Worth Knowing*, 108–10, quoting 109; my emphasis. *Pivotal* is at best a half-rhyme, but Muldoon's practice is – as throughout his work – freewheeling and permissive.

114 James C. Nohrnberg, *The Analogy of The Faerie Queene*, xi.

115 Brogan, 'Rhyme', 1060.

shades of awareness.'[116] I suggest that the interrogation of key rhymes is one way to achieve such nuanced awareness – one which is both sensuously in touch with the surface of the text and rigorously alert to its affective possibilities.

Any attentive reading is conscious of the way in which large portions of *The Faerie Queene* are made up of variation with difference. Though I am sceptical about Lethbridge's claim that Spenser countenanced 'a certain amount of deliberate and systematic automation', there are moments where this seems like a reasonable characterisation.[117] Consider two stanzas from III.xi, the C-rhymes of which describe cognate activities:

> There they dismounting, drew their weapons bold
>   And stoutly came vnto the Castle gate;
>   Whereas no gate they found, them to withhold,
>   Nor ward to wait at morne and euening late,
>   But in the Porch, that did them sore amate,
>   A flaming fire, ymixt with smouldry smoke,
>   And stinking Sulphure, that with griesly hate
>   And dreadfull horrour did all entraunce choke,
> Enforced them their forward footing to reuoke. …
>
> Therewith resolu'd to proue her vtmost might,
>   Her ample shield she threw before her face,
>   And her swords point directing forward right,
>   Assayld the flame, the which eftsoones gaue place,
>   And did it selfe diuide with equall space,
>   That through she passed; as a thunder bolt
>   Perceth the yielding ayre, and doth displace
>   The soring clouds into sad showres ymolt;
> So to her yold the flames, and did their force reuolt. (III.xi.21, 25).

The C-rhyme clusters are closely linked phonetically and semantically. In stanza 19, the C-rhyme describes the fire which guards the House of Busirane; in stanza 25, the same rhyme position shows Britomart surmounting the barrier and forcing the flames back. The two clusters assonate – *smoke: choke: reuoke* anticipates *bolt: ymolt: reuolt* – and each cluster takes the same grammatical form of noun: verb: verb. From Lethbridge's point of view, this is perhaps a good illustration of poetic 'automation': Spenser needs to describe roughly the same sort of action in two proximate stanzas, so that the second cluster is a variation on the terms of the first. In each

116 Leah Whittington, 'Wallowing and Getting Lost: Reading Spenser with Heather James'.
117 Lethbridge, 'The Bondage of Rhyme' in Brown and Lethbridge, *A Concordance*, 134.

case, the final verbs have cognate meanings: in 19, it is Britomart and Scudamour who have to turn back their footing because of the fire, in 25, Britomart forces the fire to turn back in its turn. Arguably, 'reuolt' is simply a rhyming synonym for 'reuoke', which demonstrates the pressure on the poet to come up with new rhymes as occasion demands.[118] The fact that this is the only rhyme on 'reuolt', and its only occurrence in the poem, suggests the term's value is primarily synonymic:[119] in Lethbridge's model, Spenser would probably have used 'reuoke', had he been able to make it rhyme with 'bolt' and 'ymolt'

I remain resistant to this view because it minimises the poetic force of variation with difference in rhyme, and because in this fictional context it plays down the possibility that the parallel gestures of advancing and being turned back may themselves return (and re-turn) us to broader questions of interpretation. The point can be expanded in relation to the character of Britomart and her symbolic function in Book III. Judith Anderson's observation that Britomart '*makes* metaphor instead of merely being its embodiment' is pertinent.[120] Although the gesture of knights being turned back – revoked through superior force – is familiar from two earlier episodes, what happens outside the House of Busirane is different in terms of the obstacle faced by Britomart and Scudamour and the narrative context.[121] Stanzas 21 and 25 follow a long passage (III.xi.7–20) in which forward momentum is stayed as Britomart tries to raise the prone Scudamour from 'the grownd' on which he is 'groueling' (III.xi.8). Anticipating the fictional setting of *Daphnaïda* (1591), in which the poet-narrator tries to comfort the grief-stricken Alcyon, this canto dramatises some of the impatience which is perhaps supressed from the mourning decorum of the complaint written for Arthur Gorges.[122] Though Britomart sympathises

118 See "revoke, v.6" citing II.viii.39c ('forst his foot reuoke'), and "revolt, v.5", citing this passage, in *OED Online*. OED identifies both usages as obsolete.
119 Brown and Lethbridge, *A Concordance*, 303, 437.
120 Judith H. Anderson, 'Britomart', 114. See also her earlier discussion in *The Growth of a Personal Voice*, 98–103, 'Although Britomart is a figure in an allegorical romance and clearly has metaphorical dimensions, she too is made to appear less simply a metaphor and more simply herself' (100). On both occasions, Anderson's focus is on the early cantos of Book III, but the observation holds good for Britomart's role throughout the poem.
121 See I.i.12b, where Una and Recrosse discuss the dangers of entering Error's cave ('shame were to reuoke/The forward footing for an hidden shade'), and II.viii.39c, where Arthur repulses Cymochles ('twise him forst his foot reuoke'). See Kenneth Gross, *Spenserian Poetics*, 157–60, who reads the present episode in terms of the negotiation of thresholds.
122 For the prostrated Alycon, see *Daphnaïda*, ll.185 ('fell to ground for great extreamitie') and 543 ('As if againe he would have fallen to ground'). Miller, 'Laughing at Spenser's *Daphnaida*', uncovers some of the potentially subversive notes in the complaint, while

with Scudamour, from the outset of their encounter, her 'pitty' and her 'patience' are in tension:

> Still as she stood, she heard with grieuous throb
> Him grone, as if his hart were peeces made,
> And with most painefull pangs to sigh and sob,
> That pitty did the Virgins hart of patience rob. (III.xi.8)

At one level, Britomart becomes impatient not so much with Scudamour, but with the social convention which dictates she shouldn't disturb him ('the braue Mayd would not for courtesy,/Out of his quiet slomber him abrade'), yet this distinction becomes harder to maintain as the episode develops. Scudamour repeatedly droops, whilst Britomart continually tries to raise him up. Unlike *Daphnaïda*, this narrative is amenable to a kind of ironic tolerance in its handling of both protagonists, as Britomart's optimism ('Perhaps this hand may helpe to ease your woe'; III.xi.15) abrades against Scudamour's defeatism ('What boots it plaine, that cannot be redrest'; III.xi.16–17).[123] In a sense, the first part of the canto turns on the ethics of turning back versus giving up, which suggests in turn that the rhyming clusters in stanzas 21 and 25 are neither purely synonymic nor purely ornamental. The contrast between the two clusters is thus semantically telling: where in 21, Busirane's magic leads to defeat and Scudamour's despair (see stanzas 22–24), in 25, Britomart's crossing the flame anticipates her ultimate triumph over Busirane.

In my reading, 'reuolt' is a significant variation through which Spenser stresses Britomart's role as a maker, or in context an undoer, of metaphor, who will undermine the force of Busirane's enchantment. As Kenneth Gross notes, 'reuolt' raises transgressive mythological echoes; the simile implicitly aligns Britomart with Zeus, while her earlier allusion to the Titans ('the Earthes children', III.xi.22) ironically jars with the way in which she crosses the threshold 'as a thonder bolt': 'While the absence of the likely divine name seems to demythologize the lightning figure, that name's phantom possibility still resonates within it and heightens the more than natural imagery of violent transgression.'[124] If 'reuolt' were no

---

Jonathan Gibson, 'The Legal Context of Spenser's *Daphnaïda*', explores its complex relationship with Gorges. *Daphnaïda* is of course a rewriting of Chaucer's *Book of the Duchess*; see for example Duncan Harris and Nancy L. Steffen, 'The Other Side of the Garden'.

123 See Anderson's comments on the freedom of humour which Britomart gives Spenser, in 'Britomart', 114; see also Gross, *Spenserian Poetics*, 160, for a discussion of the episode in terms of 'the comedy of [Scudamour's] narcissistic pride'.

124 Gross, *Spenserian Poetics*, 159.

more than a synonym, this would hardly be the case, while 'reuoke' does not carry such transgressive associations.[125] Spenser's synonymic variations for rhyme may thus profitably be read in terms of his broader allegorical poetics.

Related choices of diction which impinge on rhyme in this passage are singular enough to merit comment. When Scudamour describes Busirane's torture of Amoret, he uses the strong preterite of 'yield' to describe her devotion to him: 'to yield to him loue she doth deny,/Once to me yold, not to be yolde againe' (III.xi.17). Spenser's usual form is 'yielded', used seven times in the poem as a whole, whereas 'yold[e]' occurs on four occasions, three of which are in this episode.[126] Scudamour's line catches the edginess between amorous devotion and bragging machismo which many critics have seen in him; as Lesley Brill puts it, 'He stands both as Amoret's fulfillment and her affliction.'[127] The use of 'yold' in the final line of stanza 25 suggests the difference between Britomart and Scudamour: 'So to her *yold* the flames, and did their force re*uolt*'.[128] Again, Spenser's rhymes imply moral and psychological discriminations between his characters. Where Scudamour boasts of Amoret's yielding, Britomart melts the fire's resistance and undoes its power to hurt. And where Scudamour is repeatedly unable to pass the fire, because of his 'greedy will and enuious desire' (III.xii.26), Britomart is by virtue of her sex and innocence able to 'make [her] progresse' into the House of Busirane (III.xi.20).[129] Moreover, the close assonance and alliteration between *yold* and *reuolt* – an effect which would have been blunted had the line read 'So to her yold the flames, and did their force reuoke' – argues for the deliberation of Spenser's choice of rhymes in this passage. While I remain agnostic about whether such inlaying of related terms makes *The Faerie Queene* into a kind of endlessly attenuated lyric, it seems clear that the rhymes here are at once decorative and semantic.[130]

125 See "revoke, v." *OED Online*.
126 Brown and Lethbridge, *A Concordance*, 423. See also Sugden, *The Grammar of Spenser's Faerie Queene*, 97. The other 'yold' is in The Mutabilitie Cantos, and is the last term of a C-rhyme cluster: 'To reape the ripened fruits the which the earth had yold' (VII. vii.30). This emphasizes the singularity of 'yold' in III.xi in the editions published during Spenser's lifetime.
127 Brill, 'Scudamour', 635. See also David Lee Miller, *The Poem's Two Bodies*, 283.
128 My emphases.
129 For Britomart's innocence, see Anderson, 'Britomart', 114.
130 See Wilson-Okamura, *Spenser's International Style*, 70–139, for a brilliant discussion of the stylistic contexts of *The Faerie Queene*'s lyrical, or 'flowery', features.

Rhyme as a trope of recurrence inevitably brings with it the broader question of how episodes (and books and poems) close. For Spenser, as the writer of an incomplete epic which seldom decisively seals off its episodes, this remains a question which further raises the relationship between form and content. The different endings of Book III in the 1590 and 1596 editions are a touching yet notoriously problematic instance of this, which in turn enable some reflection on the broader phenomenon of rhyme in *The Faerie Queene*. What is the reader to make of the gulf between the 1590 ending, in which the reunited Scudamour and Amoret are compared to the statue of the Hermaphrodite (III.xii.43–47, 1590), and the revised 1596 ending, which postpones that reunion outside of the poem as we have it? Influential commentary has drawn attention to the extraordinary hermeneutic difficulties of the original ending. For Harry Berger, 'The happy ending … does not solve the problems posed by Busirane; it gets rid of them by sweeping them under the rug'; similarly, David Lee Miller emphasises the problematics of the Hermaphrodite simile, which 'offers a distraction of the kind to which the lovers are momentarily immune, and the fact that no one knows what "rich Romane" Spenser is talking about only heightens the distraction.'[131] The 1590 ending is certainly beautiful, but is its image of the 'sweet countervayle' – another striking one-off rhyme – between Scudamour and Amoret fully convincing (III.xii.47, 1590)?[132] The 1596 ending is less heightened, less resonant, less often discussed. Where 1590 offers extraordinary richness of imagery and suggestion, the new ending is curtailed and seemingly deliberately edited down.[133] In place of the seven langourous lines of pastoral which evoke the poet's weariness with his 'iournall toyle' in 1590, 1596 allows the poet-narrator just one out-of-breath hemistich. And by prolonging the isolation of Scudamour from Amoret, Spenser recurs to the flat, *Daphnaïda*-like[134]

131 Harry Berger Jr, 'Busirane and the War between the Sexes', in *Revisionary Play*, 193; Miller, *The Poem's Two Bodies*, 285. See also Gross's brilliant discussion of the iconoclasm of the erasure of the 1590 ending: 'Difficult as the stanzas are in themselves … we must also try to make sense of their cancellation from the six-book version of the poem in 1596', in *Spenserian Poetics*, 171–74 (173).
132 See Brown and Lethbridge, *A Concordance*, 215, 467. There are rhymes on *counteruaile* (VII.vi.49b) and *counteruayld* (II.vi.29b). The use of the term is however semantically distinct in Book III, where it has the sense of 'reciprocation' rather than 'resisted'; see Hamilton's notes in *FQ*, 208, 406, and "countervail, v." *OED Online*, particularly 2.b and 3.a. In effect, 'sweet counteruayle' is an adjectival noun constructed from this verb.
133 See Gross, *Spenserian Poetics*, 173–74.
134 'Sad' is something of a signature adjective in *Daphnaïda*, used on eight occasions, and usually describing 'sad *Alycon*' (ll.6, 525); compare with Scudamore as 'sad man' above, and III.xi.18.

misery of Scudamour's exclusion from the House of Busirane in the previous canto:

> But he sad man, when he had long in drede
>   Awayted there for *Britomarts* returne,
>   Yet saw her not nor signe of her good speed,
>   His expectation to despaire did turne,
>   Misdeeming sure that her those flames did burne;
>   And therefore gan aduize with her old Squire,
>   Who her deare nourslings losse no lesse did mourne,
>   Thence to depart for further aide t'enquire:
> Where let them wend at will, whilest here I doe respire. (III.xii.45, 1596)

Nothing is concluded with this sign-off: the 'returne' is postponed indefinitely, expectation retreats 'to despaire'; the B-rhyme resolves almost remorselessly from the possibility of a return to the shared but dissimilar mourning of that oddest of odd couples, Scudamour and Glauce. As I noted at the beginning of this chapter, William Scott's *Model of Poesy* enthusiastically characterises rhyme as a device of 'proportionable return' within elaborate stanza forms.[135] In the context of this stanza as a substitute for the 1590 ending, the 1596 text is perhaps not so much an act of 'literal iconoclasm' than a more characteristic gesture of deferral and movement in process.[136] The reader, like Scudamour, must indefinitely await 'for *Britomarts* returne', while the poet more briefly 'respire[s]' in the gap between the two instalments, where Book IV waits over the page (or in the next volume) rather than as a promise the poet has yet to deliver on. Spenserian rhyme is, in this view, a form of sonal and semantic deferral, which is always in the process of pausing for breath, and awaiting the 'returne' of fresh incidents, characters, and rhymes.

This chapter has tried to capture something of the complexity in which Spenser uses rhyme as a trope of recurrence. Through Book III Canto iii, I have shown the ways in which Spenser flaunts and capitalises on morphological distortion in the construction of his poem: the very oddness of *The Faerie Queene*'s rhyming idiom is made in this episode to underline the transgressive and enstranging cast of Merlin's prophecy. I have then turned to the ways in which Spenser adopts and adapts the idiom of Chaucer, stressing the way in which his rewriting of 'The Squire's Tale' in Book IV is a critical updating of Chaucer's practices, and an almost

135 Scott, *The Model of Poesy*, 63.
136 Gross, *Spenserian Poetics*, 173.

obsessional development of some of the devices he found in *Troilus and Criseyde*. Finally, I have concentrated on a few rhymes at the climax of Book III to shed light on the ways in which Spenser uses rhyme as a non-linear device, which suggests both the inevitable return of narratives and characters, alongside the perhaps disturbing, unresolved circularity of those events and motifs. Running throughout these sections has been implicitly the relationship between rhymes and stanzas, so it is now appropriate to turn to the broader question of how rhymes work within the conceptual 'grid' of that most specialist of poetic forms, the Spenserian stanza.

4

Unusual staff: the archaeology of the Spenserian stanza

In the early 1590s, Henry Gurney, an amateur poet and Norfolk farmer, sat down to read a borrowed copy of *The Faerie Queene*. Though he didn't get very far, he was sufficiently underwhelmed to record why he disliked the poem. His disappointment was rooted in its forms:

> ould outworne wordes, this aucthor does observe
> And vsuall staff, or measure, doth reiect
> if praise or blame, therfor he do deserve
> I cannot Iudge, although I may suspect
>   that when a woorke is strang & new devised
>   the aucthor is Invyed, or dispised[1]

Gurney is an important example of the effect Spenser's poem had on some readers during the 1590s, not because he is an original critic, but rather because his objections surface the group-think which surrounded *The Faerie Queene*, and which is more shrewdly observed in Everard Guilpin's 'Satire VI'.[2] In Gurney's view, archaism goes hand in hand with Spenser's choice of an '[un]vsuall staff'[3] – the innovation of the nine-line form. In a prose comment, he makes this disdain explicit, noting that the Spenserian stanza bears 'great fame, but not in my Iudgement'.[4] As Steven May explains,

---

1 Steven W. May, 'Henry Gurney', 183–223 (191); Gurney's manuscript is Bodleian Tanner MS. 175; see May, 'Henry Gurney', 184–85, for a full description.
2 Guilpin, *Skialetheia*, 89–90. See Chapter 1 above.
3 'Staff' is the habitual Elizabethan term for stanza; see Puttenham, *The Art of English Poesy*, 155, and Whigham and Rebhorn's notes in ibid., 154, 447. See also "staff, n.1, 19.b" *OED Online*. Oxford University Press, June 2016.
4 May, 'Henry Gurney', 191.

Gurney's ideas about poetry were conservative and utilitarian: in decasyllabic lines he insisted on the 4/6 pattern, disliked assonantal rhymes, and showed a consistent preference for clarity of structure and content; in his own words, 'A Perfect verse much matter must containe/fit woordes & knowne, none forced nor in vayne'.[5] His views on literary form thus mirror those of Gascoigne and Puttenham. Gurney's critical dismay is nicely registered in this text, as it uses the *Ababcc* sixain, one of the most widely used forms in the later sixteenth century, and follows his strictures about line and rhyme form. The implication is clear: had Spenser chosen a more conventional stanza form, such as the sixain itself or rhyme royal, then Gurney would have found the poem less 'strang & new devised'.[6] Gurney responds to the Spenserian in the same way that conservative listeners responded to synthesisers in later twentieth-century popular music: as a new, controversial technology, which adversely affected music.[7]

My argument in this chapter is that during the 1590s the Spenserian stanza was a new and controversial poetic technology, which both transformed how poets wrote and provided them with a template against which they could react. The analogy with synthesisers is again pertinent: even if you didn't approve of them, during the 1970s and 1980s, it was imperative for musicians and journalists (and so their audiences) to have a view on them, so that reaction to this technology was constitutive both of the music which depended on it and the music which reacted against it.[8] Any new technology comes from somewhere, and it's the same with the Spenserian stanza. Yet discussion of the sources of the Spenserian has been fitful in the last fifty years, almost as though this is no longer a question which matters. This is an oversight, since Spenser lived and worked in a literary culture which was – as Gurney shows – sophisticated in its use and reading of stanzaic verse. To state the point bluntly: the stanzas of *The Faerie Queene* are central to the impact the poem makes on its readers. My argument is that the stanza should be read in the contexts of its construction to appreciate the complex amalgam of influences and ambitions which are layered into this structure. The bulk of this chapter therefore considers the chief competitors to the Spenserian – the

5 May, 'Henry Gurney', 193–97 (196).
6 See May, 'Henry Gurney', 194, for his reading of Blenerhasset and his praise of *The Mirror for Magistrates*, in which rhyme royal is extensively used.
7 See for example Simon Reynolds, *Rip It Up and Start Again*, 400, for contemporary debates around the pros and cons of synthesisers.
8 The Musicians' Union in the UK contemplated a boycott of synthesisers in 1982 because of fears of the impact they would have on string players' incomes; see www.muhistory.com/contact-us/1971–1980/ [accessed 5 September 2016].

sixain, rhyme royal, and *ottava rima* – to understand what was new about Spenser's stanza. By extension, as a hybrid form devised for the purpose of writing a national epic, the Spenserian demands a quasi-archaeological approach to uncover its sources. It is not simply a new version of existing forms but is, rather, a synthesis of radically disparate impulses and motifs which enables new ways of writing, which in themselves embody new ways of thinking and feeling in writing. The Spenserian changes subsequent poetry, not just in the sense that it provides the stimulus for imitative or parodic texts like Giles Fletcher's *Christ's Victorie, and Triumph*, Donne's *Metempsychosis*, or Ralph Knevet's *A Supplement of the Faery Queene*,[9] but in the broader way in which it contributes to what David Scott Wilson-Okamura has described as 'period style'.[10] As a controversial, widely debated and imitated innovation, the Spenserian stamps its mark on English poetry as surely as the bleeps and blirts of the Moog and pastel washes of the Mellotron reshaped popular music in the later twentieth century.

New forces to learn: reading Una and Redcrosse

How far is not very far? Conceivably, it was writing like the first description of Una which helped to shape Gurney's negative impression of *The Faerie Queene*. We do know that he read this, because he copied the first five stanzas into his manuscript book:

> A louely Ladie rode him faire beside,
>> Vpon a lowly Asse more white then snow,
>> Yet she much whiter, but the same did hide
>> Vnder a vele, that wimpled was full low,
>> And ouer all a blacke stole she did throw,
>> As one that inly mournd: so was she sad,
>> And heauie sate vpon her palfrey slow:
>> Seemed in heart some hidden care she had,
> And by her in a line a milkewhite lambe she lad. (I.i.4)[11]

Failures to enjoy are important because they can tell us much about the mentalities of readers. Gurney's earnest copying out of these opening stanzas alongside his notes in prose and verse show a reader bemused by

---

9 For Fletcher, see William B. Hunter, Jr (ed.), *The English Spenserians*, 8–108; Ralph Knevet, *A Supplement of the Faery Queene*, ed. Christopher Burlinson and Andrew Zurcher.

10 Wilson-Okamura, *Spenser's International Style*, 8–11.

11 May, 'Henry Gurney', 190–91. As well as these stanzas, Gurney also transcribed the first eight dedicatory sonnets and some of the commendatory poems, 191–92.

modernity. From the point of view of the professional Spenserian, I.i.4
marks an important change in pace and tone from the apprentice hero
sketched in the first three stanzas. It introduces a second character, distinctly
different from the Red Crosse Knight. Where Redcrosse manfully subdues
his 'angry steede', Una sits heavily 'vpon her palfrey slow'; where Redcrosse
is bound 'To prove his puissance in battle braue' against the dragon, Una
is enigmatically still, 'sad', mournful.[12] And where the hero is coloured by
the 'bloodie Crosse' – 'The deare remembrance of his dying Lord' – Una
is monochrome. Whiter than her 'lowly Asse more white then snow', her
colour is relieved only by her spondaic 'blacke stole' (I.i.1–3). She rides,
but slowly; she's veiled, but seems tantalisingly on the verges of legibility,
as though the reader can infer mood and demeanour from her pace and
clothing. This is a poetry which responds well to the story of Alexander
Pope reading a canto of Spenser to an old lady who 'said that I had been
showing her a collection of pictures', an observation which might open
up the question of Spenser's use of pictorialism and ecphrasis.[13] Yet it is
a stanza form which is in crucial ways permissive and not as syntactically
disciplined or predictable as the writing Gurney preferred. Caesurae are
unfixed or absent: the 4/6 pattern is strongly felt only in the fourth line;
syntax is accretive and decorative as the object of the writing is significant
chiefly for its layered enigmas. When Gurney began to read 'A louely
Ladie rode him faire beside', he probably expected to have that lady more
defined by the end of the stanza, yet what in fact happens is that the
description – assisted by the rhyme scheme and the strategically vague
approach to caesurae – contributes to an impression of not clarifying Una.

The description, and the stanza, is indeed pervasively and self-consciously
allegorical. We go back to it because it communicates much of what will
be of the first importance to making sense of the symbolic schema which
underpins Book I. Kathryn Walls's book-length study of Una devotes four
pages to the stanza, focusing with gathering frustration on the way in
which it reveals – or more precisely *fails* to reveal – Una to the reader:

> hidden as she is by a black stole covering a long (and, presumably, white)
> veil, Una is (as a number of commentators have remarked) emblematic of
> allegory itself … In his commentary on Una's appearance the poet-narrator
> is nearly as muffled as Una herself. First, he points to a possible but uncertain

12 Although Una's sadness is anticipated, and possibly triggered by, Redcrosse's being 'too
    solemne sad' (I.i.2); see further below.
13 Pope in Alpers (ed.), *Edmund Spenser: A Critical Anthology*, 96. On pictorialism, see
    John B. Bender, *Spenser and Literary Pictorialism*.

correspondence between Una's black stole and her evident (but unconfirmed) sadness … He then attributes her sadness *per se* – once again without any certainty – to 'some hidden care'. His vagueness seems particularly studied in the light of the information he goes on to supply in the following stanza, which is that Una's royal parents have been expelled from their estate by an 'infernal feend'.[14]

Walls's interrogation – nicely caught by the parentheses noting what the reader may infer but not conclude – of the narrator's evasive description prepares the ground for the critical account she presents of Una as a morally flawed heroine. It is Walls's argument which ultimately generates her desire to unmuffle Una, to make the text disclose more of the mysterious figure 'hidden'-and-disclosed in this stanza. And yet – 'as a number of commentators have noted' – it is the condition of this allegorical poetry not to reveal all, particularly in the opening stages of the narration. The narrator does not need at this moment to be any clearer about who or what Una is or may represent. He needs the reader's attention first of all, and he gets it through the provocative yet 'uncertain' details Walls itemises. Like any good thriller writer, Spenser uses suspenseful 'vagueness' to stimulate readerly curiosity.

My interest is on the stanza form as a form of narration: how Spenser tells his story in carefully regulated lines of verse which conform to an exacting stanza form. As we read about the enigmatic Una, we are also in the process of getting used to Spenser's idiosyncratic stanza. If the first-time reader has read sequentially from the opening, this is, including the proem, only the seventh Spenserian stanza s/he has read.[15] I want to get at that sense that this is a new form which designedly keeps, as in the eighth line, some crucial aspects of itself undisclosed, unstated. 'Seemed in heart some hidden care she had' provokes the reader with what s/he doesn't yet know, and with what the poet is not yet willing to unveil.

How, then, should we describe the poetic structure of this stanza, beyond the tabular notation of the *Ababbcbcc* rhyme scheme? This is a deceptively easy question to frame since it assumes that it is possible to read stanzas in isolation, or that a description of one stanza will work for all. As we shall see throughout this chapter, *Faerie Queene* stanzas are almost always experienced relationally to one another in the fictive context of a given episode. While this is true of most stanzaic poems, the combination of

14 Kathryn Walls, *God's Only Daughter*, 6–8.
15 See Kaske, *Spenser and Biblical Poetics*, 3–4 and passim, for a related concern for the hermeneutic processing done by novice readers.

Spenser's syntactic permissiveness, and interstanzaic rhyming, makes it a particularly prominent facet in reading *The Faerie Queene*, conditions which do not obtain in a poem like (say) Churchyard's 'Thomas Wolsey'.[16] I.i.4 is hinged most strongly to I.i.2 in terms of the poetic work being done – both are blazons of the main characters – and in specific twists of rhyme and lexis. I want to compare the organisation of syntax in these two stanzas in the poetic context of the rhyme scheme. This is, however, not a simple task. From a formal point of view, I.i.2 is a simpler piece of narrative than I.i.4, which almost seems to have been written as a test case of Paul Alpers's model of the independent, heavily endstopped Spenserian line, as each new line adds to or modifies what has gone before. It does not exhibit the periodic syntax and antithetical, witty style of (for example) Shakespeare's *Venus and Adonis* and *Lucrece*. However, as a consequence of the theological issues it raises – issues which reverberate throughout the Book – there are hazards in a purely formal analysis of this stanza. Similarly, any theological reading has to engage with its constitutive resistances of grammar:

> And on his brest a bloodie Crosse he bore,
> The deare remembrance of his dying Lord,
> For whose sweete sake that glorious badge he wore,
> And dead as liuing euer him ador'd:
> Vpon his shield the like was also scor'd,
> For soueraine hope, which in his helpe he had:
> Right faithfull true he was in deede and word,
> But of his cheere did seeme too solemne sad;
> Yet nothing did he dread, but euer was ydrad. (I.i.2)

The difficulties of this stanza have been well elucidated by Darryl Gless, who drew attention to the ambiguous pronouns and shifting conjunctions which modify tone and theological meaning unexpectedly. My quotation reproduces the text given in Hamilton's second edition of the poem, following the 1590 *Faerie Queene*, where stanza 2 begins with 'And' – and which was the text transcribed by Henry Gurney. In 1596, 'And' was changed to 'But', a change which may represent Spenser's second thoughts. As Gless notes, the revised reading 'hints that a conflict exists between the simply romantic or earnestly moral activities referred to at the end of stanza 1 and the subject introduced in stanza 2'.[17] That subject is in

---

16   See Chapter 2 for discussion of this poem.
17   Darryl J. Gless, *Interpretation and Theology in Spenser*, 51–52, and 225 n.9. See also Hamilton's note in *FQ*, 31. Either reading can be defended: 1590 allows greater concessive power to the 'Buts' and 'Yets' which follow later in this stanza and in stanza 4. As Gless suggests, 1596 highlights the uncertainties which proliferate within the stanza.

turn made awkward by Spenser's almost prodigal ambiguity of pronoun throughout this stanza. Gless highlights the uncertainties around lines 3–7; line 7 is particularly striking, as 'he' hovers between Redcrosse and Christ. These ambiguities are connected with the complex theologies which underlie the stanza, in particular the Pauline idea that the Christian must 'put on' Christ as a kind of spiritual clothing:

> the uncertain syntax of those lines induces readers to hesitate between interpreting the 'he' in 'Right faithfull true he was' as Red Cross or as 'his dying Lord'. Expectations oriented toward the discovery of theological meaning can realize either of these constructions, and will probably realize both, in rapid alternation. This alternation produces a striking and complex image of the Legend's announced theological subject, 'Of Holinesse', for we 'perceive' that Red Cross' first appearance in the poem represents the doctrinal idea that to be holy is to 'put on' Christ, to exist in grace 'in him'. The enigmatic commingling of pronoun references, that is, enables readers to experience something comparable to a photographic double exposure, a perception that merges Red Cross and his 'dying Lord'.[18]

What at one level looks like a wilful failure to resolve ambiguous pronouns is likened to a new technology of poetic perception, which fuses multiple perspectives in a single stanzaic space which the reader experiences 'in rapid alternation': the blazon of the knight repeatedly evokes 'The deare remembrance of his dying Lord'. The device of straying, ambiguous pronouns is a trick Spenser uses throughout *The Faerie Queene*, most famously in I.ix, where Redcrosse's encounter with Despair enables the reader to realise that the dialogue may also be construed as a monologue, or duologue, as Redcrosse recognises the justness of Despair's accusations.[19] Though the stanza form does not mandate ambiguous pronouns, it is certainly the case that Spenser often exploits such metrically flexible monosyllables to further a sense of enigma or confusion. Despite, or because of, the restrictive grid of its rhyme scheme, the stanza stylistically tends towards multiplicity of perspective and referent, and paradoxically enables a range of contrasting subunits within the nine-line stanza form. Singularity of poetic perspective is in this reckoning unlikely, fugitive; the reader looking for certainty from *The Faerie Queene* is almost foredoomed to frustration.

18 Gless, *Interpretation and Theology in Spenser*, 54; see 45–46, 53 for 'putting on' Christ.
19 See in particular I.ix.41.7, and 48.1, where 'his speach' is similarly permissive. The affective potential of these ambiguities was beautifully brought out in a performance of this passage at the *Spenser, Poetry and Performance* conference held at The Globe Theatre in June 2017, in which, at key moments, the actors playing Redcrosse and Despair spoke these stanzas in unison.

This latter point is well shown by the contrast between I.i.2 and I.i.4. In stanza 2, the floating syntax is partly anchored by stanzaic subunits: the *Abab* quatrain focuses on the 'bloodie Crosse' on the knight's breast, which each succeeding line amplifies. Lines 5–6 – spliced between the B- and C-rhymes – form a second unit explaining how the decoration of the shield follows that on the breast. Lines 7–9 shift from description to moral depiction, and the chancier terrain of inferring the knight's interiority from his appearance. Syntax and line shape still cohere, but what changes is the semantic relationship between lines. 'Right faithfull true he was in deede and word' builds on but is syntactically isolated from line 6, an isolation emphasised by the colon at the end of the latter.[20] Line 8 qualifies all of the stanza up to this point but without a necessary connection to line 7, beyond resolving the pronoun confusion set up by '*he* was in deede and word'.[21] 'But of his cheere did seeme too solemne sad' re-evaluates Redcrosse's appearance with a certain degree of scepticism, which the alexandrine immediately qualifies with a statement which squares uneasily with the poem's opening stanza. If Redcrosse had not wielded 'armes till that time' (I.i.1), the assertion of the alexandrine's second hemistich – 'but euer was ydrad' – seems a peculiar form of wishful thinking, as though the narrator is verbalising what the knight wants to feel about himself rather than an objective condition. Who at this stage in Book I might plausibly dread, or have dreaded, this novice? The contradictory cast of the last three lines is shown by the quick succession of alternating conjunctions: '*But* of his cheere', '*Yet* nothing did he dread, *but* euer'.[22] This is in sharp contrast with the opening six lines of the stanza in the 1590 *Faerie Queene*, where conjunctions are additive and almost Maloryesque, as the blazon manoeuvres between 'Ands' (ll. 1, 4) and 'Fors' (ll.3, 6). This is not to privilege 1590's reading over 1596's, but to suggest the value of the sometimes minute discriminations involved in the choice of conjunctions.[23]

20 This is not to suggest that the punctuation is authorial, but rather that the colon recognises the semantic pause between lines 6 and 7.
21 My emphasis; see Gless, *Interpretation and Theology in Spenser*, 55, noting the theological tension between lines 7 and 8, as the latter 'introduces a hint of insecurity' in relation to Redcrosse's election.
22 My emphases.
23 Unsurprisingly, these conjunctions are extremely common: *and* is the most frequently used word in *The Faerie Queene*, with 10,864 instances, comfortably outscoring *the* in second place (8235). *But* has 2403 instances, while *yet* occurs 989 times. In the light of these statistics, the change to the more discriminatory 'But' seems like the kind of change the writer alone would have made. See Brown and Lethbridge, *A Concordance*, 451, and Judith Anderson, 'What Comes after Chaucer's *But* in *The Faerie Queene*?', 42–53.

If Spenser did make this change, then it is a move towards semantic complexity.

Though I.i.4 follows I.i.2 in being structured as a blazon, the stanzaic organisation offers a significant contrast, pointing at this early stage in the poem to the inherent flexibility of Spenser's form. Although individual lines retain the quality of syntactic independence described by Alpers, this stanza has the first enjambment in the poem proper (between lines 3 and 4),[24] and has semantic units which infringe line boundaries. Initially, phrase units are in couplet form. Lines 1–2 describe Una's appearance, while lines 3–4 complicate that appearance: 'Yet she much whiter, but the same did hide/Vnder a vele, that wimpled was full low'. Once again, the concessive force of the 'Yet … but' double should not be underestimated: appearance is deceptive, and no sooner has the narrator said that Una is whiter than the ass than that whiteness is covered up. Una's appearance is increasingly occluded as the conjunctions of line 3 signal. This impression is confirmed in the next truncated semantic unit: 'And ouer all a black stole shee did throw,/As one that inly mournd'. Though the next hemistich takes up directly from this pause – 'so was she sad' – the reader is clearly intended to hear an imitative or sympathetic break to these lines, a sympathy partly verbalised in line 8, 'Seemed in heart some hidden care she had', with its unambiguously trochaic opening.[25] Read in this way, the final phrase unit is the alexandrine as a discrete unit; like the alexandrine of stanza 2, it is something of a semantic orphan, although the additive connection 'And by her' registers that it is part of the stanza's description of Una's appearance.

There's a further aspect to the relationship between these stanzas which merits commentary, since it touches both on the question of interstanzaic links and on the related issue of rhyming distortion. The C-rhyme of stanza 2 cues the C-rhyme of stanza 4, with reciprocal relationships in lexis and referent – *had: sad: ydrad* leads to *sad: had: lad*. In effect, Spenser rhymes Una with Redcrosse: 'so was she sad' irresistibly looks back to 'did seeme too solemne sad'.[26] Similarly, 'some hidden care she had' modifies 'which in his helpe he had' in ways which are related to Gless's reading

---

24 There are several enjambments in the Proem (1.7–8; 2.2–4, 6–7; 3.2–3; 4.3–4); indeed, the syntactic fluidity of the Proem is in marked contrast to the stanzas which immediately follow. The enjambment in I.1.4 is perhaps not felt as much of a distortion, since lines 3–4 follow a similar phrase pattern to lines 1–2.

25 I.i.4 has the first trochaic line openings in the poem proper in lines 4 and 8 – '*Vnder* a vele'; '*Seemed* in heart' (my emphases). There are similar lines in I.Proem 3.9 and 4.2.

26 See *FQ*, 32, for Hamilton's note on the proleptic qualities of I.i.2.8.

of the ominous note in Redcrosse's sadness: there is 'a hint of insecurity … not fully compatible' with the suggestion in the first half of stanza 2 that the knight is one of the elect.[27] The reader troubled by Redcrosse's mood should have that concern magnified by Una's enigmatic, existential state of mourning. These are not particularly unusual rhymes, but their close proximity conditions the reader at this early stage to look back; this is a condition which becomes something of a reflex the more experienced the reader becomes in the ways of the poem.[28] The shared rhymes also underline the point that it is difficult to discuss individual stanzas in isolation. For *The Faerie Queene*, the individual – whether this is a line, a stanza, a rhyme, a character, or a book – is always part of a larger process of poetic interrelationship.

At the same time, the key point about the Spenserian is that – as Una veils her whiteness – it veils its difficulty behind its characteristic forms of expression. This pressure to disclose and withhold at the same time is visible in the way that the apparently regular syntax hides the pressures the rhyme scheme places on morphology. Spenser's practice differs from that of imitators like Byron and Shelley: because of the verbal character of his rhyming, his stanzaic writing is not a form of blank verse with dampened-down rhymes.[29] As in the previous chapter, my argument is that though Spenser's rhymes can be unobtrusive, they are nevertheless intended to be heard by the reader. This is aptly shown by the final C-rhyme of this stanza, where the rhyming distortion 'lad' replaces the normal preterite 'led'.[30] For students today, such lapses into linguistic eccentricity could provide a reason not to continue reading: 'If he's going to cheat on the rhymes, what next?' 'Cheating' isn't quite the *mot juste* for Spenser's practice; he lived at a time when English was more mobile than it is now, and where tricks – or more properly, variants – of this kind were frequent, albeit frowned on by stylistic conservatives like Puttenham and

27 Gless, *Interpretation and Theology in Spenser*, 56.
28 See Brown and Lethbridge, *A Concordance*, 365, 376, 431: though rhymes on *had* and *sad* are very common (respectively, 70 and 40 rhymes apiece), their close proximity this early in the poem is remarkable. For rhyme as a practice which assumes the reader must turn back, see Brown, '"Charmed with Inchaunted Rimes"', in Brown and Lethbridge, *A Concordance*, 4–9, and Chapter 3 above.
29 See Addison, 'Rhyming Against the Grain', 341–46, for comparisons of Spenser's use of the stanza with the practices of Shelley, Keats, and Byron. For the idea that the Spenserian anticipates blank verse, see Lethbridge, 'The Bondage of Rhyme' in Brown and Lethbridge, *A Concordance*, 77–84.
30 See Brown and Lethbridge, *A Concordance*, 367, 266. Of the nine rhymes on *lad*, eight are verbal, with only one on the noun (III.v.24b). *Led* outscores *lad* with twenty-nine instances; all these rhymes are verbal; *A Concordance*, 368, 269.

Gurney.[31] One small example: substituting *than* for *then* in rhyme was common, as in Churchyard's 'The Siege of Leith' (1575), a poem in rhyme royal, where 'Lord *Skrope* the Marshall than' (i.e. *then*, at that time) is rhymed with 'can' and 'man'.[32] Nevertheless, the *lad* rhyme and similar distortions manifest the pressure the Spenserian generates for the poet in the manufacture, as it were, of fresh rhyming combinations for each new demanding stanza. To an extent, interstanzaic rhyming shows both Spenser's mastery of rhyme and his ready exploitation of shortcuts to formal compliance: repeating the verbal patterning of 'which in his helpe he had' for 'some hidden care she had' is valuable because it shows you ways you might satisfy the form over again. Distorted morphology is a similar shortcut, suggesting that Spenser used all the plastic resources of Early Modern English which he had to hand in the stanzaic construction of *The Faerie Queene*. Once again, Spenser's practice shows that he did subdue 'rough words' through 'Vse' (*Prose*, 16).

We don't know precisely when Henry Gurney finally put the poem down, but this approach highlights some of the novelties he may have found disconcerting in the new stanza. Alongside its formal intricacy, it is syntactically permissive with a tendency to ambiguous or unresolved statements. As we have seen, its caesurae are not fixed in the 4/6 'chant' preferred by writers of the so-called 'drab' period.[33] Gless's analysis of the theological implications of 'Right faithfull true he was in deede and word' is suggestive of some of the reluctances Gurney may have had.[34] More immediate, perhaps, is the sense that Spenser made Gurney feel intellectually inadequate – an emotion which is not unfamiliar to many first-time readers of *The Faerie Queene* today. Gurney's suspicion that the aesthetic wool was being pulled over his eyes by Spenser is clear in another short poem he wrote, this time about his failure to 'get' *Mother Hubberds Tale*. As May

31 See Brown, '"Charmed with Inchaunted Rimes"' in Brown and Lethbridge, *A Concordance*, 26–27, 63–66, for discussion with examples. For Puttenham's strictures against *rime riche* and feminine rhyme, see 2.8 in *The Art of English Poesy*, 169–70. Gascoigne, with the more generous perspective of a practising poet, assimilates such devices under the broad heading of 'poeticall licence', which he characterises as 'a shrewde fellow'; *Certaine Notes of Instruction*, in Smith (ed.), *Elizabethan Critical Essays*, I.53.
32 In Churchyard, *The firste parte of Churchyardes chippes*, sig. A1v. There are only two such rhymes in *The Faerie Queene*; see Brown and Lethbridge, *A Concordance*, 328, 381.
33 Wilson-Okamura, *Spenser's International Style*, 31.
34 See May, 'Henry Gurney', 191, for reflection on the irony that Gurney – a conservative Protestant – would have found much to admire in the glorification of Protestant England, had he continued with the poem.

notes, Gurney did not detect any satire of the Cecils (which would have
further damned the poem in his eyes), and again focuses on the sense
that its style escapes him in some way. For Gurney, it is precisely in
Spenser's stylistic oddity that his own shortcomings as a reader are
uncomfortably exposed:

> No point of praise ther soundeith in myn eare
> in poem wch such speciall fame doth bear
> yt halteth oft aswell in Ryme as feet
> hath Theame obscure & verse more harsh than sweet
> myn Ignorance I rather yet Suspect[35]

It's always hard to like something which makes you feel stupid, particularly
when everyone else is maddeningly praising it. Gurney's frank expression
of his discomfiture is valuable because it gives stylistic grounds for these
feelings. Halting in rhyme and feet, and sounding harsh implies (rather
surprisingly) Gurney's failure to hear Chaucer in *Mother Hubberd*. Gurney
was perhaps as ignorant and provincial as he paints himself, but this poem
does raise the question of how Spenser was read in the early 1590s, and
what sort of stylistic referents readers reached for when trying to assimilate
this new poem. I have just suggested that Gurney could not cope with
the freewheeling aspects of Spenser's syntax – compared with the stanzaic
poems he was familiar with, *The Faerie Queene* seemed intimidatingly
loose. This comment on *Mother Hubberd* raises the further possibility – also
signalled by Guilpin – that early readers of Spenser often failed to read
him in terms of his literary antecedents. Another way of putting this
might be that while it's one thing to say to close literary friends that you
'hope to ouergo' *Orlando Furioso*, it's quite another to expect your readers
to be as well read as you are (*Prose*, 471).[36] To explore this issue in greater
detail, the next section turns to the question of the sources and analogues
of the Spenserian stanza. I want to reopen the dig into this particular ruin
to suggest that an old answer as to its likely sources is probably still the
best one available.

Things lost and laid amiss: analogues and origins

Part of what makes Gurney a valuable witness is that his response to *The
Faerie Queene* underlines the extent to which Elizabethan readers were

35 May, 'Henry Gurney', 192–93.
36 This is Harvey repeating to Spenser what the latter 'flatly professed your self in one of
    your last Letters'.

almost instinctively stanzaic; that this was a culture which had a marked tendency to think and conceptualise in stanzas, for whom stanzaic form was intimately allied with the idea of poetry. Even in denouncing the pre-eminent stanzaic epic of the period, Gurney does not renounce stanzas *per se*. When Donne reaches for a literary image to describe the canonisation of a love affair, he homes in on the physical shape of the stanza on the page as spatial metaphor for the transcendence he seeks to inscribe:

> Wee can dye by it, if not live by love,
>   And if unfit for tombes and hearse
> Our legends bee, it will be fit for verse;
>   And if no peece of Chronicle wee prove,
>   We'll build in sonnets pretty roomes;
>   As well a well wrought urne becomes
> The greatest ashes, as halfe-acre tombes,
>   And by these hymnes, all shall approve
>   Us *Canoniz'd* for Love.[37]

Since the lovers' story – using the teasingly Spenserian word 'legend' – is 'unfit' to be displayed on tombs, or as part of 'Chronicle' history (one thinks irresistibly of the stanzaic verse chronicles of *The Faerie Queene* II.x and III.iii, Daniel's *Civil Wars*, and Drayton's *Barons' Wars*), Donne turns to the 'well wrought' form of 'sonnets' in 'pretty rooms' as a samizdat representation of a love which cannot officially be disclosed.[38] Donne's own innovative form – an *Abbacccaa* stanza, in which each 'pretty room' is locked in by the *rime riche* repetition on *Love* – snakes inventively across the page, prompting the reader to compare it with the implicitly drabber forms of funerary epitaphs and verse chronicles. These are, we are intended to think, truly lovers who both 'live[d] by love', which – in the interlocking forms of 'The Canonization' – inevitably also means through the shaping constraints of stanzaic poetry. To think poetically was for poets of different generations to think in stanzas; Spenser and Donne worked in and reshaped what might be called a stanzaic poetic culture.

The sixain and stanzaic culture

Consider two examples of being in two minds in the same stanza form, both written just after the first publication of *The Faerie Queene*. The first

37 John Donne, *Poems* (1633), 203.
38 See Donne, *The Complete English Poems*, ed. Robin Robbins, 153, for a defence of the manuscript reading of 'legend'. Though Robbins only cites *The Golden Legend*, either reading may comprise a Spenserian allusion.

is from *Venus and Adonis*, the second from one of Southwell's devotional lyrics:

> A thousand spleens bear her a thousand ways;
> She treads the path that she untreads again.
> Her more than haste is mated with delays,
> Like the proceedings of a drunken brain,
>> Full of all respects, yet naught at all respecting,
>> In hand with all things, naught at all effecting.
>
> One foote he often setteth forth of dore,
>> But t'others loath uncertaine wayes to tread;
> He takes his fardle for his needefull store,
>> He casts his Inne where first he means to bed:
> But still ere he can frame his feete to goe,
> Love winneth time, till all conclude in no.

Comparing Southwell with Shakespeare is perhaps unlikely, given their different literary affiliations and audiences. Where the former was writing for English Catholics looking for spiritual reassurance, the latter aimed at *bien-pensant* readers familiar with Ovid, like the poem's dedicatee, the Earl of Southampton, who was (curiously enough) related to Southwell.[39] Nevertheless, *Venus and Adonis* and Southwell's poems are related in terms of their popularity and their shared stanza form. The poetic subjects could not be more different, though both are suffering the torments of misprized love. In the first, Venus tries to track down the hunting, soon-to-be-gored, Adonis; in the second, Joseph – 'stranger yet to Gods intent' – pauses on the point of leaving the wife he believes has been impregnated by another man.[40] Where Shakespeare presents Venus's indecision through the 'thousand ways' she goes and ungoes to try to find Adonis, Southwell – perhaps even more brilliantly – half animates Joseph to walk away with 'One foote', while 't'other' resistantly holds him at home.[41] In both cases, the subject treads a poetic dance which leads to stasis – 'naught at all effecting', 'all conclude in no'. Where Shakespeare's poem is sexy and sexualised throughout its long description of Venus's unsuccessful seduction, Southwell's focuses on Joseph's suspension between suspicion and love to

---

39 See Anne Sweeney's Introduction in St Robert Southwell, *Collected Poems*, xiii–xiv, for Southwell's poetry as a substitute for outlawed preaching, and for his family relationship with Southampton.

40 Shakespeare, *Venus and Adonis*, ll.907–12, in *The Complete Sonnets and Poems*, 223; Southwell, 'Josephs Amazement', ll.19–24, 3, in *The Poems*, 21.

41 't'others' is the manuscript reading preferred in *The Poems* and *Collected Poems*; the first printed edition has 't'other'; see Robert Southwell, *Saint Peters complaint*, 70.

magnify the devotional miracle which this poem cannily edits out of its bewildered complaint.[42]

Though himself an earnest Protestant, Gurney admired Southwell, writing of the 1595 edition of *Moeoniae*,[43] 'For matter form Choise woordes and fittest phrase … thes poemes may we blase/& compt for woorkes of speciall estimation'. As May comments, Gurney 'must have found it easy to approve Southwell's style because of its reliance on conventional Elizabethan metres and stanzas, especially its repeated use of "sixain" stanzas'.[44] Indeed, despite their differences of intent and inspiration (it is difficult to imagine Southwell enjoying the *Metamorphoses*), Shakespeare's and Southwell's use of the sixain stanza is remarkably consistent. Syntax is delivered through units of two lines almost in the fixed manner of Latin elegaic couplets. Both Shakespeare's 'A thousand spleens bear her a thousand ways;/She treads the path that she untreads again' and Southwell's 'One foote he often setteth forth of doore,/But t'others loath uncertaine wayes to tread' take the same form of semantically complete sentences of twenty syllables, in which the second line either expands on or completes the thought of the first. There is a pronounced tendency to antithesis and parallelism. This is why the manuscript of Southwell's line as 'But t'others loath uncertaine wayes to tread' is superior to the printed version, where 't'other' replaces 't'others'. Though the print version seems more modern, it blunts the verbal parallelism with the preceding line, in which (a) Joseph *sets* one foot outside, but (b) the other foot *is* loath to leave. Caesural pauses tend to be after the fourth or fifth syllable; thus the Quarto of *Venus and Adonis* prints line 908 as 'She treads the path, that she vntreads againe', making the 4/6 pattern graphically evident.[45] Endstopping similarly is enforced by end-of-line punctuation which in both cases – at least in the printed versions – is decisive and directive.[46] Venus and Joseph may

---

42 See Anne R. Sweeney, *Robert Southwell*, 125, for the 'unusual' avoidance of a closing prayer or consolation in the poem.

43 'Josephs Amazement' was first published in 1602 (*Saint Peters complaint*, 69–72). It is in all the five major Southwell manuscripts described by McDonald and Pollard Brown in *The Poems*, xxxvi–li. The poems collected in *Moeoniae* display similar stylistic features – for example, some of the poems later collected as 'The Sequence on the Virgin Mary and Christ' (*The Poems*, 3–12) are all in iambic pentameter sixains, though set as blocks of undifferentiated verse paragraphs in 1595; see Robert Southwell, *Moeoniae*, 1–10.

44 May, 'Henry Gurney', 208.

45 Shakespeare, *Venus and Adonis*, F4r.

46 See Southwell, *Collected Poems*, 19, for a text based more directly on that of the 'Waldegrave' manuscript than that used in the Oxford edition, *The Poems*. In this case, the only punctuation is a full stop after the final 'noe'. Even without punctuation, however,

be in two minds, but the poets and their compositors present them in syntactic, semantic, and stanzaic forms which are unwavering.

'Josephs Amazement' and *Venus and Adonis* are part of the writing which follows *The Faerie Queene*; Shakespeare's poem in particular reacts to and exploits aspects of Spenser's Ovidianism. Because the sixain is arguably the quintessential Elizabethan stanza form, it has been burdened with the a-historical tag of 'the *Venus and Adonis* stanza'. True, Shakespeare used it, but in adopting this form, he was following a zeitgeist – what A. E. B. Coldiron calls 'a veritable sixain explosion' – which took place during the Elizabethan period.[47] It might be better described as 'the *Tottel's Miscellany* sixain', 'the Gascoigne sixain', or indeed '*The Shepheardes Calender* sixain'.[48] Its ubiquity is shown by the fact that Anthony Copley deployed it in his 'Catholic response to *The Faerie Queene*', first published in 1596, a text which also shows the viability of the sixain as an epic stanza.[49] The question I want to explore is why Spenser did not use it or other competing forms for *The Faerie Queene*. Everybody was writing sixains, partly following Spenser's own precedent, so why did he not use that form for his own epic?

This question is in turn related to the issue discussed by David Scott Wilson-Okamura, whose work helps to explain why stanzaic verse was appropriate for epic poems during the sixteenth century.[50] I want to go in a different direction: why was this particular form – the *Ababbcbcc* stanza, with all its inherent difficulties and peculiarities – the solution which Spenser opted for? Arising from that, where does this stanza come from – what are its parents, its antecedents – where is the literary archaeology for the Spenserian stanza? The origins of sixains, in contrast, are easier to account for – as Coldiron suggests, the *Ababcc* stanza is a direct

Southwell's syntactic intentions are clear, with the only enjambment coming in the couplet, as the subject and main verb are delayed to the start of the final line, 'Love wynneth time …'.

47 A. E. B. Coldiron, 'French Presences in Tudor England'. See also Coldiron, *Printers Without Borders*, 210–211, 212–213, 221, 225–226, 227–228, for the use of this 'dominant English workhorse form' (210) in a range of printed texts, from broadsheets to more courtly and ambitious poems.

48 Tottel includes some thirty sixains: see Holton and MacFaul (eds), *Tottel's Miscellany*, 538. For Gascoigne's sixains, see *The Poesies*, 38–42, 93–95, 116–17, amongst others. In *The Shepheardes Calander*, 'Januarye', 'August' and 'December' follow the *Ababcc* pattern, while 'October' has the more complex variant *Abbaba*.

49 See Anthony Copley, *A Fig for Fortune*, 1. See 32–33, for Susannah Brietz Monta's remarks on Copley as a reader of Spenser, and his sophisticated engagement with *The Faerie Queene* as an allegorical epic.

50 Wilson-Okamura, *Spenser's International Style*, 18–49.

import from France: it is in effect the sestet of a French sonnet, repurposed into an independent stanza form. Its Elizabethan vogue is a significant part of the underrated 'French presence' within the English Renaissance. Similarly, the origins of rhyme royal are not mysterious: the form was first used in English by Chaucer for *Troilus and Criseyde*, again adapting precedents in French and Italian sources.[51] We know Spenser invented his stanza, but arguably we don't fully appreciate why or what he encoded in his new structure – Henry Gurney's experience suggests that this bemusement at the new form was widespread. Elizabethan readers understood forms like sixains and fourteeners; the Spenserian was more of a conceptual challenge.

The Elizabethan culture of stanzas, and the thinking implicit in that culture, finds its fullest expression in Book 2 of Puttenham's *The Art of English Poesy*, which gives an illustrated catalogue raisonné of stanza forms and some of the expectations which were attached to different forms. There are caveats to make about Puttenham. Although published in 1589, Puttenham's examples – and therefore the poetry he was describing – tend to come from the 1560s and 1570s (Gascoigne and Turberville are frequent touchstones), despite his reliance on more recent manuscript verse. The value of *The Art of English Poesy* is more what it tells us about the poetry of the immediate past than any light it sheds on Spenser's practice. Though in bulk *The Art of English Poesy* is by far and away the most detailed poetics in English, Puttenham was not an original thinker. He drew on Julius Caesar Scaliger's encylopaedic *Poetices Libri Septem* (1561), and shows some acquaintance with contemporaneous Italian criticism.[52] This is part of his value – he voices the literary truisms of his culture – but it also constitutes an important limit on the credence modern scholars should give his work. As Steven May has argued, the claim that *The Art of English Poesy* is a coherent 'courtly poetics' based on close association with the court does not square with the evidence.[53] Puttenham does not seem to

51 See Martin Stevens and T. V. F. Brogan, 'Rhyme Royal', 1065, and Theodore Maynard, *The Connection Between the Ballade, Chaucer's Modification of It, Rime Royal, and the Spenserian Stanza*, 64–92.
52 See Whigham and Rebhorn in Puttenham, *The Art of English Poesy*, 35–40.
53 Steven W. May, 'George Puttenham's Lewd and Illicit Career', 143–76. A further problem Puttenham raises is the relationship of life to theory: the documentary evidence shows him to have been a sexual predator, guilty of amongst other things domestic violence and rape; see May, 'George Puttenham', 150–59. Without palliating these actions, Whigham and Rebhorn provide a measure of contextual empathy, viewing Puttenham's actions as those of a younger son excluded from inheritance. They make suggestive analogies between his 'injured' and 'bellicose' nature and that of Edmund in *King Lear*;

speak for any coterie or group; rather, as May puts it, his work 'provides by far the most complete insight into the role of poetry in genteel but non-courtly Renaissance society'. His own poetry – which he uses repeatedly for examples in *The Art of English Poesy* – is at best merely competent and at worst inept and tactless.[54] Puttenham therefore needs to be read with a measure of caution, particularly in relation to the poetry of the 1590s, which he did not live to witness, and which it is likely he would not have fully understood.

Puttenham builds on the terse, pragmatic account of stanza form given in Gascoigne's *Certayne Notes of Instruction* (1575). In one long paragraph, Gascoigne describes rhyme royal, sixain, a variety of ballade stanzas, and the sonnet. As throughout this elliptical text, Gascoigne's advice is studiedly modest and characteristically mercurial; the paragraph ends 'let this suffise (if it be not to much) for the sundrie sortes of verses which we vse now adayes'.[55] For the casual or indeed the courtly reader, Puttenham's account risks being 'to much', with its lengthy descriptions, diagrams of the spatial dynamics of stanza forms, and its bespoke technical vocabulary, which is one of the treatise's originalities.[56] Puttenham's debt to Gascoigne is readily apparent. His characterisation of rhyme royal as 'the chief of our ancient proportions used by any rhymer writing anything of historical or grave poem' draws on Gascoigne's wording: 'surely it is a royall kinde of verse, seruing best for graue discourses', as both men have the work of Chaucer and Lydgate in mind.[57] Again like Gascoigne, Puttenham's descriptions are evaluative inasmuch as he is concerned to give directive, practical advice about how to write. In his estimation, the shortest conceivable stanza is the quatrain. Five-line stanzas are 'seldom used', and the sixain represents a happy medium: it 'is not only the most usual, but also very pleasant to the ear'.[58] Notions of pleasantness to the

---

see Puttenham, *The Art of English Poesy*, 5–15 (7). An apter Shakespearean analogy might be with Malvolio: an ill-intentioned social climber, frustrated in his larger ambitions for property and influence, yet capable of enforcing his will on the servants he abused.

54 See May, 'George Puttenham's Lewd and Illicit Career', 165–71 (171).

55 Gascoigne in Smith (ed.), *Elizabethan Critical Essays*, I, 56. For a reading of *Certayne Notes* as an ironic familiar letter, see Gillian Austen, *George Gascoigne*, 101–03.

56 For Puttenham's innovative lexis, see *The Art of English Poesy*, 242, and for sympathetic discussion, Whigham and Rebhorn's Introduction, 58. This discussion relates chiefly to the anglicisations of rhetorical terms in Book 3, such as '*Metonoymy*, or the Misnamer', rather than the present passage; 265.

57 Puttenham, *The Art of English Poesy*, 155 and n.6; Gascoigne, *Certayne Notes of Instruction*, in Smith (ed.), *Elizabethan Critical Essays*, I, 54.

58 Puttenham, *The Art of English Poesy*, 155.

ear connected with musicality form an important part of Puttenham's thinking. As he notes in a later chapter, 'our maker by his measures and concords of sundry proportions doth counterfeit the harmonical tunes of the vocal and instrumental musics'.[59] Though the discussion of stanza is not a sustained consideration of the relationship between form and genre, he was certainly right about the connection between sixain and song throughout the Elizabethan period. Of the twenty-one songs in Dowland's *First Book of Songs* (1597), ten follow the *Ababcc* form, with one in the related *Aabbcc* form.[60]

That the sixain is the Goldilocks stanza – not too short, not too long – is further emphasised as Puttenham relates stanza length to the syntactic units it contains:

A staff of four verses containeth in itself matter sufficient to make a full period or complement of sense, though it do not always so, and therefore may go by divisions. … A staff of six verses is very pleasant to the ear, and also serveth for a greater complement than the inferior staves, which maketh him more commonly to be used. A staff of seven verses, most usual with our ancient makers, also the staff of eight, nine, and ten, of larger complement than the rest, are only used by the later makers, and unless they go with very good band, do not so well as the inferior staves.[61]

Puttenham's articulation of his thinking is typically clotted, and is not always helped by unusual locutions such as 'complement' and 'band'.[62] Nevertheless his central point is straightforward: there is a complex relationship between stanza forms and sentences. The sixain is a good compromise between the 'inferior' (that is, shorter) quatrain and longer stanzaic forms, because the sixain allows more space for a unit of thought to be developed. Puttenham is less enthusiastic about longer forms because the longer the stanza, the greater the risk there is of losing syntactic coherence.

59 Puttenham, *The Art of English Poesy*, 174.
60 John Dowland, *The First Booke of Songes or Ayres*, sigs. A1v–B2r, D1v–D2r, E1v–E2r, G1v–H1r, H2v–I1r, I2v–K1r, K2v–L2r.
61 Puttenham, *The Art of English Poesy*, 156–57.
62 Whigham and Rebhorn gloss 'complement' as 'completion' here, adding 'amplitude' for the third usage. A clearer definition would be 'capacity'; see "complement, n." *OED Online*, 4a: 'The quantity or amount that completes or fills; complete quantity, provision, or set; full allowance, totality', citing this passage. My thanks to David Lee Miller for this point. For 'band', see below. In Puttenham, *The Art of English Poesy*, 156.

This emphasis on the relationship between sentence structure and stanza form partly explains what Puttenham meant by 'band'. He expands on what he means by this term in a later chapter:

> ye may perceive by these proportions before described that there is a band to be given every verse in a staff, so as none fall out alone or uncoupled, and this band maketh that the staff is said fast and not loose: even as ye see in buildings of stone or brick the mason giveth a band, that is a length to two breadths, and upon necessity divers other sorts of bands to hold in the work fast and maintain the perpendicularity of the wall. So, in any staff of seven or eight or more verses, the coupling of the more meters by rhyme or concord, is the faster band; the fewer, the looser band; and therefore in a huitain, he that putteth four verses in one concord and four in another concord, and in a dizain five, showeth himself more cunning, and also more copious in his own language. For he that can find two words of concord, cannot find four or five or six, unless he have his own language at will.[63]

Whigham and Rebhorn's gloss of 'band' is worth quoting: it is the 'connective or unifying force which structural elements (such as rhyme scheme, refrain, sestina repetition) impart to a stanza of poetry'. This is based on an analogy with bricklaying where the term 'is defined as that which a mason gives to a wall by alternating bricks laid with the short side showing (called band-stones) and those with the long side showing', a way of strengthening the structural integrity of the wall.[64] As Gavin Alexander wryly comments, 'Architectural metaphors are of fundamental importance to Renaissance versification, but few theorists take them this literally.'[65] Though Puttenham's literalism makes the analogy difficult to visualise, the key point is that the poet should avoid 'uncoupled' verses and that rhyme schemes – 'a band to be given every verse in a staff' – serve to bind the stanzaic structure as tightly as possible. The edifice of the stanza should not fall away from 'the perpendicularity of the wall', an image which does not allow for the subversive white spaces which surround and encroach on individual stanzas on the printed page.

Puttenham's feeling for the structural shapes of stanza forms and the binding work done by rhyme schemes is illustrated by his diagram included in an earlier chapter (Figure 1). This passage underlines that Puttenham's interest was in stanzas of between four and seven lines. Within the dizzying array of forms illustrated, his major concern is the *Ababcc* sixain and the

---

63 Puttenham, *The Art of English Poesy*, 178.
64 Puttenham, *The Art of English Poesy*, 443.
65 Gavin Alexander (ed.), *Sidney's 'Defence of Poetry'*, Penguin ebook.

Befides all this there is in *Situation* of the concords two other
points,one that it go by plaine and cleere compaffe not intangled:
another by enterweauing one with another by knots,or as it were
by band,which is more or leffe bufie and curious, all as the maker
will double or redouble his rime or concords,and fet his diftances
farre or nigh,of all which I will giue you ocular examples,as thus.

Concord in

Plaine compaffe ⌒ Entertangle.

And firft in a *Quadreine* there are but two proportions,
for foure verfes in this laft fort coupled,
are but two *Difticks*, and not a ftaffe *quadreine* or of foure.

The ftaffe of fiue hath feuen proportions as,

whereof fome of them be harfher and vnpleafaunter to the eare
then other fome be.

The *Sixaine* or ftaffe of fixe hath ten proportions,wherof fome
be vfuall, fome not vfuall,and not fo fweet one as another.

The ftaffe of feuen verfes hath feuen proportions,whereof one
onely is the vfuall of our vulgar, and kept by our old Poets *Chaucer* and other in their hiftoricall reports and other ditties: as in the
laft part of them that follow next.

The

Figure 1 Puttenham, *The Art of English Poesy* (1589)

Ababbcc rhyme royal stanza, since these are 'the usual of our vulgar'.[66]
The diagrams throughout *The Art of English Poesy* are perhaps best
understood as evidence of Puttenham's absorption of some aspects of
Ramism. He owned a copy of Ramus's *Dialectique*, and the visual representations of stanza forms are at least in part evidence of the runaway success
of the Ramist 'visualizable schematization' in the mid-sixteenth century
European thought.[67] Yet their main purpose is architectural rather than
rhetorical: as with the metaphor of 'band', Puttenham saw stanza in
structural terms as a sequence of interlocking 'entanglements' via rhyme
which the diagrams render visually.

The success of the diagrams is shown by the adoption of a similar
device by Drayton in his note in *The Barons' Wars* explaining his decision
to rewrite the poem from rhyme royal into *ottava rima*, which is discussed

66 Puttenham, *The Art of English Poesy*, 177.
67 For Puttenham's Ramus, see *The Art of English Poesy*, 41; for Ramist visualisation, see
 Walter J. Ong, *Ramus, Method, and the Decay of Dialogue*, particularly 171–95; 'visualizable
 schematization' is from Whigham and Rebhorn's Introduction in *The Art of English
 Poesy*, 53 n.117.

To'the Reader.

all, but the same better aduise which hath caused me to alter the whole ; And where before the stanza was of seauen lines, wherin there are two couplets, as in this figure appeareth,

the often harmonie thereof sofined the verse more then the maiestie of the subiect would permit, vnlesse they had all been Geminels, or couplets. Therefore (but not without new fashioning the whole frame) I chose Ariostos stanza of all other the most complete, and best proportioned, consisting of eight, sixe interwouen, and a couplet in base.

The Quadrin doth neuer double, or to vse a word of Heraldrie, neuer bringeth foorth Gemells . The Quinzain too soone. The Sestin hath Twinnes in the base , but they detaine not the Musicke, nor the Cloze (as Musitions terme it) long enough for an Epick Poem ; The stanza of seauen is touched before; This of eight both holds the tune cleaue through to the base of the columne (which is the couplet at the foote or bottom) & closeth not but with a full satisfaction to the eare for so long detention.

Figure 2 Drayton, *The barrons vvars* (1603)

below.[68] As Figure 2 shows, these diagrams make readily visible the spatial structure of the rhyme scheme. Compared with the completist elaboration of Puttenham's illustrations, which attempt to visualise every permutation of rhyme scheme, Drayton's are noteworthy for their focused concentration on the two forms in question – note the counting of couplets which is a key part of his claim that *ottava rima* is the superior stanza.

Puttenham's preference for sixains emerges throughout Book 2, where the complications inherent in longer stanza forms are repeatedly canvassed. The sentence beginning 'So, in any staff of seven or eight or more verses' quoted above proposes that longer stanzas are more structurally sound when they 'couple' more lines with the same rhyme than when they use a greater number of rhymes. Puttenham seems to mean that a huitain

---

68 Drayton, *The barrons vvarrs*, sig. A2v–A3v. This text was reprinted with minimal revisions in the collected *Poems* of both 1605 and 1619.

should be rhymed *Ababab* and a dixain *Abababab*,[69] though these are not patterns which are diagrammed on the preceding pages. In some ways, his model anticipates the complex 'entertangle' of the *Ababbcbcc Spenserian*.[70] It should be noted that this paragraph goes on to express doubts about the couplet closes of both rhyme royal and the sixain: since the final couplets are unconnected with the preceding rhyme clusters, this makes 'but a loose rhyme', although Puttenham immediately notes that 'the double cadence in the last two verses serve the ear well enough'.[71] In the case of these medium-length forms, congruity of sound partly eclipses the need for a binding structure. The overarching point is that Puttenham does not wholeheartedly recommend longer stanza forms. Although the mastery of such forms would reveal a 'copious' poet who has 'his own language at will', the risks of 'the looser band' are considerable. As a theorist, Puttenham was as haunted by the loss of structural integrity as he was as a litigant by the loss of property.[72] In these contexts, the sixain represents a familiar poetic structure, akin to poulter's measure and the fourteener. We might put it like this: although they were not the most exciting or experimental of verse forms, they were poetic technologies with which readers and writers were familiar. They were the default formal settings of mid-century verse, and indeed for some decades to come.

Rhyme royal

Rhyme royal and *ottava rima* present different but related problems. Rhyme royal had period form. In addition to its extensive use in post-Chaucerian literature, it features in *Tottel's Miscellany*,[73] while it is the dominant stanza in *The Mirror for Magistrates*. Of the thirty-three poems in Lily B. Campbell's edition, only six use different stanza forms.[74] *The Mirror's* reliance on rhyme royal helps to gloss Puttenham's formulation that the form was

69 Possibly Puttenham had something like the dixain used in 'King Richard the Second' from *The Mirror for Magistrates*; see note 74 below.
70 Puttenham, *The Art of English Poesy*, 176, 177, where analogies are made between rhyme form and 'interweaving one with another by knots' (176).
71 Puttenham, *The Art of English Poesy*, 178.
72 For Puttenham's disastrous court cases, see May, 'George Puttenham's Lewd and Illicit Career', 146–59.
73 See Amanda Holton and Tom MacFaul (eds), *Tottel's Miscellany*, 538, for listings of the different verse forms used in the *Miscellany*. Holton and MacFaul count 21 poems in rhyme royal; this compares with 30 poems in the sixain.
74 See Campbell (ed.), *The Mirror for Magistrates*. The six non-rhyme royal poems are: 'King Richard the Second' (dixains rhyming *Ababbaabab*; 111–18); 'King Henry the Sixth' (hexameter quatrains rhyming *Aabb*; 212–18); 'King Edward the Fourth' (douzains rhyming *Ababbcbccdcd*; 236–39); 'Lord Hastings' (octaves rhyming *Aabbccdd*; 268–96);

'used by any rhymer writing anything of historical or grave poem'. For Puttenham, there was a strong connection between rhyme royal and Chaucer and his followers. Although he does not explore the question in detail, he implies a fit between this 'ancient' form and the historical matter of *Troilus and Criseyde* and Lydgate's *The Fall of Princes*.[75] Puttenham's remark and the practice of Elizabethan poets points to a felt connection between form and content, as rhyme royal comes to seem the natural form for complaint and medieval epic. This gravity of tone and historical subject matter are evident throughout *The Mirror*. Thomas Sackville, Earl of Dorset's 'The Induction' exemplifies these attributes in a poem which embraces debts to Chaucer in its stanza, while Virgil presides over its ecphrastic account of the Fall of Troy and its *Aeneid* VI-lite katabasis.[76] Spenser clearly studied 'The Induction'. The personification of Sorrow stands behind Verlame in *The Ruines of Time*, while the steady handling of metre, stanzaic form and apostrophe in a context of lament and suffering showed how the virtues of Chaucer might be updated for sixteenth-century audiences.[77] A stanza such as

> But Troy alas (mee thought) aboue them all,
> It made myne iyes in very teares consume:
> When I beheld the wofull werd befall,
> That by the wrathfull wyl of God was come:
> And Ioues vnmooved sentence and foredoome
> On Priam kyng, and on his towne so bent.
> I could not lyn, but I must there lament[78]

directly informs a passage in *The Ruines of Time*:

> O *Rome* thy ruine I lament and rue,
> And in thy fall my fatall overthrowe,
> That whilom was, whilst heavens with equall vewe
> Deignd to behold me, and their gifts bestowe,
> The picture of thy pride in pompous shew:
> And of the whole world as thou wast the Empresse,
> So I of this small Northerne world was Princesse. (ll.78–84)

'The Blacksmith' (this poem has a central section in *Aabbcc* sixains, framed by rhyme royal; 402–18); 'King James the Fourth' (*Ababbcbc* ballade stanzas; 483–87). Other editions of *The Mirror* were more metrically adventurous than the text printed by Campbell; see Harriet Archer, "'Those chronicles whiche other men had"', 154–55.

75 Puttenham, *The Art of English Poesy*, 155. See further Richard Danson Brown, 'Wise Wights in Privy Places'.

76 See Wilson-Okamura, *Virgil in the Renaissance*, 164–65.

77 See Woods, *Natural Emphasis*, 108–09.

78 In Campbell (ed.), *The Mirror for Magistrates*, 313.

The connections are not just at the level of epic apostrophe or the perception of civic mutability, important though these are. Spenser's manipulation of the syntax of rhyme royal is, like Sackville's, closely modelled on Chaucer's. Many of the stanzas of 'The Induction' follow the syntax adumbrated above, where the stanza falls into two unequal portions: an *Abab* quatrain followed by a *Bcc* tercet. Sackville begins with his tears over the fall of Troy (ll.1–4), and then focuses on Priam's fate (ll.5–7). This pattern is found repeatedly in *Troilus and Criseyde*, as in this stanza which follows Troilus's death:

> And whan that he was slayn in this manere,
> His lighte goost ful blisfully is went
> Up to the holughnesse of the eighthe spere,
> In convers letyng everich element;
> And ther he saugh with ful avysement
> The erratik sterres, herkenyng armonye
> With sownes ful of hevenyssh melodie.[79]

In the quatrain, Troilus's spirit travels to the spheres; in the tercet, he looks around and hears the music of the spheres, as the 'bliss' of the journey upwards is succeeded by the 'ful avysement' of the intellectual understanding he has been missing up until this point. That Elizabethan readers felt that rhyme royal mandated a major pause between the quatrain and the tercet is neatly shown by Drayton's *Mortimeriados*, a poem later revised into *ottava rima*. The *mise en page* of the 1596 quarto indents every fifth line, whether or not the sense pauses at the end of the fourth line, as is shown by the opening two stanzas (Figure 3), where the second follows this pattern, whereas the first has a full stop at the end of the fifth line.

Despite the frequent occurrence of this pattern, the formal advantage of rhyme royal is that it is permissive, and admits of many permutations, as the beginning of *Mortimeriados* exemplifies.[80] Such permissiveness is a key difference from the sixain, where the even number of lines tends to produce the regular syntax observed in Shakespeare and Southwell. In

79 *Troilus and Criseyde* V.1807–13 in Chaucer, *The Riverside Chaucer*, 584. For the sixteenth-century text, see Chaucer, *The Works*, sig. Qq2v. Apart from some differences of wording, the major difference is the almost complete absence of punctuation from the texts printed by Thynne, Stow, and Speght. Even without modern editorial apparatus, however, the change of direction between the fourth and fifth lines is readily signalled by the 'And' which begins l.1811.
80 Not every rhyme royal poem of the period follows this *mise en page*. Sir John Davies's *Orchestra* (1596) indents each closing couplet from the preceding five lines. Davies's syntax is less Chaucerian than Drayton's, as in the first two stanzas, where the *Bbcc* couplets tend to syntactic independence; see sig. A3r, and *The Poems*, 90.

Mortimeriados.

THE lowring heauen had mask'd her in a clowde,
Dropping sad teares vpon the sullen earth,
Bemoning in her melancholly shrowde,
The angry starres which raign'd at *Edwards* birth,
     VVith whose beginning ended all our mirth.
Edward the second, but the first of shame,
Scourge of the crowne, eclipse of Englands fame.

VVhilst in our blood, ambition hotely boyles,
The Land bewailes her, like a wofull Mother,
On euery side besieg'd with ciuill broyles,
Her deerest chyldren murthering one another,
     Yet shee in silence forc'd her griefe to smother:
Groning with paine, in trauaile with her woes,
And in her torment, none to helpe her throwes.
         B.   VVhat

Figure 3 Drayton, *Mortimeriados* (1596)

rhyme royal, the fourth line works as a hinge between the two 'halves' of the stanza, either completing a train of thought (as with Sackville and Chaucer) or extending the sentence into the fifth line (as with Spenser). By continuing the sense from the fourth line into the fifth, Spenser contrives a definitive pause at the end of the fifth line which in turn serves to isolate the closing couplet, a distinction further emphasised by the slightly strained feminine rhyme *Empresse: Princesse*.[81] Indeed, Spenser's stanza shows how rhyme royal maybe organised to underline the double couplet structure. A celebrated stanza which contains this structure comes just before the death of Troilus, where the first five lines deploy the same rhyme:

> Go, litel book, go, litel myn tragedye,
> Ther God thi makere yet, er that he dye,
> So sende myght to make in some comedye!
> But litel book, no makying thow n'envie,

---

81 See Puttenham, *The Art of Enlish Poesy*, 170–71, for advice against half-rhyme. Puttenham goes on to display a measure of pragmatism in the suggestion that it is better 'to help the rhyme by false orthography than to leave an unpleasant dissonance to the ear'. Spenser does not use either of these words for rhyme in *The Faerie Queene*; see Brown and Lethbridge, *A Concordance*.

But subgit be to alle poesye;
And kis the steppes where as thow seest pace
Virgile, Ovide, Omer, Lucan, and Stace.[82]

Chaucer's syntax insists on the double-couplet close: 'But litel book, no makying thow n'envie,/But subgit be to alle poesye' is cut off from the opening three lines and is more directly linked with the final couplet, as Chaucer modestly places his 'litel book' in relation to Classical poetry. Though not as grandiloquent as this, Spenser's rhymes on the closely related diphthongs *rue: vewe* and *overthrowe: bestow: show* has a similar effect. The rhyming structures of rhyme royal lend themselves to a range of syntactic patterns and thus to a variety of different tones. This is one of the reasons why it is such an effective unit for narrative poetry: 'Ample enough for narrative purposes, the stanza is also suited to description, digression, comment, and literary burlesque', as the examples demonstrate.[83]

My suggestion, then, is that rhyme royal is the clearest harbinger of the Spenserian stanza.[84] Spenser's extensive use of the form elsewhere – in *The Ruines of Time*, *Fowre Hymns*, and the *Ababcbc* variant he devised for *Daphnaïda* – suggests that he considered using it for *The Faerie Queene*. That he ultimately did not choose it had implications for the stanza's currency. Something odd happens to rhyme royal towards the end of the sixteenth century.[85] Though it was still used in a number of important texts, the dominance which it enjoyed over other stanza forms from roughly the death of Chaucer to the 1580s begins to recede. Poems like Shakespeare's *Lucrece* (1594), Drayton's *Legends* (from 1595), and indeed *The Ruines of Time* and *Fowre Hymns*, all look back to the historical and literary past, as though the choice of rhyme royal were in some way a formal signal of an antiquarian agenda. Though it works in a different stylistic range, the same is true of Sir John Davies's *Orchestra* (1596), a poem which wittily attempts to prove '*The Antiquitie of Dancing*'.[86] By the end of the 1590s,

---

82 *Troilus and Criseyde* V.1786–92 in Chaucer, *The Riverside Chaucer*, 584. Thynne's text of the middle portion of this stanza is different enough to merit quoting: 'There god thy maker yet er that I dye/So sende me might to make some comedye/But lytel boke/ make thou none enuye'; Chaucer, *The Works*, sig. Qq2v.

83 Stevens and Brogan, 'Rhyme Royal', 1066.

84 Brown, 'Wise Wights in Privy Places'.

85 See Whigham and Rebhorn's note in Puttenham, *The Art of English Poesy*, 405, where they see Drayton's revision of *Mortimeriados* from rhyme royal to *ottava rima* in *The Barons' Wars* (1603) as 'marking the end of rhyme royal's dominance as the great heroic measure'.

86 *Lucrece* and the *Legends* both work in the tradition of *The Mirror*, drawing on either classical or medieval sources. While *Fowre Hymnes* does not fit into this category, Spenser contextualises the first two as products of '*the greener times of my youth*'

the stanza ceases to be a part of the current stylistic repertoire of most poets. Drayton's revision of the rhyme royal *Mortimeriados* into *ottava rima* for *The Barons' Wars* in 1603 shows this change in the process of happening. The ostensible reason he gives for the alteration is aesthetic: rhyme royal's double-couplet structure '*softned the verse more than the maiestie of the subiect would permit*'. Conversely, *ottava rima* '*hath in it a maiestie, perfection, & soliditie, resembling the piller which in Architecture is called the Tuscan*'. If majesty is what you want, Drayton suggests, the solidity of the eight-line form is unassailable. Nevertheless, the suspicion remains that the change was more motivated by the sense that the older form was not as current as 'Ariostos *stanza*', or indeed that of '*our first late great Reformer Ma. Spenser*'.[87] Drayton's epistle betrays the impulse to be up to date, and the anxiety that the stanza of Chaucer and *The Mirror* would no longer serve. It is unsurprising that Donne does not use rhyme royal in any of his surviving poems,[88] and that Herbert uses it only once.[89]

The progressive obsolescence of rhyme royal may be further associated with Reformation attitudes towards the medieval past. Steven Mullaney's retelling of the Protestant desecration of bones from St Paul's ossuary in 1549 describes an attempt to uproot the ancestral past: 'It was an effort to dislocate the dead from human feeling as well as local habitation; to root them out from the hearts and minds of their survivors'.[90] Though poetic forms are different from the bones of the dead, the comparison is not too far-fetched. As the medieval dead had become unacceptable to the duke of Somerset's radical Protestant regime, so the 'grave' rhyme royal becomes less usable, less acceptable, by the 1590s. In this context, Davies's adoption of rhyme royal for *Orchestra* is provocative, because this text seeks to flaunt the agedness of dance – as Antinous incredulously asks Penelope, 'How justly then is Dauncing termed new/Which with the world in point of time

---

because of their sexual content; *The Shorter Poems*, 690. For *Orchestra*, see Davies, *The Poems*, 90–126, quoting the marginal gloss to stanza 17 (94). These glosses were added to the 1622 edition; see Davies, *Nosce teipsum [and] Orchestra, or A poeme of dauncing*, sig. H7v.

87 Drayton, *The barrons vvarrs*, sig. A3r–v.

88 See Pierre Legouis, *Donne the Craftsman*, 14–16, for an inventory of the forms in 'Songs and Sonnets'. The closest Donne gets to rhyme royal is the *Ababccc* stanza, with a variety of different line lengths, used in five of the 'Songs and Sonnets'.

89 See 'The Bunch of Grapes', the precise form of which is $A10b6a10b8b8c10c10$. Herbert used seven line forms for 'Sunday' and 'Vanitie (I)', which are variants of the *Daphnaïda Ababcbc* form, and for 'The Flower', which is in the original form of $A8b10a8b10c4c4b8$. See Herbert, *The English Poems*, 448–52, 270–75, 307–10, 566–70.

90 Steven Mullaney, *The Reformation of Emotions in the Age of Shakespeare*, 3.

begun?'[91] If you're writing about the distant past when the universe was created, Davies insinuates, rhyme royal is the proper measure. Mullaney describes an aggressive process of cultural erosion: the Reformers worked to eradicate memory through the spoliation of the bones of the dead. Poets did not stop writing poems in rhyme royal during the 1590s but the form becomes less often used, in the same way that traditional religious practices went underground or died out during the Elizabethan period.[92] It is perhaps appropriate that Spenser's most antiquarian poem, *The Ruines of Time*, a text vested in and obsessed with the passage of time, should be written in rhyme royal.[93] Like the dead lamented in that poem – notably the vanished Roman city of Verulamium, Leicester, and Sidney – the form of the poem looks forward to its own disappearance. Verlame 'Is turnd to smoake', even as the poem perilously asserts the prerogatives of poetry to preserve the past through the tropes of literary immortality (l.123). It is not impossible to hear this as a proleptic lament for the rhyme royal stanza, particularly since the poem closes with a visionary pageant in which four of the Seven Wonders of the World – symbols of the 'vaine labours of terrestrial wit' – crumple 'sodainlie to dust' (ll.512, 517).

Ottava rima

Drayton's laborious recasting of *Mortimeriados* into *ottava rima* for *The Barons' Wars* demonstrates the complex issues of genre and tone which were at stake in the selection of stanza forms. Contemporary parallels would be Robert Lowell's restless rewriting of the sonnet sequences *Notebook* and *History* in the early 1970s, or Kate Bush's re-recording of songs from *The Sensual World* and *The Red Shoes* in *The Director's Cut*.[94] Lowell, however, did not change his form of the unrhymed sonnet – he remade published sequences into new collections. The textual rewiring done by Drayton remains an impressive testimony to Renaissance stanzaic thinking alongside the imperative to be *à la mode*. What is implicit in Drayton's change is that '*the same better aduise which hath caused me to alter the whole*' was connected with the felt need to update his verse form.[95] Yet he skates over the perhaps more interesting question of why, having decided

91 Davies, *The Poems*, 96.
92 For changes in ritual practice in the period, see Eamon Duffy, *The Stripping of the Altars*.
93 See Helfer, *Spenser's Ruins*, 136–67, for *The Ruines of Time* as a poem in dialogue with the processes of 'inevitable decay' (167). See Brown, *The New Poet*, 99–132, for my earlier work on the poem as a bridge between tradition and novelty.
94 Ian Hamilton, *Robert Lowell: A Biography*, 419–27; Kate Bush, *The Director's Cut* (2011).
95 Drayton, *The barrons vvarrs*, sig. A3r.

to recast the poem in a different form, he did not opt for the Spenserian, particularly given his professed admiration for '*that excellent Master*'.[96] There is a partial explanation in the admission that

> *generally all stanzas are in my opinion but tyrants, and torturers, when they make inuention obey theyr number, which sometime would otherwise scantle it selfe. A fault that great Maisters in this Art striue to auoyde.*[97]

As was noted in Chapter 2, this passage is valuable because of its frank recognition by a practitioner of the costs of the subordination of '*inuention*' to formal pattern. Read alongside Puttenham, Drayton offers a refreshingly modern recognition that form may degenerate into formalism – the empty compliance with more or less 'tyrannical' restrictions. Drayton was, however, also a man of his time, and this comment mirrors the caution found in Gascoigne and Sidney about verse form overriding '*inuention*'. The real force of the analogy with '*tyrants, and torturers*' is the sense that the rhyme scheme may usurp the writer's 'first determined Inuention'; as Gascoigne puts it, you should 'rather search the bottome of your braynes for apte wordes than chaunge good reason for rumbling rime'.[98] What Drayton does not say directly here is that *ottava rima* is less tyrannical than the Spenserian because it puts slightly less of a premium on the search for rhymes. Conversely, *ottava rima* is slightly less syntactically permissive than the Spenserian.

In terms of the syntactic organisation of materials, *ottava rima* in English is more like the sixain than rhyme royal. Stanzaic forms with an even number of lines in decasyllabic verse tend to resolve the sense into the form of four connected units of two lines each. Consider two examples chosen more or less at random from Harington's translation of *Orlando Furioso* and Fairfax's *Godfrey of Bulloigne*:

> It fortund as they carryd him to slaughter,
> Among the rest that did the same behold,
> Was *Alessandra, Oronteas* daughter,
> A fine young girle, about twise eight yeare old,
> *Elbanio* humbly as he went besought her,
> To be a meane this foule death to withhold,
> That like a man he might be kild at least,
> And not be drawne to slaughter like a beast.[99]

96 Drayton, 'To the Reader', the preface to the *Legends* in *Poems*, 312.
97 Drayton, *The barrons vvarrs*, sig. A3v.
98 Gascoigne, *Certayne Notes of Instruction*, in Smith (ed.), *Elizabethan Critical Essays*, I.52.
99 Ludovico Ariosto, *Orlando Furioso Translated into English Heroical Verse* (1591), 20.30, 155. Robert McNulty's edition has slightly different *mise en page*, justifying all lines of

> *Erminia* fled, scantly the tender grasse
> Her *Pegasus* with his light footesteps bent,
> Her maidens beast for speed did likewise passe;
> Yet diuers waies (such was their feare) they went:
> The squire who all too late return'd (alas)
> With tardie newes from Prince *Tancredies* tent,
> Fled likewise, when he saw his mistresse gone,
> It booted not to soiourne there alone.[100]

Harington's stanza is almost as regular as the sixains of Southwell and Shakespeare. Each couplet unit focuses on a discrete incident: Elbanio being carried to execution (ll.1–2), Alessandra in the crowd (ll.3–4), Elbanio's opening supplication to her (ll.5–6), followed by its development into a concrete image (ll.7–8). Though in this case, Harington is digesting the matter of several stanzas in Ariosto, the stanza serves as a compact demonstration of *ottava rima*'s tendency to resolve syntax into successive couplets.[101] The same tendencies are evident in Fairfax. Indeed, his poem has often been cited as precursor of the closed couplet form of Waller and Dryden.[102] In this case, ll.3–4 take a slightly different route by having a major pause at the end of the third line so that the fourth line is felt as a change of direction, cued by the concessive 'Yet'. Interestingly, Fairfax was not responding to pressures in the Italian, which reads 'Fugge ancor l'altra donna, e lor quel fero/con molti armati seguir non resta'.[103] This being said, *ottava* is not intrinsically a rigid form. The slight enjambment Fairfax displays between lines six and seven – 'The squire … Fled likewise' – closely follows Tasso's original: 'il buon scudiero/con tarda novella arriva in questa,/e l'altrui fuga ancor'.[104] The tendency for *ottava rima* in English to resolve into couplets is strong enough to be registered in contemporary fiction. Ali Smith's *The Accidental* (2006) contains a comic pastiche in which a philandering literature lecturer, Michael, tries his hand firstly at

---

the stanzas to the left, where Field's 1591 indents all lines after the first line of each stanza throughout. McNulty also has end of line punctuation (based on his collation of early editions); see *Orlando Furioso Translated into English Heroical Verse* (1972), 222.

100 Torquato Tasso, *Godfrey of Bulloigne* 6.111, trans. Fairfax, 239.

101 See Ludovico Ariosto, *Orlando Furioso* 20.37–41, ebook. Harington's radical abridgement adapts material particularly from stanzas 37 and 41.

102 See Katherine M. Lea and T. M. Gang's General Introduction in Tasso, *Godfrey of Bulloigne*, 37–49.

103 'The other woman also fled, and the savage [knight, i.e. Poliferno] did not rest from following them with many armed men'.

104 Torquato Tasso, *Gerusalemme liberata* 6.111, ebook. 'The good squire, who arrived with this late news, fled as well'.

a sonnet sequence and then at *ottava rima* in a vain attempt to capture his infatuation with a mysterious stranger. Sure enough, Smith's comedic, deliberately off-key *ottava* replicates the pattern observed above:

> Michael went to the village for a walk.
> That was the kind of thing a chap like him did,
> Holiday stroll to the village, hand in pock
> ets, casual, professional, on a whim, did.
> He sat outside the church and got a shock.
> It sounded more strenuous than a gym did!
> People were clearly fucking in that church.
> It was the sound of Michael in the lurch.[105]

Smith's deliberately deflationary Byronic *ottava* tends to pause after every second line, or to separate individual lines for comic effect as in the couplet. This pattern is observable through all fourteen stanzas of Michael's poem.

One of the consequences of the translation of *ottava rima* from Italian into English is a slightly narrower approach to syntax on the part of the translators, mirrored by the *mise en page* adopted by printers.[106] Consider the opening of *Orlando Furioso* Book 1. In his intricate resumé of Orlando's peregrinations after falling in love with Angelica, Ariosto assembles a long and winding sentence which stretches over two stanzas. What starts in the fifth stanza with 'ORLANDO, che gran tempo inamorato/Fu de la bella Angelica' is concluded at lines 6–7 of the sixth with 'A destruttion del bel Regno di Francia'.[107] In effect, the sentence mimics the errancy of its protagonists, travelling 'in India, in Media, in Tartaria' before arriving at the Pyrennes.[108] This technique of stretching sentences across and

---

105 Ali Smith, *The Accidental*, 174. The irony is compounded for the reader by the fact that the couple Michael overhears are the object of his affections, Amber, and his stepson, Magnus.

106 This tendency is apparent in Harington's arguments, which almost invariably mimic the form described above. Compare the arguments of Books 9 and 10 in Ariosto, *Orlando Furioso Translated into English Heroical Verse* (1591), 65, 73; where the first follows the four couplet rule rigidly, the second suggests an enjambment between lines 6 and 7: '*He flying in the aire from thence perceaus,/Renaldos musters*'. The comma in the 1591 edition is dropped by McNulty; *Orlando Furioso Translated into English Heroical Verse* (1972), 111.

107 Ariosto, *Orlando furioso* (1556), 2. 'Orlando, who had been in love with the beautiful Angelica for a long time … to the destruction of the beautiful kingdom of France'.

108 Ariosto, *Orlando furioso* (1556), 2. The full clause means '… and had left for her in India, Medea and Tartary infinite immortal trophies'. As Bigi and Zampese note, Ariosto's place names designate a generalised idea of the Orient; see Ariosto, *Orlando furioso* 1.5, ebook note. Harington's version is considerably vaguer: 'for her sake/About the world, in nations far and neare/Did high attempts performe and undertake'; in Ariosto, *Orlando Furioso Translated into English Heroical Verse* (1972), 20.

between stanzas is common in Italian epic, and is one of the ways in which Ariosto and Tasso fashion an epic syntax similar to that of Virgil and Homer in the different form and register of rhyming stanzas.[109] Harington's version keeps much of the sense, yet is punctuated in such a way as to promote stanza form at the expense of syntactic sense. The transition from stanza 5 to stanza 6 has an emphatic full stop at variance with the sense:

> And with the force of Germanie and France,
> Neare Pyren Alpes his standard did advance.
> 6
> To make the Kings of Affricke and of Spaine,
> Repent their rash attempts and foolish vaunts,[110]

This may be evidence of what Wilson-Okamura characterises as an English distaste for 'leaking' stanzas 'that will not stay shut', though Harington's plumbing is relatively makeshift – most experienced readers will take the full stop after 'advance' as a rhetorical marker of the stanza-fringe rather than as a grammatical distinction.[111] Nevertheless, this rhetorical punctuation of English *ottava rima* stanzas is not unusual, and bespeaks a way in which English poets domesticated this continental form into familiar spatial patterns.[112] In *The Barons' Wars* Canto 1, Drayton has a long sentence describing the alienation developing between Edward II and Isabella, which stretches from stanza 16 to stanza 18. That the sentence overrides stanza boundaries is signalled by the 'Which' and 'That' at the start of stanzas 17 and 18. Yet in all early editions, *mise en page* overrides grammatical considerations.[113] As Figure 4 demonstrates, though the stanzas could have been more lightly punctuated, Drayton and his compositors chose a visual formatting which stresses the hard edges of individual stanzas: each couplet close is indented, and each stanza is numbered. *The Barons' Wars* precedes *The Faerie Queene* in numbering stanzas – numbers were

109 Wilson-Okamura, *Spenser's International Style*, 29–30.
110 Ariosto, *Orlando Furioso Translated into English Heroical Verse* (1591), 1. Again, I have preferred the 1591 edition because McNulty does not reproduce this punctuation.
111 Wilson-Okamura, *Spenser's International Style*, 29–30. For an alternative reading of the English tradition, see Chapter 3 above. See also Lethbridge, 'The Bondage of Rhyme' in Brown and Lethbridge, *A Concordance*, 106–07, for Lethbridge's suggestion that the punctuation in the early editions is unreliable as a guide to Spenser's own punctuation: 'that the majority of Spenser's stanzas end with a full stop does not entail that the majority of the stanzas end with the end of the sentence' (107). Harington's punctuation lends support to this view.
112 For the likely development of *ottava* from Italian and occitan sources, see Alex Preminger, Christopher Kleinhenz and T. V. F. Brogan, 'Ottava Rima', 871.
113 See also Drayton, *Poems* (1619), 4–5.

Figure 4 Drayton, *The barrons vvwars* (1603)

added to the latter only in Matthew Lownes's 1609 folio. English poets and their publishers contrived to make *ottava rima* have the look of a fixed form with unambiguous borders. As the quotation from Harington shows, the insertion of stanza numbers enhances the tendency of English *ottava* stanzas to disrupt and disguise the progressive syntax derived from Ariosto.

Spenser's own experiments with *ottava rima* (which are still surprisingly neglected by historians of form) suggest that, like rhyme royal, this was a stanza to which he gave sustained consideration as a vehicle for epic. Though it might go without saying, both *Virgils Gnat* and *Muiopotmos* are virtuoso demonstrations of how *ottava rima* might be anglicised, with the caveat that Spenser's stanzas are very different from the comic effects Byron later achieved with the same form. *Virgils Gnat* and *Muiopotmos* show a poet with international sympathies using a modish form with originality for the purposes of complex narrative poetry. In the case of *Virgils Gnat* this comes with the further complication of the almost unparalleled use of a rhyming stanza form to translate dactylic hexameter.[114] *Muiopotmos* is probably the later of the two poems, and shows Spenser adopting aspects of the Ariostan syntax described above for an original poem with significant narrative debts to Ovid and Virgil. A sequence of three stanzas from the heart of the poem – the butterfly woven by Pallas and its effect on Arachne – illustrate the variety of syntactic effect Spenser gets from the *ottava* stanza.

Unlike Arachne herself, the text of 1591 quarto passes into modern critical editions almost unaltered. Both Oram and McCabe correct the mistaken full stop at the end of line 346 to a comma to read 'she attempted,', but otherwise retain the punctuation from the quarto.[115] It is arguable, however, whether Spenser's syntax is best served by the quarto's conservative, or English, pointing. The 1591 text presents three sentences in three stanzas, yet as J. B. Lethbridge has argued, readers may be misled 'by attending too closely to mere punctuation and not clause-structures'.[116] In this case, as with the passage from *The Barons' Wars*, there are grounds for arguing that the three stanzas present one long sentence, moving from Pallas's perfect butterfly (ll.329–36), Arachne's jealous reaction to this 'workmanship so rare' (ll.337–44), then to her 'hideous' transformation (ll.345–52). The connecting clauses 'Which when *Arachne* saw' and 'That shortly from the shape' imply a continuation of related ideas so that the quarto's full stops might be better understood as half stops, or commas. Comparison with Drayton is instructive. Both poets use the 'Which … That' formula to link successive stanzas, yet the allocation of materials to stanzas is significantly clearer in Spenser. Even if these stanzas are best read as a long sentence, stanzaic form dictates the contents of individual stanzas, as outlined above. Drayton assays a similar structure. Stanza 16 narrates Isabella's exclusion from Leeds castle, stanza 17 highlights the growing influence of the Spensers on Edward, while stanza 18 shows Isabella becoming increasingly disaffected from the King's party. Yet in comparison with *Muiopotmos*, Drayton's stanzas are confusing in terms of how stanzas articulate with one another and the referents of pronouns. Consider the anaphoristic phrase 'more and more'. When first used in stanza 16, it applies to the Leeds castle incident as one of a number of incidents which

---

114 See Brown, '"And dearest loue": Virgilian half-lines in Spenser's *Faerie Queene*', 59–61, for Spenser's manipulation of *ottava rima* to translate the hexameters of the pseudo-Virgilian *Culex*.

115 See *Yale*, 790 and Spenser, *The Shorter Poems*, ed. Richard A. McCabe, 'Textual Apparatus' (ebook), for details.

116 Lethbridge, 'The Bondage of Rhyme' in Brown and Lethbridge, *A Concordance*, 107.

accelerates 'this great mischiefe'. The same phrase is used to introduce stanza 17 with a different referent – 'Which more and more, a kingly rage increast'. Arguably, this abrupt change of referent dilutes the affective potential of the repetition. Spenser's use of the same device demonstrates the focus Drayton has forfeited here. In the couplet of the third stanza, 'And her faire face' and 'And her fine corpes' both apply to Arachne and are positioned in strict lineal and metrical parallel. Even a reader who doesn't know anaphora from antistrophe will recognise the functional juxtaposition of related verbal structures, as the rhetorical device enforces the transformation from beautiful to hideous.[117] Drayton's ongoing revisions bespeak his sense that the poem had not reached a final form.[118] This comparison suggests that he had not fully absorbed Spenser's radical combination of stanzaic form with syntactic experimentation. The comparison of *Muiopotmos* with *The Barons' Wars* reveals that Spenser's stanzaic syntax was more akin to that of Ariosto and Tasso than anything produced by any other English poet at this time.

The *Complaints* quarto signals Spenser's consistent preference for strong end-of-line pauses. As Figure 5 demonstrates, the only unequivocal enjambments in this passage are at ll.345–46 – 'from the shape of womanhed/ Such as she was', and in the same stanza, 'her white straight legs were altered/To crooked crawling shankes' (ll.349–50). Lineal form becomes permeable as Arachne's own shape alters in front of us. As in *The Faerie Queene*, Spenser is expert in the arrangement of endstopped lines for descriptive purposes. The *Abcc* section of the first stanza (ll.333–36) is an accumulative ecphrasis where each new line further develops the illusionism of l.332, 'That seem'd to liue, so like it was in sight', moving from the sensuous feel of the butterfly's body to the glitter of its eyes. Such writing is congruent with descriptive passages in the 1590 *Faerie Queene* like the Seven Deadly Sins in I.iv, and it is notable how many of these lines either explicitly or implicitly follow the 4/6 pattern.[119] These stanzas exemplify some of the syntactic permutations Spenser got out of the *ottava rima* stanza. Where the first stanza operates on the principle of two balanced quatrains (the *Abab* unit sets up the description developed in the *abcc*

---

117 Puttenham, *The Art of English Poesy*, 282–83. Puttenham links anaphora with antistrophe ('when ye make one word finish many verses in suit') as related devices of repetition.

118 Drayton, *Poems* (1619), 4–5, shows numerous small changes in wording, some of which do help to clarify who is doing what and to whom. The 'more and more' phrases remain in place.

119 Ll.329, 330, 333–34 all suggest a caesura after the fourth syllable (e.g. 'The velvet nap || which on his wings doth lie'), while the pattern is explicitly marked in l.332. Compare also ll.338, 340, 342, 344, 346, 348, 351–52.

Muiopotmos.

Emongſt thoſe leaues ſhe made a Butterflie,
With excellent deuice and wondrous flight,
Fluttring among the Oliues wantonly,
That ſeem'd to liue,ſo like it was in ſight :
The veluet nap which on his wings doth lie,
The ſilken downe with which his backe is dight,
His broad outſtretched hornes,his hayrie thies,
His glorious colours,and his gliſtering eies.

Which when *Arachne* ſaw,as ouerlaid,
And maſtered with workmanſhip ſo rare,
She ſtood aſtonied long,ne ought gaineſaid,
And with faſt fixed eyes on her did ſtare,
And by her ſilence,ſigne of one diſmaid,
The victorie did yeeld her as her ſhare :
Yet did ſhe inly fret,and felly burne,
And all her blood to poyſonous rancor turne.

That ſhortly from the ſhape of womanhed
Such as ſhe was,when *Pallas* ſhe attempted.
She grew to hideous ſhape of dryrihed,
Pinèd with griefe of follie late repented :
Eftſoones her white ſtreight legs were altered
To crooked crawling ſhankes,of marrowe empted,
And her faire face to fowle and loathſome hewe,
And her fine corpes to a bag of venim grewe.

Figure 5 Spenser, *Muiopotmos*, ll.329-52, from *Complaints* (1591)

section), the next two work have a more discernible 6 + 2 format, as the
closing couplet either shifts the narrative focus ('Yet did she inly fret …'),
or summarises what has gone before into the unsettling anaphoristic
rendering of Arachne's metamorphosis (ll.351–52). As I have commented
elsewhere, the close of the poem, where the butterfly Clarion is murdered
by the spider Aragnoll (ll.377–440), shows the tendency of the sixth line
of each stanza to enjamb into the seventh, a technique which shows *ottava*'s
suitability for narrative.[120]

This passage suggests that Spenser used *Muiopotmos* to test *ottava
rima*, and to experiment with the syntactic effects and freer caesurae he
found in Ariosto and Tasso. As I have noted, the poetic opulence of
Muiopotmos lies in its seemingly effortless adoption of *ottava rima* to an
Ovidian narrative, in which through the 'wondrous slight' of syntax and
lineation, Spenser achieves uncanny mimetic effects. The poignance of
Spenser's Arachne is perhaps that in her amazement at the art she witnesses
– 'And with fast fixed eyes on her did stare' – she mirrors the reader's

120 Brown, 'Wise Wights in Privy Places'.

response to Spenser's own 'workmanship', a word, it should be noted, which was often used to designate poetic as much as artistic refinement.[121] The 1591 quarto of *Complaints* shows the English *ottava* stanza at a transitional moment, when the form might have developed in the permissive and sinuous direction pursued by the Italians. It is texts like Harington's *Orlando*, with its handy stanza numberings, which contribute to the development of the English *ottava* stanza into a more restrictive form.

Spenser could then certainly have adapted *ottava rima* for the greater task of *The Faerie Queene*. That he chose not to suggests that at some point during the late 1570s or early 1580s, he decided to design a new form with a double couplet structure and an odd number of lines, which was thus more aligned with rhyme royal than *ottava rima*. The decision implies some reluctance about the latter, possibly connected with the tendency of even-line stanza forms to fall into regular syntactic patterns, alongside the ambition to 'ouergo' Ariosto – what better way to do that than with a new, even tricksier, stanza form? Indeed, the social and biographical motivations for his choice are not mysterious: the Spenserian is designed to show a poet 'copious in his language', who has that language 'at will'. The formal mechanism of the stanza is a bravura device which implicitly challenges rivals – one again thinks of Donne – to equal its accomplishment and ingenuity. The final poem in the Commendatory Verses appended to the 1590 *Faerie Queene* implies such an understanding. Signed by the aptly named 'Ignoto', this poem is an elegant piece of doublethink which simultaneously advertises the value of Spenser's poem ('*I here pronounce the workmanship is such,/As that no pen can set it forth too much*') while insisting that such praise is unnecessary.[122] This is done through an analogy with inn keeping: '*when men know the goodness of the wyne,/T'is needlesse for the hoast to haue a sygne*', an image which deliciously conjures the idea of Spenser as the winner of the Good Pub award for 1590. More seriously, the tavern conceit enables Ignoto to represent his own poem as '*a garland at the dore*' of *The Faerie Queene* on the strength of custom, '*And customes very hardly broken are*'. The customary character of the poem is shown by its use of the *Ababcc* sixain.[123] By implication, the forms which are suited

---

121 See "workmanship, n." *OED Online*, and below on the Ignoto dedicatory poem.
122 *FQ*, 725. See L. G. Black, '*The Faerie Queene*, commendatory verses and dedicatory sonnets', 292.
123 In a nicely Spenserian twist the third stanza rhymes *Ababaa*. The repeated rhyme cluster, *such: tuch: such: much* is further underlined by the repetition of *such* in mid-line position in the final stanza. There is a distant family resemblance to the two-rhyme stanzas in *The Faerie Queene*; on this phenomenon, see Brown, '"Charmed with Inchaunted Rimes"' in Brown and Lethbridge, *A Concordance*, 69–70.

to commendatory poems are handsomely bested by those of the poem they recommend. The Spenserian was designed to impress its readers, and Ignoto does his or her best to make sure that the reader gets the point and '*giue[s] your hoast his vtmost dew*'.

No lesse encombrance: negotiating the Spenserian

The previous section has argued that during the late sixteenth century, poetry in English exhibits a high degree of stanzaic awareness. Through the work of Puttenham and Drayton, I have observed discriminations between forms which articulate the fit between genre and stanza, ascribing different moods to different modes, such as the association of rhyme royal with historical content and tragic narrative. Alongside their generic readings of forms, Puttenham and Drayton visualise stanza shapes diagrammatically. The space on the page becomes a counter which can be detached from the words of actual stanzas as the new technology of print gave to writers innovative ways of explaining the structures and problematics of rhyming stanzas. In turn, *mise en page* contributes to the understanding and development of these forms, and is suggestive of the conventions through which stanzas were read. Stanzaic form, particularly in the guise of the *Ababcc* sixain, was the equivalent of a tweet – a culturally determined form conforming to normative expectations. So pervasive were these structures that for readers like Henry Gurney the sixain pattern almost becomes constitutive of what is admissible as poetry. What you read determines what you think of as readable. As Louis MacNeice puts it, 'A poem, to be recognizable, must be traditional; but to be worth recognizing, it must be something new'.[124] Gurney's failure to 'get' the Spenserian dramatises the first half of this truism: it was a form which was alien to his experience as a reader, and he had little interest in novelty for its own sake. When Jacques asks Amiens 'Call you 'em *stanzos*?', his main target is trendy jargon – *OED* records Puttenham as being one of the first to use the word in English – rather than the forms themselves.[125] Later in the scene, Jacques shows himself to be an adept parodist of Amiens's intricate stanza.[126] Stanzas were ubiquitous on the page and on stage, in

---

124 MacNeice, *Selected Literary Criticism*, 12.
125 "Stanza, n." *OED Online*.
126 Shakespeare, *As You Like It*, 211–14 (2.5.15–56), and *The First Folio of Shakespeare*, 210 (Folio pagination, 192); Amiens's stanza is in the form *Aabbc3a4c3*, modulated to *Aabbc3c4c3* by Jaques. Folio lineation shows signs of cropping for space, as the first line of Jaques's response is printed '*If it do come to passe, that any man turne Asse:*',

song and in poetry. As I have suggested throughout, they were not simply vehicles through which text was delivered in a shapely fashion but were – like the internet pages of a later age – windows through which reality was apprehended and experience was structured.

In the final section of this chapter, I examine a number of stanzas from Book VI Canto iv to develop these observations in the context of *The Faerie Queene*. The syntactic structure of the Spenserian is dictated by the key decision to opt for an odd number of lines. The Spenserian moves away from the more unambiguous allocations of syntax typical of the sixain and *ottava rima*, while updating the double couplet structure of rhyme royal. In what follows, I illustrate some of the varied permutations Spenser gets from his ostensibly cumbersome stanza. VI.iv is a canto of action, which thematises states of encumbrance in ways which are relevant to stanzaic form. The canto is not, of course, 'about' stanzas; the point is rather that this section of the poem enables us to see Spenser manipulating his verse form to narrate incidents which are concerned with the interplay between the tricks of fortune and the constraints he imposes on his characters. Although the canto is comparatively short at forty stanzas, the argument contrives to skip the final episode, in which Calepine resettles the baby he has rescued from the bear with the childless Matilde.[127] Even within its breathless array of incident, however, the canto finds room for a characteristic moment of suspension:

> Much was he then encombred, ne could tell
>   Which way to take: now West he went a while,
>   Then North; then neither, but as fortune fell.
>   So vp and downe he wandred many a mile,
>   With wearie trauell and vncertaine toile,
>   Yet nought the nearer to his iourneys end;
>   And euermore his louely litle spoile
>   Crying for food, did greatly him offend.
> So all that day in wandring vainely he did spend. (VI.iv.25)

---

which suggests that the sixth line of each stanza – the refrain '*Heere shall he see no enemie*' could reasonably be printed as two dimeter lines. Thus Jaques's version should read '*Heere shall he see/Grosse fooles as he*', making the overall stanza form *Aabbc3aa2c3*; compare Donne's form for 'Song' ('Sweetest love, I do not go'): *A4b3a4b3c2dd3c4*.

127 While the argument concentrates on the salvage man rescuing Calepine from Turpine and the fight with the bear, it omits the salvage man's attempts to cure the wounded Serena; see VI.iv.arg. Spenser's confusion is evident in Vi.v.arg, which has '*Matilda*' in place of '*Serena*', presumably as the episodes blended together in his mind; see *FQ*, 632.

After rescuing the baby, Calepine finds himself in the middle of nowhere, surrounded by 'nought but woods and forrests farre and nye' (VI.iv.24). To capture this state of affairs, Spenser organises his syntax triadically. The first six lines split into two three-line expositions of the state of being lost. If Calepine tries navigating according to two of the cardinal points in the first triplet (*Aba*),[128] in the second he abandons all pretence at method (*bbc*). The care with which Spenser was writing is shown by the close phonetic proximity of the A- and B-rhymes: the similarity of sound between the *–ell* cluster and the *–ile/oile* cluster is at one level a relentless reminder that Calepine's 'wearie trauell' is leading him nowhere. At the same time, syntax cuts against rhyme scheme through the strong pauses at the ends of lines 3, 6, and 8. Although the A- and B-rhymes suggest homogeneity, the punctuation insists on the sovereignty of the individual sentence or phrase unit. Thus the last three lines vary the triadic structure. In case the reader has forgotten that Calepine is literally holding a baby, lines 7–8 refocus attention on his hungry 'litle spoile', cued by the trochaic inversion which begins line 8 '*Crying* for food' (*bc*).[129] The alexandrine is an independent summary, which throws metrical and semantic emphasis onto the key phrase 'wandring vainely' (*c*): this stanza is a protracted close-up on fruitless activity in the syntactic permutation of 3 + 3 + 2 + 1. As Hadfield and Stoll comment, it aligns Calepine with Serena and others in a book 'which is full of characters who have no idea where they are going because they have not been given proper guidance'.[130] Calepine is reminiscent of Shakespeare's Venus and Southwell's Joseph as a character who doesn't know where to turn next, yet such a comparison necessarily draws attention to the great differences between the two stanza forms. Instead of the constrictive form of the sixain, the Spenserian is an expansive space which can organise its materials more freely, on this occasion to mirror the directional uncertainties of Calepine's travelling.

Of course, Spenser might be accused of spinning out his copy to satisfy the demands of his stanza, much in the way that in *Virgils Gnat*, he expands *Culex* in order to construct semantically discrete *ottava rima* stanzas.[131]

---

128 See *FQ*, 629, for Hamilton's note that in relation to Ireland, Calepine's orientation would take him outside the English Pale. See also Richard McCabe, *Spenser's Monstrous Regiment*, 232–51.

129 My emphasis. Calepine does seem to manage to conceal the baby in his later conversation with Mathilde, who is produced rather like a rabbit from a hat in stanza 35: 'Lo how good fortune doth to you present/This litle babe'.

130 In Spenser, *The Faerie Queene Book Six and The Mutabilitie Cantos*, 61.

131 Brown, '"And dearest loue": Virgilian half-lines in Spenser's *Faerie Queene*', 59–61.

Such an approach underestimates the extent to which Book VI is concerned
with directionlessness, as well as the prominence of encumbrance in the
Calepine/Serena narrative; Spenser wants to concentrate the reader's
attention on this particular state of being. 'Encombred' and related forms
reverberate throughout the canto. The first use shows Serena's reaction to
the salvage man's defeat of Turpine:

> For though she were right glad, so rid to bee
> From that vile lozell, which her late offended,
> Yet now no lesse encombrance she did see,
> And perill by this saluage man pretended;
> Gainst whom she saw no meanes to be defended (VI.iv.10)

This is the only instance of 'encombrance' in *The Faerie Queene*, and
though similar terms like 'combrous' and '(en)combred' are used sparingly
elsewhere, Spenser seems to have focused these terms on Book VI.[132] The
one-off rhyme on 'encomberment' occurs just prior to the climax of the
Serena narrative as the salvages prepare her for the table through an
unlikely rest treatment: 'Sleepe out her fill, without encomberment:/For
sleep they said would make her battil [i.e. fatten] better' (VI.viii.38). Andrew
Zurcher's pioneering work insists on the legal associations underlying
this terminology – to encumber someone is 'to burden with duties or
obligations; spec. to charge an estate with debts and liabilities'. Zurcher's
glosses of this part of the poem stress the opposition between the natural
law represented by the salvage man and the embattled civility represented
by the initially terrified Serena.[133] Yet in Canto iv, *OED*'s first definition
of 'encumber' is arguably more relevant: 'To hamper, embarrass (persons,
their movements, actions, etc.) with a clog or burden.'[134] *OED*'s quotation
from *The Parson's Tale* offers a suggestive analogy in particular for Calepine's
position in stanza 25: 'Of Accidie comth first that a man is anoyd and
encombred for to doon any goodnesse.'[135] I am not suggesting that the
Canto is in any mechanistic way concerned with the psychological effects
of sloth, but rather that the more generalised, existential sense of blockage

132 Brown and Lethbridge, *A Concordance*, 392, 396. 'Encombrance' and 'encomberment'
    occur only in Book VI; 'encumber' once in Book IV; 'combred' occurs in Books I, V
    and VI; 'combrous' is used twice in Book VI and once in Book II; 'encombred' is used
    three times in Book I, and once each in Books II, V and VI. The raw totals are collected
    but not collated in the 'All Words' index in our published *Concordance* (see above).
133 Zurcher, *Spenser's Legal Language*, 254, 67–68; see also 59.
134 "encumber, v." *OED Online*.
135 *The Riverside Chaucer*, 311; *The Parson's Tale*, 687.

and burden articulated by Chaucer underlies Spenser's use of the term in this passage. Serena in particular is characterised through her fear of 'encombrance'. Given the incurable wound she receives from the Blatant Beast, there is a grim humour at work in the idea that she might sleep 'without encomberment', since she is effectively defined by her 'mortall wound' (VI.v.28).[136]

Encumbrances though can be shed as well as shouldered. The third instance in VI.iv comes in Calepine's fight with the bear. This passage merits quoting at length because in its embodiment of the theme of encumbrance, it illustrates the flexibility and paradoxical freedom which I am suggesting underlies Spenser's stanzaic writing:

> Well then him chaunst his heauy armes to want,
>   Whose burden mote empeach his needfull speed,
>   And hinder him from libertie to pant:
>   For hauing long time, as his daily weed,
>   Them wont to weare, and wend on foot for need,
>   Now wanting them he felt himselfe so light,
>   That like an Hauke, which feeling her selfe freed
>   From bels and iesses, which did let her flight,
> Him seem'd his feet did fly, and in their speed delight.

> So well he sped him, that the wearie Beare
>   Ere long he ouertooke, and forst to stay,
>   And without weapon him assayling neare,
>   Compeld him soone the spoyle adowne to lay.
>   Wherewith the beast enrag'd to loose his pray,
>   Vpon him turned, and with greedie force
>   And furie, to be crossed in his way,
>   Gaping full wyde, did thinke without remorse
> To be aueng'd on him, and to deuoure his corse.

> But the bold knight no whit thereat dismayd,
>   But catching vp in hand a ragged stone,
>   Which lay thereby (so fortune him did ayde)
>   Vpon him ran, and thrust it all attone
>   Into his gaping throte, that made him grone
>   And gaspe for breath, that he nigh choked was,
>   Being vnable to digest that bone;
>   Ne could it vpward come, nor downward passe,
> Ne could he brooke the coldnesse of the stony masse.

136 A. Leigh DeNeef, 'Serena', 637.

> Whom when as he thus combred did behold,
>   Stryuing in vaine that nigh his bowels brast,
>   He with him closd, and laying mightie hold
>   Vpon his throte, did gripe his gorge so fast,
>   That wanting breath, him downe to ground he cast;
>   And then oppressing him with vrgent paine,
>   Ere long enforst to breath his vtmost blast,
>   Gnashing his cruell teeth at him in vaine,
> And threatning his sharpe clawes, now wanting powre to straine.
>   (VI.iv.19–22)

In set piece combats, *The Faerie Queene* shows a tendency towards devices of repetition, such as interstanzaic rhyming and restriction of vocabulary, to render the heavy metal clashes of chivalric combat.[137] In contrast, Calepine's pursuit of the bear turns on the alternance between images of 'libertie' and of restraint. Stanza 19 is a skilful realisation of this dynamic: freed from the 'heauy' burden of his 'armes', the pedestrian Calepine becomes a hawk freed to pursue the bear at will.[138] As A. C. Hamilton notes, 'The simile prepares for an elaborate play: not encumbered with arms, Calepine may overtake the bear encumbered with the child. When the bear is encumbered instead with the stone … [Calepine] is left "Much … encombred" with the child.'[139] The simile is indeed a highly turned example of illusionism which concentrates on the elated perception of a temporary freedom. As Calepine feels himself liberated from the hindrance of armour, so the hawk feels 'her selfe freed/From bels and iesses'; the feelings are real enough, but the reader is tacitly reminded that just as the hawk will be returned to captivity, Calepine will be re-encased in armour, just as in turn, Calidore's pastoral séjour later in the book is a suspension of his knightly role rather than an abrogation of it (see VI.ix.31). Spenser necessarily articulates this sense of freedom in verse constructed through intense formal constraint. Consider the alexandrine. This begins with the crucial qualification that what we're reading is based on Calepine's interpretation: '*Him seem'd* his feet did fly, and in their speed delight'.[140]

---

137 See Chapter 3 above for discussion of the use of rhyming repetitions in IV.iii.
138 For Spenser's use of tropes from falconry, see Catherine Bates, *Masculinity and the Hunt*, 237–324, and Constance B. Hieatt, 'Falconry', 298–99. Spenser is ornithologically vague, but 'Hauke' probably refers to either a goshawk or a sparrowhawk, both of which were used in falconry; see George Turberville, *The booke of faulconrie or hauking*, 58–72.
139 *FQ*, 628.
140 My emphases.

The line then continues the metaphor of flight from falconry, falling into the orthodox syllabic pattern of 6 + 6 – it is a balanced and largely monosyllabic realisation of lineal form the reader has experienced many times before.[141] What's new is the use of such a familiar line shape to render the exhilaration of taking wing. The poetic trick is again connected with the organisation of syntax in a stanza with an odd number of lines. Spenser adopts a 3 + 2 + 4 model, clearly shown in the punctuation of the 1596 *Faerie Queene*, which is reproduced in most modern editions.[142] Lines 1–3 establish that Calepine is lucky not to be armed. A syntactic development is cued by the colon at the end of line 3, which introduces lines 4–5 as an expansion of the opening – because armour is his 'daily weed', and because he is unused to travelling 'on foot', Calepine is 'Now' (at the beginning of line 6) in a unique position. This sets up the *cbcc* portion of the stanza as a focused development of the hawk simile, in which the quatrain form is legible as a coherent grammatical subunit. Spenser constructs an image of unfettered freedom in highly fettered verse which paradoxically contrives to sound anything but constrained. On the contrary, when the alexandrine sets Calepine's feet in motion, the reader is intended to share his sense of delighted elevation.

This reading of stanza 19 aims to disclose Spenser's habitually careful yet varied artifice in the construction of his stanzaic syntax. As I have suggested, the decision to construct a stanza with an odd number of lines was crucial because it moves the Spenserian away from the clearer allocations of syntax to line typical of both *ottava rima* and the *Venus and Adonis* sixain. The odd number of lines reveals the root of the new structure in the paradigmatic shape of the rhyme royal stanza. William Empson long ago drew attention to the fifth line as the stanza's key unit: 'stanzas may … be classified by the grammatical connections of the crucial fifth line, which must give a soft bump to the dying fall of the first quatrain, keep it in the air, and prevent it from falling apart from the rest of the stanza'.[143] In VI.iv.19, the fifth line is a necessary connective between the narration of the unarmed Calepine and the defining simile – in Empson's terms, it keeps the stanza in the air through the development which the simile provides of the opening description. As we shall see, the fifth lines work differently in stanzas 20–22. For the moment, it is worth emphasising

141 John Hollander, 'Alexandrine', 15, and Chapter 2 above.
142 Spenser, *The Faerie Queene* (1596), 404.
143 Empson, *Seven Types of Ambiguity*, 33. For further discussion, see Brown, 'Wise Wights in privy places'.

that Spenser works to create discrete units of meaning, which are comprehensible first in their own terms. At the same time, the individual stanza is almost always closely connected with its neighbours: in the broader structures of episode, canto, and book, stanzas are part of a broader narrative matrix where the discrete unit must plausibly be connected with the rest of the poem.

This excerpt raises naturally the question of 'leaking' stanzas and the connections *The Faerie Queene* establishes between blocks of text which give the appearance of independence. Should we – as I have suggested above in relation to the punctuation of stanza 19 – heed the pointing of the early editions, which presents these as four syntactically discrete stanzas, or do we – following Lethbridge and the sinuous development of incident in this passage – adopt a more sceptical attitude to their printed forms? We can get some purchase on these issues by looking at the incidence of lead words in stanzas. Do they vary according to the kind of passage Spenser was writing? That is, is the incidence of simple connectives like 'So', 'But', and 'Whom' – all of which imply the protraction of syntax in the passage above – greater in passages of action than elsewhere? More broadly, what can lead words tell us about Spenser's stanzaic writing? The evidence which I have assembled suggests that it is not the case that Spenser uses more simple connectives in passages of action. While, as might be expected, conjunctions, articles, and pronouns are the most numerous words used to introduce *all* stanzas, there is no significant difference between the totals for a canto of action (such as iv) as against a canto which is more descriptive (such as x). In terms of the Book as a whole, the commonest lead words are: 'But' (65), 'The' (39), 'So' (33), 'And' (29), 'Then' (18), 'Yet' (14), 'With' (13). For cantos iv and x, the tallies are (excluding words used only once or twice): for Canto IV, 'But' (6), 'The' (3), 'And' (3), 'Then' (3), 'So' (3); and for Canto X, 'And' (4), 'But' (3), 'So' (3).[144] There are differences of allocation – Canto IV uses only twenty-three different lead words in forty stanzas, whereas Canto X is slightly more expansive in using thirty-two different lead words in forty-four stanzas; it would be hard to connect such incidences with the content of the cantos. The critical point is that Spenser tends to rely on the same or similar groups of words to kick stanzas off throughout the book. The dominance of 'But' and related conjunctions like 'Yet' further suggests the extent to which *The Faerie Queene* is committed to tropes of

---

144 See the Appendix for a count of all the stanza lead words. My thanks again to Julian Lethbridge for the data sets on which this count is based.

qualification and modification. This is keenly showed by stanza 21, which begins with a pair of conjoined *Buts*: 'But the bold knight no whit dismayd,/ But catching vp in hand a ragged stone'. In the second line, 'And' would have served grammatically as well if not better than 'But', yet the repetition conveys Calepine's resilience and his determination not to let his lack of weaponry hold him back in the struggle with the bear. This 'But/But' structure is mirrored with an answering 'Ne/Ne' pattern in the final couplet, which describes the unfortunate bear's attempts to get rid of the stone: 'Ne could it vpward come, nor downward passe,/Ne could he brooke the coldnesse of the stony masse'. The preponderance of simple connectives as stanza lead words points to the organising tension within the fabric of *The Faerie Queene* between the individual stanza and its connectedness to the poem as a whole. So, But, Whom, Then, For, Which: these are easily overlooked process words which insist that the reader carries on, despite the temptations of somnolence, or indeed the oddness of the stanza form.[145]

So do these stanzas 'leak'? This data on lead words suggests that Spenser's trick of conveying change of pace is more plausibly connected with the organisation of syntax within and across stanzas. In other words, changes of mode of writing are not signalled by different kinds of stanza lead word – simple connectives predominate, whether Spenser is describing the bear hunt or Calidore watching Colin piping to the Graces. This observation forces us to look anew at the syntax within stanzas, and the rhetorical force of stanza close punctuation in the early editions. While much of the punctuation is too authoritative to destabilise, there is room to suggest that the full stops after the alexandrines are sometimes (as in the reading of *Muipotmos* above) best interpreted as half stops.[146] This tactic provides a good way of responding to the cue words at the beginnings of stanzas 20–22: 'So', 'But', and 'Whom' all in different ways insist on the continuity of action and readerly attention across stanza boundaries. The full stops at the ends of the stanzas signal that the usually unvarying stanzaic form has been satisfied, but they do not automatically demand that the reader pauses, or – as in Krier's suggestive work – surrenders to the semantic drift implicit in the white gaps which surround each discrete stanza.[147]

---

145 For readerly somnolence in the gaps between stanzas, see Krier, 'Time Lords', 5.
146 See for example the colon at the end of the third line of stanza 19: the grammatical marker introduces the explanatory 'For' clause which expands on why Calepine is unarmed.
147 Krier, 'Time Lords'.

Such surrenders may arguably be better placed during moments of reflection within the narrative, rather than in passages of continuous action. In this passage, it is imperative that the reader continues to concentrate through these boundaries. Consider the join between stanzas 21 and 22. Stanza 21 showcases a radical realisation of the nine-line stanza: the grammatical subunits are 7 + 2, in which the reader must breathlessly process the *Ababbcb* unit 'all attone' before reaching the relative calm of the *cc* couplet. This is mimetic writing with a vengeance, as Spenser uses enjambment to a much greater extent than usual. As Calepine brutally grapples with the bear, the absence of end-of-line punctuation in lines 3–5 of the 1596 edition is striking – 'thrust it all attone/Into his gaping throte, that made him grone/And gaspe for breath'.[148] These lines are almost Donnean in their transgression of Alpers's rule of the independent sovereignty of the line. They also show Spenser ignoring the first couplet of his stanza as a potential pause in order to convey the sense of narrative progress in the struggle; though in my view such writing is far from blank verse, the 7 + 2 arrangement demonstrates the Spenserian's inherent flexibility as a narrative form. As I commented earlier, the final couplet is noteworthy for its replication of the grammatical form of the stanza's first two lines, by being structured as two successive 'Ne-' clauses. Syntax is stretched by the 7 + 2 format, but stanzaic arrangement in the elegant disposition of rhymes and repeated clauses is perhaps almost too neatly enforced by this horrible anaphoristic climax.

Stanza 21 thus ends with the cliffhanger of the bear choking on the stone, unable either to vomit or to digest 'the stony masse'. The beginning of stanza 22 suggests direct continuity with the accusative pronoun 'Whom', but focus shifts to Calepine, who is in the process of realising that he has the advantage – it is now the animal who is 'thus combred'. Pronouns are confused in the opening lines: the 'he' of line 1 is Calepine, but in line 2 it is the bear who is 'Stryuing in vaine that nigh his bowels brast', while in lines 3–4 it is again Calepine who takes the lead in 'laying mightie hold/Vpon his throte'. There is a sense that Spenser's uncertain pronouns enact something of the intimate confusion of the struggle, as well as suggesting some of the complex mirrorings which run throughout Book VI between the ostensibly civilised and the ostensibly wild.[149] In terms of

---

148 Arguably ll.2 and 6 are also enjambed into the succeeding subclauses: 'a ragged stone,/ Which lay thereby' and 'he nigh choked was,/Being vnable' would still make sense without the commas.
149 See Humphrey Tonkin, *Spenser's Courteous Pastoral*.

syntax, stanza 22 returns to a more orthodox pattern as the bear is vanquished. Lines 1–5 form a coherent subunit which climaxes with Calepine toppling the bear – 'him down to ground he cast'; in the ensuing four lines, Calepine seems finally to kill the bear. This 5 + 4 pattern is the inverse of the 4 + 5 arrangement of stanza 20, where the first quatrain narrates Calepine overtaking the bear, while the next five lines narrate the bear's outraged reaction to his assailant. Following Empson's comments quoted above, these stanzas show contrasting realisations of the fifth line as a structural marker: in stanza 22, the first couplet is a necessary prelude to the subunit of the last four lines, whereas stanza 20 enforces a strong semantic break between the fourth and fifth lines so that the first couplet is not registered as such by the reader. 'Compeld him soone the spoyle adowne to lay' is a completed grammatical action, cued by the full stop at the end of the line. 'Wherewith the beast enraged to loose his pray' initiates the second half of the stanza, and is effectively a redirection of narrative interest from Calepine to the bear – as we have seen in stanzas 21 and 22, poetic focus oscillates rapidly from one protagonist to the other across and between these stanzas; indeed, part of the purpose of these stanzas is precisely to shuffle bear with knight to suggest their similarities. Like 'So', 'But', and 'Whom', 'Wherewith' is a transactional conjunction which enforces the connection between the two 'halves' of stanza 20.[150] In truth, however, where and how Spenser makes the breaks within stanzas is negotiated afresh with each new one; in comparison with the sixain, each Spenserian is significantly more unpredictable in terms of where and how syntax is broken or protracted. What is relatively certain is that the stanza will end or seem to end with a definitive pause in sense, underlined by rhyme. In some cases, however, the full stop seems more of a rhetorical reminder – a placeholder, a poetic intent – rather than a 'brick-wall' stop.[151] We may legitimately, according to poetic context, read the closes of these stanzas as more akin to commas – half stops – than modern full stops; narrative action is certainly drawn out through these stanzas, and it is only with the beginning of stanza 23 – 'Then tooke he vp betwixt his armes twaine/The litle babe' – that the reader feels the conflict has been closed off. This is partly because of the ambiguity of

150 See "wherewith, adv. (and n.)." *OED Online*, particularly 3, 'with which as cause or occasion'.

151 I have borrowed the idea of a 'brick-wall stop' from Dodie Smith, *I Capture the Castle*, in which the narrator, Cassandra Mortmain, cautions against the 'brick-wall happy endings' of romantic fiction, 235.

Spenser's stanza lead words, but is also in this case because of his tactical elision between stanzas 22 and 23 of the question of whether the bear has finally been killed. Line 7 and stanza 22 implies his demise – 'Ere long enforst to breath his vtmost blast' – yet it is an entirely characteristic suspension of narrative, information flow, and stanzaic form, that the death of the bear is not decisively narrated.

Both the passages examined in detail in this chapter suggest the unusually permissive syntax which was paradoxically licensed by the Spenserian stanza. *The Faerie Queene* is written in a poetically complicated form which at the same time, partly because of its origins in rhyme royal, could be pointed syntactically in a number of divergent, contrasting, and interconnected ways. Providing the poet has the technique to write the Spenserian more or less 'at will', it is a form which will enable an almost infinite range of syntactic permutations – in other words, the restraint of the form is seldom a restraint on how Spenser organises his material. It is the still resistant complexity of the Spenserian which in turn may account for Spenser's intricate mirrorings and reduplications of lexis between stanzas; a stanza with one rhyme repeated three times and another four times necessarily generates a quasi-symphonic web of opportunities for repetition. I have considered inter-stanzaic repetitions of rhyme elsewhere, so I conclude by looking at a pair of simpler repetitions within this passage.

Like the blurry pronouns in stanza 22, Spenser's choice of word tends to elide the differences between the antagonists in ways which are characteristic of Book VI as a whole and, indeed, his practice as a poet alert for the affective values of strategic repetition.[152] As he reclaims (or steals) the baby from the bear, so Calepine is merged with the bear both physically and lexically. Semantic mirrorings of this kind occur both in and out of the *Ababbcbcc* rhyme scheme. Firstly, in stanza 20, the baby is described in relation to the 'greedie' bear as 'the spoyle'; then in stanza 25, the hungry baby becomes Calepine's 'louely litle spoile'.[153] Despite the differences of orthography, there is little change in the two uses of 'spoyle'.[154] What is

152 See Humphrey Tonkin, '*The Faerie Queene*, Book VI', 283–87, and bibliography.
153 'Greedie' is here a transferred epithet in the description of the bear's angry reaction to Calepine's assault, 'with greedie force/And furie'.
154 See "spoil, n." *OED Online*. In both cases, Spenser's meaning fits with *OED* I.1: 'any goods, property, territory, etc., seized by force, acquired by confiscation, or obtained by similar means; booty, loot, plunder'. Figuratively at least, both Calepine and the bear are freebooters.

modified is poetic context and usage. In the second case, 'spoile' is the final part of the B-rhyme – the orthographic change is precisely to engineer a successful eye-rhyme with the preceding rhyme word 'toile' – while the qualifying phrase 'louely litle' helps to differentiate Calepine's attitude towards the baby from the bear's.[155] While it is still a nuisance, it is a nuisance he has to feed rather than feeding on it himself. The second example tells a similar story. The C-rhyme of stanza 22, *paine: vaine: straine* focuses on the agonised bear's final struggles, with the characteristically ambiguous pronouns noted above. The eighth line in particular – 'Gnashing his cruell teeth at him in vaine' – anticipates the alexandrine of stanza 25, 'So all that day in wandring vainely he did spend'. Here 'in vaine' moves from the rhyming position to the middle of the line, but the congruity enforced by the repetition is clear. If the bear cannot rid itself of the stone, Calepine is rendered equally useless by being lost, though as the canto goes on, Calepine's sense of encumbrance is fortuitously relieved by the Matilde narrative.[156]

This chapter has tried to convey a sense of the strangeness of the Spenserian in its immediate literary and social contexts, alongside a re-evaluation of its predecessors. In my view, the Spenserian is a direct development of the rhyme royal stanza of Chaucer, which extends that form's narrative plasticity into an even more permissive structure. What made Spenser difficult for readers like Henry Gurney was not so much the intricacy of his syntax – indeed, as Alpers long ago demonstrated, decoding Spenser grammatically is significantly easier than decoding Drayton or Marlowe – but was the radical unpredictability of the stanza in action. My illustrations from Books I and VI underline this quality: although the Spenserian is a fixed and restrictive form in terms of the rhyme pattern, Spenser uses it in such a way as to showcase its seemingly endless plasticity, as stanza leads onto stanza, and the narrative of the poem is protracted, modified, paused, taken up anew with each fresh unit.

I conclude with two contrasting observations which have a purchase on the ongoing enigma of the Spenserian stanza. The first is from Catherine

---

155 For the importance of eye rhyme to the printing of *The Faerie Queene*, see Suzuki, 'Irregular Visual Rhymes in *The Faerie Queene, Part I* (Books I–III)'. For rhymes on 'spoile' and 'spoyle', see Brown and Lethbridge, *A Concordance*, 379.
156 See Frederick Kiefer, 'Fortune', 312–13, who notes that Book VI contains more references to Fortune than any other book, and bibliography. The allusions to fortune in this canto are in stanzas 2, 15, 21, 25, 26 (two contrasting references: Calepine experiences 'good fortune' in overhearing Matilde, while she her 'fortune oft defyde'), 30, 35.

Bates's *Masculinity and the Hunt* (2013). Bates's pioneering study begins with two related propositions about the unattainability of desire and the 'non-recuperable' quality of subjectivity. In relation to the latter, she writes that there is 'a permanent condition of non-coincidence and self-division in which the subject's striving for integrity and the prospect of achieving a "whole" self to which to be true is, no matter how devoutly to be wished, structurally unachievable (the ego is not master in its own house)'.[157] Spenser is close to the heart of Bates's work on the hunt as a trope of abject masculinity, and this formulation – despite its focus on the enduring issue of what Stephen Greenblatt called Renaissance Self-Fashioning – is also suggestive of the way in which Spenserian stanzas work within *The Faerie Queene*. Each stanza strives for integrity of form – an integrity which is by no means realised in every case – while being structurally connected to the larger whole of the unfinished poem. Few egos within that poem – whether they are characters like Calepine or Serena, or larger structures such as episodes – achieve 'a "whole" self', while the poem as a whole is even as we make that statement, necessarily fragmented, ruinous, and – in Matthew Lownes evocative choice of word – 'vnperfite'. We study a poem which repeatedly gestures towards coherence and totality, and yet which on every page reminds us of its patchiness. The difficult-yet-permissive stanzaic form analysed in this chapter is simply another reminder of that fact.

My second observation is from Louis MacNeice's 'Eclogue by a Five Barred Gate'. This poem introduces two remarkably dim shepherds, hooked on the beautiful and narcotic qualities of poetry, who have a fateful encounter with Death. The latter gives the shepherds a forceful tutorial in poetry which they ultimately – inevitably – ignore. Death's lesson nevertheless stands as a stark warning to any formal reading which seeks what one of the shepherds calls 'The sleeping beauty behind the many-coloured hedge':

> Poetry you think is only the surface vanity,
> The painted nails, the hips narrowed by fashion,
> The hooks and eyes of words; but it is not that only

This chapter has necessarily focused on 'the hooks and eyes of words' to explain the novelty of the Spenserian stanza as a piece of poetic technology, 'but it is not that only'. Death of course never states decisively what poetry

157 Bates, *Masculinity and the Hunt*, 35.

is, but the reader infers something of what he means as the heedless shepherds skip through the gate 'together to these pastures new'. Yet, as Death caustically reminds the reader in the final lines, 'They are gone and I am alone/With a gate the façade of a mirage'.[158] Poetry such as Spenser's, though almost superlatively invested in 'the surface vanity' of formal devices, always has other agendas, other designs on its readers.

---

158 MacNeice, *Collected Poems*, 11, 14. 'Eclogue' was first published in MacNeice's *Poems* (1935) and is part of his repudiation of the aestheticism and escapism which characterised that volume; see Richard Danson Brown, *Louis MacNeice and the Poetry of the 1930s*, 18, 59.

5

Another cast in different hews: canto form

There is a sense that whenever we talk about *The Faerie Queene*, we talk about cantos. Most readings begin with an excerpted canto or episode in an anthology. As teachers, we set individual cantos on the basis that they may prove more digestible to students than the larger book or the enormous poem. Roger Sale speaks for generations of teachers: 'No one will be badly mistaken about Spenser's understanding of temperance by reading the Bower of Bliss episode by itself.'[1] Like diminished Hazlitts tendering brevity for 'brilliancy of fancy', we pragmatically offer the canto as a partly self-contained, not too time-consuming, potentially even enjoyable artifact, to students who might otherwise be put off by *The Faerie Queene*'s enormity.[2] Yet such use of the canto is largely opportunistic – used in this way, cantos are flags of convenience rather than discrete formal units. So is the Spenserian canto simply a proxy term for a convenient division in a long work? This chapter aims to probe the question of how Spenser's cantos work through the juxtaposition of two different parts of the poem: I consider Spenser at his most fractured and seemingly casual, in the second installment at the heart of Book VI, with its incomplete narratives, and explore questions of canto structure and the role of the narrator. I then move on to the more networked composition which characterises the first installment,

---

1 Roger Sale, 'Canto', 135.
2 In Alpers (ed.), *Edmund Spenser: A Critical Anthology*, 133. I have participated in this ritual myself: see Brown, 'The Renaissance Epic', which introduces students to the poem via an excerpt from I.ix, and the whole of II.xii. My choices illustrate the tendency of teachers to choose the more celebrated cantos and episodes – allegorical cores and narrative climaxes – over cantos of incident.

to look at thematic connections across sequential cantos where narrative connections are less clear cut. We begin, however, with a cliffhanger.

Serena's 'cast'

At the end of Book VI Canto VIII, Calepine is at last reunited with Serena. Yet the reunion is both incomplete and, to Serena at least, terrifying and shaming. Calepine frees her from the chiaroscuro nightmare of being sacrificed by the saluage nation 'by th'vncertaine glims of starry night,/ And by the twinkling of their sacred fire' (VI.viii.48), but in that half light of her rescue, her nakedness and insecurity dominate, and the lovers do not recognise one another:

> From them returning to that Ladie backe,
> Whom by the Altar he doth sitting find,
> Yet fearing death, and next to death the lacke
> Of clothes to couer, what they ought by kind,
> He first her hands beginneth to vnbind;
> And then to question of her present woe;
> And afterwards to cheare with speaches kind.
> But she for nought that he could say or doe,
> One word durst speake, or answere him a whit thereto.
>
> So inward shame of her vncomely case
> She did conceiue, through care of womanhood,
> That though the night did couer her disgrace,
> Yet she in so vnwomanly a mood,
> Would not bewray the state in which she stood.
> So all that night to him vnknowen she past.
> But day, that doth discouer bad and good,
> Ensewing, made her knowen to him at last:
> The end whereof Ile keepe vntill another cast. (VI.viii.50–51)

This is a piece of writing very much in keeping with Book VI as a whole: characters stumble across friends and lovers without recognition; narrative tropes and turns of phrase are repeated and recycled in slightly different, slightly unsettling ways.[3] Serena's 'vncomely case' – with the inevitable *double entendre* which circulates around the term – echoes the opening of the canto, where the narrator urges his female readers to profit from

---

3 Compare the meetings of Arthur and Timias in VI.v.23–24 and VI.viii.4, and see Harry Berger, 'A Secret Discipline', for a comprehensive description of the patterns of transition and duplication in the Book; in *Revisionary Play*, 217–19.

Mirabella's example: 'And as ye soft and tender are by kynde,/Adorn with goodly gifts of beauties grace … Ensample take of *Mirabellaes* case (VI.viii.2).[4] Book VI is a sequence of more or less unfortunate cases, and yet no two are quite the same.[5] Where the behaviourist punishment of Mirabella – a court of love boot camp, determined to take down a 'proud and insolent' erotic prima donna – aims to inculcate a chauvinist moral against feminine 'cruelty and hardnesse' (VI.vii.29; VI.viii.2), Serena's plight is even more troubling.[6] Naked, ashamed, and seemingly at the point of a violent death, her 'vnwomanly' turning in on herself – 'Would not bewray the state in which she stood' – shows an impulse to resist exemplarity, to 'couer her disgrace' in ways which the solicitous but dim Calepine does not register, with his almost comic oversight of Serena's 'lacke/Of clothes to couer'. It's a provocative way to end Canto VIII, which returns Serena to the predicament she has endured since Canto III, when she was wounded by the Blatant Beast, a shame wound, which we subsequently discover can be cured only through abstinence from pleasure of all kinds (VI.vi.13–15). As Thomas P. Roche noted, this ending leaves the reader's desire for closure terminally unsatisfied: 'At this point, Calepine and Serena leave the narrative. Spenser's promise to finish their tale is in the manner of Ariosto, but, unlike Ariosto, Spenser never provides the promised conclusion.'[7] The close of VI.viii is not unusual in *The Faerie Queene*, but it remains a striking example of the way in which Spenser's literary artifice controls his narrative materials. Humphrey Tonkin comments: 'In the *Faerie Queene* stories repeatedly end inconclusively … because the poem is like life, and because one episode is subsumed in another in an endless series, but in the case of Serena the uncertainty is especially puzzling and frustrating.'[8]

4 See Hamilton's note on 'vncomely case' as a metonymy for Serena's 'daintie parts' (VI.viii.42–43) in *FQ*, 659, related to "case, n.2.", particularly 8, *OED Online*. This sense of 'case' is much less available in VI.viii.2, which derives more directly from "case, n.1." *OED Online*, sense 2. See also Zurcher, *Spenser's Legal Language*, 247, for two legal senses which are particularly relevant to Mirabella.

5 See Tonkin, *Spenser's Courteous Pastoral*, 35, for the squire's 'haplesse case' (VI.i.12) as an initial indication of the Book's 'inordinate stress on the vagaries of fortune'.

6 For my earlier reading of the Mirabella episode, see Brown, '"Charmed with Inchaunted Rimes"' in Brown and Lethbridge, *A Concordance*, 32–38.

7 In Spenser, *The Faerie Queene*, ed. Thomas P. Roche. Penguin ebook, note to VI.viii.51.9. See also Berger's brilliant formulation: 'The sudden shift from the problems of murder to those of modesty is characteristic of the disequilibrium Spenser maintains in this book', 'A Secret Discipline', in *Revisionary Play*, 218 n.5.

8 Tonkin, *Spenser's Courteous Pastoral*, 104. Tonkin goes on to suggest that Serena's shame derives from her consciousness of her disregard of the Hermit's teaching and her earlier resentment of Calepine (105–06). Earlier, he canvasses the possibility that the missing

The mechanics of writing in cantos are visible as the narrator juxtaposes the unfinished story with his own contingent yet undisclosed reasons for not pressing ahead.[9] Tonkin's sense that this point of closure is unusually unsatisfying is justified by Spenser's wording. While 'But day, that doth discouer bad and good,/Ensewing, made her knowen to him at last' suggests that a resolution is just around the corner, the hierarchy of terms – in which the unrhyming 'bad' precedes and overshadows 'good' – reveals the resistances and emotional complexities which still obtain between Serena and Calepine. Similarly, the rhyming locution 'another cast' recalls through alliteration and assonance 'vncomely case'. One might summarise that the 'case' needs another 'cast' to bring it to an 'end', but that the tone of that prospective ending is – on this evidence at least – ominous and unsettled. Though 'cast' is not an unusual word in *The Faerie Queene*, it is much commoner in verbal forms than as a noun.[10] When Calepine is initially separated from Serena, 'Vpon a day he *cast* abrode to wend,/To take the ayre, and heare the thrushes song' (VI.iv.17), the word has the sense of to purpose or determine.[11] The most frequent verbal use is in the sense of 'to throw', as in a passage which immediately follows Calepine and Serena's reunion, describing Calidore's persistence in his quest: 'Full many pathes and perils he hath past ... In that same quest which fortune on him cast' (VI.ix.2). This suggests that the close of Canto VIII is not simply a wording imposed on Spenser by the exigences of rhyme; rather, he chooses to describe his cantos as rolls of the dice.[12] It's almost as though the narrator is saying that, given another throw, he *may* return to this story but is – prophetically, as it turns out – making no promises; in this context, 'Ile keepe vntill another cast' nicely conveys the poet's control of his materials. The seeming randomness of fictional events, alongside the unusual prominence of Fortune in Book VI, means that once we turn the page to Calidore's 'quest which fortune on him cast' – again the coupling

---

narrative of Serena and Calepine's 'return to society ... is perhaps subsumed in the return of Calidore and Pastorella' (54).

9 See Patricia A. Parker, *Inescapable Romance*, 108, for the observation that the 'marking of transitions and the careful interweaving of episodes throughout Book VI contribute to this sense of artifice, an impression which Spenser usually mutes'.

10 See "cast, v.", and "cast, n." *OED Online*. There are 117 instances of the word in *The Faerie Queene*: see Brown and Lethbridge, *A Concordance*, 391; 450; and Lethbridge's unpublished Concordance, 320–21. For cast as a noun, see III.x.35, VI.iv.9, VI.vii.9. Hamlet's 'pale cast of thought', with the sense of tinge of melancholy, was apparently a Shakespearean coinage; see Shakespeare, *Hamlet*, ed. G. R. Hibbard, 241.

11 My emphasis. See "cast, v.", VII.44. *OED Online*.

12 See "cast, n." 3.a and quotations, *OED Online*.

of *quest* with *cast* through alliteration and half-rhyme enforces the suggestion of a reciprocity between these terms – the reader is profoundly attuned to Spenserian doublethink.[13] On the one hand, episodes are narrated fortuitously; on the other, that sense of chance is poetically determined – cast – by Spenser's mercurial narrator.

There is a further 'cast' which is worth noting. Just before his ill-judged yet accidental interruption of Calepine and Serena's lovemaking ('He chaunst to come whereas a iolly Knight … did safely rest/To solace with his Lady in delight', VI.iii.20),[14] Calidore copes with one of the cruxes in his role as the Knight of Courtesy: does he reveal to Priscilla's class-conscious father everything he knows about her relationship with the lower-ranking Aladine? At the beginning of the Book, the narrator aligns Courtesy with truth-telling when he states that it is the 'roote of ciuill conuersation', and identifies Calidore as a paragon who 'loathd leasing, and base flattery,/ And loued simple truth and stedfast honesty' (VI.i.1, 3). Yet he gives his word to help Aladine and Priscilla, so has to contrive a way out his conundrum. As many commentators have noted, Calidore's equivocation derives from Stefano Guazzo's advice in his conduct manual *Civile Conuersation* that 'it is commendable to coyne a lye at some time … so that it tend to some honest ende'.[15] In framing his response, Calidore thinks through what he needs to do: 'He can deuize this counter-cast of slight,/To giue faire colour to that Ladies cause in sight' (VI.iii.16). 'Counter-cast' is an unusual formulation – *OED* records only this example, defining it as 'an antagonistic contrivance or artifice'.[16] Spenser's coinage gets to the heart of Calidore's courtly contrivance: Courtesy is partly a rhetorical 'deuize' which 'giue[s] faire colour' to what Calidore needs Priscilla's father to believe. But this also suggests that in the writing of Book VI – which Tonkin has characterised as an unusually self-conscious text, a poem about poetry – Spenser used 'cast' as a way of conveying the relationships

13 For Book VI and the quest motif, see Tonkin, *Spenser's Courteous Pastoral*, 6–8, and passim, and Bates, *Masculinity and the Hunt*, 282–87.

14 On this interruption, see Sean Henry, 'Getting Spenser's Goat', 312: 'I am inclined to think that Calidore has caught them *in flagrante*, given the nature of the wounds Serena suffers from the Blatant Beast'.

15 Stefano Guazzo, *The Civile Conuersation*, sig.F3r. Also cited by Tonkin, *Spenser's Courteous Pastoral*, 48 n.14, and in *FQ*, 620.

16 See "†'counter-cast, n." *OED Online*. John Weever's 'In Vulpem puritanem' (1599) makes extensive play on various meanings of 'counter' and 'cast', including the suggestion that its puritan subject 'had been in the Counter [prison] cast'. Given Weever's praise of Spenser in the *Epigrammes*, it is not inconceivable that this poem registers the influence of this stanza; see E. A. J. Honigmann, *John Weever*, 17, 18, and sig. F4r.

between poetic contrivance, Fortune, and episodic narrative.[17] To think about a canto as a cast of the poetic dice in the context of a book where the word is spliced with 'counter' at a crucial moment for how we understand Courtesy in action gives some purchase on one of the least discussed aspects of the forms of *The Faerie Queene*: the canto as a narrative unit.

Reception and critical problems

While canto form has been neglected, it has not been ignored entirely. The main approaches to the problem have all been broadly formalist, from the comparative work of Alpers, to numerological analyses, to an approach informed by Book History which offers a radical recontextualisation of *The Faerie Queene*'s running headers. According to Alpers, the canto is a key unit of narration, intimately related to the poem's 'rhetorical mode' – as he puts it, 'the basic large unit in *The Faerie Queene* is the canto, not the book.'[18] Alpers cashes this claim in part through his magnificent readings of individual cantos: he illuminates the connections between the Cave of Despair and the opening conversation between Una and Arthur (I.ix) in terms of Spenser's 'radical criticism of human heroism.'[19] At the same time, although, in James Nohrnberg's words, *The Poetry of The Faerie Queene* 'remains perhaps the one study the serious student of Spenser cannot afford to ignore, cannot afford not to be instructed by', the perception of the primacy of the canto is an aspect of Alpers's instruction which has fallen by the interpretative wayside.[20] The book rather than the canto remains the constitutive unit in criticism, and it is studies of individual books which have had the most continuous influence on Spenser studies since the 1950s.[21] More recently, the tendency has been

---

17 Tonkin, *Spenser's Courteous Pastoral*, 13–17, and passim.
18 Alpers, *The Poetry of The Faerie Queene*, 107; for 'rhetorical mode', see 3–35. See also Sale, 'Canto', for a statement of the interdependence of lines, stanzas and cantos which draws on Alpers's work: 'consideration of his cantos best begins with a consideration of his lines and stanzas' (134).
19 Alpers, *The Poetry of The Faerie Queene*, 349–61 (349). Note also the following comment: 'Critics invariably neglect this episode [Arthur's account of his upbringing and his falling in love with the Fairy Queen] when they discuss the encounter with Despair, but its relevance is a striking indication of the fact that Spenser thinks of a canto as a poetic unit' (350). Alpers sees this relevance in terms of the valuing of human feelings, and the way in which Arthur's relationship with the Redcrosse Knight anticipates the latter's with Trevisan (350–51).
20 James C. Nohrnberg, 'Paul Alpers, *The Poetry of The Faerie Queene*'.
21 Consider (in order of publication) Harry Berger, Jr, *The Allegorical Temper* (on Book II); Thomas P. Roche, *The Kindly Flame* (on Books III and IV); T. K. Dunseath,

for the installment and edition to dislodge the Book. There are good reasons
for this: cantos are grouped in books, and whatever the problematics of the
Letter to Raleigh, Spenser composed in books which he viewed as linked
narrative and philosophical explorations of abstract concepts. Book head-
ings, with their firm annunciations of allegorical intent, remain consistent
across the two volumes published in Spenser's lifetime.[22] Pragmatically,
whatever the vagaries of narrative in Books III and IV, the book remains a
coherent grouping for study and analysis, which – to paraphrase Sale – will
not badly mislead the student who reads only one about *The Faerie Queene*
as a whole.[23] Nevertheless, a structural problem remains between on the
one hand books which are uneven and dissimilar in terms of narrative
structure (even though each contains the same, *Aeneid*-echoing number
of cantos) and on the other hand cantos which vary enormously in length,
focus, and structure.

Problems of this kind are at the root of numerological approaches
which attempt to relate the numbers of the different components of *The
Faerie Queene* – books, cantos, lines – to the poem's symbolic agendas.
Alastair Fowler's *Spenser and the Numbers of Time* has a chapter on canto
placement, which explains the occurrence of episodes in relation to his
argument that the poem is structured around the Pythagorean monad.
Fowler's ground-breaking work shows little interest in whether cantos
have a form: his chapter exemplifies a book-centric view of form, in which
certain types of episodes recur at predetermined places within each Legend.
Though conceding that 'narrative requirements, after all, must sometimes
have decided the sequence', Fowler's observations are rooted in examples
like Arthur's tendency to appear in the eighth canto, and the appearance

---

Spenser's Allegory of Justice in Book Five of The Faerie Queene; Jane Aptekar, *Icons of Justice* (on Book V); Tonkin, *Spenser's Courteous Pastoral* (on Book VI); Angus Fletcher, *The Prophetic Moment* (on Book V); Jonathan Goldberg, *Endlesse Work* (on Book IV); David Lee Miller, *The Poem's Two Bodies* (on the 1590 *Faerie Queene*). More recent work continues similar trends: Jane Grogan (ed.), *Celebrating Mutabilitie* (an essay collection on the Mutabilitie Cantos, almost as a quasi-book), Walls, *God's Only Daughter* (a monograph on Una), and Daniel Moss, *The Ovidian Vogue* (which considers the Ovidian echoes in Book V).

22 Compare *The Faerie Queene* (1590), 389, and *The Faerie Queene* (1596), 389; I quote here from the latter – the former has the same text, with slightly modified conventions in terms of capitalisation: 'THE THIRD/ BOOKE OF THE/ FAERIE QVEENE./ Contayning,/ THE LEGEND OF BRITOMARTIS./ OR/ Of Chastitie.'

23 In this context, the Hackett series, primarily aimed at school students, is interesting: Hackett has five individual volumes, two of which contain more than one Book: *The Faerie Queene: Books Three and Four*, ed. Dorothy Stephens, and *The Faerie Queene: Book Six and the Mutabilitie Cantos*, ed. Andrew Hadfield and Abraham Stoll.

'in every book except IV' of 'an elaborately described image of evil' in the eleventh canto.[24] From the same period, Michael Baybak, Paul Deleny, and A. Kent Hieatt's influential article, 'Placement "In the Middest" in *The Faerie Queene*', argues that narrative structure in the poem is partly conditioned by 'the arithmetically central stanza' in each book of the 1590 installment, a structure which was 'disturbed' by changes in the 1596 edition; they conclude that Spenser's 'interest in numerical composition was strong enough during the process of original composition for him to have built significant numerical midpoints into all of the Books of the first edition'.[25] Again, the canto is subservient to the book.

Canto-specific numerology includes Maren-Sofie Røstvig's 'Canto Structure in Tasso and Spenser', which reads Tasso's and Spenser's cantos based on an Augustinian understanding of artistic patterning and the symbolic potential of numbering. Røstvig compares *Gerusalemme Liberata* canto 15 (Rinaldo's journey to Armida's bower) with *The Faerie Queene* II.x. Spenser's canto follows Tasso's in being based on a numerical pattern which implicitly adumbrates an Augustinian allegory: where Tasso's is structured on a '"providential"' 2:1 ratio, Spenser's canto is also, differently, based around 'the number of redemption, 33'.[26] Røstvig's argumentation depends as much on close reading and a sensitivity to Spenser's recursive patterns of phrasing and rhyming as on intricate numerical work, all of which tends to support the observation that 'Spenser's manipulation of canto structure' is significant.[27] Jerry Leath Mills's 'Spenser and the Numbers of History' also explores the chronicle history cantos, arguing that they are underpinned by multiples of seven and nine, which he connects with Jean Bodin's numerological schema around the climacteric. As Mills puts it, 'the structure invests the theory of Bodin in a pattern which throws into relief the three great events of the coming of Christianity, the coming of

---

24 Fowler, *Spenser and the Numbers of Time*, 53–54.
25 Michael Baybak, Paul Deleny, and A. Kent Hieatt, 'Placement "In the Middest" in *The Faerie Queene*', 227, 233. The article was first published in 1969, and then reprinted in Hamilton (ed.), *Essential Articles for the Study of Edmund Spenser* (1972). Hieatt's *Short Time's Endless Moniment* (1960) on *Epithalamion* was in large measure the inaugurator of numerology in Spenser studies; see Dunlop, 'Modern Studies in Number Symbolism', 512–13. See also Hieatt, 'Three Fearful Symmetries and the meaning of *Faerie Queene* II'.
26 Røstvig, 'Canto Structure in Tasso and Spenser', 186. Røstvig gets her thirty-threes from the observation that Arthur reads sixty-six stanzas on the Briton kings which 'divide into two equal halves: thirty-three on Brutus and his progeny, and thirty-three on the generations from the English Numa, Dunwallo' (186). For Augustine, see 177, 196.
27 Røstvig, 'Canto Structure in Tasso and Spenser', 197.

Arthur, and the coming of Henry Tudor.'[28] Numerology remains speculative, but Mills's essay is persuasive because of its basis in a contemporaneous source of which Spenser was aware; such perspectives further suggest the careful arrangement of stanzas within cantos to produce symbolic patterns.

Kenneth Borris and Meredith Donaldson Clark's article, 'Hymnic Epic and *The Faerie Queene*'s Original Printed Format' (2011), offers an original perspective on what we mean when we talk about Spenser writing in cantos. Based on the examination of a range of contemporary works in English and Italian, Borris and Clark home in on the eccentricity of the abbreviation used in early editions of *The Faerie Queene*. The conventional assumption is that '*Cant.*', which stands at the head of every canto except I.i, and is used in the running heads throughout the 1590 and 1596 editions, signifies 'canto'. Through detailed comparisons, Borris and Clark argue that since '*Cant.*' is not used for 'canto' elsewhere, the term 'would have more readily suggested *canticle*, a hymn or spiritual song'.[29] In problematising *Cant.*, this article throws renewed attention on the novelty of the Italian word 'canto' during the 1590s. Through comparisons with the translations of Italian epic by Sir John Harington, Richard Carew, Robert Tofte, and Edward Fairfax, Borris and Clark underline the sense that 'canto' was seen as a Spenserian property: 'The norms of these published translations confirm that, in English usage, the word *canto* appeared to be an Italianate Spenserism throughout the 1590s, for these texts predominantly avoid it, as if it were beyond the bounds of English diction at that time'.[30] Borris and Clark's work suggests the inadequacy of the ways in which Spenser scholarship has conceptualised the canto as an innovation in literary praxis and terminology in the 1590s. This is chiefly connected with the overlooking of 'canticle' as a generic intertext. In reading Spenser's divisions solely as Italianate 'cantos', we have assumed that he was flaunting a literary genetics from Ariosto, Tasso, and, more distantly, Dante, rather than considering the ways in which the biblical 'canticle' allies *The Faerie Queene* with the metrical psalter and the Song of Songs.[31]

This observation, however, does not displace the Italian intertexts. The 1590 *Faerie Queene* unambiguously claims 'canto' through the heading 'Canto I' at I.i, which is likely the first such usage of the term in English

---

28 Jerry Leath Mills, 'Spenser and the Numbers of History', 285.

29 Borris and Clark, 'Hymnic Epic', 1149, 1152.

30 Borris and Clark, 'Hymnic Epic', 1158–59. See also 1161–62, which allies Spenser's innovative usage with his stanza form and arguments.

31 Borris and Clark, 'Hymnic Epic', 1162–64.

for a division in a long poem.[32] Though the *OED* entry for 'canto' has not
been updated since the nineteenth century, a search using the *Early Modern
Print* database suggests that *The Faerie Queene* has priority.[33] In John
Florio's *First Fruites* (1578), a passage from *Orlando Furioso* is sourced
'*al Canto trentesimo*', which is Englished as 'at the thirtye song'.[34] The song,
we might say, does *not* remain the same across languages. By implication,
Borris and Clark draw attention to a related peculiarity of the early editions:
this is in the single appearance of the word 'canto' in the 1590 installment.
Moreover, as a part of the poem's lexis, the word occurs only in Books
IV–VI, where it is used nine times, in each case as part of self-conscious
canto signs-offs: 'for my Muse her selfe now tyred has,/Vnto an other
Canto I will ouerpas' (IV.xi.53).[35] Though Books I–III do contain similar
cliffhangers, such self-conscious markers of the canto edge are significantly
more prevalent in the second installment, and seem to be associated, as
Patricia Parker has noted, with an enhanced sense of artifice.[36] Like the
introduction of feminine rhyme to Books IV–VI, Spenser seemed to want
to underline the novelty of his forms more systematically in 1596 than
he had in 1590. Thus while I agree with Borris and Clark that 'canticle'
provides a valuable context for Book I, this association recedes as the
poem goes on; indeed, the repeated use of the word 'canto' in Books IV–VI
has the effect of blunting the reader's sense of canto-as-canticle.

32 Borris and Clark, 'Hymnic Epic', 1154–55 (with facsimile).
33 See *Early Modern Print: Text Mining Early Printed English*, at https://earlyprint.wustl.edu
    [accessed 28 August 2017]. A single-term search on 'canto' shows the word occurring
    in a range of foreign language contexts, but no use of the word to denote a division in
    a poem before the 1590 *Faerie Queene*. My thanks to David Lee Miller for pointing
    me to this resource.
34 See "Canto, n." *OED Online*, and Florio, *Florio his firste fruites*, sig. L3r.
35 See Brown and Lethbridge, *A Concordance*, 391. The nine instances are: IV.ii.54; IV.ix.41;
    IV.x.58; IV.xi.53; V.v.57; V.vii.45; VI.ii.48; VI.iii.51; and VI.x.44; see the unpublished
    Lethbridge Concordance, 316.
36 Parker, *Inescapable Romance*, 108. There are five cantos which end self-consciously in
    Books I–III, three of which are book-enders, two for the different endings of Book III:
    I.vi.48; I.xii.42; III.vi.53–54; III.viii.52; III.xii.45 (*1596*); III.xii.47 (*1590*). In contrast,
    there are twenty-two such cantos in Books IV–VI; the following list cites only those
    not already included in the previous note: IV.iv.48; IV.v.46; IV.vi.47; IV.vii.47; IV.xii.35;
    V.iii.40; V.viii.51; V.xii.43; VI.i.41; VI.vii.50; VI.viii.51; VI.ix.46. My criterion for self-
    conscious canto edges is explicit reference to a deferred point or place of narrative.
    IV.vii.47 is prototypical: 'I will deferre the end vntill another tide'. In contrast, the next
    canto end refers to the end of the story but does not refer to the poem as narration:
    'as shall appeare by his euent' (IV.viii.63). Self-conscious endings are so prevalent in
    Book IV (nine out of twelve cantos on this reckoning), that it is hard not to read the
    same sorts of gestures throughout.

Alpers's assertion of the canto's primacy underlines one of the major eccentricities of *The Faerie Queene*: that it has both cantos *and* books. *Orlando Furioso* and *Gerusalemme Liberata* follow the romance tradition in having cantos as their main structural units. In the English tradition – informed by both the *Aeneid* and *Troilus and Criseyde* – long poems prior to *The Faerie Queene* tend to adopt a book structure, or are compilations made up of more or less discrete sections, like *The Mirror for Magistrates*. Graham Hough provides a useful overview of the competing options in the sixteenth century:

> Cantos are merely slices of convenient length, broken off wherever the narrator or the audience is in need of a rest; often, indeed most commonly, in the middle of a story. *Quel che segui ne l'altro canto e scritto*, as Ariosto is constantly saying. Whereas a book (though not originally so) was by this time conceived as an integral section of the plot – a member of the whole, but a member with some provisional completeness and unity of its own. *The Faerie Queene* … looks like an attempt to combine the features of the formal and the informal methods of construction.[37]

Another way of putting this would be that Spenser's forms constitute an enormous and ambitious 'Both And', which lays claim to the epic and romance traditions within the same oeuvre. I turn now to the discontinuous use of cantos in Book VI. Such discussion foregrounds the still controversial sense that the plots and forms of the poem abrade and buckle as Spenser continues to write: loose ends are not tied off and promised resolutions are postponed beyond the textual ken of the poem. The second half of the chapter therefore returns to Book III, where similar devices of happenstance and narrative discontinuity are woven together by other means. The question I want to explore through these readings is the extent to which Spenser's composition in cantos changed through the writing of *The Faerie Queene*.

Discontinuous canto form

Hough's summary offers a perhaps blunt response to the question I posed at the outset: cantos are tranches of narrative to be broken off whenever poet or reader fancies a convenience break. As the rather jaded narrator of Book IV is fond of saying: 'here my wearie teeme nigh ouer spent/Shall breath it selfe awhile, after so long a went' (IV.v.46). Since IV.v has forty-six

---

37 Hough, *A Preface to* The Faerie Queene, 85–86.

stanzas – in *Faerie Queene* terms a below average rather than an epic 'went' – the reader may detect elements of special pleading, and look for other explanations of this trope.[38] Nevertheless, we should not underestimate the innovation inherent in the notion that readers of long poems might need or want such breaks; medieval long poems such as *Troilus and Criseyde* – in which individual books stretch to 1800 lines – and verse romances, generally do not display this kind of readerly concern. The unit of narration is as long or as short (if we think of 'Sir Thopas') as the audience has patience; Spenser is more keenly conscious of his readers' comforts.[39]

Hough's sense that cantos are an 'informal method' of construction is borne out by the wide range of canto lengths in *The Faerie Queene*. At the furthest extremes, II.xii has 87 stanzas (783 lines), while V.1 has 30 stanzas (270 lines); by my calculations the average length of canto is 51.5 stanzas.[40] It is difficult to see this data as unambiguous evidence that Spenser was writing to strict, preconceived lengths.[41] The data is perhaps most suggestive of variety and change within a project that was itself

---

38 See "went, n." *OED Online*, for 'went' as a journey or movement (1.b). For the growing narratorial fatigue and sourness as the poem goes on, see Dees, 'Narrator of *The Faerie Queene*' (1990), 499.

39 See *Bevis of Hampton* in Ronald Herzman, Graham Drake, and Eve Salisbury (eds) *Four Romances of England*, 200–321, which prints the poem as 4620 uninterrupted lines; as the editors explain, *Bevis* is an episodic narrative, and scholars have conjectured a five part structure, roughly corresponding to what would be feasible in a recitation session; see 189–96. Print technology tended to impose narrative divisions onto such texts, as in William Copland's 1560 edition of *Bevis*; see *Syr Beuys of Hampton*, sig. C3v, where a woodcut facilitates a new heading. Rubrication of initial capitals in manuscripts could provide some of the effects of a chapter pause; see *Octavian* l.532 in Harriet Hudson (ed.) *Four Middle English Romances: Sir Isumbras, Octavian, Sir Eglamour of Artois, Sir Tryamour*, 57, 91. For sixteenth-century editions of *Bevis* and their influence on Spenser, see King, *The Faerie Queene and Middle English Romance*, 30–34, 129–45. My thanks to Jane Grogan for this point.

40 The basis of this calculation is that *The Faerie Queene* has 74 completed cantos in the 1609 edition, and excludes the 'vnperfite' two-stanza Canto VIII of Mutabilitie and the proems. I have preferred the 1596 edition over the 1590 – thus I.xii has 55 stanzas, and III.xii has 45 (54 and 47 respectively in 1590). This produces a sum of 3809 stanzas divided by 74 cantos, which produces the figure 51.472972973.

41 See Fowler, *Spenser and the Numbers of Time*, for the argument that Spenser 'arranged for the stanza-totals of certain of its cantos to be arithmetical means between the totals of corresponding cantos in Books I and III' (15–16). Stanza numbering is only introduced as part of the poem's *mise en page* in 1609; this does not disprove Fowler's schema, but it does make the reader's arithmetical work harder, as do the textual discrepancies between the 1590 and 1596 editions in terms of stanza totals. As throughout, my position is sceptical rather than hostile; more work needs to be done around the relationship between number and compositional units both in Spenser and in Renaissance poetry more generally.

mutating through composition – thus book lengths in the second installment tend to become slightly shorter than in the first installment.[42] Though there are instances where consecutive cantos are of the same length, canto lengths in themselves are not predictive. A sequence of three cantos with 46 stanzas each is followed by the shorter measure of 38 stanzas (II.ii–v); the just over average IV.xi (53 stanzas) is followed by the substantially under par IV.xii (35 stanzas), and then the even more slender V.i (30 stanzas). Such statistical variation suggests randomness rather than homogeneity – a canto was as long as Spenser needed it to be. As Hough argues, it seems likely that Spenser's conception of the canto was 'informal' – that is, not of a fixed length, and with parameters chiefly dictated by 'narrative requirements'.[43]

Daniel Javitch's essay, 'Cantus Interruptus in the *Orlando Furioso*', offers a parallel for this unfixed model of composition. Though Javitch's work does not extend to Spenser, his findings are relevant to *The Faerie Queene* in terms of the poetics of interruption. Drawing on the sixteenth-century controversy in Italian criticism about the *Furioso*'s extravagant and repeated shifts of narrative focus in mid-story, Javitch argues that Ariosto was deliberately subverting Aristotelian expectations of coherence and clarity for the didactic purpose of training his readers in enduring frustration:

> The deprivation experienced by the reader when Ariosto prematurely interrupts his engrossing narratives is meant to *duplicate* the similar experience that so often besets various characters in his poem. ... [O]ne of the poem's didactic aims ... is to make us aware that in a world without constancy ... we must be elastic enough to bear the unpredictable frustration of our designs and aspirations. This resilience can be developed, Ariosto seems to believe, by accustoming oneself to disappointment.[44]

My point is not that Spenser's technique was the same as Ariosto's, nor indeed his didactic goal; but rather that his self-conscious manipulation of narrative structure, with a readiness to embrace what Javitch calls 'the abrupt and disquieting manner in which [interruptions of narrative] usually occur' has Ariostan features, and suggests that the interruptive cast of the *Furioso* was much in Spenser's mind when he was drafting his poem.[45]

42 See Fowler, *Spenser and the Numbers of Time*, 16, for stanza totals in tabular form. The totals are (here excluding proems and all of Mutabilitie and again based on 1596): I (617 stanzas), II (683), III (677), IV (599), V (565), and VI (554). If there is a pattern, it is towards concision.
43 Fowler, *Spenser and the Numbers of Time*, 53.
44 Daniel Javitch, 'Cantus Interruptus', 78, 79, original emphasis.
45 Javitch, 'Cantus Interruptus', 67. See Sale, 'Canto' for the view that Spenser 'may have derived much from Dante and Ariosto but not his use of the canto' (134).

Book VI, for example is critically notorious for Calidore's interruptions, first of Serena and Calepine, and second of the Dance of the Graces (VI. iii.21 and VI.x.18). If Ariosto uses the repeated trope of interrupted narrative as a way of training his readers in the art of coping with disappointment and shortfall, Spenser in Book VI thematises frustration (whether amatory or poetic) through Calidore's repeated blunderings. Calidore becomes a kind of lumbering parody of the poet himself, not only in the ambiguities of courtesy and slander, but in the randomness of his peregrinations and the artful chances which determine his narrative.[46]

Yet Spenser's cantos are different from Ariosto's: he is seldom as prodigal of incident or as rapid in change of focus. There is nothing in *The Faerie Queene* which precisely mirrors an incident like the abrupt transitions in and out of the story of Rinaldo mustering support in Scotland in Canto 8. In stanza 21, the reader is told '*Io lascerò Ruggiero in questo caldo,/E giro in Scotia à ritrovar Rinaldo*', but by stanza 29, Ariosto has moved on already: '*Mentre à dir di Rinaldo attento sono,/D'Angelica gentil m'è souenuto*'.[47] Ariosto's narrator is skittish and mercurial, prone to be reminded of one story by another in the way that the speaker of Paul Muldoon's 'Something Else' flits in the space of fifteen lines from lobsters, to inks, to Nerval's suicide, and finally to 'something else, then something else again'.[48] Though Spenser's cantos are of widely varying lengths, they tend to cover two distinct portions of narrative. Book VI Canto III begins with the conclusion of the story of Aladine and Priscilla (stanzas 1–19), and then initiates the story of Calepine and Serena (stanzas 20–51), as Calidore disappears from the book until Canto IX. Similarly VI.x has two segments: the Dance of the Graces (1–30), which is followed by further developments in the story of Calidore among the shepherds (31–44). Even in the cantos which are at the extremes of the narrative range, a two-incident structure is usually discernible: II.xii starts with the sea voyage to the Bower of Bliss (1–38), then concludes with its destruction (39–87); V.i starts with Astraea's education of Artegall (1–12), and concludes with the story of Sanglier (13–30).

46 Compare VI.iii.21 'since it was his fortune, not his fault' with VI.x.20 'Right sory I … That my ill fortune did them hence displace'. See David Lee Miller, 'Calidore', 128, for the caveat against 'too ironic a reading of Calidore': 'Calidore's problem – how to represent true courtesy in action – is also the poet's'.
47 Ariosto, *Orlando Furioso* (1556), 72–73. Harington loosely translates: 'To Scotland now I will returne againe/And of *Renaldo* talke a word or twaine … While *Renald* here is cheard with great excesse … I meane to tell how that faire Ladie sped', in *Orlando Furioso* (1972), 92. Compare the examples discussed by Javitch, 'Cantus Interruptus', 66–68.
48 Paul Muldoon, *Poems 1968–1998*, 173.

Bool VI Canto III and VI.x contrast strongly as narratives. The former is a canto of action: Calidore rescues Priscilla, walks in on Calepine and Serena, who is then mauled by the Blatant Beast, which Calidore pursues; Calepine nurses Serena, tries to get help from the discourteous Turpine in crossing the river, then pleads for shelter in Turpine's castle, before having to rough it 'vnderneath a bush' (VI.iii.44). At the climax of the canto, the unarmed Calepine shelters behind the wounded Serena as Turpine murderously attacks him. In contrast, Canto X juxtaposes an allegorical core with a pastoral narrative. It begins with Calidore seeing the Graces dance on Mount Acidale, a moment of equipoise which he characteristically interrupts. Colin Clout explains what Calidore has witnessed: the dance encapsulates a notion of 'Ciuility' as a model of decorous social behaviour (VI.x.23). In its second half, the canto returns to action: Calidore courts Pastorella, persuading her of his superiority to Coridon through his dispatch of a timely tiger, which enables Calidore to prosecute his suit successfully with the implication that his 'humble seruice' leads to the satisfaction of his erotic 'will' (VI.x.38). The canto ends with another cliffhanger, as the Brigants exploit Calidore's absence to abduct the remaining shepherds.

As this summary indicates, in both cantos, there are significant elements of inversion, mirroring, and reduplication. Straightforwardly, Priscilla's nursing of Aladine is inverted by Calepine's nursing of Serena. With greater complexity, the image of Colin's 'Grace' in the dance reflects both Pastorella and Gloriana, as the narrator tells us in the opening stanzas (VI.x.4). In turn, Colin's model of 'Ciuility' meshes uneasily with Calidore's more instrumental pursuit of Pastorella. Seemingly random incidents – the illusion of fictive happenstance – structure how the cantos are organised and the images which Spenser uses. To give one further example: Calidore's exit from the poem for five cantos is curiously unheralded. The manic chase of the Knight after the Beast is at once urgent and static, almost like an ecphrastic image of a hunt:[49]

> But follow'd fast the Monster in his flight:
> Through woods and hils he follow'd him so fast,

---

49 A search for images of Renaissance and Early Modern images of hunting underlines a curious factor in Calidore's pursuit of the Beast: that he hunts alone. Most of the celebrated Early Modern images of hunting – Uccello's *Hunt in the Forest* in the Ashmolean, the Victoria and Albert tapestry of a boar and bear hunt – depict it as a complex social activity with multiple participants. The only analogous image I know of is Titian's magnificent *Death of Actaeon* in London's National Gallery, and even here, Diana is assisted by Actaeon's Ovidian dogs and a murky rider in the distant trees.

> That he nould let him breath nor gather spright,
> But forst him gape and gaspe, with dread aghast,
> As if his lungs and lites were nigh a sunder brast. (VI.iii.26)

The particular flows into the general: the 'couert shade' where Calepine
and Serena were 'resting' fades into a background scenery of 'woods and
hils' (VI.iii.20). The life-and-death pursuit – 'fast' in one line, 'so fast' in
the next as though the narrative is trying to catch up with its own immobile
conceptions of pace – is carefully aestheticised and arrested by the simile
which inevitably raises the question of the reality of the hunt: if the Beast's
'lungs and lites' are on the point of breaking, why introduce the line with
'As if', unless you know that this pursuit will in fact be endless? That this
is an aestheticised violence – where the sense of randomness is part of
the poet's design – is confirmed in the fight between Turpine and Calepine
which recapitulates the earlier chase:

> after long weary chace,
> Hauing by chaunce a close aduantage vew'd,
> He ouer raught him, hauing long eschew'd
> His violence in vaine, and with his spere
> Strooke through his shoulder, that the blood ensew'd
> In great aboundance, as a well it were,
> That forth out of an hill fresh gushing did appere.
>
> Yet ceast he not for all that cruell wound,
> But chaste him still, for all his Ladies cry,
> Not satisfyde till on the fatall ground
> He saw his life powrd forth dispiteously:
> The which was certes in great ieopardy,
> Had not a wondrous chaunce his reskue wrought,
> And saued from his cruell villany.
> Such chaunces oft exceed all humaine thought:
> That in another Canto shall to end be brought. (VI.iii.50–51)

The inversion is disturbing because in this case it is Calepine rather than
the Beast who is the object of the 'long weary chace'. Spenser's characteristic
pronominal confusions work to enhance the transgressive horror of what
we read as both hunter and hunted travesty chivalric custom: Turpine
through his assault on an unarmed knight; Calepine through finding that
'his best succour and refuge was still/Behinde his Ladies backe', an image
which in turn inverts the opening of the canto where Priscilla and Calidore
carried Aladine (VI.iii.49). The well simile at the end of stanza 50 seems
to suggest that Calepine's life will imminently be 'powrd forth dispiteously'.
But in this case the violence of the wound is suddenly staunched by the

narrator's explicit intervention: 'a wondrous chance' breaks the 'fatall' trajectory of the fight, and almost jauntily suggests that when we turn the page 'in another Canto', things will be different. In this sense, the adversative doubling of the first two lines of the stanza – '*Yet* ceast he not ... *But* chaste him still*' – anticipates the 'wondrous ... reskue' of the final four lines as Spenser serves to arrest the expected trajectory of the simile from the previous stanza.[50] This combination of factors – an inversion of the earlier beast chase, the interjection of the narrator and the curious dominance of adversative conjunctions – suggests the careful construction of cantos as linked and coherent units of narrative. At the same time, such complexity coexists with a countervailing rhetoric of narrative casualness previously noted. This suggests that we need to pay more attention to the figure of Spenser's narrator.

By late ensample: framing the cantos

As interstanzaic rhyming shows the careful interweaving of stanzas within and across episodes, Spenser's episodic structure is itself subject to rhetorically elaborate sequencing which moves both forwards and backwards. Often Spenser's narrator reflects on the canto just finished and can anticipate events yet to come. Structurally, they are persuasive in the sense that they are indicative of a poet seeming in command of, or responsive to, his narrative materials. Thus III.viii.1 is at once an enactment of the narrator's 'meere compassion' for the hapless Florimell, an allusion to Ariosto's related exordia on Florimell's prototype, Angelica, and covertly an anticipation of Florimell's ongoing trials.[51] Poised between the fictive incidents we have just read and those we are yet to encounter, the canto openings are Janus-faced markers of artistic self-consciousness which demand the reader's active involvement. Jerome S. Dees notes that the narrator voice is 'an aspect of the poem's rhetorical structure' – a manifestation of its didactic intent – and a potential hurdle between reader and poem:

> The reader is left uncertain whether to accord authority to the mimesis – thus perceiving the narrator to be unreliable, falsely confident, impercipient, or

50 For adversative pronouns in the Proem to Book VI, see Anderson, 'What Comes After Chaucer's *But* in *The Faerie Queene?*', in *Reading the Allegorical Intertext*, 42–53, and below.
51 For the narrator's poignant involvement in his tale, compare I.iii.2. For Angelica, see *Orlando Furioso* (1556), VIII.66–67 (76), and *Orlando Furioso* (1972), VIII.58: 'The thought hereof in me such pang doth breed/I can no further in this tale proceed' (96). For the anticipation of Florimell's incarceration by Proteus, see Hamilton's notes in *FQ*, 362.

overhasty in his assessment of the complexities of lived human experience – or to privilege the narrator's reflective, sober, usually discriminating judgments.[52]

David Lee Miller offers a robust way through such uncertainties by arguing for an ironic rather than a Romantic narrator: Spenser defers textual authority to his readers and expects them to notice when his narrator misspeaks. As he suggests, much is at stake in how we respond to this voice: 'What values does the poem convey? How deliberate are its effects? How deep do its ironies go, and how frequent are they?', then warning, 'the text continually invites *and* frustrates the tracing of its "continued Allegory, or darke conceit"' through the pervasiveness of its ironic strategies.[53]

Consider VI.iii.1–2 as the narrator interprets the action we've just read in Canto II, where Calidore comes to the aid of Priscilla and Aladine, in terms of the debate about the origins of courtesy. These stanzas show a Spenser not only backing what is, from a modern perspective, the wrong historical horse of aristocratic blood being the best guarantor of 'gentle manners,'[54] but citing Chaucer in support of this position in a passage which in fact says the opposite:

> TRue is, that whilome that good Poet sayd,
>   The gentle minde by gentle deeds is knowne.
> For a man by nothing is so well bewrayd,
>   As by his manners, in which plaine is showne
>   Of what degree and what race he is growne.
> For seldome seene, a trotting Stalion get
>   An ambling Colt, that is his proper owne:
> So seldome seene, that one in basenesse set
> Doth noble courage shew, with curteous manners met.
>
> But euermore contrary hath bene tryde,
>   That gentle bloud will gentle manners breed;
>   As well may be in *Calidore* descryde,
>   By late ensample of that courteous deed,
>   Done to that wounded Knight in his great need,
>   Whom on his backe he bore, till he him brought

52 Dees, 'Narrator of *The Faerie Queene*' (1990), 499.
53 David Lee Miller, 'Dan Edmund Meets the Romantics', 710–12.
54 Compare Tonkin, *Spenser's Courteous Pastoral*, 43, who warns against 'adopting too rigidly doctrinaire an attitude towards Spenser's exploration of the question', with Richard Neuse, 'Book VI as Conclusion to *The Faerie Queene*', 341, who argues in the context of VI.v.1–2 (on the Salvage Man's 'gentle bloud') 'These two stanzas, then, seem to me to maintain the aristocratic fiction at the expense of a great deal of irony'.

> Vnto the Castle where they had decreed.
> There of the Knight, the which that Castle ought,
> To make abode that night he greatly was besought. (VI.iii.1–2)

The Chaucerian intertext is from 'The Wife of Bath's Tale', where the wife in the tale gives the knight a tutorial based on Roman history and literature:

> "Thenketh hou noble, as seith Valerius,
> Was thilke Tullius Hostillius,
> That out of poverte roos to heigh noblesse.
> Reedeth Senek, and redeth eek Boece;
> Ther shul ye seen expres that it no drede is
> That he is gentil that dooth gentil dedis.["]^55

One is tempted to warn Spenser's narrator to check his sources. In place of Chaucer's democratic sense that gentility is a product of behaviour, Spenser's narrator narrows The Wife's formulation into what Hamilton characterises as the 'essentially aristocratic' terms of the second stanza: 'euermore contrary hath been tyde,/That gentle bloud will gentle manners breed', a position apparently evidenced by Calidore's behaviour in the previous canto.^56 Indeed, the initial citation – 'The gentle mind by gentle deeds is knowne' – dilutes the sense of absolute identity which Chaucer expresses between action and essence by replacing the parallelism 'he *is* gentil that *doth*' with the auxiliary expression 'is knowne'; Spenser's narrator focuses on the exteriors of how behaviour is interpreted socially.^57 Even the usually stabilising deployment of proverbial lore – 'seldome seene, a trotting Stalion get/An ambling colt' – repoints the proverb 'Trot sire, trot dam, how should the foal amble?' As Thomas Wilson explains, the usual sixteenth-century reading of this proverb was not as a proof of the power of 'gentle' heredity, but rather as an illustration of the reverse: 'when bothe father and mother were noughte, it is not like that the childe wil proue good, without an especial grace of God.'^58 The semantic difference is small

55 'The Wife of Bath's Tale', 1165–70, in *The Riverside Chaucer*, 120; see also *The Works 1532*, sig. K4r, where the text is very similar. See also Charles G. Smith, *Spenser's Proverb Lore*, 125, for the proverb which lies behind both Chaucer and Spenser, 'Gentle is that gentle does'.
56 In *The Faerie Queene* (1977), 640.
57 My emphases.
58 Smith, *Spenser's Proverb Lore*, 268; Wilson, *The Arte of Rhetorique*, sig. R2r. Wilson goes on to cite John Heywood's *A dialogue conteinyng the nomber in effect of all the prouerbes in the englishe tongue*, which contains an even more emphatically unSpenserian version of the same proverb: 'Colts … may proue wel, with tatchis yl/For of a ragged colt there comthe a good horse', sig. D3r. See also *The Faerie Queene Books Six and Seven*, 198, for Upton's suggestion that Spenser was thinking of Horace, *Odes* 4.4.29–32, an aristocratic assertion of pedigree. Spenser's wording, however, clearly alludes to the proverb.

but significant: the narrator reinterprets familiar texts to wrest the narrative to his own interpretation.

The reader's difficulty is how to respond to this authoritative or even authoritarian summarising – should we historicise the aristocratic politics adumbrated here (since Spenser did consistently align himself with aristocratic patrons), persuade ourselves that Spenser's meaning is less restrictive than it initially seems, or do we look to 'the mimesis' – the narrative of the poem – to assess the gaps between story and reflection?[59] From Dees's perspective, the narrator perhaps embodies 'a "provisional" authority ... though never the complete truth'.[60] This passage, however, responds better to Miller's ironic reading: the narrator's understanding is confused in both conceptual and narrative terms, and Spenser expects his readers to register that critically. The narrator offers an idiosyncratic summary of the end of Canto II, while his praise of Calidore proves unconvincing in the light of what follows.

To begin with the former point: 'Whom on his backe he bore, till he him brought/Vnto the Castle' focuses exclusively on Calidore's efforts, eliding what is for the reader the provocative image of the wounded Aladine being carried both by Priscilla and Calidore as a 'coportion' (VI.ii.47). Stanzas VI.ii.46–48 and VI.iii.4 are closely linked in terms of different meanings of 'bear' and 'bier'. The word morphs from the figurative sense of to harbour a feeling ('the courteous care, which [Calidore] did beare' to Aladine and Priscilla), into the more literal sense of to carry (Priscilla's reluctance 'him to beare'), then to the etymologically unrelated yet orthographically identical noun 'an hollow beare', which 'both with parted paines did beare' (VI.ii.46–48).[61] The repetition of these terms through rhyme – the *rime riche* effects of VI.ii.48b are particularly insistent – is carried over into VI.iii.4: 'With bleeding wounds, brought home vpon a Beare,/By a faire Lady, and a stranger Knight'.[62] Though 'bear' is present

59 See McCabe, *Ungainefull Arte*, 239–52, for Spenser's pursuit of courtly patronage. See Tonkin, *Spenser's Courteous Pastoral*, 44, for an example of the middle position: Book VI is properly concerned with 'the problems of ordinary educated Elizabethans, and ordinary social beings', not just the aristocracy.

60 Dees, 'Narrator of *The Faerie Queene*' (1990), 499.

61 See "bear, v.1.", 9 and 1a; and "bier, n.", *OED Online*. Bears of one kind or another were on Spenser's mind in Book VI – there is the actual bear Calepine fights in Canto IV, while Calidore is compared with an angry female bear at VI.xi.25: 'He chauft, he grieu'd, he fretted, and he sight,/And fared like a furious wyld Beare,/Whose whelpes are stolne away, she being otherwhere'.

62 Beginning with VI.ii.46c (*deare: beare: dreare*), the episode shows significant use of –*eare* and related rhymes: see VI.ii.48b (*beare: reare: beare: neare*), VI.iii.4b (*Beare: deare: dreare: heare*), VI.iii6.b (*cheare: appeare: geare: deare*; this stanza also includes two internal rhymes on *cheare* and *cheard*), VI.iii.12a (*teares: feares*), and

in the narrator's stanzas, the preterite form '*he bore*' emphasises the difference between what the tale reports and how the teller interprets that.[63] The tonal transition across the canto margins is complex, and it is still challenging for readers to work out how this comedy of manners should be construed. In his first edition of the poem, A. C. Hamilton confidently asserted that 'No bawdy sense is intended' by 'And him to beare, she thought it thing too base', a gloss which also takes in Calidore's even more dubious advice in the same stanza: 'Faire Lady let it not you seeme disgrace,/ To beare this burden on your dainty backe' (VI.ii.47).[64] In a perceptive review, Donald Cheney demurred:

> Although it certainly is true of the specific instance that the play on 'base' refers wittily to the relative standing of lady and burden, the episode is developed in a context of sexual anxiety and shame that is apparent from the reference in the previous line to 'her wretched case' (to which Calidore is a 'straunger' but her wounded lover by implication is not). Here as with the similar problem of Serena elsewhere in Book VI, damsels caught in compromising circumstances are consistently seen as shamed by a self-consciousness that they confuse with the external biting of the Blatant Beast.[65]

By temporarily erasing Priscilla, Spenser's narrator anticipates the ways in which some older male critics (though not Cheney) have written about the female protagonists of Book VI. Tonkin's jeremiad against Priscilla's snobbery is typical: 'Priscilla's prissiness (the term might have been invented for her) in disdaining to carry the wounded Aladine shows too great a reliance on supposedly "natural" superiority – superiority of breeding.'[66]

---

climactically, VI.iii.18b (*deare: sweare: feare: beare*), where the final rhyme is a crucial element of Calidore's 'counter-cast of slight' to maintain Priscilla's innocence through the story of the 'discourteous Knight, who had her reft,/And by outragious force away did beare'. See Brown and Lethbridge, *A Concordance*, 196–97, 552, and 23–25, 38–42, for my discussion of *rime riche* in relation to Ants Oras's argument that its incidence decreases in the second installment. The device is prominent throughout these cantos; compare VI.iii.21c, 22b.

63 My emphasis.
64 In *The Faerie Queene* (1977), 639.
65 Donald Cheney, 'A. C. Hamilton, ed. *The Faerie Queene*', 24. See also *FQ*, 617, citing Cheney for Hamilton's second thoughts: 'A bawdy sense may be implicit ... but primarily her fear is social'. While this is a reasonable reading of the first line, it does not explain the discourteous innuendo Calidore uses in the second two lines. Compare Hadfield and Stoll's gloss: 'Another of Spenser's dirty jokes', in *The Faerie Queene Book Six and The Mutabilitie Cantos*, 36.
66 Tonkin, *Spenser's Courteous Pastoral*, 223.

My point is not that Priscilla isn't snobbish – after all, complex social gradations are at the heart of her story, since she 'lou'd this fresh young Knight … though meaner borne' (VI.iii.7) – but rather that her social and amatory dilemmas are carefully structured into the image of her and Calidore carrying Aladine. 'Yet could she not deuise by any wit,/How thence she might conuay him to some place' is a practical as well as a social issue in a book which is much concerned with the physical as well as the allegorical problems of getting from A to B – this point is brutally clear in Calepine's desperate efforts to get Serena across the river in the next canto (VI.ii.47; VI.iii.30–35). It is the shared bearing of the wounded knight – 'And twixt them both with parted paines did beare' – which ultimately enables Priscilla to cure Aladine with her tears. This reading perhaps replaces masculine brusqueness with masculine sentimentality, yet this is a sentimentality which is carefully infused into VI.iii.10's empathetic feminine-signalling-masculine C-rhymes, that is, feminine C-rhymes which tend to an abjected masculine subject:

> So well she washt them, and so well she wacht him,
> That of the deadly swound, in which full deepe
> He drenched was, she at the length dispacht him,
> And droue away the stound, which mortally attacht him.

What I am suggesting, then, is that there is an aspect of the presentation of Courtesy in the overlap between Cantos II and III which is ignored by the narrator. 'The gentle mind by gentle deeds is knowne' is on this reckoning as much embodied by Priscilla as by Calidore.[67]

The narrator's comments are equally problematic in terms of what happens in VI.iii. Though the first two stanzas are couched as retrospect – 'As may well be in *Calidore* descryde,/By late ensample of that courteous deed' – the narrator evinces the same kind of absolute confidence in Calidore's exemplarity as he had earlier expressed at the start of Canto II:

> That well in courteous *Calidore* appeares,
> Whose euery act and deed, that he did say,
> Was like enchantment, that through both the eyes,
> And both the eares did steale the hart away. (VI.ii.3)

---

67 Compare also the next stanza, which depicts Aladine's empathetic involvement in Priscilla's dilemma: 'He deeply sigh'd, and groaned inwardly,/To think of this ill state in which she stood'. In the formulation of the couplet of this stanza, there is a provocative tension between Priscilla's 'noble blood' and Aladine's concern for 'her good'; see *The Faerie Queene Book Six and The Mutabilitie Cantos*, 41, for Hadfield and Stoll's useful note on the ambiguous phrase 'blam'd her noble blood'.

To be sure, Calidore's courteous mastery of speech and rhetoric is not so like enchantment as to ally him with Acrasia's erotic mastery of Verdant.[68] Yet it is the very blandness of the narrator's endorsement in these early stages of the book which makes his comments questionable.[69] If Calidore's bearing of Aladine proves his courteous heroism, the difficulty for the reader is squaring this paragon with the more fallible knight described in the rest of the canto. I have already commented on the 'counter-cast' of slight, which like the lines just quoted underscores the rhetorical and performative aspects of Courtesy. As we have seen, by persuading Priscilla's father that she is 'Most perfect pure, and guiltlesse innocent ... Since first he saw her', Calidore inevitably raises the question of how Courtesy relates to truthfulness (VI.iii.18). Where the narrator celebrates a straightforward hero, whose 'manners' amplify the sense of his noble origins, the narrative displays a resourceful courtier, expert in the rhetorical arts; thus Guazzo praises 'fine Oratours' for teaching 'men to insinuate, & by coloured wordes to creepe into mens boosomes, and to winne the fauour of Princes & Magistrates'.[70] This is not to satirise Calidore – to a large extent, he is our central guide to Courtesy until we meet Colin Clout – but to insist that the terms of his description by the narrator are unsettled and inconsistent.[71] The very blandness of the editorial frame at VI.iii.1–2 draws attention to the chancy and interrogative character of Spenser's canto form. Though Book VI is in some ways a special case because of its proliferation of unfinished narratives, such moments draw attention to the taut interplay between what is narrated and how it is framed. I turn now to a sequence of cantos in Book III to develop these observations; I return to the role of the narrator at the end of Chapter 6.

68 Compare II.12.80: 'O horrible enchantment, that him so did blend'. Even including related words like 'enchanter', 'enchantment' is used sparingly in *The Faerie Queene*, with only three instances in this form; see Brown and Lethbridge, *A Concordance*, 396.

69 The false A-rhyme here – *appeares: eyes* – may be an indication of the narrator's reluctance about Calidore; Hadfield and Stoll's note on this stanza suggests that 'Calidore is shown to be persuasive and impressive, perhaps blinding everyone to his limitations', in *The Faerie Queene Book Six and The Mutabilitie Cantos*, 23. See also Brown and Lethbridge, *A Concordance*, 190. This rhyme may be a transcription error, so that the lines should read: 'that through both the eares,/And both the eyes', as noted by Ralph Church; see *The Faerie Queene* (1758), Vol 4, 230. The Variorum editors adopted this reading; see *The Faerie Queene Books Six and Seven*, 16, 471.

70 Guazzo, *The Ciuile Conuersation*, sig. E1v.

71 In this context, many critics have rightly noted Calidore's solitariness – that he has no squire or page, and turns Tristram down for this role because of the terms of his quest (VI.ii.37).

Networked canto form

Spenser's tendency towards narrative errancy is hard-wired into the structure of *The Faerie Queene*. As soon as Redcrosse encounters Error in the first canto, the poem shows a proneness to wander from its ostensible 'great aduenture' into a series of subsidiary avenues (I.i.3, 11–13). Redcrosse maybe at fault here, but his readiness to be diverted bespeaks an impulse which is profoundly Spenserian: because of the superfluity of possible routes, the condition of protagonists, readers, and the narrator will continuously be one of 'diuerse doubt' (I.i.10.9). Nevertheless, in terms of top level narrative, in the first two Books Spenser largely does not lose sight of Redcrosse and Guyon; Arthur's incursions enrich and complicate the narrative line, yet the succession of cantos is still demonstrably determined by a focus on the questing hero and his need to achieve his mission.[72] Although we lose sight of Redcrosse in I.iii and vi, these deviations are temporary – filling in what happens to Una, '*Forsaken Truth*', after their separation in I.ii – and the next canto in each case recurs to Redcrosse and his travails (I.iii.arg).

All of this changes by the time we get to Book III. While Britomart remains the poem's most compelling and individuated character, her quest bears little structural comparison to those of Redcrosse and Guyon.[73] She disappears at III.iv.18, and doesn't resurface until III.ix.12, a gap of nearly five cantos. David Lee Miller's account of Book III in terms of the descent into eroticism is highly suggestive of the role cantos play as independent, narratively discontinuous units in the organisation of its disparate contents:

> In Book III, the basic contrast we have often observed between chance and providence works itself out in a marriage of entrelacement with allegory, which tends to unify episodes at a fairly high level of abstraction. Thus characters, events, and images that seem discontinuous at the literal narrative level are dialectically gathered into a network of analogies.

Book III marks a change in canto structure and narrative organisation – a retraction from sequential to thematic narrative – because its more distributed, multifarious allegorical agendas dictate such a formal mutation: 'While Books I and II focus on the harmonious reduction of the many

---

72 Although note that it is one of the truisms of *Faerie Queene* criticism that the narrative of Book II fails to match up to the description of the narrative in the Letter to Raleigh: where the latter describes the Palmer coming to the Faery Queen's court with Ruddymane (*FQ*, 717), II.i describes Guyon and the Palmer meeting Amavia 'by a forest side' (II.i.35).

73 See Anderson, 'Britomart', 114.

into one (Una, wholeness, the frame of temperance, the glorified body of history), Book III repeatedly focuses on the multiplication of one into many.[74] Another way of putting this would be that Spenser's conception of Chastity produces what the Proem calls 'mirrours more then one': the abstinent Belphoebe is offset by the chaste yet sexual Amoret, Florimell, and Britomart, as well as the unchaste Malacasta, Hellenora, and so on (III.Pr.5).[75] Miller reveals a complex mirroring between Cantos V and VI through discontinuous narratives: the fable of Chrysogone at the beginning of Canto VI serves 'to mediate between the allegories of virginity and procreativity: where canto 5 projects the cultural "line of succession" available to virginity, canto 6 opens by looking back to its *natural* genealogy'. Similarly, at the level of stanza numbering, Miller discerns echoic play between III.v.52 and III.vi.52: 'At the end of canto 5 [the poet] urges young female readers to frame themselves an example from Belphoebe's perfection, and at the end of canto 6, he says the same thing about Amoret'; that which appears casual is carefully sequenced.[76] What I am interested in here is Miller's 'network of analogies': his chapter does much work to uncover the pervasive contrasts between Cantos V and VI in terms of allegories of sexuality; I want to extend those observations. Spenser's construction of cantos at this point in the poem maybe characterised as networked composition, where verbal cues such as rhymes and repeated formulations serve to combine related yet different narratives.

Consider in this light the transitions from the end of Canto V to the beginning of Canto VII. Canto V concludes with the white-washing of a cliffhanger: Timias's fruitless erotic love for Belphoebe becomes a protracted praise of her 'stedfast chastity' which seems to end on a point of epideictic equipoise, marrying her signature virtue with 'goodly modesty,/That seemed those two vertues stroue to fynd/The higher place in her Heroick mynd' (III.v.55).[77] Timias's love is impossible, the narrator implies, but Belphoebe's manifold excellences create something which is perfect in itself, and which provides a model for female behaviour (III.v.52). In narrative terms, III.v.55 dissipates the tension which the preceding canto has taken such pains to establish: as a paragon of chastity and modesty, Belphoebe closes the page as 'a perfect complement'; Timias's erotic wasting sickness of III.v.49 is,

74 Miller, *The Poem's Two Bodies*, 221, 222.
75 See Kaske, *Spenser and Biblical Poetics*, 18–64, for images repeated *in bono et in malo*.
76 Miller, *The Poem's Two Bodies*, 235, 237.
77 Note that this is apparent rather than actual conflict: the next line (which marks off the last four lines of the stanza as a quatrain unit) emphatically notes 'So striuing each did other more augment'; in Belphoebe, tension is repeatedly resolved into self-sustaining unity.

for the moment at least, swept from view. In this profoundly allegorical context – where the narrator stresses Belphoebe's abstract qualities – III.vi.1 seems to show the triumph of etiological narrative over Ariostan romance:

> VVEll may I weene, faire Ladies, all this while
> Ye wonder, how this noble Damozell
> So great perfections did in her compile,
> Sith that in saluage forests she did dwell,
> So farre from court and royall Citadell,
> The great schoolmistresse of all courtesy:
> Seemeth that such wild woods should far expell
> All ciuile vsage and gentility,
> And gentle sprite deforme with rude rusticity.

As Canto V's conclusion suggests, the narrative has reached a point of stasis. In consequence, the new canto offers a mythological account of Belphoebe's excellence in terms which will explain how a country dweller might excel (a rhyme Spenser perhaps surprisingly doesn't use here) the 'faire Ladies' of 'court and royall Citadell'.[78] The connection is, as Miller notes, abstract: Belphoebe's story stimulates – so we are told – female readers' curiosity about her origins; the narrator thus proffers an explanation in this canto. As Colin Burrow dryly notes, 'No readers in their right mind – let alone someone reading Ariosto – would have been worrying about where Belphoebe came from'; Spenser's narrative technique is backward-looking in attempting to short-circuit the dangerous sexuality of his Ariostan source, in which Angelica comes upon the wounded Medoro, with whom she falls in love.[79] If we want to hear more about Timias, we will simply have to wait, and for some time.[80] This opening stanza is closely linked with the canto's last stanza, neatly demonstrating the high degree of coordination across cantos thematically even as narrative strands diverge. This stanza, however, heralds the recrudesence of romance:

> But well I weene, ye first desire to <u>learne</u>,
> What end vnto that fearefull Damozell,
> Which fled so fast from that same foster <u>stearne</u>,
> Whom with his brethren *Timias* slew, befell:
> That was to weet, the goodly *Florimell*;
> Who wandring for to seeke her louer <u>deare</u>,

78 See Brown and Lethbridge, *A Concordance*, 234, for rhymes on 'excell'. The closest to this passage at III.vi.29b; note also III.viii.8c and III.viii.46b, both focusing on, and including, '*Florimell*'.

79 Colin Burrow, *Epic Romance*, 113.

80 His narrative resumes in IV.vii, and later in VI.v. In comparison with *Orlando Furioso*, *The Faerie Queene* takes the poetics of deferred gratification to new extremes.

> Her louer <u>deare</u>, her <u>deare</u>st *Marinell,*
> Into misfortune fell, as ye did <u>heare</u>,
> And from Prince *Arthur* fled with wings of idle <u>feare</u>. (III.vi.54)[81]

The stanzas initially seem identical in function and lexis: 'Well may I weene' morphs to 'But well I weene', where in each case 'well' anticipates the B-rhyme; 'how this noble Damozell', describing Belphoebe, becomes 'What end vnto that fearefull Damozell', describing Florimell.[82] And yet the proximity between the stanzas also underlines a difference: where the stanza on the 'noble Damozell' emphasises the poem's commitment to allegory in the sense of its readiness to break narrative continuity to introduce the etiological myth, the 'fearefull Damozell' stanza almost breathlessly returns the reader to the action which seemingly lapsed several cantos ago. This difference is semantically audible in the B-rhymes: we are now once again interested in what *befell* Florimell, who *fell* 'Into misfortune' in her pursuit of Marinell; the rhymes are certainly decorative, but they also contrast with III.vi.1's B-rhyme cluster (*Damozell: dwell: Citadell: expell*) in their focus on romance action. Indeed, breathless, almost mimetic narration characterises the next stanza, III.vii.1 over the page of the 1590 edition,[83] which is in turn hinged by rhyme and repetition to its immediate predecessor:

> LIke as an Hynd forth singled from the <u>heard</u>,
> That hath escaped from a rauenous beast,
> Yet flyes away of her owne feet <u>afeard</u>,
> And euery leafe, that shaketh with the least
> Murmure of winde, her terror hath encreast;
> So fled <u>fayre</u> *Florimell* from her vaine <u>feare</u>,
> Long after she from perill was releast:
> Each shade she saw, and each noyse she did <u>heare</u>,
> Did seeme to be the same, which she escapt <u>whileare</u>.

In contrast with III.vi.1, this is an urgent canto opener: there is no space for moralising reflection. The narrator's impatience to get back to Florimell's story is shown both by the hind simile, and by the unusually intense

---

81 Underlinings in this stanza and below are mine.
82 See Brown and Lethbridge, *A Concordance*, 243, 362, for rhymes on '*Florimell*'. Including one variant, Spenser rhymes on the name on thirty-four occasions, which points to its utility as a rhyming prop. '*Damozell*', in contrast, is a relatively rare rhyme, with only eight instances (including variants), seven of which come from Book III; 'dame' in contrast is used sixty-three times; see *A Concordance*, 216–17, 356–57. Note also the internal rhymes on 'well' and 'fell', and that III.vi.1a *while: compile* echoes these sound patterns.
83 *The Faerie Queene* (1590), 493–94. III.vi.54 is on Hh8r, so the reader turns the page to get to III.vii.1 on Hh8v.

enjambment in the centre of the stanza – 'And euery leafe, that shakest with the least/Murmure of winde' – a disruption to the poem's habitual lineation cued by the trochaic inversion in the first foot.[84] Spenser is at his most Ariostan here, and wants readers to register Florimell's utter terror more forthrightly than is his norm. The proximity to the preceding stanza is evident in the closely related C-rhymes: *deare: heare: feare* becomes *feare: heare: whyleare*. As the underlinings in the quotations above indicate, this is only to note the most obvious carry through from one canto into the next: in the space of thirteen lines, Spenser produces eleven full or half rhymes which serve to connect the two cantos. It is difficult to see these poetic effects as only decorative: a passage like 'her louer deare,/ Her louer deare, her dearest *Marinell*', for instance, all but transforms anaphora into a mimetic trope as repetition underscores anxiety, thus anticipating the syntactic distortion of the next stanza. Similarly, though the rhyming terms are semantically close, there is a subtle choreography of meanings across these stanzas, either to differentiate or intensify. '[A] s ye did heare' addresses the reader as audience, reminding her of things she has previously read, but 'each noyse that she did heare' turns directly to Florimell. '[I]dle feare' anticipates III.vii.1's depiction of Florimell 'of her owne feete afeard' and 'her vaine feare' as the narrator (for the moment at least) seeks to assuage readerly anxiety about the fleeing heroine.[85]

The critical importance these stanzas give to Florimell's fear in turn recalls the earlier description in the runaway Cupid passage, of the god's 'cruell deedes' at court, in a stanza whose C-rhyme is almost duplicated by III.vii.1:[86]

> Ladies and Lords she euery where mote heare
> Complayning, how with his empoysned shot
> Their wofull harts he wounded had whyleare,
> And so had left them languishing twixt hope and feare. (III.vi.13)

84 Rhythmically, this line mirrors '*Seemeth* that such wilde woodes should far expell' in III.vi.1 (my emphasis). The earlier line works in Alpers's terms as a sovereign, independent line, whereas the syntax in the present stanza insists on the link to the previous line because of its mimetic intent; we are in effect *with* Florimell in the imagined forest, 'of her owne feete afeard', and the feet of Spenser's lines twitch to register that terror. Hamilton connects the simile with the earlier image of Florimell as a dove (III.iv.49), though that is an image focused on the bird's 'pineons' rather than the animal's feet; *FQ*, 352.

85 For the link between 'vaine feare' and Horace, see John E. Curran, 'Florimell's "Vaine Feare": Horace's Ode 1.23 in *The Faerie Queene* 3.1.1', 215–18.

86 *Heare: whyleare: feare* becomes *feare: heare: whileare*. This the only case of duplication for this cluster, though V.ii.3b adds *cheare* to the three terms, and VI.xi.37a rhymes on *feare* and *whyleare*. See Brown and Lethbridge, *A Concordance*, 342, with III.vii.1 listed under *whyleare*, the 1596 reading.

Florimell has of course fled from the same court when she hears the news about Marinell (see III.v.10), and the diagnosis of erotic dysfunction – 'languishing twixt hope and feare' – holds good for many of the Book's protagonists. As becomes apparent in the Maske of Cupid, fear is a key part of the erotics of Book III. The personification 'Feare' recaps Florimell's condition of self-flight: he 'feard each shadow mouing to or froe,/And his owne armes when glittering he did spy,/Or clashing heard, he fast away did fly' (III.xii.12). This suggests that the ostensibly functional rhymes which stitch together Cantos VI and VII are deeply imbricated in the workings of the Book's overall concern with 'How diuersely loue doth his pageants play' (III.v.1). The canto form which emerges in the centre of this Book is, properly speaking, neither Ariostan romance, nor allegory, nor indeed etiological fable, but an aptly 'diuerse' amalgam of competing motifs, in which the reader must be alert to Spenser's linguistic play in order to follow the disparate threads which connect his narratives.

These moments of hurried flight are only the fringes of the verbal coordination between cantos V–VII. I turn now to Spenser's use of rhyming terms like *hew, grew,* and *subdew* both in and out of rhyming position, further to demonstrate the high degree of thematic and lexical coordination between these cantos.[87] Unlike in Chapter 3, my concern is less with rhyme as a poetic device and the semantics of rhymes per se, but rather focuses on the ways in which rhyming terms and related lexis serve to combine different textual elements in the shaping of cantos and narratives. Canto form is not only a matter of romance fortuity, but can be seen as a consequence of the way in which Spenser manipulates his medium. I thus focus on rhymes which interleave episodes as a way of emphasising Spenser's interweaving of related narrative actions: as Timias responds to Belphoebe, so the Witch and her son respond to Florimell; where Timias attempts to 'subdew' his love for Belphoebe, in the Gardins of Adonis, 'reasonable sowles' are sexually 'indew[ed]' in physical bodies (III.v.44; III.vi.35).

---

87   The full listing of rhymes is *rew: vew: hew: grew* (III.v.30); *subdew: vew: hew: reuew* (III.v.44); *sew: hew: vew: crew* (III.v.47); *dew: shew* (III.vi.3); *vew: blew: grew* (III.vi.6); *crew: rew: dew: hew* (III.vi.17); *hew: grew: new* (III.vi.33); *knew: rew: t'indew: hew* (III. vi.35); *grew: vew* (III.vi.52), and *dew: vew: hew: crew* (III.vii.11). This excludes the repetition of key terms in non-rhyming positions and half-rhymes, noted below. *Hew, grew,* and *vew* are common rhymes (with, respectively, seventy, forty-three, and ninety instances in the poem as a whole), but the data sets suggest an unusual proliferation of such rhymes in these cantos. This is also shown by the fact that Book III has the largest, or joint largest, instances of these rhymes (thirteen rhymes on *hew,* eleven on *grew,* and eighteen on *vew*); see Brown and Lethbridge, *A Concordance,* 364–65, 382.

Why these rhymes in particular? First, because there are a lot of them in these cantos: Spenser rhymes on these sounds in nine different stanzas, with a further five uses of the same or similar words in non-rhyming positions, and at least two connected half-rhymes.[88] The majority of these uses are in Cantos V and VI, which have a total of 109 stanzas, so that these repetitions are easily noticeable, though not obtrusive. After the opening of Canto VII, Spenser abandons these rhymes for the rest of the canto, suggesting their importance for the episodes of Timias with Belphoebe, and the etiological fables of Canto VI. Second, and more importantly, these rhymes are semantically close to the central allegorical issues of Cantos V, VI, and even VII: Belphoebe, her origins, and the connection between strict chastity and the reproductive sexuality explored in the Gardins of Adonis. In these cantos, Spenser relentlessly plays with *hew* and its rhyming variants in such a way as to insist on the interconnectedness of the romance stories of Timias and Belphoebe, the flight of Florimell, and the myths of origin in the Gardins of Adonis.[89]

The first instance comes at the point where Belphoebe chances on the wounded Timias. It establishes a series of waveforms which ripple through the ensuing cantos:

> Saw neuer liuing eie more heauy sight,
>> That could haue made a rocke of stone to rew,
>> Or riue in twaine: which when that Lady bright
>> Besides all hope with melting eies did vew,
>> All suddeinly abasht she chaunged hew,
>> And with sterne horrour backward gan to start:
>> But when shee better him beheld, shee grew
>> Full of soft passion and vnwonted smart:
>> The point of pitty perced through her tender hart. (III.v.30)

Colin Burrow's reading of this stanza, informed by Angelica's 'insolita pietade' for the wounded Medoro, focuses on Spenser's struggle to contain the 'massive erotic dynamism' of Ariosto's original; he concludes (after

---

88 Would half-rhymes have counted to Spenser? Probably not in absolute terms – Puttenham argues against them (see *The Art of English Poesy*, 170–71) – yet the coincidence of clusters like III.vi.33c (*hew: grew: new*) with III.vi.34a (*sow: grow*) makes it unlikely that he did not intend the reader to hear these semantic and sonal joins. See Brown, '"Charmed with Inchaunted Rimes"' in Brown and Lethbridge, *A Concordance*, 27, for an example of where Spenser seems to prefer half-rhyme over morphological distortion, a device he uses extensively elsewhere.

89 Judith H. Anderson, '"In liuing colours and right hew"', notes the importance of 'hew' particularly in relation to Spenser's ambivalent mirroring of Queen Elizabeth in Belphoebe.

an illuminating discussion of the ambiguity of whether it is Timias's or Belphoebe's eyes which are 'melting' in line 4), 'Spenser is fighting pity … he only succeeds by emptying his hero of emotion: Belphoebe's feelings, after this early burst of compassion, are left largely undescribed.'[90] Certainly in comparison with Ariosto, Spenser has inextricable narrative difficulties: Belphoebe may be the object of sexual passion, but cannot, because of her allegorical and epideictic role, return that passion, hence the overlay of a quasi-ideological assertion of the values of strict chastity in the canto's closing stanzas.[91] At the same time, what Spenser is doing in these cantos is more than emulating Ariosto, or praising Elizabeth. The B-rhymes establish what I have called waveforms – poetic signals which are developed, altered, and punned on in what follows. The *rew: vew: hew: grew* cluster focuses on the emotive response to Timias while touching on issues which are developed later. *Hew* is initially a marker of physical difference which shades into more metaphysical questions of identity and origin. 'All suddeinly abasht shee chaunged hew' implies that Belphoebe is blushing, presumably because of her realisation that the wounded 'youth' is also a man.[92] Contra Burrow, Spenser *is* precise about Belphoebe's reaction: shame fights with compassion, and the verse works hard to verbalise the tensions implicit in her astonishment. Thus the violence of the next line – 'And with stern horror backward gan to start' – aptly suggests the tensions between shame and pity, and that the 'vnwonted smart' Belphoebe evinces will not develop erotically. Abashment in this view leads to a kind of self-policing jolt: Belphoebe's heart is 'tender' perhaps but not as 'melting' as the eyes of line 4.[93] For Burrow, the stanza suffers from syntactic ambiguity

90 Burrow, *Epic Romance*, 111, engaging with Hamilton's commentary on the stanza in *The Faerie Queene* (1977), 350; see *FQ*, 336. 'Insolita pietade' – unaccustomed pity – is Ariosto's description of Angelica's reaction to Medoro in *Orlando Furioso* XIX.20.

91 See also II.iii.42 for Braggadochio's 'filthy lust' for Belphoebe, and compare with the earlier blazon of her in stanzas 21–31, in particular with the incomplete alexandrine of II.iii.26, which may – in Hamilton's phrase – indicate 'the poet's distraction when he contemplates Belphoebe's genitalia', *FQ*, 184. On both passages, see Anderson, '"In liuing colours and right hew"', 172–76, who is illuminating on Belphoebe's anomalous status in relation to Timias.

92 See "abash, v." *OED Online*. *OED*'s first definition is particularly opposite: 'To cause (a person) to lose his or her self-possession or confidence, esp. as a result of a sudden sense of embarrassment, shame, or humiliation'.

93 Hamilton sees an implied proverb here: 'she retreats in horror because "pity melts the mind to love"', *FQ*, 336, citing Smith, *Spenser's Proverb Lore*, 217. Note that the jolt is metrically audible in the spondaic twist of 'And with *sterne horr*or backward gan to start' (my emphases).

as a consequence of its 'urgent need to protect Belphoebe ... from unchaste thoughts', but it is equally possible to read it as a dramatic underlining of Belphoebe's existential oddity – she isn't at all what she seems, or even what she thinks she is.[94] This is why I would argue that III.vi.1 (discussed above) is less funny than Burrow finds it. While from a narrative perspective, he is right that this stanza offers to satisfy a curiosity the reader is unlikely to have felt, in terms of Canto V's ambiguity about Belphoebe, the shift of focus is almost logical.[95]

The next *hew* rhyme underlines Belphoebe's questionable identity:

> Long while he stroue in his corageous brest,
>   With reason dew the passion to subdew,
>   And loue for to dislodge out of his nest:
>   Still when her excellencies he did vew,
>   Her soueraigne bountie, and celestiall hew,
>   The same to loue he strongly was constraynd:
>   But when his meane estate he did reuew,
>   He from such hardy boldnesse was restraynd,
> And of his lucklesse lot and cruell loue thus playnd. (III.v.44)

Timias has already been told that Belphoebe isn't a goddess, in imitation of Aeneas's encounter with Venus in *Aeneid* I – 'No Goddesse I, nor Angell, but the Mayd,/And daughter of a woody Nymphe' (III.v.36) – but the answer isn't altogether satisfying, and Timias's sense of her 'celestiall hew' is constitutive of the way he feels erotically about her.[96] Reason 'dew' should 'subdew' his passion, but Timias is caught in a 'lucklesse lot' which 'constrayn[s]' him for the rest of the poem. The deliberation and design underpinning these terms is emphasised by their almost immediate translation into Timias's own complaint (initiated in this

---

94 Burrow, *Epic Romance*, 111. Compare Anderson, '"In liuing colours and right hew"', 175. Close reading the phrases 'none liuing' and 'her ensample dead' in III.v.54, she argues that the latter 'continues Belphoebe's movement away from an earthly reality and suggests the only possible solution of Timias' dilemma ... to be the symbolic or actual transfiguration of Belphoebe into pure spirit'.

95 Burrow, *Epic Romance*, 113, quipping that this passage features 'the funniest lines in *The Faerie Queene* (this, perhaps, indicates that its humour is not exactly side-splitting)'. Burrow reads Spenser through Ariosto-tinted glasses, while implying that the humour of *The Faerie Queene* still remains an under-researched topic.

96 See *FQ*, 337, for the Virgilian intertext, and Anderson, '"In liuing colours and right hew"', 172. A connected play on *hew* is present in the previous stanza where Timias asks Belphoebe who she is, although not in the rhyming position: 'what grace is this,/ That thou has *shewed* to me sinfull wight' (III.v.35; my emphasis).

stanza), which produces a related B-rhyme sequence three stanzas later:

> But foolish boy, what bootes thy seruice bace
> To her, to whom the heauens do serue and sew?
> Thou a meane Squyre, of meeke and lowly place,
> She heauenly borne, and of celestiall hew.
> How then? of all loue taketh equall vew:
> And doth not highest God vouchsafe to take
> The loue and seruice of the basest crew?
> If she will not, dye meekly for her sake;
> Dye rather, dye, then euer so faire loue forsake. (III.v.47)

In James Bednarz's phrase, Timias is 'Trapped in the Petrarchan double bind', as Spenser ventriloquises Ralegh in an episode which fictionalises Ralegh's complex relationship with the Queen.[97] Indeed, this stanza replicates III.v.44: the '(re)vew' of Belphoebe does little more to Timias than confirm his own abjection: 'The loue and seruice of the basest crew' cannot hope to have an impact on this 'heauenly borne' and resistantly 'celestiall' figure. As Timias suspected earlier, his best option would be 'With reason dew the passion to subdew', but the poem has no intention of letting him off so lightly. The final appearance of this cluster in Canto V comes in stanza 53, as the narrator tells the 'Fayre ympes of beautie' to employ what Anderson calls the '*rosa moralis universalis*' in their own flower arranging in support 'Of chastity and vertue virginall'.[98] This is an explicit glance back to stanza 44, but with the difference that where Timias inevitably fails to control himself, this stanza imagines the chaste imps or offspring effortlessly embodying the virtue the squire cannot: 'And to your willes both royalties and Reames/Subdew, through conquest of your wondrous might'. At the end of Canto V, then, the erotic has been 'subdewed', or sublimated, in the 'faire ensample' of Belphoebe, while the same rhetorical and rhyming patterns have underlined Timias's paralysis.

Though Canto VI aims to explain Belphoebe's origins, its focus is progressively different, and Spenser modulates the rhymes on *hew* and *grew* to underline the different fictional coordinates of the Gardins of Adonis. The first part of the canto, with the myth of Chrysogone and the delicious rewrite of Moschus's 'The Fugitive Love', initially seems to recuperate the lexical energies of the previous canto, as in stanzas 3 and 6:

97 Bednarz, 'The Collaborator as Thief', 287.
98 Anderson, '"In liuing colours and right hew"', 172.

> Her berth was of the wombe of Morning dew,
> And her conception of the ioyous Prime,
> And all her whole creation did her shew
> Pure and vnspotted from all loathly crime,
> That is ingenerate in fleshly slime.
> So was this virgin borne, so was she bred,
> So was she trayned vp from time to time,
> In all chast vertue, and true bounti-hed
> Till to her dew perfection she was ripened. (III.vi.3)

> In a fresh fountaine, far from all mens vew,
> She bath'd her brest, the boyling heat t'allay;
> She bath'd with roses red, and violets blew,
> And all the sweetest flowres, that in the forrest grew. (III.vi.6)

Chrysogone's innocent impregnation chimes with the praise of Belphoebe's rose from the preceding canto. In this case, the *-ew* rhymes amplify the sense that what is being *shew*[n] to the reader is a further example of miraculous chastity: Chrysogone is metonymically fertilised by the 'Morning dew', and in a pointed mid-line *rime riche*, her fecundity reveals 'her *dew* perfection'.[99] If, *pace* Burrow, the end of Canto V works hard to exonerate Belphoebe 'from all loathly crime', the beginning of Canto VI works rather less hard to tell a story which is at once tall and lightly erotic. In the transition from stanzas 3 to 6, Spenser moves from the abstract assertion of Chrysogone's innocence to a more localised image of private bathing 'farre from all mens vew', a 'vew' which implicitly invites the reader to imagine the scene and which places the unwary heroine in an organic, vegetative context of 'all the sweetest flowres, that in the forrest grew'.

An analogous pressure towards the erotic is shown in stanza 17, which places Venus in the role of Actaeon, discovering Diana bathing with her nymphs:

> Shortly vnto the wastefull woods she came,
> Whereas she found the Goddesse with her crew,
> After late chace of their embrewed game,
> Sitting beside a fountaine in a rew,
> Some of them washing with the liquid dew
> From off their dainty limbes the dustie sweat,
> And soyle which did deforme their liuely hew;
> Others lay shaded from the scorching heat;
> The rest vpon her person gaue attendance great. (III.vi.17)

99 My emphasis. III.vi.7 clarifies that Chrysogone is impregnated by 'The sunbeames bright' which 'vpon her body playd', in what is arguably a more deliberately funny stanza than III.vi.1.

As Andrew Hadfield comments, Spenser was 'the most visual of all Elizabethan poets', so it is hard not to translate such passages into the terms
of contemporaneous art; this Venus and Diana seem palpably close to
Clouet's *The Bath of Diana* (c.1565), or Titian's *Diana and Actaeon*, painted
for Philip II.[100] That proximity, I suggest, is vividly apparent in the rhyming
structures which physicalise and sexualise terms which in the previous
canto had not had that value. The focus on the bathing nymphs removing
'the dustie sweat' with 'the liquid dew' participates in the same voyeuristic
game as the Clouet and Titian paintings, disclosing that which shouldn't
be seen for the diversion of its spectators.[101] Once again, the internal
rhyme, 'their *embrewed* game' is functional because of its specificity about
the hunt: the nymphs are soiled with the blood of their prey, which is
why they are discovered 'Sitting in a fountaine'.[102] Thus 'And soyle which
did deforme their liuely hew' begins the movement of the key term 'hew'
away from the evocation of Belphoebe as a goddess towards its more
complex role in the Gardins of Adonis. In this stanza, Spenser is as clear
as Clouet and Titian that Diana's nymphs are 'liuely', not 'celestiall', women
who feel the heat of the sun.[103]

Once the poem gets to the Gardins of Adonis, *hew* can usefully be
related to what Miller describes as the principle of substitution at work
in these cantos. Miller's focus is on narrative substitution, but what I want
to suggest is that this also takes place lexically, as *hew* moves from a
marker of appearance into one of form. As Miller puts it with characteristic
brio, 'we seem to slide laterally', yet deceptively into the Gardins passage
through a process of association:

> We see Timias substituted for the boar, and later Adonis for Timias, with
> the boar safely contained. We see Belphoebe's 'rose' and its Platonic offspring

---

100 Hadfield, *Edmund Spenser: A Life*, 90, commenting on the tapestries and frescos at Hill
     Hall, collected by Sir Thomas Smith. For Clouet, see http://mbarouen.fr/en/oeuvres/
     the-bath-of-diana [accessed 11 October 2017]; for Titian, see www.nationalgallery.org.uk/
     paintings/titian-diana-and-actaeon [accessed 11 October 2017]. See also Bates, *Masculinity
     and the Hunt*, 251, for the sense that this is a 'moment redolent of mythological suggestion'.
     More broadly, see Bender, *Spenser and Literary Pictorialism*.
101 See in particular stanza 19, which mimics the gestures of partial covering shown in
     the paintings: 'Soone her garments loose/Vpgath'ring, in her bosome she compriz'd,/
     Well as she might'. Though this stanza doesn't use the –*ew* rhymes, it does replicate
     Belphoebe's gesture of abashedness on seeing Timias: 'She was asham'd to be so loose
     surpriz'd'.
102 My emphasis. See "imbrue, v." *OED Online*. Oxford University Press, June 2017.
103 Clouet's painting is a visual historical allegory of real members of the French court;
     see http://mbarouen.fr/en/oeuvres/the-bath-of-diana for a who's who [accessed 11
     October 2017].

substituted for the child she will not bear, and then her own immaculate conception substituted for the etiological fable of the rose. We see Diana substituted for Venus in the Timias episode and its Virgilian prototype; Venus's descent from her 'house of forms' substituted for the sun's 'impression' of generative power on Chrysogonee; then Amoret, or wedded love, substituted for the love bandit Cupid that Venus seeks; and so on, as characters, events, and images that seem discontinuous at the literal or narrative level are dialectically gathered into a network of analogies.[104]

Substitution depends on a principle of flexible analogy, whereby Spenser expects his readers to recognise mutations between related narratives and mythological allusions. That same principle is at work in the repeated words I have been following, and again tells against the view that Spenser's diction is inexpressive. To be sure, Spenser tolerates a lot more in the way of phatic diction and seemingly empty repetition than Milton or Browning do, but the playing on, with, and against expectations which we see in these cantos surely speaks to a 'thick' rather than a 'thin' conception of the role of poetic language.[105] Thus the next instances of *hew* and the increasingly prevalent *grew* repurpose them for the discourse around the rebirth of the soul developed in the Gardins passage:

> Some thousand yeares so doen they there remayne,
> And then of him are clad with other hew,
> Or sent into the chaungefull world agayne,
> Till thither they returne, where first they grew:
> So like a wheele arownd they runne from old to new.

> Ne needs there Gardiner to sett, or sow,
>   To plant or prune: for of their owne accord
>   All things, as they created were, doe grow
>   And yet remember well the mighty word,
>   Which first was spoken by th'Almighty lord,
>   That bad them to increase and multiply: (III.vi.33–34)

I have allowed the quotation to run on into the next stanza because the half-rhyming join between the C-rhyme of stanza 33 and the A-rhyme of stanza 34 is clearly semantic and stresses the importance of these terms. The past tense of 33.8 morphs to the eternal present of 34.3 as Spenser emphasises the full force of the originating 'mighty word'. *Grew* is provocative in these clusters partly because Spenser had used it sparingly in Canto

104 Miller, *The Poem's Two Bodies*, 241.
105 See Lethbridge, 'The Bondage of Rhyme', in Brown and Lethbridge, *A Concordance*, 159.

V – the only example is stanza 30, where Belphoebe 'grew/Full of soft passion and vnwonted smart', describing an emotional rather than an organic process. In Canto VI, the growing is decidedly vegetative and sexual.[106] In this context, the 'other hew' of 33.6 is further sign from poet to reader that his diction is changing. Where in Canto V and the first half of Canto VI, *hew* has primarily denoted external appearance and complexion, as in the critical moment of Belphoebe blushing, now it returns to the primary, though closely related, sense of form and shape.[107] This is the sense in which the word is used with singular emphasis in mid-line five stanzas further on:

> The substance is not chaungd, nor altered,
>   But th'only forme and outward fashion;
>   For euery substance is conditioned
>   To change her hew, and sundry formes to don,
>   Meet for her temper and complexion: (III.vi.38)

Spenser uses a striking 4/6 line, with a heavy pause after the fourth syllable, to glance backwards to the preceding stanzas. We have already been told about Genius cladding souls 'with other hew'. Here the poet makes the metaphysical distinction between substance and complexion; *hew* is the key word because of the way it mediates between notions of appearance and those of structure. In Miller's terms, it substitutes for itself as its meanings dilate and mutate across these cantos. We might say that the 'outward fashion' of Spenser's poetry embraces a variety of *hews*, while insisting that those forms cover a single substance.[108]

Finally, the poetic value Spenser finds in this lexis is shown by the extravagant pun ten stanzas later:

> For that wilde Bore, the which him once annoyd,
>   She firmely hath emprisoned for ay,
>   That her sweet loue his malice mote auoyd,
>   In a strong rocky Caue, which is they say,
> Hewen vnderneath that Mount, that none him losen may. (III.vi.48)

---

106 See III.vi.45.1 and III.vi.52a. The latter looks back to the exemplary description of Belphoebe in III.v.52 to emphasise the differences between chastity and married love.

107 "hue, n.1." *OED Online*. In 33.6 and 38.4, Spenser uses the term in the sense of the first definition, 'Form, shape, figure; appearance, aspect; species'. Before this point his usage accords with the second meaning of 'External appearance of the face and skin, complexion'. See also Hamilton's gloss in *FQ*, 347.

108 For a contemporaneous text which also plays with a range of meanings of 'hue'/'hew', see Shakespeare's Sonnet 20, and Helen Vendler, *The Art of Shakespeare's Sonnets*, 127–29.

It's hard to miss the poetic force of the alexandrine. Not only does this line transvalue the noun which has been played with so extensively in Cantos V and VI into the unrelated yet (in Spenser's text) orthographically identical verb, but metrically the emphasis thrown onto the first syllable of the line makes the pun unavoidable. Like the 4/6 line in stanza 38, *mise en page* emphasises poetic intent, as does the change in poetic register from the colourless rhyming filler of the end of the eighth line – 'which is they say' – into the almost too precise imagery of the alexandrine. Somehow the appearances and forms we have been used to are repurposed again in the context of Spenser's queasy-yet-witty construction of Venus's mount as what Miller calls 'an anamorphic pudendum'.[109] At the literal level, Spenser means simply that the boar's cave has been sculpted 'vnderneath that Mount'.[110] Metaphorically, however, it is difficult to reconcile the imagery with the physical objects it purports to describe; as Lauren Silberman puts it, 'The dualism of spirit and matter, permanence and change, male and female is resolved in an unsettling image of inclusiveness.'[111] The pun is in this context both spectacularly apposite and spectacularly alarming: apposite inasmuch as the plays on *hew* through Cantos V and VI have implied the female genitalia Belphoebe keeps hidden and which Chrysogonee, Diana, and the nymphs are unable to keep from the reader's textual gaze; alarming inasmuch as the *vagina dentata* Silberman imagines seems violently constructed from the physical and the metaphysical. *Hewen* jolts metre and reader in one abrupt gesture of defamiliarisation.

This is not the end of this sequence of rhymes; Spenser's manipulation of these clusters suggests a further connection between and across Cantos V, VI and VII. The Witch's son is a maimed parody of Timias's Petrarchan anguish, or in A. C. Hamilton's apt phrase, a 'low-life version' of the squire.[112] When Timias falls in love, the process is intimately related to the curing of his original wound in a beautiful conflation of the physiological with the psychological: 'She his hurt thigh to him recurd againe,/But hurt his hart, the which was before was sound' (III.v.42). In contrast, the Witch's son shows the deflection of love into physical desire, so that when the narrator mentions the son's heart – 'Yet had he not the hart, nor hardiment,/As vnto her to vtter his desire' – Spenser displaces what had been a complex,

---

109 See Miller, *The Poem's Two Bodies*, 275, and Lauren Silberman, *Transforming Desire*, 47–48.
110 "hew, v." *OED Online*. Oxford University Press, June 2017. See especially meaning 7.
111 Silberman, *Transforming Desire*, 48.
112 *FQ*, 354.

multivalent term into a simple metonymy for an absence of erotic courage
(III.vii.16).[113] Before this, he critically recycles the sequence of rhymes on
hew and *vew* to show the Witch's reaction to Florimell:

> Tho gan she gather vp her garments rent,
>   And her loose lockes to dight in order dew,
>   With golden wreath and gorgeous ornament;
>   Whom such whenas the wicked Hag did vew,
>   She was astonisht at her heauenly hew,
>   And doubted her to deeme an earthly wight,
>   But or some Goddesse, or of *Dianes* crew,
>   And thought her to adore with humble spright;
> T'adore thing so diuine as beauty, were but right. (III.vii.11)

Fairly obviously, this cluster hearkens back to the preceding cantos. Line
5 is a close copy of both 'Her soueraine bountie, and celestiall hew' and
'She heuenly borne, and of celestiall hew' (III.v.44, 47), while line 7 gestures
back to III.vi.16 and 17, describing 'the secret haunts of *Dianaes* company'
and 'the Goddesse with her crew'. Spenser rhymes Florimell with Belphoebe
to force a thematic connection between them – like Belphoebe, Florimell
appears to be a goddess, particularly in the 'gloomy' milieu of the Witch's
cottage (III.vii.6). However, that this is only a partial substitution is
underlined by its almost immediate parody in stanza 13 when the son
sees Florimell:

> He comming home at vndertime, there found
>   The fairest creature, that he euer saw,
>   Sitting beside his mother on the ground;
>   The sight whereof did greatly him adaw,
>   And his base thought with terrour and with aw
>   So inly smot, that as one, which had gaz'd
>   On the bright Sunne vnwares, doth soone withdraw
>   His feeble eyne, with too much brightnes daz'd,
> So stared he on her, and stood long while amaz'd.

What happens here is that phonetically similar *–aw* rhymes replace the
–ew sequences which have underpinned Cantos V and VI to produce a
low-life version of Belphoebe's existential otherness; Florimell is certainly

---

113 See "heart, n., int., and adv." *OED Online.* In III.v.42, Spenser conflates the organ
(meaning 1) with the metaphorical idea of the heart as the seat of the affections (meaning
10). In III.vii.16, the term more simply denotes courage or morale (meaning 11). The
earlier passage is indebted to Ariosto's description of Angelica falling in love with
Medoro, on which see Burrow, *Epic Romance*, 110–11.

dazzling – 'The fairest creature, that he euer saw' – but Spenser focuses on the son's faulty cognition, 'as one, which had gaz'd/On the bright Sunne vnwares'. The parodic substitution is crystallised by the pun in line 4, where 'adaw' means both daunt or confound, and at the same time labels the son as 'a daw', that is, as a fool or simpleton.[114] Even in the diminished context of the Witch's cottage, a distinction is made between the Witch's faulty yet perceptive appreciation of Florimell's 'heauenly hew' and the son's terrified reaction – 'with aw' – to something he cannot possibly understand. The final rhyme itself signals the 'withdraw[al]' from these kinds of connections back to Cantos V and VI, as Florimell's story is developed in new directions.

These two stanzas springload Florimell's forest séjour in such a way as to remind the reader both of the action of Canto V and the origin myth of Canto VI. Indeed, the narrative substitution of Florimell for Belphoebe and the Witch's Son for Timias again points up the oddness of the Gardins of Adonis in terms of the images of sexual satisfaction at its core: love in general in Book III does not produce the images of careless physical mutuality which are at the heart of Canto VI. Rather, those images offer a counterpoint to the narratives of frustrated search and longing which characterise the Book as a whole. Spenser's canto form, on this reckoning, is a careful amalgam of hints picked up from Ariosto with an idiosyncratic way of sequencing narrative; as Burrow puts it, 'Spenser's most characteristic technique is to unfold his meaning by *plot*, the order in which events are related, rather than by *story*, the actual order in which events occur'.[115] Indeed, in cantos V–VII, the 'actual order in which events occur' is a more or less theoretical concept: of course Chrysogone's pregnancy chronologically precedes Timias's falling in love with Belphoebe, but there is little sense in *The Faerie Queene* of what time has elapsed between these two events. Beyond young, how old are Timias, Belphoebe, Amoret, and Florimell? These are not questions experienced readers of Spenser generally ask, and for the good reason that, as Burrow insists, plot dominates story;

---

114 See "adaw, v.2.", and "daw, n." *OED Online*. Though Spenser doesn't use 'daw' in *The Faerie Queene* it does figure in the self-consciously 'base' *Mother Hubberds Tale* at the climax of the description of the suitor's condition at court: 'Who ever leaves sweete home … And will to Court for shadowes vaine to seeke,/Or hope to gaine, himselfe will a dawe trie' (ll.44, 909–13), meaning 'will prove himself to be a jackdaw' or fool; see Aikin in Spenser, *The Minor Poems: Part Two*, 371. See Brown and Lethbridge, *A Concordance*, 393, for the absence of 'daw' from *The Faerie Queene*. Spenser shared his culture's prejudice against corvids, which are in fact among the most intelligent of birds; see https://en.wikipedia.org/wiki/Corvidae [accessed 11 October 2017].

115 Burrow, *Epic Romance*, 110.

we allow ourselves to heed the dynamics of a plot which is told in connected cantos which look both forwards and back, and which expect us as readers to track back right to left within the poem as well as the more usual direction of left to right. This is the force of the rhymes on *hew* and related terms discussed in this chapter: they enable us to see Spenser sequencing different sections of plot through related and contrasting pieces of lexis. How these sequences of cantos function in Books and contribute to the overall structure of the poem is the subject of my final chapter.

6

Spacious ways: narratives and narrators

My greatest wish – other than salvation – was to have a book. A long book with a never-ending story. One I could read again and again, with new eyes and a fresh understanding each time.[1]

Though the Letter to Raleigh is Spenser's most debated discussion of 'his *whole intention in the course of this worke*' (*FQ*, 714), the first stanza of the Proem to Book VI is perhaps a subtler evocation of *The Faerie Queene*'s emergent, dynamic structure:

> THe waies, through which my weary steps I guyde,
>   In this delightfull land of Faery,
>   Are so exceeding spacious and wyde,
>   And sprinckled with such sweet variety,
>   Of all that pleasant is to eare or eye,
>   That I nigh rauisht with rare thoughts delight,
>   My tedious trauell doe forget thereby;
>   And when I gin to feele decay of might,
> It strength to me supplies, and chears my dulled spright.

Spenser's narrator is a mental traveller for whom the physical labour of his forward motion is compensated by the 'spacious and wyde' 'waies' of 'this delightfull land of Faery'. He recommits himself to the inwoven, braided narrative structure of the *Orlando Furioso* at a point in the poem where most critics have felt that his imitation of Ariosto has waned, or moved back to the seemingly more straightforward narrative strategies of Books I and II. For this narrator, however, the 'sweet variety' of the

---

1 Yann Martel, *Life of Pi*, 207.

landscape he traverses is a ravishment which produces intellectual suste-
nance and 'strength' of purpose. Whether 'this delightfull land' is an
adequate evocation of Book VI remains an open question, though 'rauisht'
with its connotations of rape and spoliation as well as ecstatic transport
may suggest some of the complexity of the experience Spenser's otherwise
colourless adjectives mask.[2]

Though we have no concrete records of Edmund Spenser walking,
several poems are either directly prompted by walks, or evoke a situation
in which the poet has 'Walkt forth to ease my payne'; walking the literal
and metaphorical 'waies' seems to have been a Spenserian habit.[3] The
Book VI Proem intersects with a contemporary meditation on the poetics
of walking in Robert Macfarlane's lyrical sitings of fugitive and mysterious
pathways. In his description of walking the Broomway, also known as the
Doomway – a hazardous sand track from the Essex coast – he notes
'Similes and metaphors bred and budded. Mirages of scale occurred, and
tricks of depth … I recall thought becoming sensational; the substance
of landscape so influencing mind that mind's own substance was altered.'
Spenser's narrator suggests a similarly fluid understanding of the poem
he is in the process of writing: what he sees in the fictional landscape he
crosses structures and composes the poem he is writing. Where Macfarlane
sees in the actual landscape of Maplin Sands a 'mind-altering' dissolving
of concrete categories into a hallucinatory literariness, Spenser appropriates
the 'delightfull' aspects of a *locus amoenus* to 'guyde' the reader's sense of
the multifarious, unfixed text she is reading.[4] In both cases, the landscape
through which you walk is at once enticing, unstable, and visionary.

2 See "ravish, v." *OED Online.* The primary meaning here is 4.b, which is congruent with
VI.ix.26 (Calidore 'rapt with double rauishment') and VI.x.30 (Calidore's 'sences rauished'),
but given the narratives of Serena and the Salvage Nation and Pastorella and the brigands,
the term potentially has darker resonances. A Chaucerian intertext maybe relevant:
Chauntecleer is 'ravysshed with [the fox's] flaterie' in *The Nun's Priest's Tale*, l.3324. In
Chaucer, *The Riverside Chaucer*, 259.
3 See *The Ruines of Time*, ll.1–2 ('It chaunced me on day beside the shore/Of siluer
streaming *Thamesis* to bee'); *Amoretti* LXXV (a beach setting presupposes a beach
walk); and most clearly, *Prothalamion*, ll.1–20, quoted here. Though these texts suggest
a walking sensibility not unlike that of Wordsworth in *The Prelude* Book IV, Andrew
Hadfield informs me that he found no evidence of a particular interest in walking on
Spenser's part while working on his biography and concluded that ascending Galtymore
would probably have been too dangerous (email correspondence, August 2017); see
Edmund Spenser: A Life, 375.
4 Robert Macfarlane, *The Old Ways*, 74–75. See also the euphoric moment at discovering
Clachan Mhànais – 'a Richard Long sculpture, long before Long' – on the Isle of Lewis:
'Click. Alignment. Blur resolving into comprehension. The pattern clear: a cairn sequence,
subtle but evident, running up from the Dubh Loch shore', 156–57. For *locus amoenus*,
see Curtius, *European Literature and the Latin Middle Ages*, 183–202.

The spacious ways of Spenserian walking are clearly connected in the Proem to Book VI to broader questions of artistic structure and design. As we shall see, structure is a huge topic. This final chapter selectively reviews *The Faerie Queene*'s narrative structure in the light of conflicting reception histories. I largely eschew allegorical accounts of structure both because my focus in this book is on the poem's 'surface' structures, and because these continue to be a dominant tradition in Spenser studies; inevitably, my approach is informed by this influential critical literature. It is, however, salutary to hesitate in the face of what might be called the allegorical consensus. As scholars like Guy Cook and Rita Felski have argued, the discourse of 'critique', with its attendant predilection for metaphors of depth and surface, presents a powerful, cross-disciplinary hermeneutic assumption which privileges certain kinds of reading.[5] Felski counsels against both 'interpretation-as-excavation' and standing 'back from the text to scrutinize it from afar', since in each approach the work of critique produces typically 'suspicious' readings where the text is seen more as an 'inert object' than 'a phenomenon to be engaged'.[6] Allegory of course has the advantage of having a longer back story, and, in the case of *The Faerie Queene*, Spenser's own endorsement in the Letter to Raleigh with its celebrated description of the poem as '*a continued Allegory, or darke conceit*' (*FQ*, 714). Nevertheless, as the critical tradition has made clear, the poem's allegory is not the same throughout its books, whatever the reader takes '*continued*' to mean, and allegory is not the only way of making sense of the poem.[7] In this context, another contemporary fiction sheds a provocative sidelight. In his Preface to the *His Dark Materials* trilogy, Philip Pullman – a writer deeply conscious of *The Faerie Queene* – discusses his working methods and his discovery that privileging theme over plot was counterproductive. For Pullman, 'the story should lead, and the theme will emerge in its own time and its own way' because 'if you're

5 Guy Cook, 'Genes, Memes, Rhymes', 376–78; Cook's work is particularly useful in terms of devices like rhyme and the serious attention it plays to verbal randomising devices which criticism often discounts; see also Brown, '"Charmed with Inchaunted Rimes"' in Brown and Lethbridge, *A Concordance*, 16–17. Rita Felski, *The Limits of Critique*, 60–61, 69–84.

6 Felski, *The Limits of Critique*, 61, 70, 84. I compress Felski's brilliant exposition of the metaphors of depth and surface, and their various debts to the Marxist, Freudian, and Foucauldian traditions.

7 My suggestion here is that allegorical readings (both of *The Faerie Queene* and other texts) are proleptic of the tendencies Felski observes in her discussion of 'deep' readings, not that such readings are all vested in what she calls (following Ricoeur) 'a *hermeneutics of suspicion*' (*The Limits of Critique*, 1). For the background to allegory as a series of interpretative manoeuvres, see Hough, *A Preface to The Faerie Queene*, 100–37, and Gordon Teskey, 'Allegory', 16–22.

working as seriously as you know how to, for a matter of years, then a theme will emerge whether you want it to or not … Once you know what it is, you can shape the story more precisely to help it show up, but it's a mistake to rely on the theme to lead the story for you.'[8] Pullman is of course a product of a different literary culture from Spenser, and his preface tells us nothing about how *The Faerie Queene* was written. But it does imply the ways in which story shapes theme and vice versa through the course of the writing of a long, symbolic work. It is analogous with aspects of my method in this chapter. As throughout this study, I focus on the most immediate aspects of the reading experience, concentrating on (to adapt Felski's phrase) the phenomena to be engaged. Thus I suggest that the ways in which the poem is narrated are most pressing phenomena to new readers. Why are there so many loose ends? What sort of a device is the narrator? To what extent is his a voice similar to that found in later fiction? These are the kinds of questions this chapter tries to answer. My concern with plot entails a panoptic comparison of the narratives of Books I and VI, then turns to the role of the narrator, particularly in The Mutabilitie Cantos. My argument is that the spacious ways of Spenser's poem remain dynamic, and that the central devices of narrative – a poetic of loose ends and a rhetorically changeable yet recognisable narrative voice – work to keep the poem unpredictable from the beginning to the end. Though it is not quite the book with 'a never-ending story' craved by the shipwrecked Pi, there are aspects to its narratives which are compatible with this fantasy.

Multiple plots and opinions

Torquato Tasso is unlikely to have approved of the narrative structure of *The Faerie Queene*. In his *Discorsi dell'arte poetica* – which Spenser may have read but which most scholars believe that he probably did not[9] – Tasso argues against the use of multiple plots in epic:

8 Philip Pullman, *His Dark Materials: Northern Lights, The Subtle Knife, The Amber Spyglass*, xxxvi. Though Milton is the dominant presence in the trilogy, Spenserian allusion is present throughout: see for example the quotation from I.ix.21 (Trevisan fleeing from Despair) used as a chapter epigraph in *The Amber Spyglass*, 771.
9 Tasso wrote the *Discorsi* in c.1562–65, but they were not published until 1587. Spenser's major engagement with Tasso's work is usually seen in *The Faerie Queene*'s creative response to the *Gerusalemme liberata* (published in a complete edition in 1581) and in the Letter to Raleigh as a parallel text to Tasso's 'Allegoria del poema'. See Lawrence F. Rhu, *The Genesis of Tasso's Narrative Theory*, 10, 17, 60–61; David Quint, 'Tasso, Torquato', 678–80; and Wilson-Okamura, *Spenser's International Style*, 7–8, who justifies his use of the later still *Discorsi del poema eroico* (1594) on the grounds that Tasso's 'struggle with style' is analogous to Spenser's (8).

[M]ultiple plots cause confusion, which could go on and on forever if art did not set and prescribe limits. The poet who treats one plot has reached his goal when that one plot has finished; he who weaves together more may interweave four or six or ten: he is no more obliged to one number than to another. Thus, he can have no sure sense at what point he had best stop.[10]

For Tasso, Spenser's shifting plan for *The Faerie Queene* – whether articulated in the Letter to Raleigh or embodied in the different models of the 1590 and 1596 editions – would have seemed like Jorge Luis Borges's unsiftable sacred text, the Book of Sand. Of course, *The Faerie Queene* is not such an unbounded book – it is easily openable, and has relatively certain textual thresholds and exit points. 'Relatively' is working hard here, however: does the poem begin with the Proem to Book I, the first stanza of Book I Canto I, or the argument to that Book? Endings are even more multiple: consider the unrevised Hermaphrodite stanzas which close Book III, or indeed, the complex not-prefatory matter of the Letter to Raleigh, Commendatory Verses and Dedicatory Sonnets, and Faults Escaped in 1590; VI.xii.41 in 1596; the 'vnperfite' ending of the Mutabilitie Cantos in 1609. The difficulty of holding the poem's unfinished structure in mind remains considerable, and may legitimately remind the reader of Borges's unsettling tome: 'The number of pages in this book is no more or less than infinite. None is the first page, none the last.'[11] Tasso's criticism of multiple plots was motivated by his tense relationship with the romantic epics of Ariosto and Boiardo, which are attacked precisely for their amorphous hugeness:

> Without doubt, those poems are faulty, and the work spent on them in good part lost, in which the reader has barely passed the middle when he has forgotten the beginning. One loses the pleasure in a poem that must be assiduously pursued by the poet as its main perfection; that is, one loses the necessary or verisimilar succession of one event after another and how one thing is linked to another and inseparable from it and, in sum, how a natural and verisimilar and surprising dénouement results from a skillful interweaving of connections. And perhaps, to one who would consider the *Innamorato* and the *Furioso* as a single poem, its length could seem excessive and unlikely to be retained by an average memory after simply one reading.[12]

Tasso is of course not an objective witness. The *Discorsi* are implicitly an *ars poetica* which defend the *Gerusalemme liberata* as a coherent epic

---

10 Tasso, 'Discourses on the Art of Poetry', in Rhu, *The Genesis of Tasso's Narrative Theory*, 119.
11 Jorge Luis Borges, *The Book of Sand*, 89.
12 Tasso, 'Discourses on the Art of Poetry' in Rhu, *The Genesis of Tasso's Narrative Theory*, 117.

based around a single action in Aristotelian terms; Tasso's vocabulary – 'versimilar succession of one event after another'; 'a natural and versimilar ... dénouement' – indicates his concern to align romantic epic with contemporaneous Aristotelian criticism.[13] From this perspective, 'the main perfection' of such a poem is lost when a poet refuses to be tied to the defining 'limits' of the first quotation; for Tasso, the 'skillful weaving of connections' is best witnessed in a poem centred on 'one plot' like the *Iliad* or the *Gerusalemme Liberata*.[14] Though Spenser may have been 'Tasso's brother in poetry', Tasso's reservations about Ariostan epic were sincere, and would almost certainly have meant that he would have been doubtful of the validity of Spenser's structuring procedures.[15]

Many actual readers of *The Faerie Queene* registered similar reservations. Thomas Rymer, who is usually seen as the epitome of neo-classical orthodoxy in England, blamed Spenser's devotion to Ariosto for *The Faerie Queene*'s eccentricities:

> [Spenser] wanted a true *Idea*; and lost himself, by following an unfaithful guide. Though besides *Homer* and *Virgil* he had read *Tasso*, yet he rather suffer'd himself to be misled by *Ariosto*; with whom blindly rambling on *marvellous* Adventures, he makes no Conscience of *Probability*. All is fanciful and chimerical, without any uniformity, without any foundation in truth; his Poem is perfect *Fairy-land*.
>
> They who can love *Ariosto*, will be ravish'd with *Spencer*; whilst men of juster thoughts lament that such great Wits have miscarried in their Travels for want of direction to set them in the right way. But the truth is, in *Spencer's* time, Italy it self was not well satisfied with *Tasso*; and few amongst them would then allow that he had excell'd their *divine Ariosto*.[16]

13   For Tasso's Aristotelianism, see Rhu, *The Genesis of Tasso's Narrative Theory*, 17–21; Quint, 'Tasso, Torquato', 679; and Wilson-Okamura, *Spenser's International Style*, 143. For an alternative view, see Burrow, *Epic Romance*, who sees the structural differences between *Orlando Furioso* and *Gerusalemme Liberata* in terms of 'the two poets' differing views of the ethos of the hero of the *Aeneid*', concluding 'Form is an ethical issue in *Gerusalemme liberata*' (84, 86).

14   For the argument that the *Iliad* is centred on a single plot – 'the wrath of Achilles' – and not the Trojan War as a whole, see Tasso, 'Discourses on the Art of Poetry', in Rhu, *The Genesis of Tasso's Narrative Theory*, 115.

15   Wilson-Okamura, *Spenser's International Style*, 8. The full quotation is 'Spenser was Tasso's brother in poetry, not his son', a distillation of Wilson-Okamura's sense that Tasso and Spenser were wrestling with analogous stylistic problems of what the proper forms were for epic in the later sixteenth century. Nevertheless, there is a risk of homogenising the two poets: *Gerusalemme Liberata* and *The Faerie Queene* structurally represent very different solutions to the problem of how to be poetically up to date.

16   Rymer, 'The Preface of the Translator', in René Rapin, *Reflections on Aristotle's Treatise of Poesie*, sig.A6v–A7r. For Rymer's neoclassicism, see Robert L. Montgomery, 'Neoclassical Poetics', 828.

The terms of Rymer's reproof echo those of the first stanza of the Proem to Book VI: 'misled by *Ariosto*' and 'All is fanciful and chimerical' suggest that Spenser was far too ravished by the delightful land of Faery, a word Rymer mockingly recycles in the second paragraph. It is a small step, we might say, from forgetting your tedious travel to miscarrying along the way 'for want of direction'. If the skittish, Ariosto lover will be 'ravish'd with *Spencer*', the savant reader must realise that this is a romantic dead end with the risk of epic miscarriage. What Rymer doesn't register (exemplifying the Augustan 'cultural smugness' noted by Paul Alpers) is that Spenser's choice of these 'waies' was deliberate and aesthetically functional.[17] Rather than 'blindly rambling on *marvellous* Adventures', the Proem insists that 'such sweet variety' of incident is precisely what Spenser intended. Like Donne's speaker in 'The Indifferent' (in which Venus swears 'by Loves sweetest Part, Variety') Spenser is – in narrative terms at least – paradoxically committed to errancy as opposed to 'dangerous constancie'.[18]

Yet the overall structure, and the structural principles on which Spenser composed *The Faerie Queene*, remain elusive and perplexing. Scholars frequently look to the Letter to Raleigh for guidance, but this document poses as many problems as it solves: why is its description of the contents of 1590 *Faerie Queene* in so many places wrong, and why was it dropped from the 1596 installment?[19] Equally, the physical form of the poem as published in 1590, 1596, and 1609 gives no unambiguous account of Spenser's overall intentions. Though Rymer is condescending, the assertion that Spenser 'wanted a true *Idea*; and lost himself, by following an unfaithful guide' may chime both with the reader's experience of the poem and with aspects of the scholarly literature which has attempted to imagine a finished

---

17 Alpers (ed.), *Edmund Spenser: a Critical Anthology*, 64. As Alpers goes on to note, 'the eighteenth-century critics who invoke Elizabethan tastes and manners to explain *The Faerie Queene* are essentially giving a generous and favourable version of Rymer's harsh strictures', 67.

18 Donne, *Poems [1633]*, 201.

19 A selective reading list: Bennett, *The Evolution of The Faerie Queene*, 24–38, on the Letter as a guide to how a putative complete poem would have been structured; W. J. B. Owen, '"In These XII. Books Severally Handled and Discoursed"', 165–72, a sceptical reading, which concludes that the Letter is 'all but irrelevant to the work it purports to describe' (172). More recent work explores and sometimes celebrates the Letter's poetic and theoretical eccentricities in the literary politics of the period; see Wayne Erickson, 'Spenser's Letter to Raleigh', 139–74; Ty Buckman, 'Forcing the Poet into Prose', 17–34; Grogan, *Exemplary Spenser*, 27–68.

Faerie Queene.[20] Because it is unfinished, and because of the way it is unfinished, '*al the discourse*' of the poem is more than usually difficult to grasp either in a handful or indeed through a protracted head scratch (*FQ*, 718). This may account for the relative paucity of contemporary work on the poem's structure. In his important contribution, Andrew King notes that there is no entry on structure in *The Spenser Encyclopedia*, an observation that could now be extended to include Richard McCabe's *Oxford Handbook*, and Andrew Escobedo's *Edmund Spenser in Context*, both of which are otherwise attentive to questions of form.[21] King's essay gives an overview of previous work on the structure, arguing that critics have either privileged the poem's Ariostan or Virgilian pedigree to the detriment of its connections to the medieval tradition.[22] King adduces three different medieval forms which may impinge on *The Faerie Queene*: the story collection, in particular *The Canterbury Tales*, the *Morte Darthur*, and manuscript anthologies of romances, which were still in circulation

20 Compare Bennett, *The Evolution of The Faerie Queene*, with Wilson-Okamura's properly rhetorical question, 'Would anyone actually read a full-length *Faerie Queene*?'; Wilson-Okamura goes on to engage in precisely this sort of imaginative exercise, pondering putative Books of Law, War, and Planting and their appropriate styles; *Spenser's International Style*, 199, 203–07.

21 Andrew King, '"Well Grounded, Finely Framed"', 25, noting that Book form and structure have eclipsed 'the overall design of the poem'. For formal approaches in the *Oxford Handbook*, see my review, '*The Oxford Handbook of Edmund Spenser*', 271–72. Though the *Handbook* contains thoughtful essays on, inter alia, language, metre, genre, rhetoric and allegory, as with the *Encyclopedia*, structure is not directly discussed. Similarly, Escobedo's collection includes essays on genre (by David Quint, Katherine C. Little, Clare R. Kinney, William Kerwin), theory (by Gordon Teskey and Michael Hetherington), and prosody (by Paul J. Hecht), but not structure; see *Edmund Spenser in Context*, 99–129, 148–75, 204–13.

22 King, '"Well Grounded, Finely Framed"', 22–30, with bibliography. The most influential studies have been Bennett, *The Evolution of The Faerie Queene*, 24–38; Lewis, *The Allegory of Love*, 304–05 (asserting the poem's debt to Italian romantic epic, a position he subsequently modified); Fowler, *Spenser and the Numbers of Time* (arguing the poem is structured around Pythagorean number symbolism and astrological symbolism); Alpers, *The Poetry of The Faerie Queene*, 107–34 (suggesting that larger structural questions are best seen through the lens of the poem's smaller compositional units; see the discussion below and Chapter 5 above); Burrow, *Epic Romance*, 100–46 (arguing that Spenser's epic 'tries to transcend the epic romance tradition' through a critical recoding of the ethics of pity as witnessed in Virgil, Ariosto and Tasso [101]), and Wilson-Okamura, *Spenser's International Style*, who reads *The Faerie Queene* as a complex response to European theory and practice, in particular the work of Tasso and the poets of the Pléiade, though without a detailed discussion of structure (70–137; 161–79). See also R.A. Horton, *The Unity of The Faerie Queene*; Jan Karel Kouwenhoven, *Apparent Narrative as Thematic Metaphor*; and Judith Dundas, *The Spider and The Bee*. Finally, Arnold Williams, *Flower on a Lowly Stalk*, 14–38, provides a perceptive New Critical account of the narrative patterns and structures within Book VI.

during the sixteenth century.[23] *Troilus und Criseyde* might be added to this list, with its innovative and possibly Senecan or Boethian revision of the looser structure of the *Filostrato* into a five-book form. Spenser surely recognised Chaucer's self-consciousness about *his* book form, even though *The Faerie Queene* lacks the allusion to drama which underpins Chaucer's 'litel bok … myn tragedye'.[24] Spenser's Books are not strictly 'like' Chaucer's, in terms either of length or of narrative focus; the point is rather that the *Troilus* was a major poem where the idea of the 'Book' is structurally and rhetorically dominant as a distinct unit of narrative meaning.[25]

One of *The Faerie Queene*'s key innovations, discussed in the previous chapter, is that it contains both cantos and books. King explores this question in the light of habitual associations with the *Orlando Furioso* and the *Aeneid*:

> The Virgilian Book may be a larger unit than the Ariostan canto, but it is fundamentally of the same kind: a narrative 'fragment' which represents one particular section of an overriding narrative arc. Virgil's story is a line which runs *through* his Books; the divisions between Books are less strong than the narrative continuity which binds the Books together into a work of classical unity, a work which one can best appreciate by reading 'cover to cover'. … In *The Faerie Queene*, this situation has been reversed. There is not one narrative, but several, and these narratives are contained within the Books. The divisions between the Books are stronger than any narratorial progression which is developed over the course of the work as a whole. In other words, the fundamental structural principle of *The Faerie Queene*,

---

23 King, '"Well Grounded, Finely Framed"', 30–51. See also King, *The Faerie Queene and Middle English Romance*, 38–39.

24 Chaucer, *Troilus and Criseyde with facing-page Il Filostrato*, V.1786, 421. Boccaccio does not match this apostrophe, though at the start of Part Nine he addresses his poem as 'My piteous song'; 426. For Chaucer's innovative book form, see Stephen Barney's Introduction to this edition, x, xii. Chaucer's sense of his poem as a 'book' is evident in several places, both in text (II.10; III.1818; IV.26), and in the paratextual Latin introductions and conclusions such as '*Incipit prohemium secundi libri*' or '*Explicit liber quartus*' (68, 311). These aspects of the manuscript were carried into the sixteenth-century print editions; see Chaucer, *The Works*, sig. Oo3v.

25 *Piers Plowman* may also be relevant; Crowley's 1550 second edition notes on the title page the unaccustomed quality of the poem's formal divisions: 'the boke is deuided into twenty partes called Passus'; Langland, *The Vision of Pierce Plowman*, sig. *1r. *The Faerie Queene* is similar to *Piers* inasmuch as it has a bespoke structure: as Judith Anderson notes, 'Among medieval dream poems, a series of dreams, laced with inner dreams and periodic waking intervals, is peculiar only to *Piers*. This structure not only influences directly Spenser's treatment of Redcrosse's dreaming in *FQ* I but also influences less directly other dreamlike qualities of the poem and the nature of the poet's presence in it'; in 'Langland, William', 425–26. See also "passus, n." *OED Online*. Oxford University Press, June 2017.

not explicable in terms of the influence of either *Orlando Furioso* or the *Aeneid*, is the relative *separateness* of each Book.

Taking his cue from the Letter, King adduces what he calls a 'one Book per knight' rule, which licenses comparisons with medieval texts and pageantry, and which cumulatively validates Bishop Hurd's characterisation of *The Faerie Queene* as 'Gothic'. For King, the Letter can be trusted as a 'useful initial guide to the fundamentally different nature of the poem's structure in comparison to *Orlando Furioso* or the *Aeneid*'.[26] There are two difficulties with this approach. Firstly, though it is true that *The Faerie Queene* is not structurally like the *Aeneid* or the *Iliad* or the *Odyssey*, the ambition to *seem* classical is, as elsewhere in Elizabethan culture, evident throughout.[27] This isn't simply in the imitation of the *Aeneid*, or the way that Guyon's sea journey to the Bower of Bliss mirrors the wayfarings of Odysseus and Aeneas, but is rather an attribute of the hybridised Elizabethan classicism Spenser articulates in the Letter: 'I *haue followed all the antique Poets historicall, first Homere … then Virgil … after him Ariosto … and lately Tasso*' (*FQ*, 715). *The Faerie Queene* may not be like Homer's or Virgil's poems, but Spenser nevertheless wanted to 'follow' these great forerunners and their cultural ambitions; Chaucer and Malory do not have the brand recognition of the classical past nor of the classicising present.[28] Secondly, the qualification of 'the relative *separateness* of each Book' draws attention to the degrees of this condition and the strictness of any such demarcation. To what extent are *The Faerie Queene*'s narratives *constrained* 'within the Books'? As King acknowledges, Books III and IV challenge this model, as does Arthur's role as a disruptive, free-ranging *deus ex machina*-cum-embodiment of magnificence.[29] While Books III

26   King, '"Well Grounded, Finely Framed"', 26–28.
27   See Wilson-Okamura, *Spenser's International Style*, 10, 53, on the literary and textual cast of Elizabethan classicism and *stile antico* as a visual language with which Spenser would have been familiar. That *The Faerie Queene* sounds unlike Virgil is one of Wilson-Okamura's animating concerns; see further 18–49; 53–69. Wilson-Okamura cumulatively stresses the oddness of Spenserian classicism.
28   Sidney's backhanded comment on the *Troilus* is germane here: 'Chaucer, undoubtedly, did excellently in his *Troilus and Criseyde*; of whom, truly, I know not whether to marvel more, either that he in that misty time could see so clearly, or that we in this clear age go so stumblingly after him.' Sidney hovers, like his clustered, nervously qualifying clutch of adverbs, between condescension and admiration in a way which is quite different from his praise of Virgil; in *Miscellaneous Prose*, 112.
29   King, '"Well Grounded, Finely Framed"', 28. See *FQ*, 715–16, for Spenser's description of Arthur's role, and see Hough, *A Preface to The Faerie Queene*, 90, and Bennett, *The Evolution of The Faerie Queene*, 24–30, 37–38, for the difficulties of squaring this with the poem as it stands.

and IV are the most marked example of narrative interweaving, the overflow of characters and episodes is not isolated to these books alone. Minor characters throughout the poem are relatively free-floating, popping up according to narrative need; thus Satyrane circulates in Books I, III and IV.[30] This quality will become clear in my account of Book VI below: the Book repeatedly assumes or cues the expectation that its incomplete stories will be taken up in later books. That Book VI is finished suggests that either Spenser intended to return to these incomplete narratives in subsequent books, or contrariwise, that the loose ends were a deliberate part of the design.

The larger omission in King's approach is of allegory as a unifying structure. As I noted at the outset, this has been a dominant strain in Spenser studies, which reads *The Faerie Queene* in terms of related ideas and patterns of imagery, where the poem's structure is intellectual and conceptual rather than produced through narrative. In Jason Crawford's *Allegory and Enchantment*, this critical manoeuvre is traced back to the eighteenth century: because of their discomfort with allegorical personifications, critics like John Hughes made a foundational distinction between 'the monstrous surface' of the poem and its 'mystic sense'; as Crawford puts it, 'Because the narrative surface of allegory is … secondary … it is free to indulge even in impossibility without running any danger of incoherence.' Such bracketing-off of allegory as a 'strange fiction' unlike all other kinds can be seen to inform later scholarship.[31] Thus C. S. Lewis's meditation on the Bower of Bliss and the Gardins of Adonis as linked 'allegorical cores' which display contrasting images of vicious and virtuous sexuality helps to inaugurate modes of reading which underpin work as diverse as Northrop Frye's *Anatomy of Criticism*, Thomas P. Roche's *The Kindly Flame*, James Nohrnberg's *The Analogy of The Faerie Queene*, and more recently Roger Kuin's essay on 'The Double Helix'

---

30 See Ronald Horton, 'Satyrane', 628, and Anne Lake Prescott, 'Giants', 332–33. As Prescott notes, 'Most of Spenser's heroes must confront giants (though Calidore … chases only their relative, the Blatant Beast)' (332). Other free-floating characters include Sansloy, Florimell, Marinell, Paridell, Blandamour.

31 Jason Crawford, *Allegory and Enchantment: An Early Modern Poetics*, 31. See also Crawford's later remark, again summarising the work of eighteenth-century scholars: 'To circumscribe allegory as a narrative genre … is, after all, to contain its volatile energies, to keep it from disrupting the mainline canons of narrative probability and causation' (33). The difficulty with this position is perhaps the extent to which, as Crawford notes earlier, citing Andrew Escobedo, 'before the eighteenth century there is no idea of nonallegorical fiction' (31 n.77).

(2002).[32] Frye, echoed by Roche and amplified by Nohrnberg, suggested the organising form of books paired both sequentially and concentrically: I/VI, II/V, III/IV, and I/II, III/IV, V/VI, a model which has conditioned how contemporary Spenserians think about the macroscopic forms of the poem. Narrative shortfalls, in this view, are to be supplemented symbolically by the reader; as Gordon Teskey explains in relation to Redcrosse's encounter with Sansfoy after earlier abandoning Una: 'The connections between the events must be supplied by the interpreter who brings them together in a structure of meaning; after abandoning Una, Redcrosse meets Sansfoy not merely by chance, as it seems in the text, but because loss of faith follows loss of truth.'[33] No account of the structure of *The Faerie Queene* can overlook what Teskey calls this 'interpretative play': both microscopically and macroscopically, the poem solicits participative readers, readers who are not just ready but willing to fill in these logical and narrative blanks. From this perspective, there is a strong sense in which *The Faerie Queene* does not lack structure, but rather that it has – at least by Tasso's standards – too much. There are many, many organising structures that emerge as we read, but none dominates. My focus on narrative structure is not meant to displace allegorical structure but rather to focus on an aspect of the poem's organisation which is – like its archaising lexis and its innovative stanza form – another enstranging device, particularly since in contrast with the epics of Homer, Virgil, Ariosto, and Tasso, Spenser's remains more resolutely open-ended in terms of its multiple plots.[34]

32 See Lewis, *The Allegory of Love*, 321–60, *Spenser's Images of Life*, 20–63; Northrop Frye, 'The Structure of Imagery in *The Faerie Queene*' and *The Anatomy of Criticism*, 90, for allegory as 'a contrapuntal technique'; Thomas P. Roche, *The Kindly Flame*, 195–211; Nohrnberg, *The Analogy of The Faerie Queene*, 5–19, 35, 626–27 and passim; Roger Kuin, 'The Double Helix'. See also Angus Fletcher, *Allegory: The Theory of a Symbolic Mode*, especially 270–73. See also the overviews by Teskey, 'Allegory', 16–22 (especially 20), and Kenneth Borris, 'Allegory, Emblem and Symbol', 437–61.

33 Teskey, 'Allegory', 20. See also his subsequent comment: 'We cannot perceive logical development from one episode to the next – in Dante, Langland, Spenser, or Bunyan – without engaging the text thus in interpretative play' (20).

34 See Felski, *The Limits of Critique*, 72, for the influence of Shklovsky and Russian formalism on contemporary hermeneutics of suspicion. Felski suggests that the metaphors of 'estrangement' and 'defamiliarization' have contributed to a rhetoric of critique: 'The work of critical analysis simply is this work of estrangement, the labor of disrupting continuities and severing attachments' (84). My use of Shklovsky does not mirror this work of severing; like Felski, I am more interested in the affective work done by the reader in process of reading. As described by Teskey, the reader of Spenser's allegory is congruent with the participative, 'cocreative' model advanced by Felski after her criticism of 'deep' and 'surface' readings (84).

These issues around the potentially fugitive narrative structure are usefully discussed in an older study: Graham Hough's *A Preface to The Faerie Queene* (1962), which contains a suggestive account of the poem's structure.[35] Again, I give a relatively long extract both to remind readers of a classic formalist approach, and because these evocations of structure need space to breathe; like the texts they describe, these are seldom epigrammatic one-liners. After observing the inconsistencies between the Letter and the poem, Hough moves to a description of 'the real nature of the work', which, he suggests, is not fundamentally affected by the Letter:

> [M]ost of the critical questions about the structure of *The Faerie Queene* become idle or simply disappear when it is actually read … we are always aware of being in a varied but consistent world. This unity of atmosphere … is far more of a present reality than any discontinuities in the plot. The very multiplicity of incidents is a help in this direction; the effect is of an all-over pattern rather than that of a picture composed on a few broad structural lines. *The Faerie Queene* is composed of many relatively small parts, each commanding our appreciation by itself and all harmonious with each other; and this is its structural principle. Its essence is immanent in these multitudinous local effects, not in an over-riding plan which can be abstracted and schematically displayed … The unfinished state of the poem therefore matters less than it might. It is a misfortune that half of this richly patterned page is missing; but what is left retains its full vitality. That the parts are parts of a whole need not be doubted; but they have their own life and their own kind of mutual coherence without reference to the total design.[36]

For Hough, the structure of *The Faerie Queene* is a dynamic which is produced through the activity of reading. Discontinuity of plot is subordinated to a piecemeal structure composed of 'many relatively small parts … all harmonious with each other'. These multiple parts become synecdoches for the larger structure; 'mutual coherence' is guaranteed by the liveliness of the individual effects which go to sustain the greater, unfinished whole. Hough then advances a structural account of the poem based on analogy with dreams, informed by Freud, which suggests that the disquieting familiarity of the poem, as well as its crucial difference from the work of

---

35 King, '"Well Grounded, Finely Framed"', 26, reads Hough's chapter primarily in terms of the suggestion that the *Faerie Queene* Books were 'an attempt to combine the form of the classical with that of the romantic epic', but this undersells the complexity of Hough's argument; Hough, *A Preface to The Faerie Queene*, 86.
36 Hough, *A Preface to The Faerie Queene*, 93–94.

Ariosto and Tasso, lies in its use of dream symbolism and logic.[37] Hough's approach, with its insistence on the vitality of the individual part, anticipates Alpers's exploration later in the 1960s on the poem's rhetorical mode. As Roger Sale's *Spenser Encyclopedia* entry on Canto – which begins with an Alpersian reading of I.v.46 – puts it: 'Any consideration of Spenser's larger units, cantos and books, must proceed from this understanding of how he constructs his smaller units, and of his sense of the reader's memory and proper reading pace.' Ultimately, the larger structures are subordinated to the more human scale of the 'genuine reading units' of each individual stanza.[38] This is a New Critical twist on Tasso's anxiety about the strain Boiardo and Ariosto place on their readers' memories: as the poem is constructed stanza by stanza, so Spenser takes a pragmatic view of what we will remember. The whole, in this reckoning, is subordinated to the parts; the structural problems 'simply disappear' in the act of reading the poem.

And yet, none of this is quite enough. As Hough recognised, his evocation of the structure of *The Faerie Queene* risks reanimating Hazlitt's model of the poem as 'only an enchanting fairy-tale' where allegory can be temporarily ignored.[39] The synecdochical reading, meanwhile, puts a premium on close reading practices which have been challenged by the more politicised and politically self-conscious approaches of various forms of historicism. Is it really the case that we can read the judicial violence of Book V, with its unambiguous roots in sixteenth-century political realities, as 'harmonious' with, say, the Gardins of Adonis?[40] Should we accept that the 'essence' of the poem is 'immanent' in a series of striking 'local effects' which may be compared to 'a page of medieval illumination' when we read the striking discontinuities of narrative in Book VI, with its ragged, unfinished stories of wild men and animals, judicial torture, erotic malfeasance, and pastoral violence?[41] Hough's evocation is too

---

37 Hough, *A Preface to The Faerie Queene*, 97–99.
38 Sale, 'Canto', 134. Alpers spends much of his first chapter challenging the traditional analogy between epic poem and world which Hough articulates above, thus problematising the notion that the poem is mimetic; see *The Poetry of The Faerie Queene*, 19–35.
39 Hough, *A Preface to The Faerie Queene*, 95. The recourse to the analogy with dreams is explicitly made to forestall this criticism.
40 This is not to say that Hough overlooks these aspects of Book V. Rather, like many Spenserians of this period, he palliates the book's politics by querying its aesthetics: 'Invention and narrative power are weaker, the verse is often flat, the peaks of allegorical or pictorial concentration are lacking'; *A Preface to The Faerie Queene*, 191. Compare Lewis, *The Allegory of Love*, 349.
41 Hough, *A Preface to The Faerie Queene*, 94. See Horton, *The Unity of The Faerie Queene*, 6–7, and n.5, 193–94, for a critical review of such pictorial analogies.

beautiful, too 'harmonious', to be adequate to the poem's many loose ends and moments of unexpected violence. The point can perhaps be made by reversing the terms of Hough's description: though the poem is made up of small parts, it still claims textually, rhetorically, and politically to add up to something larger. *The Faerie Queene, Disposed into XII. Bookes, Fashioning twelue Morall Vertues* is the full title used in all three of the substantive editions of 1590, 1596, and 1609; even if we discount the Letter to Raleigh, is the reader not entitled to expect that, to use Spenser's own word in describing his structure, these books will 'compile' – in the sense of construct or build – some larger, legible textual edifice?[42]

What follows is an attempt to work through some of these questions without abandoning synecdochical formalism: unless one adopts the consensus-based approach of Wilson-Okamura, selected parts must inevitably stand for the larger whole.[43] As throughout this study, I want to stress that the interrelationships between the different parts of the poem are complex; my aim is to illuminate further the openness which characterises *The Faerie Queene* as a narrative. Such openness should not be confused with indeterminacy – Spenser is not an ambiguous poet in this modern sense. Nevertheless, the books of *The Faerie Queene* are not sealed units any more than individual lines and stanzas are completely independent of the surrounding poem; I look at the variety of narrative forms Spenser explores in the ostensibly fixed and predictable form of the twelve-canto book, extending the arguments of Chapter 5 about the open, concessive form of the canto. The ultimate challenge for formal criticism is to describe the unfinished structure of *The Faerie Queene* in ways which pay appropriate attention both to what Hough calls its 'multitudinous local effects' alongside the porous and provisional cast of the poem as a whole. As in the previous chapter, Book VI is a focal text, which in this case I juxtapose with Book I. There is widespread agreement that Books I, II, and V follow the same format of largely integrated allegorical narratives centred on a titular hero whose quest illuminates the virtue he is chosen to represent. Similarly, the idea that Books III and IV represent a looser, more Ariostan episodic structure, with a focus on connected issues of love, sex, marriage, chastity,

---

42 *Amoretti* LXXX: 'After so long a race as I have run/Through Faery land, which those six books compile'. See "compile, v. 6.b" *OED Online*, citing this passage. See King, '"Well Grounded, Finely Framed"', 37 n.47, for a possible link between Spenser's structure and the medieval practice of compilation.

43 See Wilson-Okamura, *Spenser's International Style*, 4–5, for his methodological use of 'the *consensus sapientum*, the convergence of scholarly or critical opinion over a long period'.

and friendship, is commonplace.[44] The major challenge to this view has come from the elevation of the published installment over the individual book since the late 1980s.[45] But these are not exclusive approaches: it is possible to approach the installments as separate bibliographic and poetic entities while recognising the narrative filiations between Books III and IV in the adventures of Britomart, Amoret, Florimell, Scudamour, and so on. Book VI stands apart from both these patterns. This is the part of the poem where the tension between the poet's wandering aesthetic and the moral teleology of the Knight's quest is decisively apparent as Calidore abandons his quest, and the route towards an understanding of courtesy seems hopelessly compromised as events abrade against moral allegory. This is not to say that Spenser abandons the animating ambition to be moral; rather that, as in the classic expression of this view by Richard Neuse, by Book VI Spenser 'has reached the limits of his epic enterprise'.[46] At the same time, the comparison with Book I suggests that an aesthetic of aporetic loose ends is part of *The Faerie Queene*'s narrative design from the outset. In the final section, I turn to the Mutabilitie Cantos to consider their tonal relationship to the rest of the poem in terms of narrative voice.

Loose ends and antagonistic forces: book structure

Colin Burrow offers a lucid summary of the aesthetic consequences of *The Faerie Queene*'s structural indeterminacy:

44 See Hough, *A Preface to The Faerie Queene*, 85: Books III and IV 'are put together on the "interwoven" plan of Ariosto', Roche, *The Kindly Flame*, vii–viii, 209–10, and King, '"Well Grounded, Finely Framed"', 27.
45 See Miller, *The Poem's Two Bodies*, and compare with the treatments of the poem in Hadfield's *Cambridge Companion*, and McCabe's *Oxford Handbook*; Wofford, 'The Faerie Queene*, Books I–III'; Andrew Hadfield, 'The Faerie Queene, Books IV–VII (in Hadfield); Linda Gregerson, 'The Faerie Queene (1590)'; Elizabeth Jane Bellamy, 'The Faerie Queene (1596)'; and Gordon Teskey, 'Two Cantos of Mutabilitie (1609)' (in McCabe). It should be noted that these essays do not strictly follow the logic of the installment model: Hadfield, Bellamy and Teskey discuss only the additions made in 1596 and 1609, and not the six- or six-and-a-fragment-book poems as published in these years. The paradigm shift is evident when these works are compared with *The Spenser Encyclopedia*, which devotes long entries to each individual book (by Douglas Brooks-Davies, René Graziani, Thomas P. Roche, James Nohrnberg, Michael O'Connell, Humphrey Tonkin, and Sheldon P. Zitner); see 259–88.
46 Neuse, 'Book VI as Conclusion to *The Faerie Queene*', 353. For the counter view, see J. B. Lethbridge, 'Spenser's Last Days'. That moral allegory is a unifying force remains the view of many scholars, such as Horton, *The Unity of The Faerie Queene*, and more recently, Kenneth Borris, *Visionary Spenser and the Poetics of Early Modern Platonism*, 169, 186–87 n.67, who attacks Neuse for inaugurating suspicious readings which 'blatantly victimize' Calidore.

Texts which offer the appearance of resolution, but which strike one as less unified the more one thinks about them, have an enormous power. Each generation can appropriate the apparent definitiveness of such works to sanction partial readings of them, while the residue of material which a dominant reading cannot explain enables the next generation to draw out some other aspect of the master-work to relish and exaggerate. *The Faerie Queene* presents an amalgam of antagonistic forces, which appear to be melting together in myths, but which are always restlessly shifting in relation to each other, interweaving or exfoliating into confusion and uncertainty. Such a combination of apparent unity and deep thematic instability gives the poem the potential to be reread and reinterpreted in order to suit a number of different occasions and attitudes.[47]

Burrow's sketch – which pertains to the poets and translators who immediately responded to *The Faerie Queene* – may be read as a compact allegory of professional Spenser studies. Scholars of moral allegory stressed the poem's 'apparent definitiveness', while for those influenced by movements like structuralism and New Historicism, the poem's 'residue' continues to open up 'an amalgam of antagonistic forces' which ultimately destabilise even the sense that the poem might be a 'master-work'.[48] At the same time, Burrow eloquently speaks to the contemporary sense that, despite the narrator's longing for 'stedfast rest' in the poem's final fragment, *The Faerie Queene*'s different 'forces' (by which I understand as well as the larger structures of myths, characters, narratives, books, and cantos the smaller features of stanzas, images, and individual words) are 'restlessly shifting in relation to each other', producing 'confusion and uncertainty' rather than 'all things firmely stayd' (VII.viii.2).

This dynamic between a seemingly fixed form and the less certain contours of the parts of that whole can be illustrated through tabular comparisons of Books I and VI as narrative structures. Diagrams necessarily reduce complex narrative structures to their core components, but this is precisely the point of using them: they give the reader a way of visualising the 'interweaving or exfoliating' narrative forces of the poem with convenient immediacy. Nevertheless, I use this device with a certain measure of caution.[49] Visually, the tables below may suggest a restrictive, closed matrix,

---

47 Burrow, *Epic Romance*, 147.
48 Labels and flags mutate over time; see Horton, *The Unity of The Faerie Queene* (published in 1978), 1–12, for a reception history which stresses different shades of opinion within formalism. For Horton, the 'organicist criticism' of scholars like Berger and Alpers betrays a 'romantic antirationalism and aestheticism' in place of traditional moral allegory (6).
49 For theoretical and historical background, see Tim Ingold, *Lines: A Brief History*, 159–61, and Ong, *Ramus: Method, and the Decay of Dialogue*, 171–95.

whereas argumentatively, I want to stress the opposite. The narratives of *The Faerie Queene* are seldom closed even as they are contained by – rather than 'within' – cantos and Books. At the same time, diagrams can facilitate large-scale comparisons with greater economy than prose alone, while giving the reader a more immediate sense of the bigger picture. Tasso's complaint that the length of Boiardo and Ariosto's narrative made it 'unlikely to be retained by an average memory' is an issue which tabular representation may address. The tables below focus on the key structural and narrative events in Books I and VI, outlining when characters and incidents are introduced, and highlighting narrative loose ends. Although these tables necessarily focus on character and incident, they try to offset this perhaps obvious work of précis with aspects of the text that don't work, or cohere; thus, through diagrammatising these Books, I attempt to illuminate the way in which *The Faerie Queene* is multiple – and it is multiple in terms of gaps and absences as well as presences. I make no attempt to summarise the allegory, although aspects of the poem's symbolic agendas necessarily surface, as in the summaries of I.x and VI.v.

The two tables first of all demonstrate the familiar contrast between Redcrosse's teleological quest, announced in Canto I and developed with some digressions to a climax in Cantos XI and XII, and Calidore's markedly less linear quest. Where Redcrosse is the dominant figure in each canto except III and VI – which show Una's attempts 'To seeke her knight' (I.iii.3) – Calidore is absent (and largely forgotten) for five and a half cantos of Book VI, making him the least visible of Spenser's heroes apart from Cambell and Triamond, whose adventures occupy only two cantos of Book IV.[50] Even Calepine – who is usually seen as Calidore's less talented stand-in – absents himself for a significant tranche of *his* part of Book VI, not figuring for three and a half cantos.[51] This visualisation underlines *The Faerie Queene*'s predisposition to multiple, unresolved plots. Even though the twelve-canto form alludes to the twelve books of the *Aeneid*, there is little sense in which even the most straightforward of *The Faerie Queene*'s Books (and Book I would surely be the winner of this particular prize) conforms to the narrative strategies of Virgil's poem.[52] Spenser's poem is too digressive, too committed to a 'multiplicity of

50 Note too that the title page of Book IV has 'Telamond' for 'Triamond', a mistake carried through to the 1609 edition; see *FQ*, 409, and *The Faerie Queene* (1609), 189.
51 William Blissett, 'Calepine', 127, citing Donald Cheney describing Calepine as Calidore's 'less gifted surrogate'.
52 See Wilson-Okamura, *Virgil in the Renaissance*, 192, for the unexpected, incomplete sense of the ending of the *Aeneid*.

Table 1 *The Faerie Queene* Book I: narrative structure

Canto	Main incidents	Main characters present and introduced	Narrative development and loose ends
I	Introduction; Error's wood; meeting with Archimago; Redcrosse's bad dreams	Redcrosse, Una, Error and her children, Archimago	The Error story is self-contained; the visit to Archimago's house propels the subsequent narrative
II	Redcrosse's flight from Una; fight with Sansfoy; meeting with Duessa; meeting with Fradubio	Redcrosse;[53] Sansfoy, Duessa, Fradubio and Fralissa	The Fradubio narrative is self-contained and ends without resolution; the Duessa plot continues through the following cantos
III	Una alone, then with the lion, Abessa/Kirkrapine incident; meeting with Archimago disguised as Redcrosse; meeting with Sansloy and attempted rape	Una, Archimago; Lion, Abessa, Kirkrapine, Sansloy	The Abessa story is self-contained; Sansloy provides a cliffhanger taken up in Canto VI
IV	Redcrosse and Duessa to the House of Pride; Lucifera and the Seven Deadly Sins; Sansioy and Duessa conspire to kill Redcrosse	Redcrosse, Duessa; Lucifera, Sins, Sansioy	The Lucifera/House of Pride incident is self-contained
V	Redcrosse defeats Sansioy; Duessa and Night go to hell to try to save Sansioy; Redcrosse leaves the House of Pride	Redcrosse, Sansioy, Duessa; Night, Aesculapius	The Sansioy narrative is never returned to
VI	Una rescued from Sansloy by the Salvage Nation; meeting with Satyrane and background; fight between Satyrane and Sansloy	Una, Sansloy; Salvage Nation, Satyrane	The fight between Satyrane and Sansloy is never concluded

53 In this column, I list the main characters who appear in each canto. New characters are separated from ones already known by a semi-colon; thus in I.ii, the reader has already been introduced to Redcrosse, but Sansfoy, Duessa, Fradubio, and Fralissa all appear for the first (or only) time here, hence the listing above.

Table 1 *The Faerie Queene* Book I: narrative structure (Continued)

Canto	Main incidents	Main characters present and introduced	Narrative development and loose ends
VII	Redcrosse defeated by Orgoglio; Dwarf tells Una of Redcrosse's misadventures; Una's meeting with Arthur	Redcrosse, Duessa; Orgoglio, Arthur and Timias	Main narrative: Redcrosse's fall; introduction of Arthur as '*the image of a braue knight*' (*FQ*, 715)
VIII	Arthur's fight with Orgoglio; rescue of Redcrosse; stripping and escape of Duessa	Arthur, Timias, Orgoglio, Duessa, Una, Redcrosse	Main narrative: Arthur's rescue of Redcrosse; revelation of Duessa's true identity followed by her disappearance
IX	Arthur's back story; Trevisan and the Cave of Despair	Redcrosse, Una, Arthur; Trevisan (Terwin),[54] Despair	This is Trevisan's only appearance; the Despair episode is self-contained
X	House of Holiness	Redcrosse, Una; Allegorical personae of the House, including Caelia and Contemplation	The House of Holiness is self-contained, but prepares the way for the fight with the Dragon
XI	Redcrosse's fight with the Dragon	Redcrosse; The Dragon	Climax of Redcrosse's quest
XII	Betrothal of Redcrosse and Una; Duessa and Archimago's attempt to discredit Redcrosse with Una's parents	Redcrosse, Una, Duessa, Archimago; Una's parents	Main narrative: conclusion of Book I through the betrothal and Redcrosse's ongoing obligations to Gloriana

---

54 Characters who are named but absent or – in this case – already dead, are placed in brackets.

Table 2 The Faerie Queene Book VI: narrative structure

Canto	Main incidents	Main characters present and introduced	Narrative development and loose ends
I	Introduction; Calidore meets Artegall; the episode of Briana's castle, including the Squire; the killing of Maleffort; and the civilizing of Crudor and Briana	Artegall; Calidore, Squire, Maleffort, Crudor, Briana	The Crudor episode is self-contained
II	Tristram's killing the unnamed knight; Tristram back story and knighting; Calidore's rescue of Aladine and Priscilla	Calidore; unnamed knight and lady, Tristram, Aladine and Priscilla	The Tristram episode is a loose end not further developed; Aladine and Priscilla's story continues in Canto III
III	Calidore's restoration of Aladine and Priscilla to their fathers; Calidore meets Calepine and Serena; Blatant Beast attacks Serena; Calepine is attacked by Turpine and tries unsuccessfully to take shelter at his castle	Calidore, Aladine, Priscilla, the Blatant Beast; Aldus, Priscilla's unnamed father, Calepine, Serena, Turpine, Blandina, and porter	The Aladine/Priscilla narrative is concluded here; Calepine and Serena's narrative – including the Turpine episode – becomes the focus of the next five cantos
IV	The Salvage Man rescues Calepine from Turpine; Calepine with the bear and the baby; gives the latter to Matilde	Calepine, Serena; Salvage Man, bear, baby, Matilde (Bruin)	The Salvage Man is a presence through the next four cantos; the Matilde episode is self-contained
V	The Salvage Man and Serena encounter Arthur and Timias; Timias's back story including encounter with Despetto et al.; the Hermit and his chapel	Serena, Salvage Man, Arthur, Timias;[55] Despetto et al., the Hermit	Main narrative focuses on Serena's adventures; stanzas 12–24 recap Timias's narrative from IV.viii
VI	The Hermit's slander cure; first allusion to Mirabella (stanza 16); Arthur and the Salvage Man vanquish Turpine	Hermit, Serena, Timias, Arthur, Salvage Man, Turpine, Blandina	All these narratives flow into the next two cantos
VII	Turpine's attempt to kill Arthur through Enias and unnamed fellow; punishment of Turpine; first part of the Mirabella episode, in which Timias attempts to rescue her from Disdaine and Scorn	Turpine, Arthur, Salvage Man, Timias; Enias and unnamed knight, Mirabella, Disdaine and Scorn	Further development of the Mirabella narrative, continued in the next canto

55 This is the first appearance of Arthur and Timias in Book VI, but not in the poem, hence they appear in this listing as familiar characters. Compare Artegall in VI.i.

Table 2 *The Faerie Queene* Book VI: narrative structure (Continued)

Canto	Main incidents	Main characters present and introduced	Narrative development and loose ends
VIII	Arthur defeats Disdaine; Mirabella's back story; Serena captured by the Salvage Nation, then rescued by Calepine	Mirabella, Disdaine, Scorn, Arthur, Salvage Man, Serena Calepine; the Salvage Nation	Mirabella's penance continues without resolution; this is the last we see of the Salvage Man (stanza 30); Calepine and Serena's story ends without resolution at the canto close
IX	Calidore's pastoral séjour: conversation with Meliboe and pursuit of Pastorella in competition with Coridon	Calidore; Pastorella, Meliboe, Coridon	Return to Calidore's narrative through the pastoral digression
X	Calidore with Colin and the Graces at Mount Acidale; Calidore's successful seduction of Pastorella after tiger-slaying; abduction of Pastorella et al. by the brigands.	Calidore, Pastorella, Coridon, Meliboe; Colin,[56] the Graces, tiger, brigands	The Mount Acidale incident is self-contained, but like the House of Holiness, informs prior and subsequent action allegorically; the brigands narrative continues in the next canto
XI	Fight amongst the brigands over Pastorella; death of Meliboe; rescue of Pastorella by Calidore and killing of the brigands	Calidore, Pastorella, Coridon, Meliboe, brigands	Initial resolution of pastoral digression
XII	Revelation of Pastorella's aristocratic identity; Calidore's return to the pursuit and (temporary) capture of the Blatant Beast	Calidore, Pastorella, Blatant Beast; Bellamoure and Claribell (Pastorella's parents)	Resolution of main quest narrative; final escape of the Beast

56 This is the first appearance of Colin in the poem, but as the narrator indicates in the line 'Poore *Colin Clout* (who knowes not *Colin Clout*?)' (VI.x.16), readers of Spenser's poetry will recognise him from *The Shepheardes Calender*, *Colin Clouts Come Home Againe*, and *The Ruines of Time* (ll.225–31). See further below.

incidents', for the analogy with Virgil to be anything more than a signifier of cultural value and aspiration. Spenser imitates Virgil not because like Tasso, Camões, or Ronsard he actually wants or expects his poem to resemble Virgil's, but more anecdotally and aspirationally, because 'Virgil' is a hallmark of poetic value almost in the manner of a prestige literary brand.

It is the final columns of these tables which are the most telling. Cumulatively, they point to the structural similarities between the two Books in terms of absences and discontinuities. They show how the narrative develops or digresses or is otherwise curtailed; in both Books there are a number of episodes and figures to which the poem does not return. The observation that Book VI includes many loose ends is of course familiar. Because the poem is unfinished, readers have long assumed that stories like those of Calepine and Serena, Tristram and the nameless lady, and the Salvage Man, would have been tidied up in a twelve- or twenty-four- book *Faerie Queene*. This is what Spenser's narrator trains us to expect: when we are tantalisingly told that the Salvage Man is another aristocratic foundling – 'certes he was borne of noble blood,/How euer by hard hap he hether came' – we are then reassured 'As ye may know, when time shall be to tell the same' (VI.v.2). John Upton's charmingly intimate paraphrase is germane: the tale will be told 'In some Book or Canto hereafter intended to be written by me: for my intent is to open things to you by little and little.'[57] Upton articulates what most readers of Book VI assume: such glitches are anomalies in the narrative weft which would have been supplemented by later Books rather than deliberate gaps in the structure. Nevertheless, the fragmentation within Book VI remains disconcerting. Not only, as we have seen in Chapter 5, are key narrative threads not developed to any sort of even provisional conclusion,[58] the Book also sees the proliferation of nameless characters.[59] This is a facet of the text which may suggest that either that the preparation of the 1596 edition was hurried – a supposition supported by other aspects of this text – or that in Neusian terms, Spenser had in some ways given up the narrative procedures which had characterised his poem up until this

---

57 In Spenser, *The Faery Queen*, II, 641.
58 See the stories of Tristram, the Salvage Man, Calepine and Serena, and the end of the quest for the Blatant Beast.
59 Williams, *Flower on a Lowly Stalk*, 73–74, explains the unnamed characters in terms of narrative rhythm: characters are named when the action is 'slow enough' for the name to be given (73).

point.[60] Unnamed characters are unusual in the rest of the poem, and the failure to name may be indicative of a loss of confidence in the poetics of naming which has been such a marked part of the poem up until this point.

This is where the comparison with Book I is instructive. Although the narrative loose ends are less pervasive than they are in Book VI, the pattern of incorporating inconclusive digressions from the main quest narrative is striking here too, as in the story of Fradubio and Fralissa and the Sansloy katabasis, and even in smaller fragments such as the unfinished fight between Satyrane and Sansloy in I.vi. These are examples of what might be called aporetic narrative. Puttenham discusses a figure of speech which he labels '*Aporia*, or the Doubtful': 'oftentimes we will seem to cast perils and make doubt of things, when by a plain manner of speech we might affirm or deny him.'[61] I mean something broader than the obfuscatory trope outlined by Puttenham: aporetic narrative is storytelling which is designed not to reach any decisive point of closure. The differences between Books I and VI in this light seem to be connected with differences of authorial planning and execution: the gaps in the stories of Fradubio and Sansioy are deliberate, and the thematic point Spenser underlines is that readers should not expect the resolutions they may have found in earlier epic romances. Fradubio is neither transformed back into a man, like Ariosto's Astolfo, nor left as a dead tree, like Virgil's Polydorus; as he explains to Redcrosse – who characteristically expects his condition maybe rectified by some form of heroic action – 'Time and suffised fates to former kind/Shall vs restore, none else from hence may vs unbynd' (I.ii.43).[62] Similarly, in Canto V, Duessa's rescue mission of the mortally wounded Sansioy is an essay in futility: Sansioy may not be saved, despite the endeavours of Aesculapius, because as the narrator explains at the outset, nobody returns from hell: 'there creature neuer past,/That backe retourned

---

60 For the printing of the 1596 edition, and Spenser's likely absence from the process, see Joseph Loewenstein, 'Spenser's Textual History', 644, citing earlier scholarship.

61 Puttenham, *The Art of English Poesy*, 311. See also Peacham, *The Garden of Eloquence*, 109–10, who notes the risk of articulating 'too many doubts' is that 'the speaker sheweth himself to be very simple, ignorant, or very forgetfull' (110).

62 See William J. Kennedy, 'Fradubio', 318, for a full listing of the motif of the speaking tree in classical and contemporaneous literature. For Astolfo's restoration to human form by Melissa, see Ariosto, *Orlando Furioso* (1556) VIII.16, 71; for Polydorus, see Virgil, *Aeneid* III.19–68 in *Eclogues, Georgics, Aeneid I–VI*, 372–77.

without heauenly grace' (I.v.31).[63] In both of these cases, and in an idiosyn-
cractic modification of the epic tradition, Spenser deploys the aporetic
loose end as a distinctive form of poetic narration; where Ariosto defers
the resolution of his stories, Spenser effectively postpones them. Redcrosse
and the reader may be sidetracked by these stories from the epic tradition,
but they are, properly speaking, poetic dead ends which the narrator
produces precisely in order to deny their romantic development: the point
is that we are given half a story; *The Faerie Queene* typically expects its
readers to fill in narrative gaps symbolically, as outlined above. Conversely,
the fight between Satyrane and Sansloy suggests an aesthetic proleptic of
the many loose ends of Book VI: as the predictably heavy metal combat
between the two threatens to erase their differences – 'with their drery
wounds and bloody gore/They both deformed, scarsely could bee known'
(I.VI.45) – so the narrative leaves their story 'deformed', with Sansloy
reappearing in II.ii, and Satyrane in III.vii without any sense that the poet
needs to fill in the narrative blanks.[64] In many ways, aporetic narrative is
the motive condition in Faery land.

When I bethinke me: thinking with and about the narrator

But if Spenser's narratives are indeed aporetic, what works to hold them
together in the experience of reading? I conclude by going back to the
figure of the narrator, initially discussed in Chapter 5 in the context of
the framing of the cantos. I noted there on the one hand the narrator's
equivocal role in summarising the narrative of Book VI. On the other
hand, the evidence of Book III showed that related rhetorical cues, deriving
in part from the precedent of Ariosto, enable Spenser to connect disparate
narratives symbolically. Now I want to look at the narrator as a facet of
the poem's structure. If Spenser was committed to an aesthetic of loose
ends, one of the key textual forces which stabilises the disintegrative aspects
of the narrative is the voice of the narrator. Put another way, the narrator
is a device which works towards tonal integration and semantic enstrangement at the same time.

---

63 See Hamilton's note on I.v.44.4–6: 'The further fortunes of Sansjoy need not be told:
none return from hell "without heauenly grace"', *FQ*, 79.
64 See II.ii.18 for the narrator's laconic reminder of who Sansloy is: 'He that faire *Vna*
lately fowle outraged,/The most vnruly, and the boldest boy,/That euer warlike weapons
menaged'.

That narrative voice is a key factor in how we read the poem can be demonstrated by considering Matthew Lownes's editorial presentation of the Mutabilitie Cantos in the 1609 folio. The explanatory subheading below the title, 'TWO CANTOS/ OF/ *MUTABILITIE:*' – 'Which, both for Forme and Matter, appeare/ to be parcell of some following Booke of the/ *FAERIE QUEENE,*' – draws attention to the plausible connections between the fragment and the rest of the poem.[65] Obviously, the Cantos are written in Spenserian stanzas, and share aspects of *mise en page* like canto divisions and arguments with the rest of the poem, on the reasonable assumption that these were present in the manuscript rather than supplied by the printer.[66] Nevertheless, both their belated appearance and their differences from the rest of the poem have led to energetic speculation about whether they are a separate poem, work in progress, or a hastily assembled coda written as Spenser realised he would never get the chance to finish the epic as he had planned.[67] In important ways, the Mutabilitie fragment is *discontinuous* from the rest of the poem. There is no titular knight, unless we consider that Mutabilitie herself could occupy that role; though the Cantos have aspects in common with the other allegorical cores, the allocation of two long cantos to such a narrative has no obvious precedents in the rest of the poem.[68] In terms of top level narrative, it is not surprising that earlier critics like Sebastian Evans were sceptical of the connections with the rest of the poem that the 1609 folio asserts.[69] Yet, as Sheldon Zitner noted, the narrator himself acts as a link between the fragment and the larger poem.[70] The voice we hear in the

65 *The Faerie Queene* (1609), 353.
66 See Andrew Zurcher, 'The Printing of the *Cantos of Mutabilitie* in 1609', 45, for what the folio tells us about the manuscript.
67 For overviews, see Zitner in Spenser, *The Mutabilitie Cantos*, 5–10, and Zitner, '*The Faerie Queene*, Book VII', 287–89. For the Cantos as 'a very late compilation' of working drafts to function as a coda, see Lethbridge, 'Spenser's Last Days', 302–10, 331–32; for the view that they are 'not conclusive but transitional', see Robert Lanier Reid, 'Spenser's Mutability Song', 61–84 (61).
68 My thanks to Syrithe Pugh for the point about Mutabilitie as potential heroine. From this angle, Mutabilitie is herself a questing heroine (or antiheroine), whose role the narrator both laments and celebrates at the same time.
69 For Evans, see Spenser, *The Faerie Queene Books Six and Seven*, 433–34.
70 In Spenser, *The Mutabilitie Cantos*, 9. Zitner's formulation is in keeping with the criticism of the 1960s and 1970s: the narrator is 'an imagined person', who he suggests maybe seen as 'an exemplification of the Christian gentleman the epic was intended to form'. My reading is less characterological: the narrator is more a tone of voice, a series of habits of rhetoric, than a Hamlet or a Tess. Inevitably, at times I refer to the narrator as 'he', but this should not be taken as meaning a belief in 'him' as a fully imagined character.

opening stanza is congruent with the narrative voice of the rest of *The Faerie Queene*. This is not to say that this voice is consistent with the narrator throughout, rather that this complex yet troubled voice is something we are intimately familiar with on the basis of the rest of the poem. Compare

> WHat man that sees the euer-whirling wheele
>   Of *Change*, the which all mortall things doth sway,
>   But that therby doth find, and plainly feele,
>   How *MVTABILITY* in them doth play
> Her cruell sports, to many mens decay?

with

> YOung knight, what euer that dost armes professe,
>   And through long labours huntest after fame,
>   Beware of fraud, beware of ficklenesse,
>   In choice, and change of thy deare loued Dame,
>   Least thou of her belieue too lightly blame,
>   And rash misweening doe thy hart remoue:
>   For vnto knight there is no greater shame,
>   Then lightnesse and inconstancie in loue;
> That doth this *Redcrosse* knights ensample plainly proue. (VII.vi.1; I.iv.1)

Though there is a direct connection in terms of the theme of Change, I chose these examples because of the adverbial collocations 'plainly feele' and 'plainly proue'. There are related examples throughout the poem: when Britomart is revealed as a woman at Malbecco's castle, 'Then of them all she plainly was espyde'; Scudamour's demeanour after a sleepless night in the House of Care shows 'The signes of anguish one mote plainely read' (III.ix.21; IV.v.45).[71] It is something of a Spenserian hallmark; as Kirsten Tranter notes, 'To the extent that anything "plaine appears" at any time in *The Faerie Queene*, its meaning must be questioned.'[72] The collocation is a habitual turn of phrase, a frequency to which *The Faerie Queene* is often tuned which, I suggest, highlights related ways of speaking and thinking in verse. These stanzas are connected at the level of authorial moralisation and commentary, but I am less interested in that than in the more fugitive or intangible qualities of a tonal idiom; in this light, the

71 See Brown and Lethbridge, *A Concordance*, 409; 'plainely' is used fourteen times and 'plainly' four.
72 Tranter, '"The sea it selfe, doest thou not plainely see?"', 95.

adverbial collocation has a slightly different function in each case. In Book I, the narrator's comment builds on the cantos we have read up to this point to suggest the shortcomings of Redcrosse's perception; the voice is leisurely, ironic, and at a complacent distance from the character it reproves: the alexandrine though morally correct is almost too pleased with its 'plain' formulation.[73] In contrast, the Mutabilitie fragment introduces a set of urgent concerns in which there is hardly a gap between the narrative voice and the 'man' who sees the wheel of Fortune and the narrator who tells us about it. 'Plainly feele' is the third member in a tripartite verb construction – 'sees' moves to 'finde' and then 'feele' with an intensification on each new word – which magnifies the reader's sense of Mutabilitie's 'cruell sports'. The voices are related in terms of moralisation, rhetoric, and characteristic turns of phrase, but what in I.iv has a tone conveying the narrator's distance from the story he relates in VII.vi has become a matter of involving concern. Nevertheless, the narrator's tonal commentary – the kinds of things he notices and the ways in which he points them out – serve to join these disparate stanzas. Like Matthew Lownes, when we read The Mutabilitie Cantos, we catch the same tone of voice as we have heard in the rest of *The Faerie Queene*.

Tone, though, is notoriously difficult to pin down.[74] This is particularly so when the voice I want to highlight is more of a rhetorical convention – a studied way of speaking in poetry – rather than the individuated poet narrator which Robert Durling styled as 'the Poet'.[75] But if we don't hear the connections between Mutabilitie and the rest of the poem, there is a risk of not heeding the way Spenser's writing works. An example of this comes in Trevor Joyce's *Fastness* (2017), a poem which aims to subvert Spenser's text in the service of Irish history, as it 'translates' the latter's 'English' perspective into one more sympathetic to Mutability's rebellion. Joyce's approach comprehensively undermines Spenser's literary rhetoric.[76]

73 See Dees, 'The Narrator of *The Faerie Queene*' (1971), 558–59, for a reading of this stanza and I.iii.1 and I.v.1 in terms of Renaissance humanism, arguing that the narrator's understanding deepens as the poem develops.
74 T. V. F. Brogan and Fabian Gudas, 'Tone', 1293, defining it as 'an intangible quality which is metaphorically predicated of a literary work'.
75 Robert Durling, *The Figure of the Poet in Renaissance Epic*, 8 and passim.
76 Trevor Joyce, *Fastness: A Translation from the English of Edmund Spenser*, xiii–xv, xvii–xx, explaining his work as a cultural reclamation from Spenser's imperial perspective. In-text references are given parenthetically hereafter. For my review (which explores the poetic discrepancies between the two texts in detail), see Richard Danson Brown, 'Joyce, Trevor. *Fastness: A Translation from the English of Edmund Spenser*'.

Though Joyce's reading of The Mutabilitic Cantos is heavily simplified, his poem has the virtue of enabling us to hear Spenser's tone through the contrast with his new version. Thus a line like 'O pittious worke of *MVTABILITIE!*' becomes the designedly casual 'Nice work there, Mutability' (VII.vi.6; 5). Joyce provides an ironic substitute for the voice of Spenserian lament, a voice which *Fastness* deliberately seeks to mute and misinterpret. This is most radically apparent in Joyce's version of the unfinished Canto VIII. As he explains in the introduction, he sees these stanzas as the intervention of 'a completely new voice', which in the final prayer conflates the hope of peace in 'Sabbaoth' with a secular prayer which 'reads perhaps most readily as the poet's putting his own faith, as English planter in a hostile land, in the religiously motivated force of Elizabeth's Protestant armies' (xiii).[77] Joyce's 'translation' works to deny the plangency which is evident from the opening of the Cantos:

> I'm sick to death of seeing
> this dodgy state of things, and alienated too
> from all attachments in this so unperfect world,
> those sky-flowers falling furiously. (81)

Though in my view this is a poetically and semantically inadequate response to Spenser's triplet of feminine rhymes in VII.viii.1, nevertheless it does draw attention to the consistency of narrative tone in The Mutabilitie Cantos. Where Joyce ventriloquises a grumpy commuter, morphing in the later lines into a delusional and probably war-mongering mystic, the Spenserian voice of lamentation is more properly absorbed with the Virgilian trope of *lacrimae rerum*; this is the voice we hear at the opening of the Cantos, reoccurring at the close of the fragment.[78] Spenser is authoritarian inasmuch as he expects his readers to share his sense of the poignancy of the work 'Of *Change*': the Cantos rehearse a conservative lament in the face of 'euer-whirling' contingency which is resolved in the final stanzas into an orthodox Christian eschatological longing for stability, for 'stedfast rest of all things firmely stayd'.[79] Yet this final word of *The Faerie Queene*

---

77 Joyce cites Hadfield, *Edmund Spenser: A Life*, 371, in support of this reading of 'Sabaoth', without noting the more complex terms Hadfield deploys: for him, the Cantos close with 'a haunting melancholy, a clear recognition that [Spenser's] own end is near and that he needs to think about the afterlife'. For the biblical pun on rest ('Sabbaoth') and armies ('Sabaoth'), see Zitner's note in Spenser, *The Mutabilitie Cantos*, 146.

78 Compare Wilson-Okamura, *Spenser's International Style*, 198, on Spenser as a chronic 'complainer, not a quitter'.

79 For the Augustinian resonances of this passage, see Zitner in Spenser, *The Mutabilitie Cantos*, 43.

as we have it is not the final word of the poem as projected. Meanwhile, to imagine that the voice Spenser so poignantly presents is simply and everlastingly the voice of the poet himself seems to solidify that dynamic process of thought – 'When I bethinke me on that speech whyleare' – into what it patently isn't, the permanent stasis of 'the pillours of Eternity' from which the poet, like his readers, is necessarily excluded (VII.viii.2).[80] In the spirit of Yeats's 'The Tower', you long for the lover you've lost, or in this case the place you can't attain, and it is this tension which generates poetry.[81] Perhaps where Joyce gets Spenser right is in the graver, Kierkgaardian sense of 'I'm sick to death', a register his breezy irony fails to catch in Spenser's lament.

The question of the narrator of *The Faerie Queene* is a familiar one, which was much debated particularly during the 1970s as scholars reacted to the radical model advanced by Paul Alpers, who stressed the poem's rhetorical mode and rejected, in his beautifully tart phrase, the practice of 'attributing the effects of Spenser's verse to the energies and will of a dramatically present human speaker.'[82] Nevertheless, the human speaker has proved to be a durable paradigm, initially buoyed by New Critical narrative theory, and which has been restated and developed by a number of writers.[83] Consider the influential work by Judith Anderson and David Lee Miller among others which has stressed the importance of the medieval antecedents to the Spenserian narrator. Earlier writers tended to see the narrator almost exclusively through the lens of Spenser's imitation of

80 See Gordon Teskey, 'Night Thoughts on Mutability', 37.
81 W. B. Yeats, 'The Tower', ll.113–14, 'Does the imagination dwell the most/Upon a woman won or woman lost?' The rest of the stanza explores only the 'lost' option. In *The Poems*, 197.
82 Alpers, *The Poetry of* The Faerie Queene, 76.
83 See Dees, 'The Narrator of *The Faerie Queene*' (1971), who inter alia provides the most comprehensive catalogue raisonné of narrative interventions, 537 and passim; Stan Hinton, 'The Poet and his Narrator', who reads the narrator explicitly in terms of New Critical narrative theory (165–67). Further back, Durling, *The Figure of the Poet in Renaissance Epic*, presents the Spenserian narrator largely as a humourless updating of his Ariostan counterpart, 211–37. For more nuanced views, see Kathleen Williams, 'The Poet's Voice in *The Faerie Queene*', arguing that the narrator is a dream-based convention; and Judith H. Anderson, 'Whatever Happened to Amoret?', considering the narrator's intrusion on IV.viii as 'a balancing corrective' to the official narrative in the canto (186). Richard Helgerson, *Self-Crowned Laureates*, 55–100, explores Spenser's self-presentations from a New Historicist perspective, outlining the 'unstable but necessary union of two ideas … shepherd and knight, Colin and Calidore' through his works (99).

Ariosto.[84] In contrast, Anderson has identified the complex intertextual
play at work in Spenser's reading of Chaucer, subtly tracing the differences between Chaucer's manifest persona in *The Canterbury Tales* as
both a character within the poem and the narrator of 'Sir Thopas' and
'Melibee', and Spenser's more withdrawn yet pervasively self-referential
character. Anderson's multivocal human speaker is best understood by
direct quotation:

> My conclusion from such striking evidence of multiple narrative voices in
> the Spenserian text would reject both the idea that there is a single Spenserian
> voice and that there is none. What I want to say instead is that complexity,
> conflict, and a multidimensional awareness – an awareness subtly, complexly,
> and equivocably patterned – are characteristic of Spenser's identity as a
> poet, the details of whose figure – '*Mulla* mine' or 'mother Cambridge' –
> elsewhere gesture pointedly enough toward his life to invite, but not to
> delimit or define, connections. Thus the poet I describe is a personal, not
> an impersonal pronoun, and he is also a figure whose essential humanity
> may lie – may even lie punningly – precisely in his decenteredness.[85]

In other words, the Spenserian narrator is a 'human speaker' in the fullest
sense that he is not a consistent or even an authoritarian voice, but is
rather a series of connected yet ultimately decentred postures deriving
from Spenser's careful study of Chaucer.[86] Anderson's sense of the complexity
and equivocation inherent in that voice may help to explain Joyce's failure
to understand the close of The Mutabilitie Cantos: given that his reading
of the poem is predicated on the notion that it articulates the same politics
as the *View of the Present State of Ireland*, Joyce must repress and ironise
Spenser's irresponsible lyricism.[87] Yet the difficulty this generates poetically
is that the Spenserian voice is not simply authoritarian or imperialistic

84 See Durling, *The Figure of the Poet in Renaissance Epic*, 211, 'Spenser adopts a discursive
    manner that is clearly based on Ariosto'.
85 Judith H. Anderson, 'Chaucer's and Spenser's Reflexive Narrators', in *Reading the
    Allegorical Intertext*, 27–41 (41).
86 See Anderson, 'Chaucer's and Spenser's Reflexive Narrators', 30–31, for what Spenser
    found in 'The General Prologue': cumulatively, indirection and the deconstructive
    techniques of *dédoublement*. I should emphasise that 'postures' is my term rather than
    Anderson's, reflecting my attempt to harmonise her work with that of Alpers.
87 See Joyce, *Fastness*, xiii–xiv, for the *View* in relation to The Cantos. Spenser's culpable
    irresponsibility in the face of Irish suffering is stated with greater force in Seamus
    Heaney's great lyric, 'Bog Oak' (1972), with its image of Spenser 'dreaming sunlight'
    while 'encroached upon by' the Irish 'geniuses' who creep directly out of the *View*'s
    description of the Munster famine. In *Opened Ground: Poems 1966–1996*, 44–45.

– in Anderson's terms, what surfaces in Canto VIII is a 'multidimensional awareness' of both transience, change, and the emotional longing for a certainty which intellectually that same voice has deconstructed in the stanzas which precede the prayer. The Spenserian voice both knows it can't have it both ways and tautly yearns for that fantasy 'Of that same time when no more *Change* shall be' in a dynamic process of thinking and rethinking.

Building on this work, and Miller's attractive model of the narrator deferring authority to the reader, my suggestion is that this sense of fictive presence is one of the rhetorical illusions which Spenser keeps in play throughout *The Faerie Queene* without ever constructing his narrator in the manner of a nineteenth-century novel, and that it is this illusory presence which serves to hold the poem together.[88] One might say that the Spenserian narrator practises cognitive dissonance – the humanity implicit in this voice is witnessed precisely in its repeated failures to achieve any absolute discursive coherence. Thus while I agree with Alpers that formal commentary should concentrate on 'the effects of Spenser's verse', the illusory narrator is (as Anderson's work insists) one of those effects: Spenser constructs an echoic voice, or rather a series of voices, which serve to strengthen the reader's sense of the connectedness of otherwise diffuse and potentially aporetic narratives.

As Anderson notes, Spenser's voice is partly constructed out of his back catalogue, producing a 'socially contextualized' and 'self-citational' figure which assumes readers are at least partly familiar with the 'contours of Spenser's own life.'[89] Such self-conscious practices frequently cross genres, meandering from one discursive framework to another with a kind of self-conscious impunity. When the narrator asks 'who knows not *Colin Clout*?' in the Acidale canto, the reference sideways to *The Shepheardes Calender* and *Colin Clouts Come Home Againe* makes the epic texture pervious to pastoral in a self-delighting apostrophe: 'Pype iolly shepheard, pype thou now apace/Vnto thy loue' (VI.x.16). At one level, this is a sophisticated form of literary branding, which Spenser employs throughout his career: the figure and voice of Colin is a hallmark which asserts kinship and value across disparate texts.[90] Self-citation reassures the reader that she is reading the same poet, a little like the way in which the logos of global capitalism assert brand and identity. Yet, at the same time Spenser

88 David Lee Miller, '*The Faerie Queene* (1590)', 155.
89 Anderson, 'Chaucer's and Spenser's Reflexive Narrators', 32.
90 See Richard A. McCabe, 'Authorial Self-Presentation', 463–64.

is expert at using such recycled tropes to mask, or to develop, what otherwise seems a familiar strategy.[91] What may seem to be a tired trope asserting common identity and continuity across different works may prove on closer inspection to be nothing of the sort. This is what I think happens in the second half of VII.vi.1. I quote here the complete stanza so that the second half is read anew in the context of the unsettled lament of its first five lines:

> WHat man that sees the euer-whirling wheele
> Of *Change*, the which all mortall things doth sway,
> But that therby doth find, and plainly feele,
> How *MVTABILITY* in them doth play
> Her cruell sports, to many mens decay?
> Which that to all may better yet appeare,
> I will rehearse that whylome I heard say,
> How she at first her selfe began to reare,
> Gainst all the Gods, and th'empire sought from them to beare.

As we have seen, the first five lines announce the subject of the Cantos with a troubled and insistent rhetoric; the second four lines, I will suggest, imply that the 'man that sees the euer-whirling wheele/Of *Change*' is the narrative voice, in the guise of spectator and witness. The 'rehearse' formula is another example of Spenserian self-citation; it is used regularly in the shorter poems, and almost always in contexts which shadow the connections between poetic recitation and the verse of the Spenserian text.[92] In *The Faerie Queene* it is used more sparingly, and this is one of only two cases where the term is used by the narrative self-consciously.[93] A more conventional inexpressibility topos is IV.xi.17 as the narrator contemplates the enormity of his task in enumerating the rivers at the marriage of the Thames and Medway: 'But what doe I their names seeke to reherse … How can they all in this so narrow verse/Contayned be [?]', with its

---

91 See Anderson, 'Chaucer's and Spenser's Reflexive Narrators', 34, for Spenserian masking: 'For Spenser, even more explicitly than for Chaucer, the idea of impersonation is thematized, problematical, and self-reflexive from the start.'

92 See 'August', ll.143, 193 (quoted below); 'Astrophel', l.216; 'The Doleful Lay of Clorinda', l.107 (quoted below); 'An Hymne of Heavenly Love', l.42; *The Ruines of Time*, ll.253–56, and *The Teares of the Muses*, ll.1–6. On the latter, see my commentary in *The New Poet*, 146–47, comparing this stanza with the beginning of *Epithalamion*, and exploring its inversion of the habitual relationship between the poet and the muses.

93 See Brown and Lethbridge, *A Concordance*, 412; 'rehearse' is used twice, and 'reherse' four times. The examples not discussed above are: I.ix.48, III.xii.36, IV.vii.15, and V.iv.28 ('rehearse'). The Dedicatory Sonnet to Lord Hunsdon concludes with the *verse: reherse* cluster also used in 'Astrophel', *The Ruines of Time* and IV.xi.17 (see previous note).

delightful, mimetic juxtaposition of the enormous breadth of the waterways and smaller 'compasse' of the Spenserian stanza. In this formulation, the job of the poet is a recitation of knowledge or text from other sources, and it is this usage which we find in the shorter poems: Cuddie 'rehearses' Colin's sestina to Perigot in 'August', Perigot then courteously praises 'How dolefully his doole thou didst reherse' ('August', ll.142, 193). More subcutaneously, the refrains of 'November' – 'O heavie herse … O carefull verse' modulating to 'O happye herse … O joyfull verse' – draw on the same associations between poetry and mortality as Colin uses the performance of his lament to suggest the magical force of poetic rehearsal.[94] As a rhyming tag, 'verse' suggests 'reherse', which composes a series of more or less predictable relationships between the poet, his speakers, and his sources.

At first glance, the Mutabilitie stanza may seem like a non-rhyming variant of this trope, offering a précis of the events which the ensuing text will describe, much in the way that the end of 'Astrophel' anticipates 'The Doleful Lay of Clorinda', and that poem in turn anticipates the succeeding poems in the *Astrophel* volume: 'Which least I marre the sweetnesse of the vearse,/In sort as she it sung, I will rehearse' (ll.215–16); 'The which I here in order will rehearse,/As fittest flowres to deck his mournfull hearse' (ll.107–08).[95] The imagined speakers of these texts decorously recite for the edification of the reader imagined laments for Sidney's belated funeral. In this reckoning, 'whylome I heard say' is a conventional phrase which defers the narrative's authority to a source beyond the text we read; this is how Joyce interprets the phrase when he renders the phrase 'I've heard how this Mutability one time/rose against all the Gods' (3). Joyce's narrator relates a tradition of hearsay, and unambiguously resolves Spenser's phrase into a kind of truistic folk wisdom. Yet Spenser's syntax, as well as his self-citational practices, are more slippery than Joyce allows for. 'I will rehearse that whylome *I* heard say' thrusts metrical emphasis on the speaker, and arguably the most natural reading of the lines is to conclude that the narrator is laying claim to being a direct witness to the debates on Arlo Hill/Galtymore.[96] This is what is implied later in Canto VI, as the

---

94 See Spenser, *The Shorter Poems*, ed. McCabe, for a note on 'November', ll.53–202, making the point that the 'herse' is not only the bier itself but the obsequies noted by E. K. in relation to line 60. Ebook note beginning '53–202 The fifteen stanza of Colin's elegy …'

95 See Patrick Cheney, '*Colin Clouts Come Home Againe, Astrophel*, and *The Doleful Lay of Clorinda* (1595)', 239, 250–51, for the suggestion that the 1595 volume should be read as a linked, 'national' volume, in which Spenser co-ordinates the literary community's laments for Sidney.

96 My emphasis. See Hadfield, *Edmund Spenser: A Life*, 375, for Spenser's physical proximity to Galtymore and its role in the Cantos.

Spenserian narrator claims ownership of the site of the debate: 'That is the highest head (in all mens sights)/Of my old father *Mole*'. Combined with the same stanza's challenge, 'Who knowes not *Arlo-hill*?' it seems perverse not to read this as a claiming of real textual presence at the debates described (VII.vi.36). Similarly, when the narrator in Canto VIII 'bethinkes me on that speech whyleare' and 'gin[s] to thinke on that which Nature sayd', Spenser's illusionism demands that we position ourselves as directly eavesdropping on these momentous events which the narrator has just witnessed.[97] This matters not because I believe Spenser wanted us to think that he witnessed the extraordinary events recounted in the Cantos, but because the narrator's comments on the poem in the fragment are unusually prominent and unusually grounded in a real-world environment, suggesting perhaps the availability of transcendent truth to the lowly Protestant believer. This is not Faery land any longer, and the deliberate repointing of the 'rehearse' formula suggests the different rules which obtain in The Mutabilitie Cantos as Spenser constructs a voice which meshes tonally with the rest of *The Faerie Queene* but which is in crucial respects distinct from the parent poem.

What I am suggesting may be made most effectively by comparing The Mutabilitie Cantos with another of the shorter poems, but this time one which is not intertextually linked with the passages we have been discussing. *Mother Hubberds Tale* is Spenser at his most Chaucerian, with a *Canterbury Tales*-imitating frame and a narrative which draws on the same background from the Reynard The Fox stories which Chaucer used for 'The Nun's Priest's Tale'.[98] It is still a neglected aspect of the Spenserian oeuvre, as at once a politically dangerous satire and a text which uses the Reynard tradition to reanimate the crucial problematics of that literature about the relationship between social action and reward; in brief, this is a narrative which imagines, laments, and even celebrates a world which is socially and politically amoral.[99] As befits its Chaucerian frame, its narrator is a prominent aspect of its literary rhetoric. The frame (ll.1–44) locates the story of the Fox and the Ape as a recreative fiction told by 'a good old woman' who seems like a cover version of The Wife of Bath 'who did farre surpas/The rest in honest mirth' (ll.34–35). The narrator, on the

---

97 Joyce's versions are again less immediate than Spenser's: 'Considering Mutability's presentation/of her case, and weighing her arguments'; 'But then I think of Nature's summing up' (81). To an extent, this distance is a function of Joyce's ironic intentions, but the diminution of intimacy remains striking.

98 See Brown, *The New Poet*, 169–212, for an exposition of *Mother Hubberds Tale*'s literary background and my earlier work on its troubled narrator.

99 For recent work on *Mother Hubberd*, see Hile, *Spenserian Satire*, 13–22, and Mark David Rasmussen's review essay, 'A Turn Towards Satire?'

other hand, is a literary sophisticate, whose friends tell him stories which
sound rather like *The Faerie Queene* or *The Canterbury Tales* (ll.28–32).
As a student of literary decorum, he is clear that Mother Hubberd's story
is an example of the low style: 'No Muses aide me needes hereto to call;/
Base is the style, and matter meane withall' (ll.43–44). Yet his text hovers
between claiming that it is a direct transcription of what Mother Hubberd
has said – 'Ile write in termes, as she the same did say' – and blaming his
memory for any lapses in the story – 'weake was my remembrance it to
hold' (ll.41, 1387). As this inconsistency implies, the narrator is a significant
figure in the tale that he tells, whether this is in the form of bitter asides
like '(God give them paine)' when the Ape becomes a shepherd and the
Fox his dog (l.304), or, more substantively, where he intervenes in the
court sections to outline a Castiglione-esque model of the ideal courtier
in defiance of the Fox and the Ape's immoral impersonations (ll.717–93),
and reproves what he sees as their perversion of poetry (ll.809–20). As I
have argued elsewhere, this conservative narrative voice can be seen to
represent a crisis in the humanistic vision of poetry as a force of moral
reformation; the Fox's and the Ape's successful impersonations repeatedly
suggest the failure of this idealism, so that the narrator becomes a locus
of lament and frustration in a text which cumulatively is sceptical about
the moral organisation of society.

  The voice we hear in *The Mutabilitie Cantos* is not precisely the same
as that of *Mother Hubberds Tale*. But neither is it altogether dissimilar: in
each case, Spenser carefully uses the traditions of lament and complaint to
dramatise the voice(s) of his poem(s).[100] Lament thrives on particularity,
on the sense of immediacy we see reified into an almost wholly aesthetic
form in 'Astrophel' and 'The Doleful Lay of Clorinda': inasmuch as these
artfully rhetorical works may still be moving, they thrive on a rhetoric
of presence which dizzingly works against the time lag from Sidney's
death to propose an ongoing present in which these laments are still
fictively being rehearsed. Conversely, the Chaucerian fiction of *Mother
Hubberds Tale* works to contain and downplay the dangerous subversive
content within the beast fable narrative. Yet the narrator, with his frequent

---

100 Roger Sale, *Reading Spenser*, 22–60, argues for the 'undramatic' qualities of Spenser's
     poetry. Sale was reacting partly to the New Critical valorisation of the dramatic and
     the way in which the term has ossified into cliché for good writing (23–24). My point
     is that in *Mother Hubberd* and the Cantos, Spenser rhetorically constructs a narrator
     who is an actor in the narrated events. In this sense, my usage is akin to Felski's
     characterisation of literary reading as 'a cocreation between actors [reader and text]
     that leaves neither party unchanged'; *The Limits of Critique*, 84.

interruptions and protests against the story he tells works to (in Nashe's phrase) 'rekindle … the sparks of displeasure': his laments make urgent and immediate what the fiction of beast fable otherwise suggests is distant, taking place in a pre-civilised world.[101] This is where, I suggest, the narrator of the Cantos may be seen as analogous: in both cases, the prominence of the narrative voice is a function of the way in which the fiction threatens to break into the real world. Thus when The Mutabilitie Cantos begin with the claim that 'I will rehearse that whylome I heard say', Spenser at once binds the fragment tonally to the rest of *The Faerie Queene* and his broader oeuvre and repeats the transgressive gesture with which Book VI closes, when the bruised voice of the unregarded poet bursts onto a 'world' overrun by the Blatant Beast: 'Ne may this homely verse … Hope to escape his venemous despite' (VI.xii.40–41). The voice of the Cantos is more thoughtful, perhaps, but it is no less mindful of the incursions of the real world on the imagined spaces of poetry.

Indeed, at these pivotal moments in Spenser's narration, stanzaic form again becomes relevant to the poem's broader processes of thinking. Stanza VII.vi.1 is a beautiful embodiment of Empson's description of the syntactic permutations of the Spenserian stanza, particularly the key role of the fifth line. In this case, that line 'complete[s] the sense of the quatrain … and the stanza will then begin with a larger, more narrative unit, *ababb*, and wander garrulously down a perspective to the alexandrine.'[102] To recap: the narrator's opening expostulation reaches an initial climax in the first couplet, 'How *MVTABILITY* in them doth play/Her cruell sports, to many mens decay?' while the new sentence introduced by 'Which that' signals a shift from the opening lament to the business of narrating Mutabilite's insurrection 'Gainst all the Gods'. Though this is not a storytelling stanza, the demarcation between quintain and quatrain is stressed both by that question mark and the archaic 'Which that' construction introducing the

---

101 In Spenser, *The Minor Poems: Part Two*, 580–81. Nashe's comment (from *Strange Newes* [1593]) comically reproves Harvey, suggesting that the latter had foolishly reignited the scandal around *Mother Hubberd* through his comments about it in his *Foure Letters* (1592). Nashe labels Harvey's intervention as a 'rehearsall', a touch Spenser may have enjoyed. The trope of distance is present both in Mother Hubberd's story, imagined as taking place 'before the world was civill' (l.45) and the dedication to Anne Spencer, which notoriously claims the poem was '*long sithens composed in the raw conceipt of my youth*' (*Yale*, 334). For commentary, see Brown, *The New Poet*, 174.

102 Empson, *Seven Types of Ambiguity*, 33. See Chapter 4 above, and note David Lee Miller's comment that this 'must be the finest page and half ever written on Spenser's style'; in '*The Faerie Queene* (1590)', 154.

quatrain.[103] This structure is in effect a motif of thinking aloud: the complaint of the quintain is redirected and pursued through different means by the quatrain; the energies of lament are turned efficiently back to the business of narration, in this case a narration which will turn back to the existential question of the opening stanza.

Curiously enough, the two stanzas of Canto VIII follow the same syntactic structure, even to the extent in VII.viii.1 of duplicating the connective: 'In all things else she beares the greatest sway./*Which* makes me loath this state of life so tickle'.[104] Similarly, VII.viii.2 (although it lacks a full stop at the end of the fifth line) pivots from the apparent stasis of 'Vpon the pillours of Eternity/That is contrayr to *Mutabilitie*' in the first couplet climax back to 'For, all that moueth, doth in *Change* delight' before the containing energies of the final prayer.[105] The syntactic movement is in each case at once logical and developmental, suggesting a clarity of thought and purpose which is sometimes at odds with the way in which ideas actually develop in these stanzas.[106] Though this pattern isn't deployed at the start of the intervening Canto VII, I would suggest that its recursion in Canto VIII suggests a degree of symmetrical design, and that Spenser expected readers to be reminded of the beginning of VII.vi as they read the unfinished VII.viii.[107] In each case, poignant lament and thinking through in verse of larger problems mandates this stately, or even 'garrulous' construction of what Empson aptly characterises as the 'perspective' of the alexandrine. Another way of putting it would be that the quintain + quatrain syntax implies that the stanzas fall into two asymmetrical halves (in which the alexandrine partly compensates for the disparity in numbers of lines) and that this apparently balanced form imparts a measured

103 See Zitner's note in Spenser, *The Mutabilitie Cantos*, 119, identifying this as a Chaucerianism.
104 My emphasis.
105 VII.viii.2.5 ends with a colon. VII.vii.59, which immediately precedes the final fragment has the same syntax, this time with a full stop at the end of the fifth line. The quintain records Nature's counsel to Mutabilitie, while the quatrain elliptically finishes the narrative: 'So was the *Titaness* put downe and whist, … And *Natur*'s selfe did vanish, whither no man wist'; *The Faerie Queene* (1609), 363.
106 Spenser uses the quintain + quatrain structure in other Proems and canto openers, but it is by no means the only permutation he employs in these moments of narrative address. The clearest analogues are II Proem 2–5, and IV Proem 1–4, but note that III Proem has only one example (stanza 2). The model of having a full stop after the fifth line is rarer still.
107 The syntax of VII.vii.1 and 2 provides a significant contrast, with uncharacteristic midline pauses (VII.vii.2.6), and repeated qualifications as the narrator mimetically gestures to 'This too high flight' of the events on Arlo Hill which he must try to narrate.

authority to the authorial discourse. Spenser accustoms us to a way of speaking which is at once unsettled – 'Her cruell sports'; 'Which makes me loath' – measured, and at odds with itself even as it seems to reach the decisive formulations of 'Short *Time* shall soon cut down with his consuming sickle' and 'O that great Sabbaoth God, graunt me that Sabaoths sight'. Stanzaic design inflects narrative voice, and the poetic heft of the 'unperfite' Canto is a consequence of its re-engagement with this particular permutation of the Spenserian. The two stanzas familiarly echo VII.vi.1, and yet at the same time stay unfinished; the tight mesh of the rhymes which asserts the poem's definitive closure abrades against an intellectual design which is unsatisfied by any easy resolution.[108] Empson's all too brief discussion ends with the remark that 'It would be interesting to take one of the vast famous passages of the work and show how these devices are fitted together into larger units of rhythm.'[109] Indeed it would, and it is provocative that for all the massive subtlety of contemporaneous Spenser studies, we have still not managed to achieve this kind of dynamic formal commentary. At the same time, I suspect that what Empson was hinting was the more you look at the way the fifth line mediates and modulates syntax, the more you appreciate both the intricacy of the Spenserian as a formal unit, and the ways in which that permissive structure serves to make connections between form and discourse. The 'vast famous passages' depend on the deployment of familiar, echoic devices like the quintain + quatrain stanza, in which the narrator – himself a trick of language, a will o'the wisp of recursive gestures and biographical fictions – gives us the illusion that 'he' speaks directly to us.

In sum, my suggestion in this chapter is one which emerges from the readings and arguments I have been making throughout this book: Spenser's forms, his choices of word, his rhythms, stanzas, cantos as well his larger, more amorphous patterns structure *The Faerie Queene* to a significant and perhaps underestimated extent. This is not to argue that we don't need to look for allegorical depth – as I have indicated, conceit of one kind or another is discernible on every page of the poem. Yet this conceit

---

108 My thinking here is again endebted to Teskey's 'Night Thoughts on Mutability': 'what could be more in the nature of the materials of poetry – diction, metre, rhythm, rhyme, enjambment, syntactical complexity, decaying and re-forming images, stanzas, structures, stories, visions – than for those materials always to long to turn into something other and better than themselves, such as the truth, even as they continually return to themselves?' (37). Spenser uses the quintain + quatrain syntax to construct stanzas which gesture towards a changeless truth they none the less concede is always still running away from them.

109 Empson, *Seven Types of Ambiguity*, 34.

remains '*darke*' rather than fixed. To return to one of my preferred terms: the conceit is dynamic, a product of style, tone, syntax, stanza form, and modes of narration, which are at least as powerful guides to the author's '*whole intention*' as the Letter to Raleigh. Often the poem suggests that we have been here before, yet we do not necessarily recognise where we are, an unsettling and disturbing narrative process which never ends.

For the epigraph to this chapter, I used a passage from Yann Martel's *Life of Pi*, in which the castaway Pi (who is trapped on a lifeboat in the Pacific Ocean with an adult male Bengal tiger called Richard Parker) laments the lack of reading matter. As I suggested earlier, the 'never-ending story' he longs for has aspects of *The Faerie Queene*, and the desire for a text which can be re-read 'with new eyes and a fresh understanding each time' echoes the experience of many professional Spenserians – think of Harry Berger's brilliant evocation of 'that poem' which 'has never let me go because it has never let me in, has kept me digging outside its crooked walls for five decades in a responsive delirium of interpretation'.[110] Pi, we might say, longs for walls like these. The novel has another passage which is relevant to the formal reading of *The Faerie Queene*. This comes right at the end of Pi's narrative, as he finally makes land in Mexico, and Richard Parker – 'awful, fierce thing that kept me alive' – disappears into the jungle without looking back. This prompts an extraordinary moment of stylistic self-consciousness by Martel's narrator, as Pi at once mourns Richard Parker's unsentimental departure and recognises his own longing for ordered forms:

> What a terrible thing it is to botch a farewell. I am a person who believes in form, in the harmony of order. Where we can, we must give things a meaningful shape. For example – I wonder – could you tell my jumbled story in exactly one hundred chapters, not one more, not one less? … It's important in life to conclude things properly. Only then can you let go. Otherwise you are left with words you should have said but never did, and your heart is heavy with remorse.[111]

Though at one level, *Life of Pi* rises to this challenge – it *is* a novel of 'exactly one hundred chapters' – at another it repeatedly pulls against 'the harmony of order', whether this is in the poignant moment of the botched farewell, or in the credulity-stretching conceit of a teenage castaway coexisting with a tiger on a tiny boat, a conceit which the novel's final

110 Harry Berger Jr, 'Archimago: Between Text and Countertext', 19.
111 Martel, *Life of Pi*, 285.

section comically problematises when Pi is interrogated by two sceptical Japanese civil servants.[112] One might say that Pi's aesthetic sense is out of kilter both with his own story and with the book he longs for earlier. In this sense, he provides a contemporary mirror for the narrator of *The Faerie Queene*, who also believes in the harmony of order, yet is forced to 'rehearse' and to a certain measure celebrate its opposites, whether these come in the shape of Mutabilitie, the Giant with the scales, or the fractured narratives of Book VI. Inasmuch as 'he' is anything beyond 'winged words' (V.ii.44), he is an articulate inexpressibility topos whose heart – at the end of The Mutabilitie Cantos at least – seems 'heavy with remorse', and yet who nonetheless 'conclude[s] things properly' on a note of what might be called unsettled equipoise.

112 *Life of Pi* is a frame tale retold by a previously unsuccessful writer, who retells the story in Pi's voice; at this moment, Pi addresses the writer ('could you tell my jumbled story[?]') directly. See 'Author's Note', xiii–xiv, and for the final section, 289–319.

Appendix: stanza lead words

The first table is based on data extracted by Julian Lethbridge, and provides frequencies of stanza lead words for the poem as a whole. It is a selective listing which includes Proems, but not Arguments, since these are written in a different stanza form. Variant spellings are homogenised and cued by an *, on the basis that for example 'She' and 'Shee' are semantically identical. The text is based on the same used for *A Concordance to the Rhymes of The Faerie Queene* (xiii–xv); it includes both the 1590 and 1596 endings to Book III, the stanza added to Book I in the 1596 edition (I.xi.3), and The Mutabilitie Cantos. Thus presented, this is largely raw data in support of arguments made in Chapter 4. I intend to come back to the question of stanza lead words at a later stage, where I will offer a fuller interpretation of the data.

The second table focuses on Book VI. As well as giving the most frequent stanza lead words, it includes the full data set for each canto with the aim of giving a detailed picture of this book.

Table A1 Stanza lead words by frequency

	Book I	Book II	Book III	Book IV	Book V	Book VI	Book VII	Totals
But*	30	46	74	42	66	67	11	**336**
And	61	47	50	48	35	30	13	**284**
The	66	52	43	22	25	40	5	**253**
So	28	31	18	34	34	33	9	**187**
Then	27	15	17	27	31	19	13	**149**
Which	9	28	9	31	22	11	1	**111**
For	7	8	17	14	23	16	4	**89**
There	12	6	14	17	19	13	1	**82**
He	16	17	13	10	8	12	0	**76**
Yet	6	5	11	20	15	14	3	**74**
With	6	16	13	12	13	13	0	**73**
At	16	7	16	12	4	11	1	**67**
Thus	7	12	13	13	9	8	1	**63**
His	22	11	10	6	5	4	0	**58**
Who	14	5	7	7	12	12	0	**57**
Her	9	12	9	7	8	5	1	**51**
In	11	14	8	7	2	8	1	**51**
That	7	9	8	8	6	7	4	**49**
Whom	7	9	6	10	7	10	0	**49**
To	4	7	5	6	12	11	3	**48**
Tho	1	5	14	5	6	14	0	**45**
As	8	10	4	6	11	2	1	**42**
It	6	6	14	8	3	4	0	**41**
All	5	6	8	8	6	5	1	**39**
She*	8	5	9	5	7	3	2	**39**
They	5	8	5	8	7	5	0	**38**
Like	0	4	6	5	10	10	1	**36**
Ne	2	5	12	4	3	7	2	**35**
Now	9	6	4	5	6	4	1	**35**
By	6	5	6	4	2	4	0	**27**
Such	4	4	1	8	5	5	0	**27**
When	6	1	0	6	6	4	2	**25**

Table A1 Stanza lead words by frequency (Continued)

	Book I	Book II	Book III	Book IV	Book V	Book VI	Book VII	Totals
Soone	4	6	6	2	5	1	0	**24**
What	7	3	4	3	5	1	1	**24**
Ah	5	3	5	3	4	2	1	**23**
Much	3	1	1	3	9	6	0	**23**
Of	1	8	2	2	2	6	1	**22**
Therewith	9	5	3	2	2	1	0	**22**
Eftsoones*	2	6	4	4	2	2	1	**21**
O	9	2	5	2	1	1	0	**20**
A	10	4	3	1	0	1	0	**19**
Long	4	1	7	3	2	2	0	**19**
Therefore	1	1	1	6	4	6	0	**19**
Well	2	3	3	3	3	5	0	**19**
Nathlesse*	0	2	1	6	4	5	1	**19**
Thereat	1	6	3	6	1	0	0	**17**
Next	0	3	6	3	0	0	5	**17**
Where	1	3	5	3	4	0	0	**16**
Full	3	0	4	4	2	2	0	**15**
One	2	2	2	1	4	4	0	**15**
Not	3	1	2	1	4	4	0	**15**
Thence*	3	3	1	3	2	1	1	**14**
Great	4	1	5	3	0	1	0	**14**
Vpon	2	3	0	1	1	5	0	**12**
These	0	1	3	4	1	1	1	**11**
After	0	5	3	0	1	1	0	**10**

* *These totals include variant spellings of these words.*

Table A2 Book VI

Proem
2: But
1: The Such Reuele Amongst Then

Canto I – 47 stanzas
5: The 4: But With 2: Of And Then Thus Who
1: Ne Now That Sir Vnhappy Not A His He Which Like They False Much To Thereof Well Nathlesse There At For All Whereof So

---

Canto II – 48 stanzas
5: But 4: Then 3: And So 2: That Whom The Which Yet All Therefore There
1: What Thereto Him Buskins For Much Of This Vnarm'd Meane Faire To Ne Thus Glad In When

---

Canto III – 51 stanzas
11: But 5: The 4: So 3: Yet 2: He Who Of Sir And
1: True Such For Which Him Streight There Most To With All Now Whom Vnknightly Full His Wherefore By

---

Canto IV – 40 stanzas
6: But 3: The And Then So 2: Yet For Well To
1: Like Till He With Long Thether During Now Whom Much At Which If Right

---

Canto V – 41 stanzas
5: So 3: Vpon 2: Whom With And
1: O That Who Tho At Bout After But Oftimes The Securely Sharpely Like Him Till Eftsoones Then Gnashing To In Let Mongst Wherewith They He Yet Therefore

---

Canto VI – 44 stanzas
6: For 4: But Yet 3: Whom 2: The Thus Which Who There
1: No Such One So Echidna To Of In Arriuing Ere Art With Whereof At Her And Whether

---

Canto VII – 50 stanzas
7: But The 3: He Then 2: Like So Nathelesse And
1: That Well To As By Not Perdie Thereof Much Wearie Whom There Whereat She Through It Fayre Ne For His This Whose

---

Canto VIII – 51 stanzas
7: The 6: But 5: And 4: So 3: Then 2: With In Tho
1: Ye Who As His It Eftsoones He For Certes Here Meane Ah Through Thereto Soone Her Those Long There From

---

Canto IX – 46 stanzas
5: But 4: So 3: And 2: There The Which Thus
1: Now Great From They Vpon Ne Her By He She Tho How Surely Therefore To Sometimes With Whylest Yet That In It Since Not One Another

---

Canto X – 44 stanzas
4: And 3: But So 2: For One It He They Such
1: Who That Ne Vpon All Looke Those She Much Not Tho These Therefore Another Sunne When In Which From Amongst With Hither

---

Appendix

Table A2 Book VI (Continued)

Canto XI – 51 stanzas

10: But 6: Tho 5: At 3: Like There 2: The So To Then When

1: Whylest By During Therewith Thus Their Who Ne Ah In Whereof Her How This

---

Canto XII – 41 stanzas

3: And The Tho But 2: Like At Thus Who Him

1: For Sir Her Nathlesse Well Both Therefore Which Much Thence Through Into From Full Or Yet Thenceforth So Ne

---

Bibliography

Primary works

Alexander, Gavin (ed.) (2004) *Sidney's 'Defence of Poetry' and Selected Renaissance Literary Criticism*. London: Penguin ebook.

Ariosto, Ludovico (1556) *Orlando Furioso Tutto Ricorreto, et di Nvove Figvre adornato*. Venetia: Vicenzo Valgrisi.

Ariosto, Ludovico (1591) *Orlando Furioso Translated into English Heroical Verse*. London: Richard Field.

Ariosto, Ludovico (1972) *Orlando Furioso Translated into English Heroical Verse*, trans. Sir John Harington. Ed. Robert McNulty. Oxford: Clarendon.

Ariosto, Ludovico (2012) *Orlando Furioso*, ed. Emilio Bigi and Cristina Zampese. Milano: BUR rizzoli classici ebook.

Ascham, Roger (1570) *The Scholemaster*, in *Elizabethan Critical Essays*, 2 vols, ed. G. Gregory Smith (1904). Oxford: Clarendon.

Aubrey, John (1949; rpt 1972) *Aubrey's Brief Lives*, ed. Oliver Lawson Dick. Harmondsworth: Penguin.

Birch, William (1562) *A new balade of the worthy seruice late doen by Maister Strangwige in France, and of his death*. London: William Owen.

Calvin, Jean (1560) *Sermons of John Calvin, Vpon the Songe that Ezekias made after he had bene sicke and afflicted by the hand of God, conteyned in the 38. chapiter of Esay. Translated out of Frenche into Englishe*. London: John Day.

Chapman, George (2017) *Homer's Iliad*, ed. Robert S. Miola. Cambridge: Modern Humanities Research Association.

Chaucer, Geoffrey (1483) *Troylus and Creseyde*. Westminster: Caxton.

Chaucer, Geoffrey (1517) *The noble and amerous au[n]cyent hystory of Troylus and Cresyde*. London: Wynkyn de Worde.

Chaucer, Geoffrey (1526) *The boke of Troylus and Creseyde*. London: Rycharde Pynson.

Chaucer, Geoffrey (1976) *The Works 1532 with supplementary material from the Editions of 1542, 1561, 1598 and 1602*, ed. D. S. Brewer. Ilkley: Scolar.

Chaucer, Geoffrey (1987) *The Riverside Chaucer*, ed. Larry D. Benson et al. Boston: Houghton Mifflin.

Chaucer, Geoffrey (2006) *Troilus and Criseyde with facing-page Il Filostrato*, ed. Stephen Barney. New York: Norton.

Churchyard, Thomas (1575) *The firste parte of Churchyardes chippes contayning twelue seuerall labours*. London: Thomas Marshe.

Copley, Anthony (2016) *A Fig for Fortune: A Catholic Response to The Faerie Queene*, ed. Susannah Brietz Monta. Manchester: Manchester University Press.

Cowley, Abraham (1656) *Poems*. London: Humphrey Moseley.

Cowley, Abraham (1915) *The Essays and Other Prose Writings*, ed. Alfred B. Gough. Oxford: Clarendon.

Daniel, Samuel (1594) *Delia and Rosamund augmented Cleopatra*. London: [James Roberts and Edward Allde] for Simon Waterson.

Daniel, Samuel (1603) *A Defence of Ryme*, in *Elizabethan Critical Essays*, 2 vols, ed. G. Gregory Smith (1904). Oxford: Clarendon.

Dante (1996; rpt 2005) *De vulgari Eloquentia*, ed. and trans. Steven Botterill. Cambridge: Cambridge University Press.

Davies, Sir John (1596) *Orchestra or A poeme of dauncing*. London: I. Robarts.

Davies, Sir John (1622) *Nosce teipsum [and] Orchestra, or A poeme of dauncing*. London: Richard Hawkins.

Davies, Sir John (1975) *The Poems*, ed. Robert Krueger and Ruby Nemser. Oxford: Clarendon.

Davison, Francis (1602) *A poetical rapsody containing, diuerse sonnets, odes, elegies, madrigalls, and other poesies, both in rime, and measured verse. Neuer yet published*. London: By V. S[immes] for Iohn Baily.

Donne, John (1970) *Poems [1633]*. Menston: Scolar.

Donne, John (2010) *The Complete Poems*, ed. Robin Robbins. Harlow: Pearson.

Dowland, John (1597) *The First Booke of Songes or Ayres*. London: Peter Short.

D[owriche], A[nne] (1589) *The French Historie, that is, A lamentable discourse of three of the chiefe, and most famous bloodie broiles that haue happened in France for the Gospell of Iesus Christ namelie, 1. The outrage called the winning of S. Iames his streete, 1557, 2. The constant martirdome of Annas Burgans one of the K. Councell, 1559, 3. The bloodie marriage of Margaret sister to Charles the 9, anno 1572*. Exeter: Thomas Orwin for William Russell.

D[rayton], M[ichael] (1591) *The harmonie of the church Containing, the spirituall songes and holy hymnes, of godly men, patriarkes and prophetes: all, sweetly sounding, to the praise and glory of the highest. Now (newlie) reduced into sundrie kinds of English meeter: meete to be read or sung, for the solace and comfort of the godly*. London: Richard Ihones.

Drayton, Michael (1596) *Mortimeriados. The lamentable ciuell vvarres of Edward the second and the barrons*. London: Humfry Lownes.

Drayton, Michael (1603) *The barrons vvars in the raigne of Edward the second. VVith Englands heroicall epistles.* London: N. Ling.

Drayton, Michael (1610) *A heauenly harmonie of spirituall songes, and holy himnes, of godly men, patriarkes, and prophets.* London: Thomas Orwin.

Drayton, Michael (1969) *Poems [1619].* Menton: Scolar.

Du Bellay, Joachim (1967) *Les Regrets, Les Antiquités de Rome, La Défense et Illustration de la Langue française,* ed. S. De Sacy. Paris: Gallimard.

Florio, John (1578) *Florio his firste fruites which yeelde familiar speech, merie prouerbes, wittie sentences, and golden sayings.* London: Thomas Woodcocke.

Fraunce, Abraham (1588) *The Arcadian rhetorike: or The praecepts of rhetorike made plaine by examples.* London: Thomas Orwin.

Gascoigne, George (1575) *Certayne Notes of Instruction,* in *Elizabethan Critical Essays,* 2 vols, ed. G. Gregory Smith (1904). Oxford: Clarendon.

Gascoigne, George (1576) *The steele glas A satyre co[m]piled by George Gascoigne Esquire. Togither with The complainte of Phylomene. An elegie deuised by the same author.* [London]: Printed [by Henrie Binneman] for Richard Smith.

Gascoigne, George (1907; rpt 1969) *The Posies,* ed. John W. Cunliffe. New York: Greenwood.

The Geneva Bible: A Facsimile of the 1560 Edition (1969; rpt 2007), ed. Lloyd E. Berry. Peabody, MA: Hendrickson.

Geoffrey of Monmouth (1966) *The History of the Kings of Britain,* trans. Lewis Thorpe. Harmondsworth: Penguin.

Guazzo, Stefano (1581) *The Civile Conuersation,* trans. George Pettie. London: Richard Watkins.

Guilpin, Everard (1974) *Skialetheia or A Shadowe of Truthe, in Certaine Epigrams and Satyres,* ed. D. Allen Carroll. Chapel Hill: University of North Carolina Press.

Harington, Sir John (1591) *A Preface, or rather a Briefe Apologie of Poetrie,* in *Elizabethan Critical Essays,* 2 vols, ed. G. Gregory Smith (1904). Oxford: Clarendon.

Henryson, Robert (1987) *The Poems,* ed. Denton Fox. Oxford: Clarendon.

Henryson, Robert (2009) *The Testament of Crisseid and Seven Fables,* trans. Seamus Heaney. London: Faber and Faber.

Herbert, George (2007) *The English Poems,* ed. Helen Wilcox. Cambridge: Cambridge University Press.

Herzman, Ronald B., Graham Drake, and Eve Salisbury (eds) (1997) *Four Romances of England: King Horn, Havelok the Dane, Bevis of Hampton, Athelston.* Kalamazoo: TEAMS.

Heywood, John (1546) *A dialogue conteinyng the number in effect of all the prouerbes in the englishe tongue.* London: Thomas Berthelet.

Holinshed, Raphaell (1577) *The firste [laste] volume of the chronicles of England, Scotlande, and Irelande conteyning the description and chronicles of England, from the first inhabiting vnto the conquest: the description and chronicles of*

Scotland, from the first original of the Scottes nation till the yeare of our Lorde 1571: the description and chronicles of Yrelande, likewise from the first originall of that nation untill the yeare 1571. London: Iohn Hunne.

Holton, Amanda and Tom MacFaul (eds) (2011) *Tottel's Miscellany: Songs and Sonnets of Henry Howard, Earl of Surrey, Sir Thomas Wyatt and Others.* London: Penguin.

Hudson, Harriet (ed.) (2006) *Four Middle English Romances: Sir Isumbras, Octavian, Sir Eglamour of Artois, Sir Tryamour.* Kalamazoo: TEAMS.

Hunter, William B. (ed.) (1977) *The English Spenserians: the Poetry of Giles Fletcher, George Wither, Michael Drayton, Phineas Fletcher and Henry More.* Salt Lake City: University of Utah Press.

Jones, Emrys (ed.) (1991) *The New Oxford Book of Sixteenth Century Verse.* Oxford: Oxford University Press.

Kerrigan, John (ed.) (1991) *Motives of Woe: Shakespeare and 'Female Complaint'. A Critical Anthology.* Oxford: Clarendon.

Kinsley, James (ed.) (1969, 1982) *The Oxford Book of Ballads.* Oxford: Oxford University Press.

Knevet, Ralph (2015) *A Supplement of the Faery Queene*, ed. Christopher Burlinson and Andrew Zurcher. Manchester: Manchester University Press.

Langland, William (1550) *The Vision of Pierce Plowman*, second edition. London: Robert Crowley.

Langland, William (1978) *The Vision of Piers Plowman: A Critical Edition of the B-Text*, ed. A. V. C. Schmidt. London: Dent.

Lucie-Smith, Edward (ed.) (1965) *The Penguin Book of Elizabethan Verse.* Harmondsworth: Penguin.

Marlowe, Christopher (1590) *Tamburlaine the Great Who, from a Scythian shephearde, by his rare and woonderfull conquests, became a most puissant and mightye monarque. And (for his tyranny, and terrour in warre) was tearmed, the scourge of God. Deuided into two tragicall discourses, as they were sundrie times shewed vpon stages in the citie of London. By the right honorable the Lord Admyrall, his seruauntes.* London: Richard Ihones.

Marlowe, Christopher (1633) *The famous tragedy of the rich Ievv of Malta As it vvas playd before the King and Queene, in his Majesties theatre at White-hall, by her Majesties Servants at the Cock-pit.* London: I[ohn] B[eale] for Nicholas Vavasour.

Marlowe, Christopher (1978, 1997) *The Jew of Malta*, ed. N. W. Bawcutt. Manchester: Manchester University Press.

Marlowe, Christopher (1981, 1999) *Tamburlaine the Great*, ed. J. S. Cunningham. Manchester: Manchester University Press.

Marlowe, Christopher (1999) *The Complete Plays*, ed. Mark Thornton Burnett. London: Everyman.

Marston, John (1598) *The scourge of villanie: Three bookes of satyres.* London: I[ames] R[oberts].

Milton, John (1971) *Paradise Lost*, ed. Alastair Fowler. Harlow; Longman.

The Mirror for Magistrates (1938, 1960) Ed. Lily B. Campbell. Cambridge: Cambridge University Press; rpt New York: Barnes & Noble.

Norbrook, David and H. R. Woudhuysen (eds) (1992) *The Penguin Book of Renaissance Verse 1509–1659*. London: Penguin.

Ovid (1567) *The. xv. bookes of P. Ouidius Naso, entytuled Metamorphosis, translated oute of Latin into English meeter, by Arthur Golding Gentleman*. London: William Seres.

Ovid (1916, 1977) *Metamorphoses*, with trans. by Frank Justus Miller, 2 vols. Cambridge, MA: Harvard University Press.

Ovid (2002) *Metamorphoses*, trans. Arthur Golding. Ed. Madeleine Forey. London: Penguin.

Peacham, Henry (1593) *The Garden of Eloquence*, London: Richard Field for H. Iackson.

Pearsall, Derek (ed.) (1990) *The Floure and the Leafe, The Assembly of Ladies, The Isle of Ladies*. Kalamazoo: TEAMS.

Petrarca, Francesco (1976) *Petrarch's Lyric Poems: The Rime Sparse and Other Lyrics*, trans. Robert M. Durling. Cambridge, MA: Harvard University Press.

Plato (1961, rpt 1989) *The Collected Dialogues*, ed. Edith Hamilton and Huntingdon Cairns. Princeton: Princeton University Press.

Puttenham, George (2007) *The Art of English Poesy*, ed. Frank Whigham and Wayne A. Rebhorn. Ithaca: Cornell University Press.

Ralegh, Sir Walter (1951) *The Poems*, ed. Agnes Latham. London: Routledge and Kegan Paul.

Ralegh, Sir Walter (1999) *The Poems of Sir Walter Ralegh: A Historical Edition*, ed. Michael Rudick. Tempe, AZ: Arizona Center for Medieval and Renaissance Studies.

Rapin, René (1674) *Reflections on Aristotle's treatise of poesie containing the necessary, rational, and universal rules for epick, dramatick, and the other sorts of poetry*, trans. Thomas Rymer. London: H. Herringman.

Robinson, Clement (1584) *A Handefull of pleasant delites, Containing sundrie new Sonets and delectable histories in divers kinds of Meeter*. London: Richard J[h]ones.

Scott, William (2013) *The Model of Poesy*, ed. Gavin Alexander. Cambridge: Cambridge University Press.

Shakespeare, William (1593) *Venus and Adonis*. London: Richard Field.

Shakespeare, William (1952; rpt. 1972), *King Lear*, ed. Kenneth Muir. London: Methuen.

Shakespeare, William (1982) *Hamlet*, ed. Harold Jenkins. London: Methuen.

Shakespeare, William (1994) *Hamlet*, ed. G. R. Hibbard. Oxford: Oxford University Press.

Shakespeare, William (1996) *The First Folio of Shakespeare*. Second Edition. ed. Charlton Hinman. New York: Norton.

Shakespeare, William (1997) *Shakespeare's Sonnets*, ed. Katherine Duncan-Jones. Walton on Thames: Thomas Nelson.

Shakespeare, William (2000) *Romeo and Juliet*, ed. Jill Levenson. Oxford: Oxford University Press.

Shakespeare, William (2002) *The Complete Sonnets and Poems*, ed. Colin Burrow. Oxford: Oxford University Press.

Shakespeare, William (2005) *Antony and Cleopatra*, ed. Emrys Jones and René Weis. London: Penguin.

Shakespeare, William (2006) *As You Like It*, ed. Juliet Dusinberre. London: Cengage.

Shakespeare, William (2006) *Much Ado About Nothing*, ed. Claire McEachern. London: Cengage.

Sidney, Sir Philip (1962) *The Poems*, ed. William A. Ringler, Jr. Oxford: Clarendon.

Sidney, Sir Philip (1973) *Miscellaneous Prose*, ed. Katharine Duncan-Jones and Jan Van Dorsten. Oxford: Clarendon.

Smith, G. Gregory (ed.) (1904) *Elizabethan Critical Essays*, 2 vols. Oxford: Clarendon.

Southwell, Robert, S. J. (1595) *Moeoniae. Or, Certaine excellent poems and spirituall hymnes*. London: John Busbie.

Southwell, Robert, S. J. (1602) *Saint Peters complaint Newlie augmented vvith other poems*. London: I. R[oberts] for G. C[awood].

Southwell, Robert, S. J. (1967) *The Poems*, ed. James H. McDonald and Nancy Pollard Brown. Oxford: Clarendon.

Southwell, St Robert, S. J. (2007) *Collected Poems*, ed. Peter Davdison and Anne Sweeney. Manchester: Carcanet.

Spenser, Edmund (1590) *The Faerie Queene*. London: William Ponsonbie.

Spenser, Edmund (1591) *Complaints. Containing sundrie small Poemes of the Worlds Vanitie*. London: William Ponsonbie.

Spenser, Edmund (1596) *The Faerie Queene*. London: William Ponsonbie.

Spenser, Edmund (1609) *The Faerie Queene*. London: Matthew Lownes.

Spenser, Edmund (1758) *The Faerie Queene*, 4 vols, ed. Ralph Church. London: William Faden.

Spenser, Edmund (1758) *The Fairy Queen*, 2 vols, ed. John Upton. London: J. and R. Tonson.

Spenser, Edmund (1909) *The Faerie Queene*, 2 vols, ed. J. C. Smith. Oxford: Clarendon.

Spenser, Edmund (1938) *The Faerie Queene Books Six and Seven*, ed. Edwin Greenlaw, Charles Grosvenor Osgood, Frederick Morgan Padelford, Ray Heffner, James G. McManaway, Dorothy E. Mason, and Brents Stirling; Vol. 6 *of The Works of Edmund Spenser: A Variorum Edition*. Baltimore: Johns Hopkins Press.

Spenser, Edmund (1947) *The Minor Poems: Part Two*, ed. Charles Grosvenor Osgood and Henry Gibbons Lotspeich; Vol. 8 *of The Works of Edmund Spenser: A Variorum Edition*. Baltimore: Johns Hopkins Press.

Spenser, Edmund (1949) *Spenser's Prose Works*, ed. Rudolf Gottfried; Vol. 10 *of The Works of Edmund Spenser: A Variorum Edition*. Baltimore: Johns Hopkins Press.

Spenser, Edmund (1968) *The Mutabilitie Cantos*, ed. S. P. Zitner. London: Nelson.

Spenser, Edmund (1977) *The Faerie Queene*, ed. A. C. Hamilton. Harlow: Longman.

Spenser, Edmund (1989) *The Shorter Poems*, ed. William A. Oram, Einar Bjorvand, Ronald Bond, Thomas H. Cain, Alexander Dunlop, and Richard Schell. New Haven and London: Yale University Press.

Spenser, Edmund (1999) *The Shorter Poems*, ed. Richard A. McCabe. London: Penguin ebook.

Spenser, Edmund (2001, 2007) *The Faerie Queene*, Revised Second Edition, ed. A. C. Hamilton with Hiroshi Yamashita and Toshiyuki Suzuki. Harlow: Pearson.

Spenser, Edmund (2006) *The Faerie Queene: Book One*, ed. Carol V. Kaske. Indianapolis: Hackett.

Spenser, Edmund (2006) *The Faerie Queene: Book Two*, ed. Erik Gray. Indianapolis: Hackett.

Spenser, Edmund (2006) *The Faerie Queene: Books Three and Four*, ed. Dorothy Stephens. Indianapolis: Hackett.

Spenser, Edmund (2006) *The Faerie Queene: Book Five*, ed. Abraham Stoll. Indianapolis: Hackett.

Spenser, Edmund (2007) *The Faerie Queene: Book Six and The Mutabilitie Cantos*, ed. Andrew Hadfield and Abraham Stoll. Indianapolis: Hackett.

Spenser, Edmund (2009) *Selected Letters and Other Papers*, ed. Christopher Burlinson and Andrew Zurcher. Oxford: Oxford University Press.

Sternhold, Thomas (1549) *Certayne psalmes chose[n] out of the Psalter of Dauid, and drawe[n] into Englishe metre by Thomas Sternhold grome of ye kynges Maiesties roobes*. London: Edouardus Whitchurche. STC (2nd edn)/2419.

Tasso, Torquato (1981) *Godfrey of Buloigne: A Critical Edition of Edward Fairfax's translation of Tasso's 'Gerusalemme Liberata', together with Fairfax's Original Poems*, ed. Kathleen M. Lea and T. M. Gang. Oxford: Clarendon.

Tasso, Torquato (2009) *Gerusalemme liberata*, ed. Franco Tomasi. Milano: BUR rizzoli classici ebook.

Tichborne, Chidiock (1586) *Verses of Prayse and Ioye written vpon her Maiesties preseruation. Whereunto is annexed Tychbornes lamentation, written in the towre with his own hand, and an aunswere to the same*. London: Iohn Wolfe.

Tichborne, Chidiock (1986) 'The Works of Chidiock Tichborne (text)', ed. Richard S. M. Hirsch. *English Literary Renaissance* 16, 303–18.

Turberville, George (1575) *The booke of faulconrie or hauking*. London: Christopher Barker.

Tusser, Thomas (1557) *A hundreth good pointes of husbandrie*. London: Richard Tottel.

Tusser, Thomas (1573) *Fiue hundreth points of good husbandry vnited to as many of good huswiferie first deuised, & nowe lately augmented with diuerse approued lessons concerning hopps & gardening, and other needefull matters: together with an abstract before euery moneth, conteining the whole effect of the saide moneth: with a table & a preface in the beginning both necessary to be reade, for the better understandinge of the booke.* London: Richard Tottel.

Tusser, Thomas (1580) *Fiue hundred pointes of good husbandrie as well for the champion, or open countrie, as also for the woodland, or seuerall, mixed in euerie month with huswiferie, ouer and besides the booke of huswiferie, corrected, better ordered, and newly augmented to a fourth part more, with diuers other lessons, as a diet for the fermer, of the properties of winds, planets, hops, herbes, bees, and approoued remedies for sheepe and cattle, with many other matters both profitable and not vnpleasant for the reader. Also a table of husbandrie at the beginning of this booke: and another of huswiferie at the end: for the better and easier finding of any matter conteined in the same.* London: Henrie Denham.

Tusser, Thomas (1984) *Five Hundred Points of Good Husbandry*, ed. Geoffrey Grigson. Oxford: Oxford University Press.

Virgil (1557) *Certain bokes of Virgiles Aeneis turned into English meter by the right honorable lorde, Henry Earle of Surrey.* London: Richard Tottel.

Virgil (1558) *The seuen first bookes of the Eneidos of Virgill, conuerted in Englishe meter by Thomas Phaer Esquier.* London: Richard Jugge.

Virgil (1562) *The nyne fyrst bookes of the Eneidos of Virgil conuerted into Englishe vearse by Thomas Phaer Doctour of Phisike.* London: Nicholas Englande.

Virgil (1570) *Pub. Virgilii Maronis opera De integro collatis probatissimae fidei exemplaribus, q diligentissimè restituta, ac doctissimis scholijs & annotationibus Pauli Manutij in margine ascriptis, illustrata.* London: Henricus Bynneman

Virgil (1573) *The whole .xii. bookes of the AEneidos of Virgill. Whereof the first .ix. and part of the tenth, were conuerted into English meeter by Thomas Phaër Esquire, and the residue supplied, and the whole worke together newly set forth, by Thomas Twyne, Gentleman.* London: Abraham Veale.

Virgil (1964) *Aeneidos Liber Secvndvs*, ed. R. G. Austin. Oxford: Clarendon.

Waller, Edmond (1668) *Poems, &c. written upon several occasions, and to several persons.* London: Henry Herringman.

Webbe, William (1586) *A Discourse of English Poetrie* in (1904) *Elizabethan Critical Essays*, 2 vols, ed. G. Gregory Smith (1904). Oxford: Clarendon.

Wesley, Samuel (1700) *An Epistle to a Friend Concerning Poetry.* London: Charles Harper.

Wilson, Thomas (1553) *The Arte of Rhetorique.* London: Richard Grafton.

Secondary works

Adams, Percy G. (1993) 'Alliteration', in *The New Princeton Encyclopaedia of Poetry and Poetics*, ed. Alex Preminger and T. V. F. Brogan. Princeton: Princeton University Press.

Addison, Catherine (2003) 'Little Boxes: The Effects of the Stanza on Poetic Narrative', *Style* 37.2, pp. 124–43.

Addison, Catherine (2005) 'Stress Felt, Stroke Dealt: The Spondee, the Text, and the Reader', *Style* 39.2, pp. 153–74.

Addison, Catherine (2006) 'Rhyming Against the Grain: A New Look at the Spenserian Stanza', in *Edmund Spenser: New and Renewed Directions*, ed. J. B. Lethbridge. Madison: Fairleigh Dickinson University Press.

Alpers, Paul (1967, 1982) *The Poetry of The Faerie Queene*. Columbia: University of Missouri Press.

Alpers, Paul (ed.) (1969) *Edmund Spenser: A Critical Anthology*. Harmondsworth: Penguin.

Alpers, Paul (1990, 1997) 'Style', in *The Spenser Encyclopedia*, ed. A. C. Hamilton et al. Toronto: University of Toronto Press.

Anderson, Judith H. (1972) 'Whatever Happened to Amoret? The Poet's Role in Book IV of *The Faerie Queene*', *Criticism* 13.2, pp. 180–200.

Anderson, Judith H. (1976) *The Growth of a Personal Voice: Piers Plowman and The Faerie Queene*. New Haven: Yale University Press.

Anderson, Judith H. (1982, 1995) '"In liuing colours and right hew": The Queen of Spenser's Central Books', in *Critical Essays on Edmund Spenser*, ed. Mihoko Suzuki. New York: G. K. Hall & Co.

Anderson, Judith H. (1990, 1997) 'Britomart', in *The Spenser Encyclopedia*, ed. A. C. Hamilton et al. Toronto: University of Toronto Press.

Anderson, Judith H. (1990, 1997) 'Cambell, Canacee, Cambina', in *The Spenser Encyclopedia*, ed. A. C. Hamilton et al. Toronto: University of Toronto Press.

Anderson, Judith H. (1990, 1997) 'Langland, William' in *The Spenser Encyclopedia*, ed. A. C. Hamilton et al. Toronto: University of Toronto Press.

Anderson, Judith H. (1996) *Words that Matter: Linguistic Perception in Renaissance English*. Stanford: Stanford University Press.

Anderson, Judith H. (1998) 'Narrative Reflections: Re-envisaging the Poet in *The Canterbury Tales* and *The Faerie Queene*', in *Refiguring Chaucer in the Renaissance*, ed. Theresa Krier. Gainsville: University Press of Florida.

Anderson, Judith H. (2008) *Reading the Allegorical Intertext: Chaucer, Spenser, Shakespeare, Milton*. New York: Fordham University Press.

Aptekhar, Jane (1969) *Icons of Justice: Iconography and Thematic Imagery in Book V of The Faerie Queene*. New York: Columbia University Press.

Archer, Harriet (2016) '"Those chronicles whiche other men had": Paralipsis and Blenerhasset's Seconde Part of the *Mirror for Magistrates* (1578)', in *A Mirror for Magistrates in Context: Literature, History and Politics in Early Modern England*, ed. Harriet Archer and Andrew Hadfield. Cambridge: Cambridge University Press.

Attridge, Derek (1974, 1979) *Well-Weighed Syllables: Elizabethan Verse in Classical Metres*. Cambridge: Cambridge University Press.

Auden, W. H. (1996) *Prose 1926–1938. Essays and Reviews and Travel Books in Verse and Prose*, ed. Edward Mendelson. London: Faber and Faber.

Aughterson, Kate (2004, online edn Jan. 2011) 'Dowriche, Anne (*d*. in or after 1613)', *Oxford Dictionary of National Biography*. Oxford: Oxford University Press.

Austen, Gillian (2008) *George Gascoigne*. Woodbridge: D. S. Brewer.

Bajetta, Carlo M. (1996) 'Ralegh's Early Poetry in its Metrical Context', *SP* 93.4, pp. 390–411.

Bate, Jonathan (1993) *Shakespeare and Ovid*. Oxford: Clarendon.

Bates, Catherine (2013) *Masculinity and the Hunt: Wyatt To Spenser*. Oxford: Oxford University Press.

Baybak, Michael, Paul Delany, and A. Kent Hieatt (1969) 'Placement "in the middest" in *The Faerie Queene*', *Papers in Language and Literature* 5, pp. 227–34.

Bednarz, James P. (1996) 'The Collaborator as Thief: Ralegh's (Re)vision of The Faerie Queene', *ELH* 63, pp. 279–307.

Bellamy, Elizabeth Jane (2010) '*The Faerie Queene* (1596)', in *The Oxford Handbook of Edmund Spenser*, ed. Richard A. McCabe. Oxford: Oxford University Press.

Bellos, David (2011) *Is That a Fish in Your Ear? The Amazing Adventure of Translation*. London: Penguin.

Bennett, Josephine Waters (1942, rpt 1960) *The Evolution of The Faerie Queene*. New York: Burt Franklin.

Berger, Harry, Jr (1957) *The Allegorical Temper: Vision and Reality in Book II of Spenser's Faerie Queene*. New Haven: Yale University Press.

Berger, Harry, Jr (1988) *Revisionary Play: Studies in Spenserian Dynamics*. Berkeley: University of California Press.

Berger, Harry, Jr (2003) 'Archimago: Between Text and Countertext', *Studies in English Literature, 1500–1900* 43.1, pp. 19–64.

Berry, Craig A. (1998) '"Sundrie Doubts": Vulnerable Understanding and Dubious Origins in Spenser's Continuation of the Squire's Tale', in *Refiguring Chaucer in the Renaissance*, ed. Theresa Krier. Gainsville: University Press of Florida.

Black, L. G. (1990, 1997) '*The Faerie Queene*, commendatory verses and dedicatory sonnets', in *The Spenser Encyclopedia*, ed. A. C. Hamilton et al. Toronto: University of Toronto Press.

Blank, Paula (2006, 2012) 'The Babel of Renaissance English', in *The Oxford History of English: Revised Edition*, ed. Lynda Mugglestone. Oxford: Oxford University Press.

Blissett, William (1990, 1997) 'Calepine', in *The Spenser Encyclopedia*, ed. A. C. Hamilton et al. Toronto: University of Toronto Press.

Blissett, William (1990, 1997) 'Spensersian Stanza', in *The Spenser Encyclopedia*, ed. A. C. Hamilton et al. Toronto: University of Toronto Press.

Bloom, Harold (1973, 1997) *The Anxiety of Influence: A Theory of Poetry*. New York: Oxford University Press.

Brill, Lesley (1990, 1997) '*The Faerie Queene*, Proems', in *The Spenser Encyclopedia*, ed. A. C. Hamilton et al. Toronto: University of Toronto Press.

Brill, Lesley (1990, 1997) 'Scudamour', in *The Spenser Encyclopedia*, ed. A. C. Hamilton et al. Toronto: University of Toronto Press.

Booth, Mark W. (1990, 1997) 'Song', in *The Spenser Encyclopedia*, ed. A. C. Hamilton et al. Toronto: University of Toronto Press.

Borges, Jorge Luis (1979) *The Book of Sand*, trans. Norman Thomas di Giovanni and Alastair Reid. Harmondsworth: Penguin.

Borris, Kenneth (2010) 'Allegory, Emblem and Symbol', in *The Oxford Handbook of Edmund Spenser*, ed. Richard A. McCabe. Oxford: Oxford University Press.

Borris, Kenneth (2017) *Visionary Spenser and the Poetics of Early Modern Platonism*. Oxford: Oxford University Press.

Borris, Kenneth and Meredith Donaldson Clark (2011) 'Hymnic Epic and *The Faerie Queene*'s Original Printed Format: Canto-Canticles and Psalmic Arguments', *Renaissance Quarterly* 64, pp. 1148–93.

Brewer, Derek (ed.) (1978) *Chaucer: The Critical Heritage*, 2 vols. London: Routledge and Kegan Paul.

Brogan, T. V. F. (1993) 'Archaism', in *The New Princeton Encyclopedia of Poetry and Poetics*, ed. Alex Preminger and T. V. F. Brogan. Princeton: Princeton University Press.

Brogan, T. V. F. (1993) 'Ballad', in *The New Princeton Encyclopedia of Poetry and Poetics*, ed. Alex Preminger and T. V. F. Brogan. Princeton: Princeton University Press.

Brogan, T. V. F. (1993) 'Ballad Meter', in *The New Princeton Encyclopedia of Poetry and Poetics*, ed. Alex Preminger and T. V. F. Brogan. Princeton: Princeton University Press.

Brogan, T. V. F. (1993) 'Broken Rhyme', in *The New Princeton Encyclopedia of Poetry and Poetics*, ed. Alex Preminger and T. V. F. Brogan. Princeton: Princeton University Press.

Brogan T. V. F. (1993) 'Masculine and Feminine', in *The New Princeton Encyclopedia of Poetry and Poetics*, ed. Alex Preminger and T. V. F. Brogan. Princeton: Princeton University Press.

Brogan, T. V. F. (1993) 'Rhyme', in *The New Princeton Encyclopedia of Poetry and Poetics*, ed. Alex Preminger and T. V. F. Brogan. Princeton: Princeton University Press.

Brogan, T. V. F. (1993) 'Rich Rhyme', in *The New Princeton Encyclopedia of Poetry and Poetics*, ed. Alex Preminger and T. V. F. Brogan. Princeton: Princeton University Press.

Brogan, T. V. F. and Fabian Gudas (1993) 'Tone', in *The New Princeton Encyclopedia of Poetry and Poetics*, ed. Alex Preminger and T. V. F. Brogan. Princeton: Princeton University Press.

Bromwich, David (1990, 1997) 'Hazlitt, William (1778–1830)', in *The Spenser Encyclopedia*, ed. A. C. Hamilton et al. Toronto: University of Toronto Press.

Brown, Richard Danson (1999) *The New Poet: Novelty and Tradition in Spenser's Complaints*. Liverpool: Liverpool University Press.

Brown, Richard Danson (2006) 'MacNeice in Fairy Land', in *Edmund Spenser: New and Renewed Directions*, ed. J. B. Lethbridge. Madison: Fairleigh Dickinson University Press.

Brown, Richard Danson (2010) '"I would abate the sternenesse of my stile": Diction and Poetic Subversion in *Two Cantos of Mutabilitie*', in *Celebrating Mutabilitie: Essays on Edmund Spenser's Mutabilitie Cantos*, ed. Jane Grogan. Manchester: Manchester University Press.

Brown, Richard Danson (2011) '"Can't we ever, my love, speak in the same language": Everyday Language and Creative Tension in the Poetry of Louis MacNeice', in *Creativity in Language and Literature: The State of the Art*, ed. Joan Swann, Rob Pope and Ronald Carter. Basingstoke: Palgrave.

Brown, Richard Danson (2012) '*The Oxford Handbook of Edmund Spenser*', *Modern Language Review* 107.1, pp. 171–72.

Brown, Richard Danson (2013) '"Such ungodly terms": Style, Taste, Verse Satire and Epigram in *The Dutch Courtesan*'. www.dutchcourtesan.co.uk/such-ungodly-terms/ [accessed 19 May 2014].

Brown, Richard Danson (2014) 'The Scope of Spenser's Strangeness', *Spenser Review* 43.3.53. www.english.cam.ac.uk/spenseronline/review/item/43.3.53/ [accessed 31 October 2014]

Brown, Richard Danson (2015) 'The Renaissance Epic: Spenser, *The Faerie Queene*', in *Shakespeare and His Contemporaries*, ed. Jonathan Gibson. Milton Keynes: The Open University.

Brown, Richard Danson (2017) '"And dearest loue": Virgilian Half-lines in Spenser's *Faerie Queene*', in *Proceedings of the Virgil Society* 29, pp. 49–74.

Brown, Richard Danson (forthcoming) 'Wise Wights in Privy Places: Rhyme and Stanza Form in Spenser and Chaucer', in *Spenser and Chaucer*, ed. Tamsin Badcoe, Gareth Griffith and Rachel Stenner. Manchester: Manchester University Press.

Brown, Richard Danson with J. B. Lethbridge (2013) *A Concordance to the Rhymes of The Faerie Queene, With Two Studies of Spenser's Rhyme*. Manchester: Manchester University Press.

Bruton, Avril (1990, 1997) 'Morphology and Syntax', in *The Spenser Encyclopedia*, ed. A. C. Hamilton et al. Toronto: University of Toronto Press.

Bruton, Avril (1990, 1997) 'Pronunciation', in *The Spenser Encyclopedia*, ed. A. C. Hamilton et al. Toronto: University of Toronto Press.

Buckman, Ty (2005) 'Forcing the Poet into Prose: "Gealous Opinions Misconctructions and Spenser's Letter to Ralegh', *Studies in the Literary Imagination* 38.2, pp. 17–34.

Burrow, Colin (1993) *Epic Romance: Homer to Milton*. Oxford: Clarendon.

Burrow, Colin (1996) *Edmund Spenser*. Plymouth: Northcote House.

Campana, Joseph (2010) '*Letters* (1580)', in *The Oxford Handbook of Edmund Spenser*, ed. Richard A. McCabe. Oxford: Oxford University Press.

Campbell, Gordon and Thomas N. Corns (2008) *John Milton: Life, Work, and Thought*. Oxford: Oxford University Press.

Carson, Anne (2013) *Red Doc>*. London: Jonathan Cape.

Carter, Ronald (2004) *Language and Creativity: The Art of Common Talk*. London: Routledge.

Chamberlain, Richard (2005) *Radical Spenser: Pastoral, Politics and the New Aestheticism*. Edinburgh: Edinburgh University Press.

Chaucer Concordance (2007) https://machias.edu/faculty/necastro/chaucer/concordance/ [accessed 2 May 2014].

Cheney, Donald (1978) 'A. C. Hamilton, ed. *The Faerie Queene*', *Spenser Newsletter* 9.2, pp. 21–25.

Cheney, Patrick (2010) '*Colin Clouts Come Home Againe, Astrophel*, and *The Doleful Lay of Clorinda* (1595)', in *The Oxford Handbook of Edmund Spenser* ed. Richard A. McCabe. Oxford: Oxford University Press.

Coldiron, A. E. B. (2010) 'French Presences in Tudor England', in *A Companion to Tudor Literature*, ed. Kent Cartwright, Kent. Oxford: Blackwell. Blackwell Reference Online. www.blackwellreference.com/subscriber/tocnode.html?id=g9781405154772_chunk_g978140515477220 [accessed 20 September 2016]

Coldiron, A. E. B. (2015) *Printers Without Borders: Translation and Textuality in the Renaissance*. Cambridge: Cambridge University Press.

Cook, Eleanor (1993) 'Lexis', in *The New Princeton Encyclopedia of Poetry and Poetics*, ed. Alex Preminger and T. V. F. Brogan. Princeton: Princeton University Press.

Cook, Guy (1995) 'Genes, Memes, Rhymes: Conscious Poetic Deviation in Linguistic, Psychological and Evolutionary Theory', *Language and Communication* 15.4, pp. 375–91.

Crawford, Jason (2017) *Allegory and Enchantment: An Early Modern Poetics*. Oxford: Oxford University Press.

Cummings, R. M. (ed.) (1971) *Spenser: The Critical Heritage*. London: Routledge & Kegan Paul.

Curran, John E. Jr (1998) 'Florimell's "Vaine Feare": Horace's Ode 1.23 and *The Faerie Queene* 3.7.1', *Spenser Studies* 12, pp. 215–18.

Curtius, Ernst Robert (1953, rpt 1990) *European Literature and the Latin Middle Ages*, trans. Willard R. Trask. Princeton: Princeton University Press.

Dees, Jerome S. (1971) 'The Narrator of The Faerie Queene', *Studies in Literature and Language* 12.4, pp. 537–68.

Dees, Jerome S. (1990, 1997) 'Narrator of *The Faerie Queene*', in *The Spenser Encyclopedia*, ed. A. C. Hamilton et al. Toronto: University of Toronto Press.

Dees, Jerome S. (1990, 1997) 'Ship imagery', in *The Spenser Encyclopedia*, ed. A. C. Hamilton et al. Toronto: University of Toronto Press.

DeNeef, A. Leigh (1982) *Spenser and the Motives of Metaphor*. Durham, NC: Duke University Press.

Dolven, Jeff (2004) 'The Method of Spenser's Stanza', *SSt* 19, pp. 17–26.

Dolven, Jeff (2007) *Scenes of Instruction in Renaissance Romance*. Chicago: University of Chicago Press.

Dolven, Jeff (2010) 'Spenser's Metrics', in *The Oxford Handbook of Edmund Spenser*, ed. Richard A. McCabe. Oxford: Oxford University Press.

Dundas, Judith (1985) *The Spider and the Bee: The Artistry of Spenser's Faerie Queene*. Urbana: University of Illinois Press.

Dunlop, Alexander (1990, 1997) 'Modern Studies in Number Symbolism', in *The Spenser Encyclopedia*, ed. A. C. Hamilton et al. Toronto: University of Toronto Press.

Dunseath, T. K. (1968, 2015) *Spenser's Allegory of Justice in Book Five of The Faerie Queene*. Princeton: Princeton Uiversity Press.

Durling, Robert (1965) *The Figure of the Poet in Renaissance Epic*. Cambridge, MA: Harvard University Press.

Edwards, Philip (1997) *Sea-Mark: The Metaphorical Voyage, Spenser to Milton*. Liverpool: Liverpool University Press.

Eliot, T. S. (1951) *Selected Essays*. London: Faber and Faber.

Empson, William (1930, rpt 1984) *Seven Types of Ambiguity*. London: Hogarth.

Erickson, Wayne (1989) 'Spenser's Letter to Ralegh and the Literary Politics of *The Faerie Queene*'s 1590 Publication', *SSt* X, pp. 139–74.

Escobedo, Andrew (ed.) (2016) *Edmund Spenser in Context*. Cambridge: Cambridge University Press.

Felski, Rita (2015) *The Limits of Critique*. Chicago: Chicago University Press.

Fenton, James (2003) *An Introduction to English Poetry*. London: Penguin.

Fletcher, Angus (1971) *The Prophetic Moment: An Essay on Spenser*. Chicago: University of Chicago Press.

Fletcher, Angus (2012) *Allegory: The Theory of a Symbolic Mode*. Princeton: Princeton University Press.

Forni, Kathleen (2001) *The Chaucerian Apocrypha: A Counterfeit Canon*. Gainesville: University Press of Florida.

Fowler, Alastair (1964) *Spenser and the Numbers of Time*. London: Routledge and Kegan Paul.

Fowler, Elizabeth (1995) 'The Failure of Moral Philosophy in the Work of Edmund Spenser', *Representations* 51, pp. 47–76.

Fried, Debra (1981) 'Spenser's Caesura', *English Literary Renaissance* 11, pp. 261–80.

Frye, Northrop (1957, rpt 1990) *Anatomy of Criticism: Four Essays*. London: Penguin.

Frye, Northrop (1963) 'The Structure of Imagery in *The Faerie Queene*', in *Fables of Identity: Studies in Poetic Mythology*. New York: Harcourt.

Gans, Nathan A. (1979) 'Archaism and Neologism in Spenser's Diction', *Modern Philology* 76, pp. 377–79.

Gibson, Jonathan (2004) 'The Legal Context of Spenser's *Daphnaïda*', *Review of English Studies*, 55.218, pp. 24–44.

Gless, Darryl J. (1994) *Interpretation and Theology in Spenser*. Cambridge: Cambridge University Press.

Goldberg, Jonathan (1981) *Endlesse Work: Spenser and the Structures of Discourse*. Baltimore: Johns Hopkins University Press.

Görlach, Manfred (1991) *Introduction to Early Modern English*. Cambridge: Cambridge University Press.

Greenblatt, Stephen (1980) *Renaissance Self-Fashioning: From More to Shakespeare*. Chicago: Chicago University Press.

Grogan, Jane (2009) *Exemplary Spenser: Visual and Poetic Pedagogy in The Faerie Queene*. Farnham: Ashgate.

Gross, Kenneth (1985) *Spenserian Poetics: Idolatry, Iconoclasm, and Magic*. Ithaca: Cornell University Press.

Gross, Kenneth (2004) 'Shapes of Time: On the Spenserian Stanza', *SSt* 19, pp. 27–35.

Hadfield, Andrew (1998) 'Was Spenser a Republican?', *English* 47, pp. 169–82.

Hadfield, Andrew (2001) 'Introduction: The Relevance of Edmund Spenser', in *The Cambridge Companion to Spenser*, ed. Andrew Hadfield. Cambridge: Cambridge University Press.

Hadfield, Andrew (2001) '*The Faerie Queene*, Books IV–VII', in *The Cambridge Companion to Spenser*, ed. Andrew Hadfield. Cambridge: Cambridge University Press.

Hadfield, Andrew (2012) *Edmund Spenser: A Life*. Oxford: Oxford University Press.

Hamilton, A. C. (1961) *The Structure of Allegory in The Faerie Queene*. Oxford: Clarendon.

Hamilton, A. C. (ed.) (1972) *Essential Articles for the Study of Edmund Spenser*. Hamden, CT: Shoe String Press.

Hamilton, A. C. et al. (1990) *The Spenser Encyclopedia*. Toronto: University of Toronto Press.

Hamilton, Ian (1982) *Robert Lowell: A Biography*. New York: Random House.

Hardison, O. B., Jr (1989) *Prosody and Purpose in the English Renaissance*. Baltimore: Johns Hopkins University Press.

Hardt, Michael and Kathi Weeks (2000) *The Jameson Reader*. Oxford: Blackwell.

Harmon, William (1990, 1997) 'Rhyme', in *The Spenser Encyclopedia*, ed. A. C. Hamilton et al. Toronto: University of Toronto Press.

Harris, Duncan and Nancy L. Steffen (1978) 'The Other Side of the Garden: An Interpretive Comparison of Chaucer's *Book of the Duchess* and Spenser's *Daphnaida*', *Journal of Medieval and Renaissance Studies* 8, pp. 17–36.

Häublein, Ernst (1978) *The Stanza*. London: Methuen.

Heale, Elizabeth (2010) 'Spenser and Sixteenth-Century Poetics', in *The Oxford Handbook of Edmund Spenser*, ed. Richard A. McCabe. Oxford: Oxford University Press.

Heaney, Seamus (1998) *Opened Ground: Poems 1966–1996*. London: Faber and Faber.

Hecht, Paul J. (2005) 'Spenser out of His Stanza', *Style* 39.3, pp. 316–35.

Hecht, Paul J. (2010) 'Letters for the Dogs: Chasing Spenserian Alliteration', *SSt* 25, pp. 263–86.

Hecht, Paul J. (2016) 'Marina Tarlinskaja, *Shakespeare and the Versification of English Drama, 1561–1642', Spenser Review* 46.1.13. www.english.cam.ac.uk/spenseronline/review/item/46.1.13 [accessed 7 December 2017].

Hecht, Paul J. (2017) 'Prosody', in *Edmund Spenser in Context*, ed. Andrew Escobedo. Cambridge: Cambridge University Press.

Helfer, Rebeca (2012) *Spenser's Ruins and the Art of Recollection*. Toronto: University of Toronto Press.

Helgerson, Richard (1983) *Self-Crowned Laureates: Spenser, Jonson, Milton and the Literary System*. Berkeley: University of California Press.

Helgerson, Richard (1992) *Forms of Nationhood: The Elizabethan Writing of England*. Chicago: Chicago University Press.

Henry, Sean (2015) 'Getting Spenser's Goat: Calepine, Spenser's Goats, and the Problem of Meaning', *SSt* 30, pp. 301–16.

Herron, Thomas (2007) *Spenser's Irish Work: Poetry, Plantation and Colonial Reformation*. Aldershot: Ashgate.

Hieatt, A. Kent (1973) 'Three Fearful Symmetries and the Meaning of *Faerie Queene* II', in *A Theatre for Spenserians*, ed. Judith M. Kennedy and James A. Reither. Toronto: University of Toronto Press.

Hieatt, A. Kent (1998) 'Room of One's Own for Decisions: Chaucer and *The Faerie Queene*', in *Refiguring Chaucer in the Renaissance*, ed. Theresa Krier. Gainsville: University Press of Florida.

Hieatt, Constance B. (1990, 1997) 'Falconry', in *The Spenser Encyclopedia*, ed. A. C. Hamilton et al. Toronto: University of Toronto Press.

Hile, Rachel E. (2017) *Spenserian Satire: A Tradition of Indirection*. Manchester: Manchester University Press.

Hill, Christopher (1993, 1994) *The English Bible and the Seventeenth-Century Revolution*. London: Penguin.

Hinton, Stan (1974) 'The Poet and His Narrator: Spenser's Epic Voice', *ELH* 41.2, pp. 165–81.

Hollander, John (1970) 'Romantic Verse and the Metrical Contract', in *Romanticism and Consciousness*, ed. Harold Bloom. New York: Norton.

Hollander, John (1988) *Melodious Guile: Fictive Pattern in Poetic Language*. New Haven: Yale University Press.

Hollander, John (1990, 1997) 'Alexandrine', in *The Spenser Encyclopedia*, ed. A. C. Hamilton et al. Toronto: University of Toronto Press.

Hollander, John (1990, 1997) 'Music', in *The Spenser Encyclopedia*, ed. A. C. Hamilton et al. Toronto: University of Toronto Press.

Honigmann, E. A. J. (1987) *John Weever: A Biography of a Literary Associate of Shakespeare and Jonson, Together with a Photographic Facsimile of Weever's Epigrammes (1599)*. Manchester: Manchester University Press.

Horton, R. A. (1978) *The Unity of The Faerie Queene*, Athens: University of Georgia Press.

Horton, Ronald (1990, 1997) 'Satyrane', in *The Spenser Encyclopedia*, ed. A. C. Hamilton et al. Toronto: University of Toronto Press.

Hough, Graham (1962) *A Preface to The Faerie Queene*. London: Duckworth.

Ingham, Patricia (1990, 1997) 'Dialect', in *The Spenser Encyclopedia*, ed. A. C. Hamilton et al. Toronto: University of Toronto Press.

Ingold, Tim (2007) *Lines: A Brief History*. London: Routledge.

Javitch, Daniel (1980) '*Cantus Interruptus* in the *Orlando Furioso*', *Modern Language Notes* 95.1, pp. 66–80.

Jowett, John (2006) 'Editing Shakespeare's Plays in the Twentieth Century', *Shakespeare Survey* 59, pp. 1–19.

Joyce, Trevor (2017) *Fastness: A Translation from the English of Edmund Spenser*. Oxford, OH: Miami University Press.

Kaske, Carol V. (1999) *Spenser and Biblical Poetics*. Ithaca: Cornell University Press.

Kennedy, William J. (1990, 1997) 'Fradubio', in *The Spenser Encyclopedia*, ed. A. C. Hamilton et al. Toronto: University of Toronto Press.

Kerrigan, John (2016) *Shakespeare's Binding Language*. Oxford: Oxford University Press.

Kiefer, Frederick (1990, 1997) 'Fortune', in *The Spenser Encyclopedia*, ed. A. C. Hamilton et al. Toronto: University of Toronto Press.

King, Andrew (2000) *The Faerie Queene and Middle English Romance: The Matter of Just Memory*. Clarendon: Oxford.

King, Andrew (2001) '"Well Grounded, Finely Framed, and Strong Trussed Up Together": The "Medieval" Structure of *The Faerie Queene*', *Review of English Studies* V52.205, pp. 22–58.

Kosako, Mararu (1995) 'Some Historical Observations on the Collocation of Noun plus Adjective in Rhyme Position of *The Faerie Queene*', *Bulletin of the Faculty of Education, Okayama University* 100, pp. 197–221.

Kosako, Mararu (1998) 'Parts of Speech in Rhyme Words of *The Faerie Queene* (from Books I to III): Verbal Icons in the Prominent Distributions', in *A Love of Words: English Philological Studies in Honour of Akira Wada*, ed. Masahiko Kanno et al. Tokyo: University of Tokyo Press, pp. 145–60.

Kouwhenhoven, Jan Karel (1983) *Apparent Narrative as Thematic Metaphor: The Organization of The Faerie Queene*. Oxford: Clarendon.

Krier, Theresa (ed.) (1998) *Refiguring Chaucer in the Renaissance*. Gainesville: University Press of Florida.

Krier, Theresa (2006) '*The Faerie Queene* (1596)', in *A Critical Companion to Spenser Studies*, ed. Bart van Es. Basingstoke: Palgrave.

Krier, Theresa (2007) 'Time Lords: Rhythm and Interval in Spenser's Stanzaic Narrative', *SSt* 21, pp. 1–19.

Kuin, Roger (2002) 'The Double Helix: Public and Private in Spenser's *Faerie Queene*', *SSt* 16, pp. 1–22.

Legouis, Pierre (1928, rpt 1962) *Donne the Craftsman: An Essay upon the Structure of the Songs and Sonnets.* New York: Russell & Russell.

Lethbridge, J. B. (2006) 'Introduction: Recuperating the Return to History', in *Edmund Spenser: New and Renewed Directions*, ed. J. B. Lethbridge. Madison: Fairleigh Dickinson University Press,

Lethbridge, J. B. (2006) 'Spenser's Last Days: Ireland, Career, Mutability, Allegory', in *Edmund Spenser: New and Renewed Directions*, ed. J. B. Lethbridge. Madison: Fairleigh Dickinson University Press.

Lethbridge, J. B. (2008) 'Introduction: Spenser, Marlowe, Shakespeare: Methodological Investigations', in *Shakespeare and Spenser: Attractive Opposites*, ed. J. B. Lethbridge. Manchester: Manchester University Press.

Lethbridge, J. B. (ed.) (nd) 'Concordance of *The Faerie Queene*', unpublished.

Levertov, Denise (1979) 'On the Function of the Line', *Chicago Review* 30.3, pp. 30–36.

Lewis, C. S. (1936 rpt 1985) *The Allegory of Love: A Study in Medieval Tradition.* Oxford: Oxford University Press.

Lewis, C. S. (1954) *English Literature in the Sixteenth Century Excluding Drama.* Oxford: Clarendon.

Lewis, C. S. (1967) *Spenser's Images of Life*, ed. Alastair Fowler. Cambridge: Cambridge University Press.

Loewenstein, Joseph (2010) 'Spenser's Textual History', in *The Oxford Handbook of Edmund Spenser*, ed. Andrew Escobedo. Oxford: Oxford University Press.

Loewenstein, Joseph (2018) 'Tudor Verse Form: Rudeness, Artifice, and Display', in *A Companion to Renaissance Poetry*, ed. Catherine Bates. Hoboken, NJ: Wiley Blackwell.

Longenbach, James (2008) *The Art of the Poetic Line.* St Paul, Minnesota: Graywolf.

Lowell, Robert (1987) *Collected Prose*, ed. Robert Giroux. London: Faber and Faber.

McCabe, Richard (2002, 2005) *Spenser's Monstrous Regiment: Elizabethan Ireland and the Poetics of Difference.* Oxford: Oxford University Press.

McCabe, Richard (2010) 'Introduction', in *The Oxford Handbook of Edmund Spenser*, ed. Richard A. McCabe. Oxford: Oxford University Press.

McCabe, Richard (2010) 'Authorial Self-Presentation', in *The Oxford Handbook of Edmund Spenser*, ed. Richard A. McCabe. Oxford: Oxford University Press.

McCabe, Richard (2016) *Ungainefull Arte: Poetry, Patronage, and Print in the Early Modern Era.* Oxford: Oxford University Press.

McEachern, Claire (2010) 'Spenser and Religion', in *The Oxford Handbook of Edmund Spenser*, ed. Richard A. McCabe. Oxford: Oxford University Press.

McElderry, Bruce (1932) 'Archaism and Innovation in Spenser's Poetic Diction', *PMLA* 47, pp. 144–70.

Macfarlane, Robert (2012) *The Old Ways: A Journey on Foot.* London: Hamish Hamilton.

McMahon, April (2006, 2012) 'Restructuring Renaissance English', in *The Oxford History of English: Updated Edition*, ed. Lynda Mugglestone. Oxford: Oxford University Press.

McMullan, Gordon and David Matthews (eds) (2007) *Reading the Medieval in Early Modern England*. Cambridge: Cambridge University Press.

MacNeice, Louis (1938) *Modern Poetry: A Personal Essay*. Oxford: Oxford University Press.

MacNeice, Louis (1987) *Selected Literary Criticism*, ed. Alan Heuser. Oxford: Clarendon.

MacNeice, Louis (2007) *Collected Poems*, ed. Peter McDonald. London: Faber and Faber.

Mack, Peter (2010) 'Spenser and Rhetoric', in *The Oxford Handbook of Edmund Spenser*, ed. Richard A. McCabe. Oxford: Oxford University Press.

McRae, Andrew (2004) 'Tusser, Thomas (c.1524–1580)', *Oxford Dictionary of National Biography*, Oxford University Press.

Maley, Willy (1994) 'Spenser's Irish English: Language and Identity in Early Modern Ireland', *SP* 91, pp. 417–31.

Maley, Willy (2001) 'Spenser Languages: Writing in the Ruins of English', in *The Cambridge Companion to Spenser*, ed. Andrew Hadfield . Cambridge: Cambridge University Press.

Maley, Willy (2017) 'Spenser and Europe: Britomart after Brexit', *Spenser Review* 47.3.42. www.english.cam.ac.uk/spenseronline/review/item/47.3.42 [accessed 7 December 2017].

Manley, Lawrence (1980) *Convention 1500–1750*. Cambridge, MA: Harvard University Press.

Marks, Herbert and Kenneth Gross (1990, 1997) 'Names, Naming', in *The Spenser Encyclopedia*, ed. A. C. Hamilton et al. Toronto: University of Toronto Press.

Marre, L. A. (1971) 'Spenser's Control of Tone'. Unpublished dissertation, University of Notre Dame.

Martell, Yann (2001, rpt 2016) *Life of Pi*. Edinburgh: Canongate.

Matsuura, Masayoshi and Takako Matsuura (2002) *A Rime Index to the Poetry of Marlowe, Shakespeare and Some Elizabethan Poets*. Tokyo: Eihōsha.

Maxwell, J. C. (1952) 'The Truancy of Calidore', *ELH* 19.2, pp. 143–49.

May, Steven W. (2005) 'Henry Gurney, a Norfolk Farmer, Reads Spenser and Others', *SSt* 20, pp. 183–223.

May, Steven W. (2008) 'George Puttenham's Lewd and Illicit Career', *Texas Studies in Literature and Language* 50.2, pp. 143–76.

Maynard, Theodore (1934, rpt 2015) *The Connection Between the Ballade, Chaucer's Modification of It, Rime Royal, and the Spenserian Stanza*. Washington, DC: Catholic University of America; rpt Folcroft: Folcroft Library Editions.

Miller, David Lee (1979) 'Abandoning the Quest', *ELH* 46.2, pp. 173–92.

Miller, David Lee (1988) *The Poem's Two Bodies: the Poetics of the 1590 Faerie Queene*. Princeton: Princeton University Press.

Miller, David Lee (1990, 1997) 'Calidore', in *The Spenser Encyclopedia*, ed. A. C. Hamilton et al. Toronto: University of Toronto Press.

Miller, David Lee (2006) '*The Faerie Queene* (1590)', in *A Critical Companion to Spenser Studies*, ed. Bart van Es. Basingstoke: Palgrave.

Miller, David Lee (2011) 'Laughing at Spenser's *Daphnaida*', *SSt* 26, pp. 241–50.

Miller, David Lee (2014) 'Dan Edmund Meets the Romantics', in *Edmund Spenser's Poetry: Authoritative Texts and Criticism, Fourth Edition*, ed. Anne Lake Prescott and Andrew D. Hadfield. New York: Norton.

Mills, Jerry Leath (1976) 'Spenser and the Numbers of History: A Note on the British and Elfin Chronicles in *The Faerie Queene*', *PQ* 55, pp. 281–87.

Milroy, James and Lesley Milroy (1985) *Authority in Language: Investigating Language Prescription and Standardisation*. Routledge and Kegan Paul: London.

Miskimin, Alice S. (1975) *The Renaissance Chaucer*. New Haven: Yale University Press.

Montgomery, Robert L. (1993) 'Neoclassical Poetics', in *The New Princeton Encyclopedia of Poetry and Poetics*, ed. Alex Preminger and T. V. F. Brogan. Princeton: Princeton University Press.

Mueller, Martin (2014) 'The EEBO-TCP Phase I Public Release', *Spenser Review* 44.2.36. www.english.cam.ac.uk/spenseronline/review/volume-44/442/digital-projects/the-eebo-tcp-phase-i-public-release/ [accessed 18 August 2016].

Muldoon, Paul (2001) *Poems 1968–1998*. London: Faber and Faber.

Muldoon, Paul (2015) *One Thousand Things Worth Knowing*. London: Faber and Faber.

Mullaney, Steven (2015) *The Reformation of Emotions in the Age of Shakespeare*. Chicago: Chicago University Press.

Nelson, William (1963, 1965) *The Poetry of Edmund Spenser: A Study*. New York: Columbia University Press.

Neuse, Richard (1968) 'Book VI as Conclusion to *The Faerie Queene*', *ELH* 35.3, pp. 329–53.

Neuse, Richard T. (1990, 1997) 'Pastorella', in *The Spenser Encyclopedia*, ed. A. C. Hamilton et al. Toronto: University of Toronto Press.

Nicholson, Catherine (2014) *Uncommon Tongues: Eloquence and Eccentricity in the English Renaissance*. Philadelphia: University of Pennsylvania Press.

Nohrnberg, James C. (1976) *The Analogy of The Faerie Queene*. Princeton: Princeton University Press.

Nohrnberg, James C. (2013) 'Paul Alpers, *The Poetry of The Faerie Queene*', *Spenser Review* 43.2.23. www.english.cam.ac.uk/spenseronline/review/volume-43/issue-432/43201-in-memoriam-paul-alpers-oct16-1932-may-19-2013/paul-alpers-the-poetry-of-the-faerie-queene/ [accessed 22 March 2017].

O'Connell, Michael (1990, 1997) 'Giant with the Scales', in *The Spenser Encyclopedia*, ed. A. C. Hamilton et al. Toronto: University of Toronto Press.

Ong, Walter J. (1958, rpt 2004) *Ramus, Method, and the Decay of Dialogue: From the Art of Discourse to the Art of Reason*. Chicago: University of Chicago Press.

Oras, Ants (1955) 'Intensified Rhymes Links in *The Faerie Queene*', *Journal of English and Germanic Philology* 54, pp. 39–60.

Oras, Ants (1960) *Pause Patterns in Elizabethan and Jacobean Drama: An Experiment in Prosody*. Gainesville: University of Florida Press.

Osgood, Charles Grosvenor (1915) *A Concordance to the Poems of Edmund Spenser*. Philadelphia: Carnegie Institute of Washington/J. B. Lippincott Co.

Osselton, Noel (1990, 1997) 'Archaism', in *The Spenser Encyclopedia*, ed. A. C. Hamilton et al. Toronto: University of Toronto Press.

Owen, W. J. B. (1952) 'In These XII Books Severally Handled and Discoursed', *ELH* 19.3, pp. 165–72.

Owen, W. J. B. (1953) 'The Structure of *The Faerie Queene*', *PMLA* 68.5, pp. 1079–100.

Owens, Judith (2002) *Enabling Engagements: Edmund Spenser and the Poetics of Patronage*. Montreal: McGill-Queen's University Press.

Padelford, Frederick Morgan (1941) 'Aspects of Spenser's Vocabulary', *PQ* 20, pp. 279–83.

Parker, Patricia A. (1979) *Inescapable Romance: Studies in the Poetics of a Mode*. Princeton: Princeton University Press.

Paterson, Don (2010) *Reading Shakespeare's Sonnets: A New Commentary*. London: Faber and Faber.

Patterson, Annabel (1992) 'The Egalitarian Giant: Representations of Justice in History/Literature', *Journal of British Studies* 31.2, pp. 97–132.

Pinsky, Robert (1998) *The Sounds of Poetry: A Brief Guide*. New York: Farrar, Strauss and Giroux.

Pope, Emma Field (1926) 'Renaissance Criticism and the Diction of *The Faerie Queene*', *PMLA* 41, pp. 575–619.

Preminger, Alex, Christopher Kleinhenz, and T. V. F. Brogan (1993) 'Ottava Rima', in *The New Princeton Encyclopedia of Poetry and Poetics*, ed. Alex Preminger and T. V. F. Brogan. Princeton: Princeton University Press.

Preminger, Alex and Ernst Haüblein (1993) 'Sexain', in *The New Princeton Encyclopedia of Poetry and Poetics*, ed. Alex Preminger and T. V. F. Brogan. Princeton: Princeton University Press.

Prescott, Anne Lake (1990, 1997) 'Giants', in *The Spenser Encyclopedia*, ed. A. C. Hamilton et al. Toronto: University of Toronto Press.

Price, Bronwen (2002) 'Women's Poetry 1550–1700: "Not Unfit to be Read"', in *A Companion to Early Modern Women's Writing*, ed. Anita Pacheco. Oxford: Blackwell.

Pugh, Syrithe (2005) *Spenser and Ovid*. Aldershot: Ashgate.

Pugh, Syrithe (2016) *Spenser and Virgil: The Pastoral Poems*. Manchester: Manchester University Press.

Pullman, Philip (2011) *His Dark Materials: Northern Lights, The Subtle Knife, The Amber Spyglass*. London: Everyman.

Quilligan, Maureen (1990) 'Feminine Endings: The Sexual Politics of Sidney's and Spenser's Rhyming', in *The Renaissance Englishwoman in Print: Counterbalancing the Canon*, ed. Anne M. Haselkorn and Betty S. Travitsky. Amherst, MA: University of Massachusetts Press.

Quilligan, Maureen (1990, 1997) 'Puns', in *The Spenser Encyclopedia*, ed. A. C. Hamilton et al. Toronto: University of Toronto Press.

Quint, David (1990, 1997) 'Tasso, Torquato', in *The Spenser Encyclopedia*, ed. A. C. Hamilton et al. Toronto: University of Toronto Press.

Quitslund, Beth (2008) *The Reformation in Rhyme: Sternhold, Hopikins and the English metrical Psalter, 1547–1603*. Aldershot: Ashgate.

Rasmussen, Mark David (2010) '*Complaints* and *Daphnaïda* (1591) in *The Oxford Handbook of Edmund Spenser*, ed. Richard A. McCabe. Oxford: Oxford University Press.

Rasmussen, Mark David (2017) 'A Turn Towards Satire?', *Spenser Review* 47.3.53. www.english.cam.ac.uk/spenseronline/review/item/47.3.53 [accessed 30 November 2017].

Rees, Christine (1990, 1997) 'Cowley, Abraham (1618–67)', in *The Spenser Encyclopedia*, ed. A. C. Hamilton et al. Toronto: University of Toronto Press.

Reid, Robert Lanier (2010) 'Spenser's Mutability Song: Conclusion or Transition?', in *Celebrating Mutabilitie: Essays on Edmund Spenser's Mutabilitie Cantos*, ed. Jane Grogan. Manchester: Manchester University Press.

Renwick, W. R. (1922) 'The Critical Origins of Spenser's Diction', *Modern Language Review* 17, pp. 1–16.

Reynolds, Simon (2005) *Rip It Up and Start Again: Post-punk 1978–1984*. London: Faber and Faber.

Rhu, Lawrence F. (1993) *The Genesis of Tasso's Narrative Theory: English Translations of the Early poetics and a Comparative Study of Their Significance*. Detroit: Wayne State University Press.

Ricks, Christopher (1963) *Milton's Grand Style*. Oxford: Oxford University Press.

Ricks, Christopher (2003) *Dylan's Visions of Sin*. London: Viking.

Riddell, James A. and Stanley Stewart (1995) *Jonson's Spenser: Evidence and Historical Criticism*. Pittsburgh: Duquesne University Press.

Rix, Herbert D. (1940) *Rhetoric in Spenser's Poetry*. State College, PA: University of Pennsylvania Press.

Robinson, Ian (1971) *Chaucer's Prosody: A Study of the Middle English Verse Tradition*. Cambridge: Cambridge University Press.

Robson, Mark (2006) *The Sense of Early Modern Writing: Rhetoric, Poetics, Aesthetics*. Manchester: Manchester University Press.

Roche, Thomas P. (1964) *The Kindly Flame: A Study of the Third and Fourth Books of Spenser's Faerie Queene*. Princeton: Princeton University Press.

Rose, Mark (1975) *Spenser's Art: A Companion to Book One of The Faerie Queene*. Cambridge, MA: Harvard University Press.

Røstvig, Maren-Sofie (1980) 'Canto Structure in Tasso and Spenser', *SSt* 1, pp. 177–200.

Røstvig, Maren-Sofie (1990, 1997) 'Tradition of Number Symbolism', in *The Spenser Encyclopedia*, ed. A. C. Hamilton et al. Toronto: University of Toronto Press.

Røstvig, Maren-Sofie (1990, 1997) 'Topomorphical Approach', in *The Spenser Encyclopedia*, ed. A. C. Hamilton et al. Toronto: University of Toronto Press.

Rubel, Veré L. (1941) *Poetic Diction in the English Renaissance from Skelton through Spenser*. New York: Modern Language Association of America.

Saintsbury, George (1923) *A History of English Prosody: From the Twelfth Century to the Present Day*, 2nd edn. London: Macmillan and Co. Ltd.

Sale, Roger (1967) 'Spenser's Undramatic Poetry', in *Elizabethan Poetry: Modern Essays in Criticism*, ed. Paul Alpers. London: Oxford University Press.

Sale, Roger (1968) *Reading Spenser: An Introduction to The Faerie Queene*. New York: Random House.

Sale, Roger (1990, 1997) 'Canto', in *The Spenser Encyclopedia*, ed. A. C. Hamilton et al. Toronto: University of Toronto Press.

Shklovsky, Viktor (1990) *Theory of Prose*, trans. Benjamin Sher. Champaign, Urbana: Dalkey Archive Press.

Silberman, Lauren (1995) *Transforming Desire: Erotic Knowledge in Books III and IV of The Faerie Queene*. Berkeley: University of California University Press.

Smith, Ali (2006) *The Accidental*. London: Penguin.

Smith, Charles G. (1970) *Spenser's Proverb Lore: With Special Reference to His Use of the Sententiae of Leonard Culman and Publilius Syrus*. Cambridge, MA: Harvard University Press.

Smith, Dodie (2004) *I Capture the Castle*. London: Vintage.

Spina, Elaine (1967) 'Skeltonic Meter in *Elynour Rummyng*', *SP*, 64.5, pp. 665–84.

Staines, John D. (2010) 'The Historicist Tradition in Spenser Studies', in *The Oxford Handbook of Edmund Spenser*, ed. Richard A. McCabe. Oxford: Oxford University Press.

Stephens, Dorothy (2010) 'Spenser's Language(s): Linguistic Theory and Poetic Diction', in *The Oxford Handbook of Edmund Spenser*, Richard A. McCabe. Oxford: Oxford University Press.

Stevens, Martin and T. V. F. Brogan (1993) 'Rhyme Royal', in *The New Princeton Encyclopedia of Poetry and Poetics*, ed. Alex Preminger and T. V. F. Brogan. Princeton: Princeton University Press.

Stevenson, Charles L. (1970) 'The Rhythm of English Verse', *Journal of Aesthetics and Art Criticism* 28.3, pp. 327–44.

Strang, Barbara M. H. (1990, 1997) 'Language, General and Resources Exploited in Rhyme', in *The Spenser Encyclopedia*, ed. A. C. Hamilton et al. Toronto: University of Toronto Press.

Sugden, Herbert W. (1936) *The Grammar of Spenser's Faerie Queene*. Philadelphia: Linguistic Society of America.

Suzuki, Toshiyuki (1993) 'Irregular Visual Rhymes in *The Faerie Queene, Part I* (Books I–III)', *Treatises and Studies by the Faculty of Kinjo Gakuin University* 149, pp. 61–80.

Suzuki, Toshiyuki (2005) 'A Note on the Errata to the 1590 Quarto of *The Faerie Queene*', *Studies in the Literary Imagination* 38.2, pp. 1–16.

Swallow, Alan (1950) 'The Pentameter Lines in Skelton and Wyatt', *Modern Philology* 48.1, pp. 1–11.

Sweeney, Anne R. (2006) *Robert Southwell. Snows in Arcadia: Redrawing the English Lyric Landscape, 1586–95*. Manchester: Manchester University Press.

Tarlinskaja, Marina (2014) *Shakespeare and the Versification of English Drama, 1561–1642*. Farnham: Ashgate.

Teskey, Gordon (1990, 1997) 'Allegory', in *The Spenser Encyclopedia*, ed. A. C. Hamilton et al. Toronto: University of Toronto Press

Teskey, Gordon (1996) *Allegory and Violence*. Ithaca, NY: Cornell University Press.

Teskey, Gordon (2007) 'Thinking Moments in *The Faerie Queene*', *SSt* 22, pp. 103–24.

Teskey, Gordon (2010) 'Night Thoughts on Mutability', in *Celebrating Mutabilitie: Essays on Edmund Spenser's Mutabilitie Cantos*, ed. Jane Grogan. Manchester: Manchester University Press.

Thompson, John (1961, 1989) *The Founding of English Metre*. New York: Columbia University Press.

Tonkin, Humphrey (1972) *Spenser's Courteous Pastoral: Book Six of The Faerie Queene*. Oxford: Clarendon.

Tonkin, Humphrey (1990, 1997) '*The Faerie Queene*, Book VI', in *The Spenser Encyclopedia*, ed. A. C. Hamilton et al. Toronto: University of Toronto Press.

Tranter, Kirsten (2006) '"The sea it selfe, doest thou not plainely see?": Reading *The Faerie Queene*, Book V', *SSt* 21, pp. 83–107.

Tuve, Rosamund (1947, 1961) *Elizabethan and Metaphysical Imagery: Renaissance Poetic and Twentieth-Century Critics*. Chicago: University of Chicago Press.

van Es, Bart (2002) *Spenser's Forms of History*. Oxford: Oxford University Press.

van Es, Bart (ed.) (2006) *A Critical Companion to Spenser Studies*. Basingstoke: Palgrave.

van Es, Bart (2006) 'Introduction', in *A Critical Companion to Spenser Studies*, ed. Bart van Es. Basingstoke: Palgrave.

van Es, Bart (2006) 'Works Published before 1589', in *A Critical Companion to Spenser Studies*, ed. Bart van Es. Basingstoke: Palgrave.

Van Ostade, Ingrid Tieken-Boon (2006, 2012) 'English at the Onset of the Normative Tradition', in *The Oxford History of English: Revised Edition*, ed. Lynda Mugglestone. Oxford: Oxford University Press.

Vendler, Helen (1997) *The Art of Shakespeare's Sonnets*. Cambridge, MA: Harvard University Press.

Vickers, Brian (1998) *In Defence of Rhetoric*. Oxford: Clarendon.

Voigt, Ellen Bryant (2003) 'Rhythm of Thought, Rhythm of Song', *Kenyon Review* NS 25.1, pp. 144–63.

Wall, Wendy (2010) 'Literacy and the Domestic Arts', *Huntingdon Library Quarterly* 73.3, pp. 383–412.

Walls, Kathryn (2013) *God's Only Daughter: Spenser's Una as the Invisible Church.* Manchester: Manchester University Press.

Ward, Alan (1990, 1997) 'Neologism', in *The Spenser Encyclopedia*, ed. A. C. Hamilton et al. Toronto: University of Toronto Press.

Webster, John (1976) 'Oral Form and Written Craft in Spenser's *Faerie Queene*', *Studies in English Literature* 1500–1900, 16.1, 75–93.

Webster, John (1990, 1997) 'Rhetoric', in *The Spenser Encyclopedia*, ed. A. C. Hamilton et al. Toronto: University of Toronto Press.

Whittington, Leah (2015) 'Wallowing and Getting Lost: Reading Spenser with Heather James', *Spenser Review* 44.3.54. www.english.cam.ac.uk/spenseronline/review/item/44.3.54-1 [accessed 23 July 2017].

Williams, Arnold (1967) *Flower on a Lowly Stalk: The Sixth Book of the Faerie Queene.* East Lansing: Michigan State University Press.

Williams, Kathleen (1966) *Spenser's Faerie Queene: The World of Glass.* London: Routledge and Kegan Paul.

Williams, Kathleen (1969) 'The Poet's Voice in *The Faerie Queene*', *ELH* 36.1, pp. 131–44.

Williams, Penry (2004) 'Babington, Anthony (1561–1586)', *Oxford Dictionary of National Biography*, Oxford University Press. www.oxforddnb.com/view/article/967 [accessed 16 August 2013].

Williams, William Carlos (1988) *The Collected Poems: Volume II 1939–1962*, ed. Christopher MacGowan. Manchester: Carcanet.

Wilson-Okamura, David Scott (2007) 'The French Aesthetic of Spenser's Feminine Rhyme', *Modern Language Quarterly* 68.3, pp. 345–62.

Wilson-Okamura, David Scott (2009) 'Belphoebe and Gloriana', *English Literary Renaissance*, 39, 47–73.

Wilson-Okamura, David Scott (2010) *Virgil in the Renaissance.* Cambridge: Cambridge University Press.

Wilson-Okamura, David Scott (2010) 'The Formalist Tradition', in *The Oxford Handbook of Edmund Spenser*, ed. Richard A. McCabe. Oxford: Oxford University Press.

Wilson-Okamura, David Scott (2013) *Spenser's International Style.* Cambridge: Cambridge University Press.

Wimsatt, W. K. (1944) 'One Relation of Rhyme to Reason: Alexander Pope', *Modern Language Quarterly* 5, pp. 323–38; also rpt in *The Verbal Icon: Studies in the Meaning of Poetry* (1954; rpt 1970). London: Methuen.

Wofford, Susanne L. (2001) 'The Faerie Queene, Books I–III', in *The Cambridge Companion to Spenser*, ed. Andrew Hadfield. Cambridge: Cambridge University Press.

Woodcock, Matthew (2004) *Fairy in 'The Faerie Queene': Renaissance Elf-Fashioning and Elizabethan Myth-Making*. Aldershot: Ashgate.

Woodcock, Matthew (2016) *Thomas Churchyard: Pen, Sword, and Ego*. Oxford: Oxford University Press.

Woods, Susanne (1984) *Natural Emphasis: English Versification from Chaucer to Dryden*. San Marino: Huntingdon Library.

Woods, Susanne (1990, 1997) 'Versification', in *The Spenser Encyclopedia*, ed. A. C. Hamilton et al. Toronto: University of Toronto Press.

Wright, George T. (1988) *Shakespeare's Metrical Art*. Berkeley: University of California Press.

Yamashita, Hiroshi (1990) *A Comprehensive Concordance to the Faerie Queene, 1590*. Tokyo: Kenyusha.

Yeats, W. B. (1983) *The Poems: A New Edition*, ed. Richard J. Finneran. London: Macmillan.

Zitner, Sheldon P. (1966) 'Spenser's Diction and Classical Precedent', *PQ* 45, pp. 360–71.

Zurcher, Andrew (2006) 'Spenser's Studied Archaism: The Case of "Mote"', *SSt* 21, pp. 231–40.

Zurcher, Andrew (2007) *Spenser's Legal Language: Law and Poetry in Early Modern England*. Cambridge: D. S. Brewer.

Main digital resources

Early English Books Online: https://eebo.chadwyck.com via the Open University Library.

Early Modern Print: Text Mining Early Printed English: https://earlyprint.wustl.edu

eChaucer website and concordance: http://echaucer.machias.edu/concordance/

Eighteenth Century Collections Online: Gale Group via the Open University Library.

English Short Title Catalogue: http://estc.bl.uk/

Oxford Dictionary of National Biography: https://oxforddnb.com via the Open University Library.

Oxford English Dictionary: https://oed.com via the Open University Library.

Index